Practical Ideas

FOR TEACHING

WRITING

AS A PROCESS

AT THE

ELEMENTARY

SCHOOL

AND MIDDLE

SCHOOL

LEVELS

1996 REVISED

EDITION

Compiled and edited by
Carol Booth Olson
Director, University of California Irvine/
California Writing Project

Prepared for publication by
The Staff of the Bureau of Publications
California Department of Education

Publishing Information

Practical Ideas for Teaching Writing as a Process at the Elementary School and Middle School Levels was compiled and edited by Carol Booth Olson, Director of the University of California, Irvine/California Writing Project. Theodore R. Smith, former Editor in Chief of the Bureau of Publications, did the initial planning and preparation of this revised edition and of the revised edition for high schools and colleges, which is also available. Preliminary reviews of the material were provided by Mae Gundlach, Diane Levin, and Kathi Cooper, Consultants, from the Language Arts and Foreign Languages Office of the Department and by Dan Holt, Consultant, Bilingual Education Office.

It was edited for publication by Janet Lundin, Associate Editor, Bureau of Publications, California Department of Education. The book, which presents techniques and practical ideas for teaching students the stages in the writing process, was first published by the Department in 1986 as a companion to the *Handbook for Planning an Effective Writing Program*. This edition of the book was completely revised and expanded to include new articles with new techniques and practical ideas for teaching writing in elementary schools and middle schools. A new design for the cover and interior and new illustrations were also created.

Practical Ideas was prepared for photo-offset production by the staff of the Department's Bureau of Publications. Cheryl McDonald, Senior Graphic Artist, designed the cover and the interior and prepared the artwork. The typesetters were Carey Johnson, Donna Kurtz, and Anna Boyd. Dixie Abbott, Staff Editor, assisted with the proofreading.

Practical Ideas was developed by the Bureau of Publications, California Department of Education, and was published by the Department, 721 Capitol Mall, Sacramento, California (mailing address: P.O. Box 944272, Sacramento, CA 94244-2720). It was distributed under the provisions of the Library Distribution Act and *Government Code* Section 11096.

ISBN 0-8011-1221-4

Ordering Information

Copies of the publication are available for $17 each, plus sales tax for California residents, from the Bureau of Publications Sales Unit, California Department of Education, P.O. Box 271, Sacramento, CA 95812-0271; FAX (916) 323-0823.

The current *Educational Resources Catalog* describing publications, videos, and other instructional media available from the Department may be obtained without charge by writing to the address given above or by calling the Sales Unit at (916) 445-1260. To charge your order to MasterCard or VISA, please telephone 1-800-995-4099.

Dedication

This book is dedicated to

George Nemetz

former English–Language Arts Consultant,
California Department of Education,

and

Theodore R. Smith

former Editor in Chief, Bureau of Publications,
California Department of Education,
for their many contributions to the enhancement
of English–language arts curriculum
and instruction in California.

Contents

Writing

Teaching Writing in the Culturally and Linguistically Diverse Classroom

Domains of Writing

Writing the Saturation Report

Point of View in Writing

Writing the I-Search Paper

Critical Thinking and Writing

Preface

If you are looking for ideas for teaching writing as a process at the elementary school and middle school levels, this book was compiled for you. It represents the collaborative efforts of teacher/consultants participating in the University of California, Irvine, California Writing Project and of special guest contributors. Their articles present some of the most innovative and effective strategies for teaching writing that have been presented over the past 17 years at our annual Summer Institute on the Teaching of Composition.

When the original version of *Practical Ideas for Teaching Writing as a Process* was released in 1986, the early stages of a reform movement in language arts instruction had begun in California. During this movement the *Model Curriculum Standards, Grades Nine Through Twelve*, which includes standards for English/language arts, and the *English–Language Arts Framework for California Public Schools, Kindergarten Through Grade Twelve*, were published. One outcome of these efforts is that the initial *Aha!* that writing is a process evolved into the broader concept that learning is a process. I would like to think that the California Writing Project, and perhaps even *Practical Ideas* itself, which has been used by over 100,000 teachers and others, contributed to the shift in emphasis from learning to read and write to reading and writing to learn and to our emerging sense that literacy is not the possession of minimal competency or basic skills but the development of a richer, deeper, and more integrated base of understanding and knowledge. We emphasize that students must know not only *what* the curriculum consists of but also *how* to solve problems and make their own meaning from what they learn.

As Dan Kirby says elsewhere in this publication, "If you are going to develop your students as thinkers, you must begin to look at knowledge and knowing in new ways." He goes on to say that this new view of knowledge does not mean that you have nothing to teach students or that textbooks are no longer valuable. What it does mean is that we have to plan for and structure our classrooms in such a way that students construct their own versions of old knowledge in new and more personal ways. Many of the new selections in *Practical Ideas* directly reflect this notion that genuine teaching and learning involve not just *transmission* but *transaction*. Reader response strategies, ideas for infusing cooperative learning into the classroom, multiple intelligence projects, alternatives to what one teacher has called the "termpapasauras rex," portfolio assessment and reflection, and an array of interactive strategies to help the growing number of culturally diverse and limited-English-proficient students in California make meaning from their educational experience all embody this constructivist approach.

Because the concept of writing as a process has revolutionized the way in which so many of us view the act of composing and is still at the heart of how we structure our classes and design our learning activities, the stages of that process—prewriting, writing, sharing and responding, revising, rewriting, editing, and evaluating—remain the most logical organization for this publication. Each section of the book begins with a well-known author/teacher presenting specific techniques for highlighting one of the stages of the writing process. After the description of each technique, commentaries are presented in which you will find testimonials, applications of writing techniques at particular grade levels, descriptions of ways to modify the strategies presented for specific audiences, new ideas that sprang from an original idea, and variations on a theme—all contributed by classroom teachers. These commentaries are intended for your use as points of departure as you experiment with the suggested approaches and develop your own curriculum.

For further study of the topics covered in *Practical Ideas*, you may want to consult the list of selected resources at the end of this publication. Here you will find citations for all sources used in the book—works of literature, works from other disciplines, and publications about writing. In this section, works of literature are cited below the titles of the articles in which they appear.

One of the most rewarding dimensions of the California Writing Project and the National Writing Project is the spirit of sharing inherent in the teachers-teaching-teachers model initiated by James R. Gray, founder of the Bay Area, California, and National Writing Projects, and discussed by him as part of the introduction to this book. This publication might be considered a product of the process of sharing that takes place at every writing project site. But it is not meant as a replacement for that process. In fact, we hope it will encourage you to become involved in a summer institute or other available workshops and conferences in your area. Take what you can use, use what you take to supplement what you already know and do well, and make the ideas that are presented your own by adapting them to your unique teaching style and classroom situation.

CAROL BOOTH OLSON
Director, UCI Writing Project

Acknowledgments

Practical Ideas for Teaching Writing as a Process at the Elementary School and Middle School Levels represents the work of many dedicated people over a period of several years. And first, we thank all of the contributing authors whose work appears on the following pages. It was your practical and innovative ideas for teaching writing and your spirit of sharing that made this book a reality. On behalf of all those teachers who will benefit from your generous contributions, we thank you:

Lois Anderson, Carl Babb, Sandra Barnes, Kathy Pierce-Beauchamp, Virginia Bergquist, Ruby Bernstein, Sheridan Blau, Rich Blough, Brenda Borron, Linda Bowe, Barbara Farrell Brand, Pam Burris, Trudy J. Burrus, Rebekah Caplan, Michael Carr, Joni Chancer, Evelyn Ching, Lynda Chittenden, Susanna Clemans, Laurel Corona, Lorna Curran, Catherine D'Aoust, Diane Dawson, Scott Edwards, Peter Elbow, Marie Filardo, Russell Frank, Anita Freedman, Patricia Gatlin, Jenee Gossard, James R. Gray, Jim Hahn, Mary K. Healy, Todd Huck, Charrie Hunter, Pamela W. Jones, Jerry Judd, Spencer S. Kagan, Mifanwy Patricia Kaiser, Lea Kiapos, Dan Kirby, Erline S. Krebs, Jim Lee, Michelle Lindfors, William Lomax, Nancy McHugh, Reba McLaughlin, Ken Macrorie, Mindy Moffatt, Barbara Morton, Greta Nagel, Michael O'Brien, Carol Booth Olson, Laurie Opfell, Linda Bautista-Pappert, Glenn Patchell, Steven Pinney, Robert E. Probst, Mark Reardon, Elizabeth Williams Reeves, Charles L. Reichardt, Gabriele Lusser Rico, Robin Scarcella, Margaret Serences, Esther Severy, Julie Simpson, Dale Sprowl, Jeanne M. Stone, Irene Thomas, Owen Thomas, Mary Turner, Karen Walden, Sue Rader Willett, and Sandi Wright.

We are also indebted to the following publishers, literary agents, and individuals for granting us permission to use copyrighted material selected from their publications:

Aesop. "The Fox and the Grapes." From *Aesop's Fables*, selected and illustrated by Michael Hague. Edited text copyright 1985 by Henry Holt and Company, Inc. Reprinted by permission of Henry Holt and Company, Inc.

Britton, James, and others. *The Development of Writing Abilities (11—18)* (Schools Council Research Studies Macmillan Education Ltd , 1975), pp. 58 and 130. Copyright 1975. Reprinted by permission of James Britton and others and of Thomas Nelson Ltd., Walton-on-Thames, Surrey, England.

Caplan, Rebekah, and Catherine Keech. *Showing Writing: A Training Program to Help Students Be Specific.* Copyright 1980. Reprinted by permission of the Bay Area Writing Project, 615 University Hall, Room 1040, University of California, Berkeley, CA 94720-1040.

Chute, Marchette. *Introduction to Shakespeare* by Marchette Chute. Copyright 1951, renewed 1979 by Marchette Chute. Used by permission of Dutton Signet, a division of Penguin Books USA, Inc.

Connell, Richard E. "The Most Dangerous Game." Copyright 1924 by Richard E. Connell, renewed 1952 by Louise Fox Connell. Reprinted from *Stories* by Richard E. Connell. Reprinted by permission of Brandt & Brandt Literary Agents, Inc., 1501 Broadway, New York, NY 10036.

Curran, Lorna. Lesson 33, "Talking Trees." From *Cooperative Learning Lessons for Little Ones: Language Arts Edition.* Copyright 1993 by Kagan Cooperative Learning. Reprinted by permission of Kagan Cooperative Learning.

Doctorow E. L. *The Book of Daniel.* Copyright 1971 by Random House, Inc. Reprinted by permission of Random House, Inc.

Einstein, Albert. "A Testimonial from Professor Einstein." From *An Essay on the Psychology of Invention in the Mathematical Field*, by Jacques Hadamard. Copyright 1945 by Princeton University Press. Reprinted by permission of Princeton University Press.

Elbow, Peter. Excerpts from *Writing Without Teachers* by Peter Elbow. Copyright 1973 by Oxford University Press, Inc. Reprinted by permission.

Enright, D. Scott, and Mary Lou McClosky. *Integrating English: Developing English Language and Literacy in the Multilingual Classroom.* Reading, Mass.: Addison-Wesley Publishing Co., Inc., 1988, p. 281. Reprinted from Robin Scarcella, *Teaching Language Minority Students in the Multicultural Classroom.* Englewood Cliffs, N.J.: Prentice-Hall, Inc., 1990, p. 79. Copyright 1990 by Prentice-Hall, Inc. Reprinted by permission of Prentice-Hall, Inc.

Gardner, Howard. *Frames of Mind: The Theory of Multiple Intelligences.* Copyright 1984 by Howard Gardner. Reprinted by permission of HarperCollins Publishers, Inc.

Jones, Grahame L. "1904—The Forgotten Games," in the *Los Angeles Times*, July 24, 1984. Copyright 1984, Los Angeles Times. Reprinted by permission of the Los Angeles Times.

Kagan, Spencer, and Laurie Robertson. "Cooperative Learning and the Writing Process," in *Cooperative Learning: Coop Across the Curriculum.* San Juan Capistrano, Calif.: Kagan Cooperative Learning, p. Language Arts: 3. Copyright 1993 by Spencer Kagan, Kagan Cooperative Learning. Reprinted by permission of Spencer Kagan.

Kalan, Robert. Brief text excerpt from *Jump, Frog, Jump!* Copyright 1981 by Robert Kalan. Reprinted in the United States, its dependencies, the Philippine Islands, Canada, and all territory outside the British Commonwealth by permission from Greenwillow Books, a division of William Morrow & Company, Inc. Reprinted in all territory within the British Commonwealth by permission from Walker Books Ltd, London, England.

Kirby, Dan. "Reforming Your Teaching for Thinking: The Studio Approach." Reprinted by permission of Dan Kirby and Carol Kuykendall: *Mind Matters* (Boynton/Cook Publishers, A subsidiary of Reed Elsevier, Inc., Portsmouth, NH, 1991).

Lurie, Toby. Poem from *Conversations and Construction.* Copyright 1978 by Toby Lurie. Reprinted by permission of Toby Lurie.

Megged, Aharon. "The Name." Translated by Minna Givton. From *Israeli Stories.* Edited by Joel Blocker. Copyright 1962 by Schocken Books Inc. Reprinted by permission of Aharon Megged.

O'Brien, Michael. "Some Techniques for Oral Evaluation," *English Journal* (January, 1982). Reprinted by permission of the National Council of Teachers of English.

Olson, Carol Booth. "Tapping Multiple Intelligences Through the Literature Book Project," *THINK*, Vol. 2, No. 2 (December, 1991). Reprinted by permission from ECS Learning Systems, Inc., publishers of *THINK* magazine.

Probst, Robert. "Dialogue with a Text," *English Journal* Vol. 77, No. 1 (January, 1988), 32–38. Copyright 1988 by the National Council of Teachers of English. Reprinted with permission.

Rosenblatt, Louise M. "Language, Literature, and Values," p. 65. Reprinted by permission of Louise Rosenblatt. In *Language, Schooling, and Society*, edited by Stephen N. Tchudi (Boynton/Cook Publishers, A subsidiary of Reed Elsevier, Inc., Portsmouth, NH, 1985).

Sandburg, Carl. "Summer Grass." From *Good Morning, America.* Copyright 1928 and renewed 1956 by Carl Sandburg. Reprinted by permission of Harcourt Brace & Company.

Scardamalia, Marlene. (1981). How Children Cope with the Cognitive Demands of Writing. In M.F. Whiteman (Ed.), *Process, Development, and Communication: Vol. 2. Writing: The Nature, Development, and Teaching of Written Communication.* (p. 81). Hillsdale, N.J.: Lawrence Erlbaum Associates, Inc. Copyright 1981. Reprinted by permission of Lawrence Erlbaum Associates, Inc., and by permission of Marlene Scardamalia.

Shaughnessy, Mina P. *Errors and Expectations: A Guide for the Teacher of Basic Writing.* Copyright 1977. Reprinted by permission of Oxford University Press, Inc.

Simon, Marcia L. *A Special Gift.* San Diego, Calif.: Harcourt Brace Jovanovich. Copyright 1978 by Marcia L. Simon. Reprinted by permission of Marcia L. Simon.

Stanford, Gene, and Marie Smith. *A Guidebook for Teaching Creative Writing.* Newton, Mass.: Allyn & Bacon, Inc. Copyright 1981 by Gene Stanford and Marie Smith. Reprinted by permission of Barbara Stanford and by permission of Marie Smith.

Stone, Jeanne M. *Cooperative Learning and Language Arts: A Multi-Structural Approach.* Copyright 1992 by Kagan Cooperative Learning. Reprinted by permission of Kagan Cooperative Learning.

Tolkien, J.R.R. *The Hobbit.* Copyright 1966 by J.R.R. Tolkien. Reprinted in the United States by permission of Houghton Mifflin Co. All rights reserved. Reprinted throughout the world by permission of George Allen & Unwin, now Unwin Hyman, an imprint of HarperCollins Publishers Limited, London.

Williams, Margery. *The Velveteen Rabbit: Or How Toys Become Real.* Copyright 1983. Reprinted by permission of Henry Holt and Company, Inc.

Introduction

The California Writing Project

By James R. Gray
Founder, Bay Area, California,
and National Writing Projects

The California Writing Project (CWP) is designed to improve the writing of students in California by improving the teaching of writing in the classroom. Teachers teaching other teachers is the project's essential component. Each year over 30,000 teachers from all levels of instruction and regions of the state participate in a variety of summer and school-year programs sponsored by the 17 local writing projects in the statewide CWP network. Each of the projects in the network is established according to the staff development model of the Bay Area Writing Project and is united with the other projects through a common commitment to a set of key assumptions:

- Universities and schools can work together as partners in a cooperative effort to solve the writing problems common to both levels. New collegial and nonhierarchical relationships among professors, instructors, and teachers are essential; the top-down tradition of past university/school programs is no longer useful as a staff development model.
- Many teachers have developed effective approaches to the teaching of writing. These successful teachers can be identified. They can be brought together through summer institutes to learn how to teach other teachers of writing in project-sponsored programs conducted throughout the school year on college campuses and in school districts.
- The best teachers of teachers are other teachers who are believable as consultants because

their ideas and the specific teaching strategies they demonstrate have been developed with students in the classroom.
- Teachers need to experience regularly what they are asking of their students and to discover and understand, through their own writing, the process (of writing) they are teaching.
- Change in classroom practice happens over time. Effective professional development programs are ongoing and systematic— programs that make it possible for teachers to come together regularly throughout their careers to evaluate the best practices of other teachers.
- Effective programs to improve student writing involve teachers at all grade levels and in all content areas. Using writing as a means of discovery and a way of learning is a compelling approach for teachers across the curriculum and across grade levels.
- What is known about the teaching of writing comes not only from research but also from the practice of those who teach writing.

In the summer institutes selected teachers are invited to college campuses as university Fellows and given modest stipends to cover expenses. These teachers demonstrate the specific teaching strategies they have found successful with their own students and, typically, involve the audience of Fellows as students. The demonstrations are considered not only for their effectiveness as approaches to writing but also for their effectiveness as demonstrations. For many teachers in the institutes, this is the first time in their careers that they have ever been asked to present what they know to another teacher. In addition to making demonstrations, teachers examine research and key texts in the field of written composition, work with occasional outside guest speakers, and meet regularly in small editing/response groups to share and examine their own manuscripts. All teachers submit articles for an anthology, which is prepared at the close of the institute.

The intensive five weeks are only a beginning. Participation in the California Writing Project does not stop with the summer institute; it continues with regular follow-up programs that include monthly meetings that bring together summer Fellows from all past institutes to continue the experience of the summer institute. The most important follow-up programs sponsored by the California Writing Project are the professional development workshops held throughout the school year in school districts near each CWP site. Conducted by the teachers from the summer institutes, these workshops are usually three-hour sessions spaced throughout the year. It is in these school district workshops and in the variety of other programs sponsored by the CWP sites that the California Writing Project achieves the ripple effect that now influences teachers in every region of California.

At least twice a year, the directors and codirectors of the 17 CWP sites meet to discuss their programs and to explore common issues. From these meetings all of those persons involved in the writing project movement in California get a sense of its continuing momentum and ever-increasing scope. Most sites now offer several programs beyond the summer institutes and the school year follow-up programs—programs for teachers of English language learners, programs for teachers in urban centers, summer programs open to all teachers who wish to participate in a CWP program, programs on special topics such as portfolio assessment, and teacher research programs. Many sites also offer programs for young writers, parents, and administrators. Increasingly, the writing project is asked to conduct writing-across-the-curriculum workshops for the entire faculty of a school. To meet this need, teachers from the various disciplines who use writing to learn are participating in the summer institutes in greater numbers.

One outgrowth of the California Writing Project is that the number and variety of publications have increased over the years. Most sites distribute quarterly newsletters to their CWP Fellows, and many publish anthologies of writing from students and teachers. Still others are producing monographs and disseminating occasional papers on some of the best practices in the teaching of writing that have originated from their respective summer institutes.

One publication effort was the development of the California Department of Education's *Handbook for Planning an Effective Writing Program,* first published in 1981. Working cooperatively with personnel from offices of county superintendents of schools and the Department of Education, representatives from 15 California Writing Project sites contributed their expertise to the creation of that document. Accordingly, the *Handbook* reflects the basic tenets of the California Writing Project:

- Writing is a tool for learning because it fosters thinking skills.
- As a learning tool, writing can be encouraged across the curriculum.
- The teacher creates an environment that is conducive to learning and to establishing a community of writers; assigning writing is not the same thing as teaching writing.
- Good teachers of writing, themselves, write; good teachers are, themselves, learners.
- Writing, itself, is a process; the act of transforming thought into print involves a nonlinear sequence of creative acts or stages.
- The goal of instruction in writing is to enable students to develop skills in fluency, form, and correctness. Fluency is stressed first because students must be able to produce text before they can edit it.

Building on and complementing the efforts of the *Handbook,* the collection of *Practical Ideas for Teaching Writing as a Process,* developed by the University of California, Irvine/California Writing Project, offers a host of how-to strategies for implementing the basic tenets of the California Writing Project. Like the summer institutes from which its articles and commentaries spring, *Practical Ideas* focuses on what works and why; the authorities are teachers teaching teachers.

Teachers teaching teachers. That is our model for success. The California Writing Project works because it puts a premium on discovering successful practices in the teaching and learning of writing. Its staff development model is not the familiar deficit model that treats teachers as if they were diseased, damaged, and in need of repair. Instead, the model celebrates good teaching and enhances the professional status of teachers. Teachers come to these university-based programs not as students but as colleagues, recognized as authorities in classroom practice, who bring their unique source of knowledge about the teaching of writing. Their commitment, enthusiasm, and desire to share is at the heart of the California Writing Project.

"We Are All Out-of-Date Scientists": New Language Research Since You Left School

By Owen Thomas

Former Professor, English, Linguistics, and Teacher Education, University of California, Irvine; and Former Codirector, UCI Writing Project

In one of S. J. Perelman's books, a character says, "We are all out-of-date scientists." I would like to explain what I think the author meant by that and then to suggest how that meaning relates to teachers of writing.

Mr. Perelman expanded on the statement by saying that our ideas of science are based on the last course we had in a particular science in school. With a very few exceptions, most of us are out-of-date, rather than up-to-date, concerning recent developments in various fields of science. Even scientists are often out-of-date in fields not directly related to their own. Physicists, for example, are often out-of-date in a field such as sociobiology. Organic chemists may well be out-of-date in mathematics. And if this is true for scientists, it is all the more true for most of us who are not working in science every day.

For example, most people assume they have at least some idea of the meaning of infinity. Many people even remember the mathematical symbol for infinity: ∞. But what most people do not know—unless they have kept up with recent developments in mathematics—is that some infinities are larger than other infinities and that there is, in fact, a subbranch of mathematics called the mathematics of infinity.

The point of the preceding example is this: Often, we all sometimes *think* we know a fair amount about a particular subject when, in fact, we are out-of-date. And the fact is that many teachers of writing are out-of-date in some important ways, and I will suggest a few of them. Other contributors to this book will suggest other ways, but none of us knew about these important developments until a few years ago. However, all of us believe that these developments have significant implications for the teaching of composition.

In the next few paragraphs, I will be concerned with two subjects: (1) what young children and adolescents know (in some sense) about language; and (2) what linguists know (in another sense) about language. Finally, I will look briefly at a third subject—namely, what these two kinds of "knowing" imply for the teaching of writing.

Most of the ideas that I am concerned with result from research in the field of psycholinguistics, and particularly in the area of language acquisition. Let us start with one of the most important of these ideas. I will ask a question, and you will believe that you know the answer. Then I will suggest (as gently as possible) that you are out-of-date.

Here is the question: What is the primary function of language?

If you are like most people, you will probably answer, "Communication." Approximately ten years ago, I would have answered the same way. But research during that time has caused me to change my answer. Now I believe the primary function of language, is, in a word, survival—and not simply survival in a social sense (that is, in the sense that, if you do not speak a standard dialect, you would have difficulty surviving in the business world or in some social situations). I mean survival as the biologists use the term. Consider an analogy with the opposing thumb. Humans have thumbs that can rotate so they "oppose" the fingers. This opposition permits us to grasp things—to hold tools—which has helped us survive by enabling us to develop such things as agriculture. In brief, the opposing thumb enhances the ability of the individual—and the species—to survive in the physical world.

Most researchers now believe that the same thing is true of language. Because we have language, we can name things, express relationships between things, develop concepts of cause and effect, and so on. And all this precedes the use of language in communication with others.

The case of Helen Keller is illustrative here. In the sense that I am now using the term *language*, Helen Keller had language long before she learned to communicate with Anne Sullivan. Miss Keller was, in fact, using her *language* to help her survive. In a loving and supportive way, Miss Sullivan was finally able to help Miss Keller relate this *language* to English. But this fact—the important fact—is that the survival language came first. This helps to explain why people are often apprehensive when we—well-meaning English teachers—try to change their language. (I will return to this subject, briefly.) Once we accept the idea of language as survival, we can more easily accept another, perhaps startling, idea: The acquisition of language is primarily a biological—rather than an intellectual—process. That is, most researchers now believe that the ability to acquire language is passed on through the DNA molecule. There is, in fact, evidence that children as young as 12 hours old have begun the process of acquiring language. Once we accept this idea, we can more readily understand several important conclusions that are derived from the idea:

- First, no language is inherently more difficult—more complex—than any other language.
- Second, any child can learn any language as a native language—given the proper circumstances.
- Third, the acquisition of language does not depend, in any way, on formal instruction. Contrary to what many people think, we do not teach language to children. Rather, they learn language biologically and, for the most part, effortlessly.

For the past 15 years, linguists have been trying to describe what it is that children (and adults) know when they know a language. The task is far from over. We have just begun to be able to describe what children "know." Still, what we have learned is, and I use the word with care, *awesome*.

I must proceed slowly here. Actually, I am trying to make two points at once, and both are important:

- First, researchers in language acquisition are convinced that a child entering school has already acquired (biologically) an enormous quantity of linguistic knowledge, particularly syntactic knowledge.
- Second, linguists are still very far away from describing, in any complete way, the precise nature of this knowledge.

As an example of syntactic knowledge, consider one use of *do* in English. There are certain questions, called tag questions, that sometimes require *do* and sometimes do not:

Statement	Related tag question
1. This is interesting.	This is interesting, isn't it?
2. You can swim.	You can swim, can't you?
3. The boy ate the hamburger.	The boy ate the hamburger, didn't he?

The rule for the use of *do, does,* and *did* in such questions is rather complex. It relates to whether the main verb in the statement is a form of *be,* and if it is not, to whether there is an auxiliary verb in the statement. My point, here, is this: Without ever receiving formal instruction in the use of *do,* most five-year-old children know when to use an appropriate form of *do* in a tag question. This is but one example out of thousands that I could cite of a child's syntactic knowledge—hence, my earlier use of the word *awesome.*

The second point is equally important. Although most linguists agree that the amount of knowledge possessed by a child is vast, they do not agree on a description of that knowledge. They do not even agree on such fundamental questions as the basic word order of an English sentence. Some say English is a subject-verb-object (SVO) language. Others say SOV. Still others say VSO.

Both these points relate to the teaching of writing. As a teacher once said to me after I had made the first point (and supported it with considerably more evidence than I have room for here), "Then our job is not to get language *into* the head of a child. Our job is to get it *out*." (The teacher said this to me almost ten years ago. It sums up my point so succinctly that I have been quoting her frequently since then.)

In brief, I believe—and I want to state this as strongly as possible—that any teacher of writing must accept, as fact, the conclusion that school-age children possess an extraordinary wealth of linguistic knowledge. The question, then, is this: How do we get this knowledge "out" in the form of writing?

Much of this book is devoted to suggesting ways of getting the knowledge out, so I will not list these ways here. Rather, I will turn again to the second point.

We know less about the nature of linguistic knowledge—about grammar, if you will—than we do about the structure of the atom. This means, among many other things, that since we do not know the true nature of grammar, we do not know of any way to use grammar when we are teaching children to write. At this point, you may be asking yourself, "But what about parts of speech, what about diagramming, what about defining compound and complex sentences?"

The facts, as briefly as possible, are these. Traditional grammar—that is, of the sort most widely taught in schools today—is an extremely inaccurate description of English. Most people's knowledge of the system of English is as out-of-date as their knowledge of infinity. Moreover, research dating back more than 50 years, and frequently reconfirmed since then, indicates that a knowledge of traditional grammar bears no relation to writing ability. Even more significantly, recent research into brain hemispheres (right and left brains) indicates that the formal study of grammar (a left-brain activity) actually interferes with writing fluency (principally, right-brain activity).

In summary, we know that most children have linguistic knowledge adequate to the skill of writing, but we do not yet know of any way to use a formal description of this knowledge to help children develop their writing skills. Some things, however, are clear:

- The starting point in the teaching of writing must be the teacher's belief that children possess the requisite linguistic knowledge.
- Teachers need to use every possible means to give their students confidence in their linguistic knowledge. (Children who believe that they "don't know any grammar" are children who also believe they "can't write.")
- "Getting language out" is a process, and teachers of writing must have an intimate knowledge of this process. The best way of gaining this kind of knowledge is in actual writing.

I have discussed the first two of the preceding points already. The third point requires some comment. In every writing project that comes under the umbrella of the California Writing Project, the Project Fellows spend a considerable amount of time writing and discussing each other's writing. This writing, in fact, is the cornerstone of the project. Usually, at the beginning of a project, the majority of Fellows think the writing segment is only a minor part of the project. The major part, they think, will be the suggestions they receive on how to teach. But by the end of the project, the great majority of Fellows see the writing segment as the single most important part. They have experienced—in a very personal way—both the hardships and the rewards of writing. They know, personally, that writing is seldom fun, seldom easy, and they also know that it can be extremely satisfying.

When they discussed writing before taking part in one of the California Writing Projects, the Project Fellows would talk about dangling modifiers, spelling, subject/verb agreement, and so on—all things that relate to the end product. After the project, they are much more inclined to talk about the process rather than the product of writing. Having shared their writing with other Fellows, they are vastly more sensitive to what a writer's real needs are. Having listened to criticism—some positive, some negative—of their own writing, they are better able to make helpful criticisms of a student's writing. It is through experiences like these that the Fellows come to appreciate—to experience—the fact that language is more than just communication. Language is associated with our sense of self, and ultimately, with survival.

In summary, in the out-of-date way of teaching writing we once subscribed to, we thought it necessary to put language into students' heads. Actually, the time we spent trying to do that was time we did not spend in real writing, in getting the language out. And it is to the task—and the joy of teaching real writing that my fellow contributors to this book now ask you to turn.

Owen Thomas died of lung cancer in March, 1990. Throughout his long and painful ordeal, the courage with which Owen faced his illness and the remarkable compassion which he demonstrated toward those he loved was truly inspirational. In December, 1989, to honor and celebrate Owen's many contributions to the UCI Writing Project, the teacher/consultants presented him with the just-completed manuscript of Thinking/Writing: Fostering Critical Thinking Through Writing, which was later published by HarperCollins Publishers (1992). Three pages in, Owen found these words:

This book is dedicated to Owen Thomas, who taught us that our job is not to put language into kids' heads but to help them express "the extraordinary 'wealth of linguistic knowledge' that each of them already possesses through writing."

The Process

Teaching Writing as a Process

By Catherine D'Aoust
Coordinator, Instructional Services,
Saddleback Valley Unified School District;
and Codirector, UCI Writing Project

I was introduced to the concept of writing as a process several years ago at a composition conference at the University of California, Irvine. At that time I was teaching composition— not very successfully—and found that the idea of writing as a process afforded me a new perspective and had tremendous implications for classroom teaching. I immediately revised my curriculum and began to see my students improve as writers. What I have provided in this essay is a general description of the stages of the writing process and a discussion of the significance of this process for both the teacher and student. Subsequent sections of this book will offer practical ideas for teaching the various stages in the writing process at all levels of the curriculum.

Identifying the Stages of Writing as a Process

When writers and linguistic researchers describe writing as a process, they are attempting to describe the incredibly complex system of transforming thought into written communication. This description has had a significant impact on the composition teacher whose demand for a product has been replaced by a concern for the series of stages, both focused and unfocused, conscious as well as unconscious, which make up the writing process. It has meant using the stage-process model—prewriting, writing, sharing/responding, revising, editing, and evaluating—as a teaching tool to facilitate student writing. To do so, the composition teacher has had to reassess his or her goals and determine how to marry his or her process as a teacher with that of the student writer to improve the ultimate product.

Prewriting

The stage-process model begins by focusing on *prewriting*. Prewriting activities are designed to stimulate the flow of ideas before any structured writing begins. Writing arises out of a sense of having something to communicate. Any exercise which stimulates the writer's inner voice to seek verbalization is a prewriting activity. Brainstorming, clustering, debating, freewriting, and fantasizing are a few of the infinite possibilities. Prewriting activities generate ideas; they encourage a free flow of thoughts and help students discover both what they want to say and how to communicate it on paper. In other words, prewriting activities facilitate the planning for both the product and the process.

Writing

With a desire to communicate, students move to the next stage, *writing*. They allow their ideas to take shape by putting words to paper. However, the writers may lack any conscious awareness of what they specifically want to communicate. Writing then becomes a discovery on the conscious level. This movement of an idea to the conscious level allows for spontaneity and creativity and must not be impeded by concerns over correctness. Writing is simplified as the writers let go and disappear into the act of writing. As Sondra Perl says in her article, "Understanding Composing" (*College Composition and Communication*, December, 1980), "Writing is a process of coming into being."

Sharing/Responding

Having expressed themselves, the students move to the next stage called *sharing*. Writing can be a very lonely process; some of the difficulty in writing comes from the fact that it is one-way communication. Unlike speech, a writer's words often go untested. The writers use their own reactions to their words for primary feedback. Frequently, writers become so engrossed in what

> *Writing, itself, is a process; the act of transforming thought into print involves a nonlinear sequence of creative acts or stages.*
>
> JAMES R. GRAY

they are saying that it is impossible to distinguish between what they want to say and what they said. Given a chance to share with others, student writers gain a sense of the power of their words to have an impact on others. They gain a sense of audience, a significant trusted other, who will be influenced by the words of the writer. It is not unusual at this phase for writers to discover an incongruity between the purpose and the effect of their writing; writers may have intended to communicate a specific idea but, through the feedback from peers, learn that they did not do so. Then writers are at liberty to revise or possibly reassess their intention.

Besides providing an audience and reactions to the writing, sharing generates enthusiasm about writing. Writers are inspired by effective student models to improve their own communication. Moreover, in *responding* to the writing being shared by others, writers gain a clearer sense of what distinguishes effective from ineffective writing. Once the students have discovered that they *can* write, the instructor can now teach revising and editing skills because the student writers will not only need them but will also request them.

Revising

Revising, then, is a *re-viewing* of the writing in light of the feedback. It is a reworking of the composition on both semantic and lexical levels; the writers are concerned not only with the words they have chosen to express their ideas but also with how these words work together. The student writers scratch out, mark over, add, rephrase, and reorder to make their words consistent with the intended meaning. It is a focused and conscious manipulation of words. Changes may be in words, phrases, sentences, paragraphs, or in the total composition.

Revision actually can occur at any time during the writing process because of the recursive nature of the act of composing. Sondra Perl further explains that writing is not simply a linear process but a "forward moving action that exists by virtue of a backward moving action." Writers put words to a page and immediately go back to see what they have created. Sondra Perl contends that writers not only go back to bits of discourse but

The result of structuring a composition course around the concept of writing as a process is that student writers come to understand that they have ideas to express.

CATHERINE D'AOUST

also return to their notion of the topic as well as to the "nonverbalized perceptions that surround the words." Student writers go backward to discover what they said and move forward to elaborate on it. The impulse to revise could occur at any time.

Editing

After addressing meaning, writers focus on correctness. This next stage in the writing process is *editing*, the imposing of correctness. Editing is a focused, deliberate, grammatical concern. The writers continue to rework their papers by adding and deleting and by correcting punctuation, spelling, and grammar. In keeping with the purpose of their work, the writers conform to the standards of written English.

During this altering and refining phase, the teacher will be called on to use his or her linguistic expertise. Appropriately, the composition teacher addresses grammar when it is relevant. Rather than using arbitrary grammar and punctuation exercises, the teacher is able to draw on the students' own writing to illustrate polishing techniques. Within that context, the writers use and increase their knowledge of the structure of the language to improve communication.

Evaluating

It is imperative during the focused, more conscious phases of the writing process that students have a clear sense of how their writing will be evaluated and by whom. The teacher and students must agree regarding the standards that will be used for evaluating writing. *Evaluation*, the next stage in the writing process, is simply the final feedback for the student writers and usually comes in the form of a grade. Often, there is a discrepancy between the criteria used by the teacher and the

students for evaluation. If a letter grade is a surprise, the writing process is flawed. This generally happens when a teacher sets the standards for evaluation, often with an undue emphasis on correctness, either without adequately communicating the standards to the class or with few or no suggestions from the students.

Dialogue between the teacher and the student writers concerning evaluation also allows the teacher more options. Optimally, the students should be able to assess their own papers. However, if the teacher assesses the writing, the students should be able to offer suggestions. One effective technique for giving students this opportunity is to have the writers attach statements to their papers in which they give the criteria they would like used in assessing their work. The writers and teacher then have complementary roles in the writing process.

Overlapping of the Stages

As the teacher facilitates the students' writing process, it becomes apparent that the writing stages overlap and sometimes compete for the students' attention. Student writers do not simply move linearly from procedure to procedure. Their own recursive inner processes dictate the sequence. Rarely do students inhibit themselves while writing from spontaneously editing, revising, and sharing. The stages are ongoing, and with the guidance of the instructor, student writers are able to direct their attention while still acknowledging the demands of their inner processes. (See Figure 1 for an illustration of this conceptual model.)

The result of structuring a composition course around the concept of writing as a process is that student writers come to understand that they have ideas to express, that they can find words to communicate those ideas, that others are interested in what they have to say, and finally that they have or can acquire the expertise to clarify that communication. The teacher facilitates all this and takes satisfaction in watching the writing of students improve. To help students discover their individual writing processes, the teacher may have to restructure the classroom and constantly reevaluate his or her role as a writing teacher. The result of this is that the teacher will probably feel better about being a teacher/facilitator of writing primarily because his or her students are becoming much better writers.

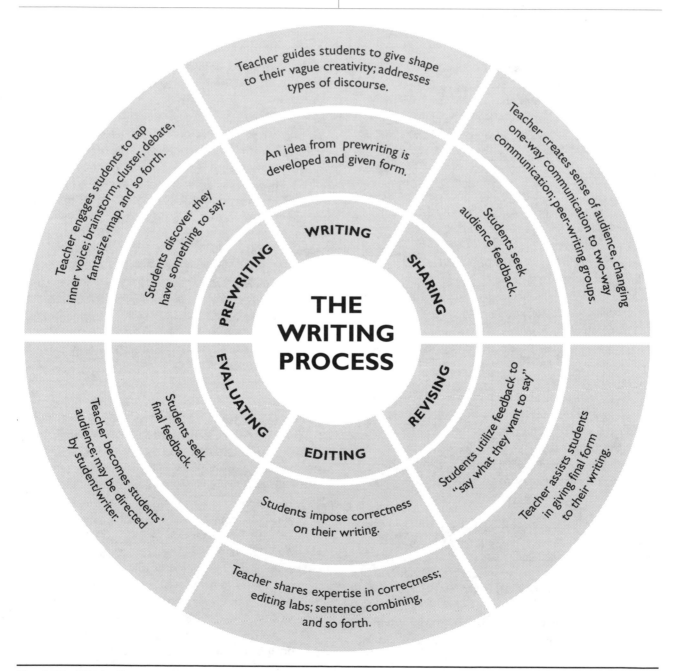

Fig. 1. The Writing Process

Practical Ideas for Teaching Writing as a Process

Introducing Teachers to the Concept of Writing as a Process

By Sue Rader Willett

English Teacher, Capistrano Valley High School,
Capistrano Unified School District;
and Teacher/Consultant, UCI Writing Project

Practice what you preach! Those few simple words have to be one of the most irritating, guilt-inducing, challenging, hackneyed, and—begrudgingly, I admit—wisest adages I know. They have certainly taunted and guided me through many personal dilemmas, classroom lessons, and, oddly enough, in-service workshops for colleagues, administrators, and lay people.

In fact, I consciously work to practice what we, the teacher/consultants from the UCI Writing Project, enthusiastically preach and teach. Much of our approach to the teaching of writing boils down to five tenets:

1. Teachers of writing should, themselves, write so that they are in touch with their own writing abilities.
2. Students should experience audiences other than the teacher as assessor. Other audiences include self, peer, and teacher as a partner in learning.
3. Peer response groups can lessen the load of correcting papers and yet ensure that the students get ample writing experiences and constant feedback.
4. Students should be involved in the evaluation process.
5. Teachers should stress the written product less and emphasize writing as a process more.

Those basic statements of philosophy can easily be translated into an in-service training design.

Planning an in-service training program to introduce the concept of writing as a process is very much like planning any lesson, meeting, or composition. One begins by forming a clear idea of the audience to be addressed and the message to be communicated. Once these two items have been defined, one has to create a procedural plan for presenting the writing process.

I believe that it is imperative to "hook" your audience within the first few seconds of your in-service training workshop, and the easiest and most effective way to do that is to immediately involve them on a very personal level. What is a better way of doing that than writing?

"The Popcorn Reminiscence," which I have used as an opening for in-service training, is a simple exercise in sensory/descriptive and narrative writing. (A little exposition might work itself in here and there, too.) Save the theory and research for later. Begin with an experience, such as the one for "The Popcorn Reminiscence" outlined below:

The Popcorn Reminiscence

1. Planning the experience (to be completed before the in-service training begins):
   a. Assemble the popcorn popper, popcorn, butter, salt, oil (preferable for olfactory impact), serving utensils, and napkins.
   b. Pop or purchase enough prepared popcorn to serve the participants.
   c. Set up your equipment and utensils near a working electrical outlet.

2. Prewriting activity
   a. While the popcorn is popping and the aroma is permeating the entire room, ask the participants to begin clustering the word *popcorn*. Direct them to include any experiences they connect with popcorn.
   b. Serve the popcorn while they cluster. Taste will spark more ideas.
   c. You may wish to use an overhead projector or chalkboard to record (cluster) their words, as shown in Figure 2.

3. Writing activity
   a. Inform the students that they should begin writing when they feel ready and believe they have clustered enough. A prompt might be:

      Write a short personal reminiscence that involves popcorn.

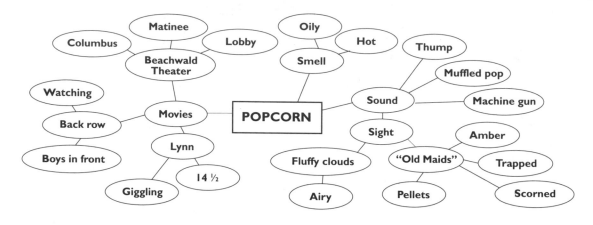

Fig. 2. The Clustering of *Popcorn*

b. Explain that what they write will be read and evaluated by others for content and any other attributes you wish to include.

c. Write with them if possible. Many will be nervous, and your openness will help.

4. Postwriting activity

a. After a few minutes of writing, ask them to finish up and quickly reread for minor editing. Stress that papers are to be read as first and very rough drafts.

b. Ask each participant to record the last four digits of his or her telephone number at the top of the page and to title the piece.

c. Conduct a "read-around" for evaluation. (See the section on read-around groups, which appears later in the book, for a description of this technique.) Direct the readers to jot down the numbers of the papers they most enjoyed.

d. After all the papers have been read, ask the participants to share the numbers of the papers they enjoyed. Record the numbers on a chart or chalkboard, and positively reinforce those whose numbers appeared.

5. Establishing closure and directing the participants to take a short break

a. During the break encourage the participants to discuss the experience they shared.

b. You may wish to join in informally or take this time to collect your thoughts or clean up the popcorn area.

After the members of your audience have written and have immersed themselves in the very activity we so quickly demand of our students,

they will be open to a fresh view of the complexity of the writing process with all its cognitive and affective variables. Marlene Scardamalia reminds us how complex the task of written composition is:

> "The proposition that it is theoretically impossible to learn to write has the ring of truth," says Peter Elbow [in *Writing Without Teachers*, 1973, page 135]. Too many interdependent skills are involved, and all seem to be prerequisite to one another. To pay conscious attention to handwriting, spelling, punctuation, word choice, syntax, textual connections, purpose, organization, clarity, rhythm, euphony, and reader characteristics would seemingly overload the information processing capacity of the best intellects.[1]

Every practicing writer intuitively knows that. We must reinforce that knowledge and use it wisely. Your audience knows that writing, good writing, is extremely difficult to achieve. Yet, they must be made aware that it can be done in a much less than chaotic, hit-or-miss fashion that many teachers practice—for want of better training and information.

Therefore, it is helpful to explain the writing process at this point in your presentation. It may include these stages:

1. Prewriting: Brainstorming, collecting material, and giving data from which an assign-

---

[1]From "How Children Cope with the Cognitive Demands of Writing," (p. 81) by Marlene Scardamalia. In *Writing: Process, Development, and Communication*, Vol. 2 of *Writing: The Nature, Development, and Teaching of Written Communication*. Edited by Marcia F. Whiteman, 1981, Hillsdale, N.J.: Lawrence Erlbaum Associates, Inc. Copyright 1981. Reprinted by permission of the author and the publisher.

ment is written (clustering, lecture, experience, discussion, and so forth).

2. Precomposing: The assignment is given, and a writing plan is formulated (mapping, outlining, and so forth).

3. Writing: Ideas from prewriting and precomposing are developed and given form in verse or prose.

4. Sharing: Writing is shared with others (partner or group) for positive feedback or suggestions for revision.

5. Rewriting: Based on the feedback received in the sharing step, additions and deletions are made on paper.

6. Evaluation: The writing is scored on the basis of a rubric, a list of desirable qualities a paper is measured against (formal or informal).

7. Rewriting and reevaluation: This is an optional step that may be used as many times as necessary.

Remind your audience that writing is a recursive process and that even though we may logically delineate its various stages, they do not occur in a nice, neat, orderly fashion. In fact, they often happen all at once or out of sequence. Writing is, indeed, one of the most complex intellectual and even emotional processes a person engages in, and it draws from the left and right hemispheres of the brain. While the process model outlined above is certainly not a perfect description of the writing activity, it does serve as a very effective teaching design, one that is readily understood by children and adults. (For more information on the process, see the Department of Education's *Handbook for Planning an Effective Writing Program*.)

After discussing the writing process generally and emphasizing the complexity of thought and the stages of the process, you might want to establish that teachers of writing can systematically work to improve writing based on the three goals of fluency, form, and correctness, as defined below:

- Fluency: Authentic voice, facility with words and phrasing, ability to be spontaneous, a "mature" or appropriate vocabulary, a sense of pacing
- Form: Logical development, adequate transition, use of supporting details, variation of sentence structure

- Correctness: Using the conventions of written English (spelling, punctuation, grammar) and departing from them only for a valid reason

We must work to refine and practice the goals of fluency, form, and correctness in our lessons and in our personal writing. I believe it would be safe to assume that these are the same goals even the most respected and prolific writers seek to perfect.

As much as we would like to believe that writing can be perfected, I am not certain that it can be. Certainly, the "greats" come close. Blasphemous as it may sound, consider that William Shakespeare, Alexander Pope, Samuel Johnson, Thomas Hardy, Raymond Chandler, D. H. Lawrence, Ernest Hemingway, Carl Sandburg, Henry David Thoreau, and all the other great writers still needed to refine certain aspects of these goals. And although our students and we writers certainly produce works that are far from perfect, we face the same task and the same problems as they did— step by step by step. *Great* writing may be a long way off, but *good* writing could be right around the corner. Just remember, Johnny can and does write with the proper guidance. Your in-service training can make a difference to Johnny's teacher if you plan it with a philosophy in mind, involve your audience as writers, present a systematic approach to teaching, and, of course, *practice what you preach.*

Talking Students Through the Thinking-Writing Process

By Jerry Judd

English Teacher, Irvine High School, Irvine Unified School District; and Teacher/Consultant, UCI Writing Project

I have always been a believer in writing with my students, becoming a partner in learning, and engaging in a true dialogue with them about the writing and learning that are occurring in my classroom. To begin this process, I direct students through prewriting activities to help them generate ideas, give them the prompt to guide them, and provide precomposing activities to aid them in translating their thoughts into print. Then the writing begins. At this point I used to sit at my desk and observe some students writing successfully; some sitting puzzled, not exactly sure what to do next; and others staring at the ceiling, blank page, or scrawling hand of the person next to them.

Since I have been exposed to the concept of metacognition, I have become aware of how important it is to model my own thinking and writing process as my students are engaged in the act of composing. *Metacognition*, in its simplest sense, can be defined as thinking about thinking. It is a conscious monitoring of one's own thinking process. It could be the ability to realize that you do not understand something another person just said. It could be paraphrasing aloud what someone has just told you to determine whether he or she will agree that that is, in fact, exactly what was meant. It could be the realization that someone does not know enough about a particular subject to write effectively about it and needs to gather more information before beginning to write. I have found that one of the most valuable uses of metacognition is as a tool for self-questioning. Rarely, if ever, have students had the opportunity to listen to how a writer thinks during the writing process. My students needed to hear how a writer progressed through the same writing assignments that they were doing.

So, now, when my students are ready to begin writing a draft, I talk them through my own thinking-writing process. I begin by thinking aloud. Those students who are working well are instructed to continue writing and to ignore me. They pause only momentarily as my voice begins; then they go back to their work. Those who are having trouble starting to write focus their attention on me and what I am saying. I admit that at first they look at me and think I am somewhat crazy talking to myself, rambling, talking off the top of my head, and jotting down ideas on the overhead projector. But they get used to this activity rather quickly. There is value in having students see *raw* words scrawled on the page, the first draft being illuminated by the light of the overhead projector.

Here is a partial list of questions to ask yourself when starting this self-talk, self-questioning, metacognitive technique:

What do I want to write about?
What do I know about this subject?
What essential knowledge do I lack about this subject?
What do I want to say about this subject?
How will I organize my piece?
Who is my audience?
What effect do I want to have on my audience?
How do I get from the beginning of this piece to the end?

The only ground rule during this process is that no one can interrupt me or ask questions. I admit, at first, this is a frightening thing to put myself through. Some teachers may want to forgo my ground rule and elicit comments and suggestions from the class if they get stuck. It is valuable, though, for teachers to become *stuck* in their thinking. Perhaps this is the best pedagogical tool of all. For it is here that students are able to see the difficulty of the writing process, even for the teacher of writing. "Let's see how he gets himself out of this one," I can almost hear a student think as he leans back in his chair against the back wall.

I go through this self-questioning/thinking-aloud process while the students listen, get ideas, and then begin their own drafts. I also do a similar process during the revision and editing stages of the writing process. I do this with my writing as an example and also with students' drafts. Sometimes, students will take my place and sit in the "writer's chair" at the overhead projector and think and write before their classmates.

I have found this technique invaluable in demonstrating to inexperienced writers how a writer thinks through the writing process. This technique brings students in the class in touch with their own problem-solving process and allows them to assess and see what *thinking* must occur before they can write.

For most of the students, they are seeing a new persona they have not encountered in a teacher before. After observing me in this process, my students look at me differently—as a writer, as someone who shares the same frustrations and triumphs as they do. Students often comment that other teachers have told them *what* to write, but I am the first one who has ever shown them *how* to write.

Prewriting

Clustering:
A Prewriting Process

By Gabriele Lusser Rico
Associate Professor, English and Creative Arts,
California State University, San Jose

Even after several years of continued experiments with clustering in my classrooms, I remain awed at its simple power, excited by its many applications, surprised at the changes it has wrought in my overall approach to teaching.

The clustering process grew out of my fascination with the findings from brain research of the past 20 years, and it represents a way to involve the talents of the mute right brain in the complex symbolic activity that we call writing. The story of specialized capacities of the two hemispheres of the brain has been told again and again. In this brief space it is enough to say that the left brain has primarily logical, linear, and syntactic capabilities while the right brain has holistic, image-making, and synthetic capabilities.

Clustering is based on the premise that any effective writing effort moves from a whole—no matter how vague or tenuous—to the parts, then back to a more clearly delineated whole. What is of overriding importance for writing is that the talents of both hemispheres of the brain be brought into play in the process. Clustering focuses on that initial whole by fashioning a trial web of knowings from the clusterer's mental storehouse.

What Is It?

Exactly what is clustering? I can define clustering as a nonlinear brainstorming process that generates ideas, images, and feelings around a stimulus word until a pattern becomes discernible. But the student evaluation of clustering, as shown in Figure 1, presents a clearer, more graphic definition. As this student indicates, clustering makes silent, invisible mental processes visible and manipulable; hence, teachable and usable. In short, clustering is a powerful mental tool.

How Does It Work?

How does clustering work? It works, very likely, by blocking the critical censorship of the analytic left

Clustering engenders and encourages expressive behavior at all levels of proficiency.

GABRIELE LUSSER RICO

brain and by allowing the synthesizing right brain to make flash-like nonlinear connections. A cluster is an expanding universe, and each word is a potential galaxy; each galaxy, in turn, may throw out its own universes. As students cluster around a stimulus word, the encircled words rapidly radiate outward until a sudden shift takes place, a sort of Aha! that signals a sudden awareness of that tentative whole which allows students to begin writing.

What Are Appropriate Instructions?

What instructions should you give to begin this prewriting process? I have found the following both appropriate and effective:

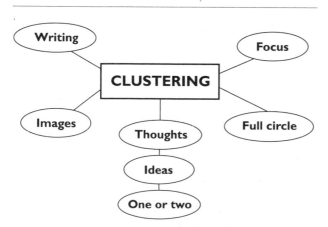

I believe that clustering is a natural process we do unconsciously in our minds. It is more helpful to do it on paper, though. Our mind clusters many ideas and thoughts, but it is unable to sort and sift the ideas into a reasonable order around one main focus. When we cluster on paper, we can visually look at our ideas and choose which ones we want to use. The thoughts in our mind are all piled together, and we see only one or two at a time. On paper, through clustering, we can see all our thoughts at once as a whole.

Fig. 1. An Anonymous Student Evaluation of Clustering

1. Tell students that they are going to learn to use a tool that will enable them to write more easily and more powerfully—a tool similar to brainstorming.
2. Encircle a word on the board—for example, *energy*—and ask students, "What do you think of when you see that word?" Encourage all responses. Cluster these responses, radiating outward. When the students have finished giving their responses, say, "See how many ideas there are floating around in your heads? Now, if you cluster all by yourself, you will have a set of connections as unique to your own mind as your thumbprint is to your thumb."
3. Now ask students to cluster a second word for themselves. Before they begin, tell them that the clustering process should take no more than one to two minutes and that the paragraph they will write should take about eight minutes. Ask them to keep clustering until the Aha! shift, signaling that their mind is holding something they can shape into a whole. In writing, the only constraint is that they "come full circle"; i.e., that they do not leave the writing unfinished. Some excellent words are *afraid* or *try* or *help*.
4. After they finish writing, ask students to give a title to what they have written that is suggestive of the whole.

Figure 2 is a cluster and paragraph by a college freshman written on the first day I introduced clustering to the class. Note the quality of wholeness—the completeness of the piece. Note the rather sophisticated stylistic devices, such as repetition and parallel construction, which increasingly become a part of student writing as students continue to cluster. Note also that this ten-minute

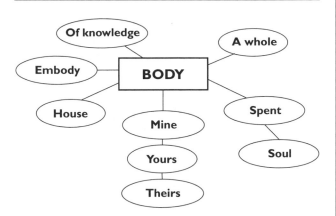

I sometimes wish for a different one—this body that is me. I am inside this scrawny hide that other people react to instead of to the real me. They look at me real funny-like sometimes; maybe they wonder what's inside. So I talk, and they hear what is inside by what I say; perhaps they see what is inside by how I move; or maybe they guess what is inside by what I do. Now, you please talk to me, so I can know something about the you inside your body.

Fig. 2. Paragraph Developed from Clustering *Body*

effort, although complete in itself, has the potential of being developed into a highly focused, longer piece of writing. The organic center is already there.

What Is the Effect of Clustering?

The writer whose cluster and paragraph are reproduced in Figure 2 discovered—even after the first time—that clustering was easy and unthreatening. Since a cluster draws on primary impressions—yet simultaneously on a sense of the overall design—clustering actually generates structure, shaping one thought into a starburst of other thoughts, each somehow related to the whole. That is why clustering so often results in writing that is naturally marked by increased coherence, increased fluency, increased concrete support, and an increased sense of how to expand ideas.

Perhaps the most significant outcome of clustering is its idiosyncratic nature. A stimulus word filtered through the singular experiential grid of each individual clusterer produces a unique constellation. The stimulus (cluster word) *fragments*, for example, produced three widely divergent responses, as shown in Figure 3.

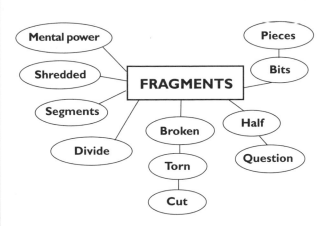

When I think of the word, fragment, it makes me try to visualize the inside of my head. It just seems as though my mind is always divided, never really coming to a whole. One half wants to do something that the other half doesn't want to do. One seems to be saying, "Come on, let's not go to class; you can do your paper later," while the other side of my mind answers back, "but I have to because I'll be missing out on my learning." These two halves go on and on like that, just bruising the inside of my mind, and, if they continue, they'll probably shred my mind all to pieces.

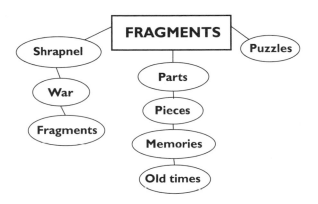

Sometimes, when I'm sitting back, relaxed and reminiscing over old times in my head, small fragments of memories will flash through my mind. They never stay long enough to be recognized by my brain as a complete thought. They seem to stay just long enough to bring back the emotion of the moment, and I will find myself smiling or frowning or wanting to cry. I wish I could grab hold of these pieces of my memory— especially the happy ones—as they fly by the recall part of my brain, but I am happy at least for the glimpses I get.

(Continued on next page)

Fig. 3. Three Responses to Clustering the Word *Fragments*

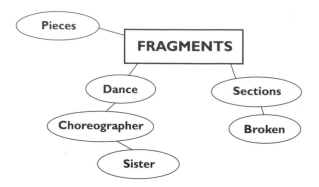

My sister choreographed a dance called "Fragments" last year for the SJSU Arts Department. The reason she named her dance "Fragments" was that the whole dance was made up of bits and pieces of dances. There were about five different movements making up the whole dance. It was as if the entire dance were broken up into five separate themes. Because there was no fixed pattern, the dance really didn't make sense. The dance definitely did not flow together. Well, that was the purpose of her dance—fragments.

Fig. 3. Three Responses to Clustering the Word *Fragments* (Continued from previous page)

In summary, clustering engenders and encourages expressive behavior at all levels of proficiency. As with any useful tool, be it pen or paintbrush, the more it is used, the more natural its use becomes. In my own teaching I have made clustering an integral part of all the writing assignments, long or short, and suggest further that it be introduced as a right-brain tool from the earliest grades onward. The most effective means for getting the *feel* of clustering is to introduce it conjointly with journal writing. Journal writing, long a part of most English curricula with limited success, will take on new dimensions through the focusing power of clustering. As students begin to experience that sense of accomplishment in actually producing a cluster, they discover that they do have something to say after all. They also discover that writing begins to flow on its own if a sense of play is allowed to enter the process. The student's evaluation of clustering in Figure 4 focuses precisely on this play-element of clustering.

Yes, clustering is "fooling around," indeed. Instead of writing as sheer labor, clustering turns writing into something closer to cultivated play. In so doing, such "fooling around" makes contact with our natural right-brain potential for creating connections, for perceiving one idea related to another, and for seeing the world whole.

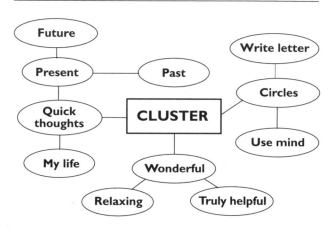

I sat down to work in order to catch up on some journal entries when my mother stood over my shoulder and noticed my clustering. Puzzled, she inquired, "Why are you fooling around making circles when you have work to do?" It seemed a silly idea to her, and it did to me also when I first encountered it. However, I have come to admire my little circles, for it is those circles with words in them that generate thoughts, bring back experiences, and enable me to use my mind to the utmost.

Clustering can be summed up in one word: wonderful. I have learned something that I will carry with me for the rest of my life; that is, I have learned to generate ideas. Thank goodness for those circles.

Fig. 4. A Student's Evaluation of Clustering

EDITOR'S NOTE: For further information on clustering, see Gabriele Rico and Mary Frances Claggett's monograph, *Balancing the Hemispheres: Brain Research and the Teaching of Writing,* which was published in 1980 by the Bay Area Writing Project, 615 University Hall, Room 1040, University of California, Berkeley , CA 94720-1040. You will also find helpful Dr. Rico's book *Writing the Natural Way: Using Right Brain Techniques to Release Your Expressive Powers,* published in 1983. It was published by J. P. Tarcher, Inc., 9110 Sunset Blvd., Suite 250, Los Angeles, CA 90069; and distributed by Houghton Mifflin Co.

Practical Ideas for Using Clustering in the Prewriting Stage

Clustering with Nonreaders/ Writers

By Michael Carr

Teacher, Valley Junior High School,
Carlsbad Unified School District;
and Teacher/Consultant, UCI Writing Project

Clustering is a method of prewriting that enables the writer to map out all of his or her thoughts on a particular subject and then to choose which ones to use. With nonreaders, clustering can be used for the same purpose. With readers, words are clustered around a central topic, as shown in Figure 5. Nonreaders can experiment with the same technique by using symbols (pictures) to represent the words. When I taught kindergarten through grade one, we started with a topic, such as being afraid, and then did a group cluster on the board. For example, I asked the children to tell me all of the things they were afraid of, and we created a cluster that looked like the one in Figure 6.

Most of our group clusters had at least 15 items. However, even though the group cluster in Figure 6 is abbreviated in scope, it contains the major topic points. After doing a group cluster, the children then do their own cluster on large sheets of news-print, using as many or as few items from the group cluster as they wish to. The children also have the option of adding items to their own cluster that were not present on the group cluster. An example of an individual cluster is shown in Figure 7.

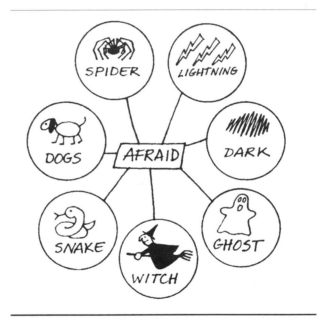

Fig. 6. Clustering with Nonreaders

Fig. 7. A Nonreader's Clustering of *Afraid*

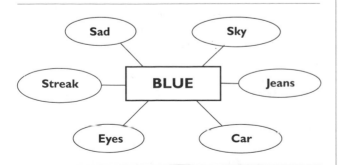

Fig. 5. The Clustering of *Blue*

> *For me, the initial delight is in the surprise of remembering something I didn't know I knew.*
>
> ROBERT FROST

From the group cluster the children choose something they wish to write about. Tony, the author of the cluster shown in Figure 7, chose to write about witches. He then did his final drawing on white ditto paper:

Tony dictated, "I am afraid of witches because they might have ghosts." His picture included other elements of things he was afraid of, such as the dark. Note that the children dictate their sentence to me; I write it on paper, and then they copy it.

In clustering with symbols, I have found that children in my class always have something to write because they do not have to worry about decoding skills that they do not possess (according to Piaget children recognize symbols before they recognize words). After a while, the children created clusters that included a few words they knew, along with the symbols for those words. By the end of the year, some of the children were able to use all the words in their cluster or a combination of words and symbols. When students are at a point where they can generate three or four sentences, I have them number the word/pictures in their cluster to help them organize their ideas.

The process I use to teach clustering to nonreaders/writers can be described as follows:

1. Introduce the topic and get a few oral responses.

2. Write the topic word on the chalkboard and circle it.
3. Draw all the children's responses to the topic cluster.
4. Have children create their own clusters on large newsprint.
5. Have the children choose those symbols from their clusters that they want to write about and draw the symbols on good paper.
6. Have the children dictate their sentences to you; then have each student copy his or her sentence. (Noncopiers may trace.)
7. Have the children read their papers in a sharing group.

This technique has produced a feeling of "can do" when it comes to writing in my classroom. All the children are able to succeed and begin to see themselves as writers. And, before they know it, they are!

Clustering in First Grade

By Kathy Pierce Beauchamp

Teacher, Melbourne A. Gauer Elementary School,
Anaheim Elementary School District;
and Teacher/Consultant, UCI Writing Project

Clustering is an open-ended, nonlinear form of sorting ideas. It is a visual structuring of concepts, events, and feelings. Once the main focus is chosen or provided, ideas may be generated around it. By clustering on paper, the children can sift and sort their thoughts into a whole. Clustering helps make writing more like the taking of a picture—thereby making writing less frightening.

In the first grade, clustering helps students generate ideas and enables them to relate to something and to write about it. Group clustering is very easy and enjoyable for the children. Using a shared experience—field trips, cooking, special events, or any created situation—students may form a group cluster on the chalkboard. Questions, especially those involving the five senses, will elicit descriptive responses. Children can then form their own sentences from the group cluster. For example, after the children made popcorn, they created the cluster shown in Figure 8.

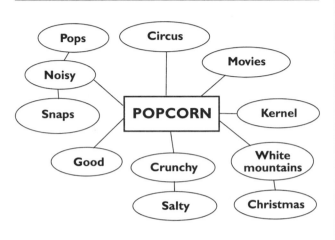

Fig. 8. Clustering of *Popcorn* by First Graders

Individual clustering is also very successful for first graders, especially if you can talk personally with each child. Use questioning to elicit a response as to what the main focus is to be. Additional appropriate questions can generate the images for children to cluster, and they can write their own stories from their clusters. After an art project, my students formed the cluster shown in Figure 9.

Using journal writing as a daily writing exercise is also a good way to get your students involved in clustering. With pictures, objects, words, or stories as stimuli, you can do the clustering on a chalkboard with the whole group. Then children can generate their own sentences in their journals.

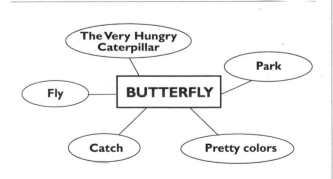

Fig. 9. Clustering of *Butterfly* After an Art Project

Clustering on Circles

By Elizabeth Williams Reeves
Teacher/Consultant, UCI Writing Project

Jefferson Newman, one of my fifth grade students when I taught at Los Alamitos Elementary School, generated such marvelous descriptive writing through his clustering that I asked him if I could share it (Figure 10).

What I think is especially interesting about Jefferson's cluster is the way his mind churns out ideas—moving from concrete to abstract, from literal to symbolic. As he writes, the language of his cluster also becomes very rhythmical (almost circular); his form reinforces his content. And it evolved, almost effortlessly, from clustering.

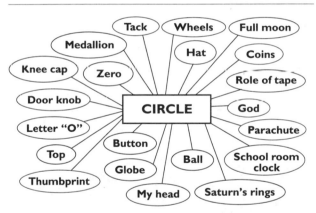

The circle is round and smooth. Coins like dimes and fifty cent pieces are in circles. A circle takes the formation of your knee cap. It is the form of Saturn's rings. The circle is the shape of a medallion glittering in the sun. A circle is like the rings of a bracelet. People get married and have a circle placed on their finger, a wedding ring. A circle shows the significance of how God is infinite. A circle takes the brightness of the full moon. I wear a button almost every day, a circle button. It reminds me of a classroom clock—ticktock, ticktock, ticking time slowly away. A circle is the egg that rests on your table. A circle is the base on which your hair rests. It is the turning of the doorknob, the orbiting of the planets, the parachute springing out as the person leaps out of the airplane. It is the thumbprint of a human being twisted and turned, making the whirls in your thumb. It is the wheel on a bicycle spinning round and round. A circle is a fascinating two-dimensional object.

Fig. 10. Paragraph Developed by Jefferson Newman from Clustering *Circle*

Prewriting in the Elementary School

A Potpourri of Prewriting Ideas for the Elementary Teacher

By Virginia Bergquist
Teacher, Meadow Park Elementary School,
Irvine Unified School District;
and Teacher/Consultant, UCI Writing Project

The prewriting stage is the main ingredient of the writing process. The writing process can be described as a sort of recipe that brings a composition into being by forming, shaping, combining, or altering ideas initiated in the prewriting stage. Just as a secret formula will not react without its catalyst, the writing process will not be successful without the stimulus of the prewriting experience.

Prewriting can be defined as anything that is done prior to composing and that creates motivation, increases conceptual knowledge, builds on to the language bank, stimulates the imagination, or spurs new thinking. The prewriting stage provides the raw materials that will be given shape by the writing process. The writing process is an act of creation.

Children, as prospective writers, especially need to spend time generating, exploring, and experimenting with ideas before they are expected to compose. The prewriting stage affords children the opportunity to generate ideas by exploring prior knowledge or new information, and it gives them time to reach into their bank of language for words to express those ideas. Taking the time to use fully this stage of the writing process ensures that children will "have something to say" when they compose. Neglecting prewriting increases the possibility of hearing the plaintive exclamation, "I don't know what to write!"

Fostering the Language Production Process

To ensure that children receive the full benefit of the prewriting process, teachers must understand the language production process and how it relates both to generating ideas and planning for the composing process.

The production of language begins when a child reacts to an experience in the environment and begins to think about it (conceptualization) and, in turn, to talk about it (verbalization). During this oral language stage, children begin to compose stories and fantasies while they are at play. This same type of activity may be used in the classroom to move children from "oracy" toward literacy. The child's stories and fantasies may be written down. Children with this experience will begin to pair speech and print perceptually; then they will gradually transcribe their own sentences and, eventually, complete stories.

Children with much practice in oral composition will progress naturally to nonverbal composition and learn the conventions of written language. It is essential that composing orally precede composing nonverbally. This is a natural sequence in language acquisition and development. Using the oral composition technique allows the child to continue building fluency in language and still learn the art of composing for writing.

On the basis of that information about language acquisition and production, I have devised a formula for the prewriting stage that can be used prior to composing orally and nonverbally (see figures 1 and 2). This formula can be used by the teacher in eliciting as much language as possible to be used in composing. "Fall Leaves," which follows, is an example of the prewriting formula put to use.

Fall Leaves

EXPERIENCE

Take the children outdoors to play in the leaves. Encourage children to watch the leaves falling, to smell the leaves, to listen to the leaves moving, to jump in the leaves, to toss the leaves, and so forth.

CONCEPTUALIZATION

Ask questions, such as: What can you do with the leaves? What do the leaves feel like? Why? What do the leaves smell like?

VERBALIZATION

Listen to the children's responses. Encourage each one to express what he or she is thinking and feeling. Praise them for the descriptive words they use.

CONSTRUCTION

Cluster or brainstorm for words and ideas that can be used when writing. This technique can be used to motivate different modes of writing: poetry, stories, an ad for raking leaves, a report on the seasons, or a book about trees. Children reach into their bank of language to express their ideas.

COMPOSING

The children can compose orally, and helpers can transcribe; or they may transcribe for themselves. The children will have ideas to write about because they have been able to act out an experience and talk about it before they were expected to write.

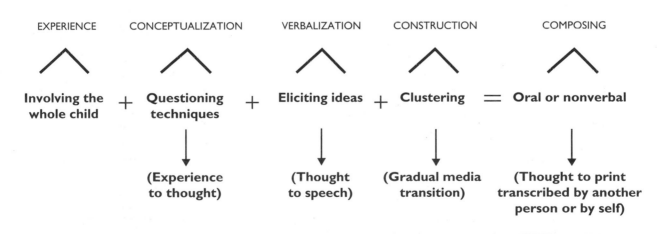

Fig. 1. The Prewriting Formula

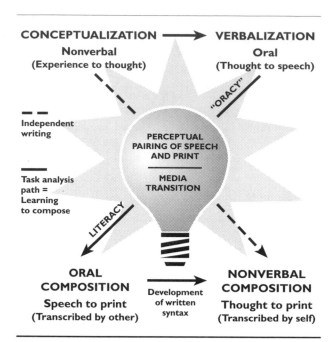

Fig. 2. Graphic Illustration of the Prewriting Formula

The following examples were developed through the process described previously:

Leaves
dusty, crunchy
falling, blowing, flying
trees, branches, colors, sun
laughing, tossing, jumping
funny, happy children.

Composed nonverbally by a third grader

The Fall Leaves

We played in the leaves today. We threw the leaves up in the air and kicked them. We ran and jumped in the leaves. The leaves were crunchy and dry. They were old. It will be winter soon.

Composed orally by a group of first graders

The only part of the prewriting formula that I have not discussed fully is construction. This step in the process is where the first shaping of ideas occurs. One of the most effective techniques that I have used for construction is Gabriele Rico's clustering.

Clustering enables children to reach into their language banks and provides a means by which they may crystallize their ideas. It is a very versatile technique and may be used prior to oral or nonverbal composition. It may be used with individuals, small groups, or entire classes. (Clustering is described in depth in the preceding section of this book.)

Finding Ideas for Prewriting

Prewriting will be most effective if you base it on something your children have a prior knowledge about—either through a lesson you conducted in the classroom or an experience they had somewhere else. Children will have more to bring to the writing process if they have had a prior experience with the topic.

Take advantage of school day happenings, such as playing marbles, eating in the cafeteria, or taking a spelling test. Special events are always great for prewriting experiences: assemblies, a visit from someone in the community, or a long-awaited holiday. Some of the best prewriting experiences are the spontaneous ones that we sometimes overlook: a windstorm, a stray dog wandering in the school yard, or a classmate who moved away suddenly.

The following are some of my favorite prewriting activities to use in the classroom. Be sure to implement them with the prewriting formula for the most success:

- *Sound Effect Sequence.* This is a good lesson to use with children to show the need for more details in a story. Play a record that contains a series of sound effects for the class. As your students listen, ask them to create a sentence for each sound effect they hear that will tell a story. The sentences can be put on an overhead projector to show the basic plot line as well as the "gaps" in the story. A group of children can work together to fill in the details.

- *Once There Was a House.* Show or draw a picture of a fantasy house. It could be made out of a shoe, an apple, a mushroom, a tree, or something else that is unusual. Ask the children to imagine who lives there. And ask other probing questions, such as, What do they do? Children may write a short story about the occupants, or they may wish to do a serial story. They will also enjoy creating their own fantasy houses and drawing them.

- *Photo Fun.* You are an Instamatic camera. Each summer your owners take you with them on vacation. Who are your owners? Where do they take you? What do you enjoy taking pictures of? Where is your favorite vacation spot? Why? Photographs may also be brought into the classroom for writing experiences.

- *Comic Dialogue.* Bring in some of your favorite comic books that you have saved, and share a few of them with the children. Talk about the dialogue bubbles and what they mean. Have a blowup of a large comic on butcher paper with blank bubbles. Discuss the pictures and create the dialogue with the group's help. Pass out individual comics with blank bubbles to the children and have them create their own dialogue. This activity can be addicting!

- *Tree for All Seasons.* I have always liked this activity because it offers an opportunity for interdisciplinary teaching. The class adopts one tree on the playground or in a nearby park or neighborhood. The class visits the tree periodically and experiences and records the changes in the tree. If they desire, the children may sit under the tree and write. They may wish to compile a book that is composed of all the activities and writing that the tree has inspired during the year. The book may contain artwork, poetry, reports, stories, photographs, and so forth.

- *Scent and Sentimentality.* Use strong scents, such as strawberry, leather, or pine. Children think of something that the smell reminds them of. Can they remember a time when they smelled this before? What were they doing? Was it a long time ago? Possibilities: a camping trip, a special Christmas, a favorite dessert, or the doctor's office.

- *Mystery Objects.* Show the class an object, such as an antique, an old pair of shoes, or a suitcase covered with travel stickers. Ask them such questions as: Whom do you think this object belongs to? What happened to it? Where has it been?

- *Dream Bus or Fantasy Jet.* Show a picture of a bus or jet and ask the children to imagine that they could go anywhere they wanted to go. Where would they go? How long would they stay? What would they do? What would the trip be like?

Using the Story Formula

The story formula, which is described below, is a versatile teaching tool to use in the classroom writing program to help students generate content and plan for form. It is adaptable for use with students who are just beginning to write narratives as well as with students who are ready to learn the intricacies of short story writing. Beginning students can write a complete story in one class period if they are directed to write two or three sentences for each part of the formula. Another way of using the formula with beginning writers is to take a day or a week to write each part of the story. Specific lessons and models may be presented to help students develop each part fully. More advanced students may use the formula in much the same way as the less advanced students use it, but they should be asked to provide more details. Lessons can be presented to help children use dialogue in their stories. "Showing, not telling," writing may be encouraged for characterization, setting, and problem. Experimenting with alternate voice and a different audience should be encouraged also.

This is the story formula:

1. Write an opening line. You may choose one from a favorite story.
2. Now, choose a main character (MC), and write a description of how your MC looks and acts.
3. Next, describe the setting of the story.
4. Write an episode that creates a problem for the MC. Make something exciting happen to the MC that causes a problem.
5. Describe the problem. How does the MC try to solve it but fails? How does the MC feel about the problem?

> *Writing, like life itself, is a voyage of discovery.*
>
> **HENRY MILLER**

The prewriting stage provides the raw materials that will be given shape by the writing process. The writing process is an act of creation.

VIRGINIA BERGQUIST

6. Now, tell how the problem is solved. Does the MC get help or solve it alone?
7. Now that the problem is solved, write about how your MC feels. What will the MC do to avoid having the same problem again?
8. Reread your story and make up a title for it.
9. Decide what parts of the story would make good illustrations.

Using Books in Prewriting

Children who are avid readers are often the best writers because they have developed a sense of written syntax, are aware of form, and have a good vocabulary. For this reason I like to use books as a prewriting experience. This technique, sometimes called "pattern writing," is a form of emulation. The child takes the pattern and uses it as a springboard for new ideas. I have used the following books to prompt writing in the classroom:

- *I Know What I Like,* by Norma Simon (Niles, Ill.: Albert Whitman & Company, 1971). This is a good book to use when introducing verbs.
- *Sara and the Door,* by Virginia A. Jensen (Reading, Mass.: Addision-Wesley Publishing Co., Inc., 1977). Use this story to prompt writing about a memory from early childhood or about a time when the student felt helpless.
- *If I Were a Cricket,* by Kazue Mizumura (New York: Harper & Row Pubs., Inc., 1973). Children can use the pattern and write what they would do for a human friend if they were an animal, plant, or insect.
- *David Was Mad,* one of the *Kin-der Owl Books* by Bill Martin, Jr. (New York: Holt, Rinehart & Winston, Inc., 1971). This is an excellent

book to use when encouraging children to "show and not tell" in their writing.
- *Nothing but a Dog,* by Bobbi Katz (Old Westbury, N.Y.: Feminist Press, 1972). Using the pattern in this book, the children in your class can write about something they have really wanted or wanted to do.
- *The Important Book,* by Margaret W. Brown (New York: Harper & Row Pubs., Inc., 1949). This is a good book to use when introducing paragraph writing. The students will choose a noun and write all the things they think are important about it.
- *Mitzi's Magic Garden,* by Beverly Allison (Westport, Conn.: Garrard Publishing Co., 1971). Children can write what they would plant in the garden and tell what would result. Imaginations will run wild. The illustrations in this book are especially amusing.
- *Janey,* by Charlotte Zolotow (New York: Harper & Row Pubs., Inc., 1973). This pattern can be used to prompt writing about memories.

Using Puppets, Role-Playing, and Story Dolls

Puppets can be used to encourage oral and written expression. Children compose naturally when they play with puppets. They can be given time to play and then be asked to compose something for a dialogue bubble, to tell a story, or to create a play. It is also fun for a group of children to work on plays together in this manner.

Another good approach for a prewriting experience is to have children role-play a situation and record it with a tape recorder. Children can replay the tape and revise it as often as they wish. One person writes down what the group has decided to keep, and the process goes on until their play is finished. This is a particularly useful lesson when you are emphasizing the importance of rewriting a piece until you are satisfied with its contents.

Children love to tell stories with the flip-over dolls that you can purchase in toy stores. They can also make up their own stories with new characters with the story doll. (See Figure 3 for instructions on how to make a story doll.) Have the children use felt scraps, crayons, and so forth to create their characters and then make up a story. The story can be in narrative form or in play form.

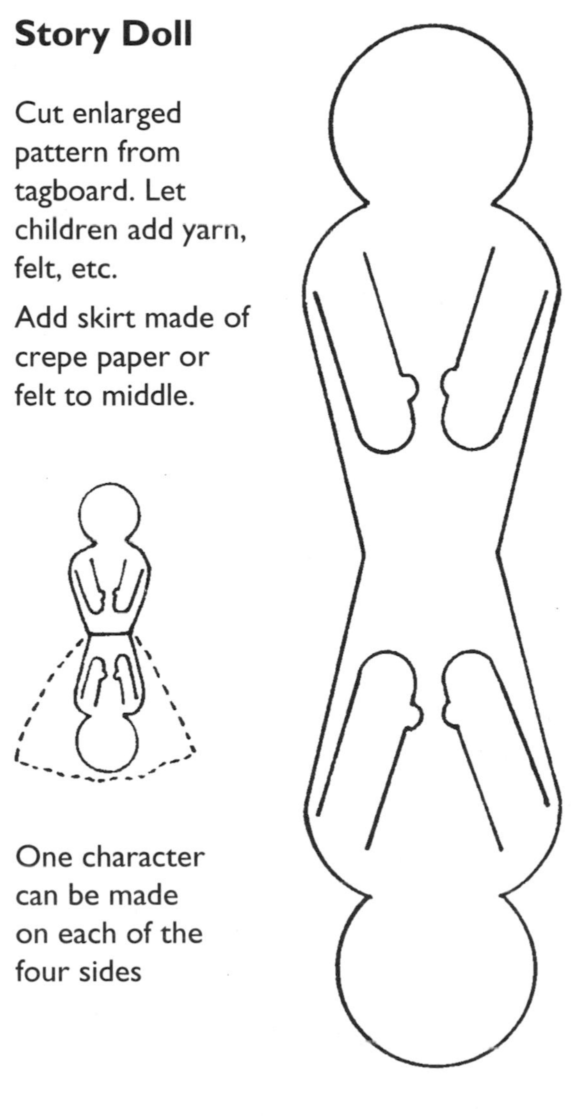

Story Doll

Cut enlarged pattern from tagboard. Let children add yarn, felt, etc.

Add skirt made of crepe paper or felt to middle.

One character can be made on each of the four sides

Fig. 3. Instructions for Making a Story Doll

Describe the Teacher's Role

If, after reading this section, you feel that the teacher's role in the prewriting stage of the writing process is a complex one, you are right! The teacher must simultaneously initiate the desire to write, induce creative thinking, and help build writing skills. Therefore, you who are teachers must approach your role with a combination of realism and assurance; and, to be successful, you must be well prepared and enthusiastic. It is important to realize that prewriting is often the most painful, the longest, and always the crucial stage of the writing process. You must be assured that there will be results; think of your own prewriting ponderings and deliberations that eventually bring forth writing. Remember that children experience the same apprehensions as you do when faced with the command to create. It is essential that you be prepared with a plan based on the following five points to encourage a successful prewriting experience:

1. Rely on the atmosphere of trust that you have created in your classroom. Children will readily express ideas without fear of ridicule.
2. Base prewriting experiences on something children have a prior knowledge about— either through a lesson you have provided or the experiences they bring to school.
3. Involve the whole child in the prewriting experience. Experiences which stimulate all of the senses have the most potential for prompting ideas.
4. Allow children the time needed to act out and talk out their ideas before you expect them to write or compose.
5. Place the most importance on the ideas which children generate. The most valued writing is based on the worth of its ideas. There is plenty of time later for rewriting and editing for correctness.

Finally, above all else, become enthusiastically involved in the excitement children feel when they are generating, thinking about, and creating ideas for writing. Personally, I find the prewriting stage to be the most exhilarating part of the process in the elementary classroom. I hope you will feel the same way. Good luck!

Practical Ideas for Prewriting in the Elementary School

Snap, Crackle, Think!

By Laurie Opfell, Sue Rader Willett, and Julie Simpson

Teachers/Consultants, UCI Writing Project

It is extremely important to provide students of all ages with prewriting activities that will enable them to generate ideas about which to write. With young children, in particular, it is also helpful to tap into concrete experiences so that what they have to say will come relatively easily and, thus, they can focus their attention on how to express it on paper.

The following lesson was designed primarily for special education teachers at the elementary level. Our goal was to demonstrate that younger students, and even students with learning difficulties, are capable of writing papers at the highest levels of critical thinking if they are provided with ample prewriting activities to develop a bank of ideas for writing and careful precomposing strategies for planning and shaping their papers. By precomposing, we mean a type of prewriting in which students focus on the transformation of ideas into written form.

Because of the skill level of the students for whom we were designing the lesson and the potential skepticism of their teachers about what they could accomplish, we felt it was essential to choose a subject that would invite active participation, enthusiasm, and interest in elementary schoolchildren and special education students at all levels and be appealing to teachers as well. So we chose cereal, something we would all have a host of memories, associations, and feelings about. What follows is a sequence of prewriting and precomposing activities that takes students from the knowledge through the evaluation levels of thinking as well as through the various stages of the writing process.

- **Prewriting**

  Step 1—*Brainstorming*. We asked our teachers/students to tell us anything they thought of when they heard the word *cereal*, and we wrote all of the suggestions on the chalkboard.

  Step 2—*Categorizing*. We passed out copies of a blank grid and asked them to record and organize on the grids the ideas from the chalkboard into basic categories, such as texture, taste, smell, and nutritional value. We also asked them to add any new information that occurred to them. The grid might look something like this:

Texture:			
crunchy			
crispy			
soggy			
lumpy			
Taste:			
sweet, etc.			

  Step 3—*Experiencing*. At this point, we wanted our audience to become involved with their subject matter, so we conducted a taste test of the cereals. As the students ate, we asked them to identify the qualities of the cereals by checking the appropriate categories on the grid and adding new information as it was needed. The grid now might look like this:

	Ratings for cereals		
Qualities	Crispies	Charms	Natural
Texture:			
crunchy			
crispy			
soggy			
lumpy			
chewy (hard)			
chewy (soft)			
spongy			

EDITOR'S NOTE: Laurie Opfell, a former English teacher, Irvine High School, Irvine Unified School District, is currently a teacher/consultant with the UCI Writing Project. Sue Rader Willett is an English teacher, Capistrano Valley High School, Capistrano Unified School District; and Julie Simpson is an English teacher, Sunny Hills High School, Fullerton Joint Union High School District.

- **Precomposing**

  Step 4—Mapping. In order for the teachers/students to make the transition from checks on a grid to writing about their subjects, we asked them to select their favorite cereal, illustrate it graphically on paper, and then to add in the checked information from the grid where appropriate. We showed them several models; then we asked them to try it on their own. Two examples are included in Figure 4.

  Mapping is a right-brain organizational tool which allows creative interpretation of information. We encouraged everyone to add in any new relevant ideas as they created their maps.

Fig. 4. Mapping the Qualities of Cereals

  Step 5—Presenting the prompt. With a visual plan of organized information to write from, we next presented the group with a series of prompts. They are graduated below from easiest to most difficult. Students can be given the option of choosing their own, or one can be selected for them. All prompts deal at the thinking level of evaluation:

  1. Select your favorite cereal and explain why you like it.
  2. Write a paragraph to persuade your mother to buy this cereal.
  3. Rank the cereals from best to worst and justify your ranking.
  4. Pretending you are the judge of a cereal "taste-off," write your choice for the best cereal and explain why.
  5. After tallying the preferences of your classmates, predict which cereal will sell the best and explain why.

  For lower-level students, prompt number 1 might be most appropriate, and a frame could be provided that might look like this:

  I like _____ because

  1._____

  _____. Also

  2._____

  _____. Finally,

  3._____

  _____.

  More advanced students might try prompt number 4 and add setting, character, description, dialogue, and the reaction of the crowd.

- **Writing**

  Step 6—Writing a rough draft. We asked our teachers/students to write a rough draft of prompt number 2 because we felt it was the one they might be likely to try with their students.

- **Sharing**

  Step 7—Providing each other with feedback. Before each writer shared his or her paper with a partner, we presented a simplified rubric, one that would be suitable for prompt number 2.

  After reviewing the rubric, each student was asked to look for the specific attributes or the lack of them in his or her partner's paper and to give each other feedback on positive aspects of the paper as well as possible corrections. Here is the rubric we presented:

 Strongly persuades and convinces. Supports with specific information.

 Suggests mother should buy the cereal. Supports with general information.

 States personal opinion without being persuasive. Gives little or no supporting reasons.

Since our primary goal was to demonstrate prewriting and precomposing strategies, we did not take the lesson beyond the first draft. However, classroom use of this lesson should include the revising, editing, and evaluating stages of the composing process. A good motivator would be to award ribbons to each writer.

The teachers who participated in our "Snap, Crackle, Think!" lesson responded enthusiastically to it. We feel a key element in its success is its hands-on quality. Even the most reluctant writers should have something to say after tasting, smelling, touching, and thinking about their subject. More important, the prewriting and precomposing activities provide the student with guidance and direction in transforming those thoughts into print.

The Rock Experience

By Erline S. Krebs
Elementary Field Supervisor,
Department of Teacher Education,
Chapman University;
and Teacher/Consultant, UCI Writing Project

"The Rock Experience" includes a series of prewriting activities that I have used successfully with elementary students; however, it could easily be adapted to any grade level. I begin this experience by reading to my class *Everybody Needs a Rock* by Byrd Baylor (New York: Charles Scribner's Sons, 1974). This book is about designing individualistic rules for finding "just the right rock for you." After I have read the story to the students, they develop some of their own "rock hunt rules," using the "how to" skills of the practical/informative domain. Then they go outside and survey the school environment for a "rock hunt adventure."

When each student has selected one "special" rock, an activity that takes approximately ten minutes, we return to the classroom and go through the process of getting acquainted with our rocks. In silence, each student examines his or her rock, focusing on the senses of smell, sight, sound, taste, and touch. Sometimes, I play soft music in the background; e.g., Johann Pachelbel's "Canon in

D." At the end of two minutes, I ring a bell. Each student now selects a partner. One person is designated "A"; and his or her partner, "B." For two minutes, "A" shares with "B" anything about his or her rock; i.e., where and how it was found, description of the rock, or personality traits of the rock. Students are encouraged to use their imagination. "B" listens (no talking whatsoever). The positions are reversed for the next two minutes. I ring a bell at the end of each two-minute segment.

This process is followed by a total group discussion, which may include some of the following "open-ended" questions:

What was this experience like for you?
Were two minutes too long, too short, just right?
Were you comfortable or uncomfortable sharing? In what ways?
Were you comfortable or uncomfortable listening? In what ways?
How did you feel about your partner as a listener?
What did you learn about yourself in this process?

Working with the same partner and using one or both rocks, the students move into a brainstorming process in order to develop a *word-bank*. I pass out five 5" x 7" cards, each of a different color (yellow, green, orange, blue, pink). One of the partners is designated the recorder. I allow approximately two to three minutes for each segment of this process. Words corresponding to different parts of speech are listed on each card, as follows:

Yellow card: Brainstorm and record all the words that could *describe* (adjectives) your rock(s); e.g., speckled, smooth, sharp, creviced.

Green card: Brainstorm and record all the words that communicate what your rock(s) *can do* (verbs); e.g., roll, skip, fall, hop.

Orange card: Brainstorm and record all the words that communicate *how* your rock(s) *can do it* (adverbs); e.g., slowly, quickly, playfully, listlessly.

Blue card: Brainstorm and record all the phrases that tell *where* your rock(s) *can do it* (prepositional phrases); e.g., under the bridge, over the water, on the sidewalk, in the car.

We discuss the individual lists and, as a group, develop a word-bank for each part of speech on four sheets of butcher paper. I color-code each list

"The Rock Experience" has given students practice in discovering, recording, describing, and sharing.

ERLINE S. KREBS

by using yellow, green, orange, and blue felt-tip pens:

Description of Our Rocks	*What* Our Rocks Can Do	*How* Our Rocks Can Do It	*Where* Our Rocks Can Do It
(List adjectives.)	(List verbs.)	(List adverbs.)	(List prepositional phrases.)

The butcher paper lists are placed on classroom walls.

Now, each pair of students takes out the *pink* card and, together, they create their own magnificent "rock sentence," using all their sentence-combining techniques and skills. I allow approximately five to seven minutes for this process. Of course, these "magic creations" are shared with the whole group.

As a follow-up, the students are usually anxious to set up a Geology Learning Center. In the process of establishing the center, they get opportunities for collecting, conducting research on, and labeling rocks. This may also lead to the following writing activities:

Sensory/descriptive domain: Describing rocks through poetry; e.g., haiku, cinquain, poetic dialogue.

Imaginative/narrative domain: "An Adventure with My Rock" or "My Adventure as a Rock"; i.e., use of visual imagery from the rock's point of view.

Practical/informative domain: Developing a handbook for beginning rock hunters or "Advanced Instructions for the Avid Rock Hunter."

Analytical/expository domain: Developing a position paper; e.g., "The Value of Rocks in the Ecosystem."

There is no doubt that "The Rock Experience" has increased my students' and my own awareness of rocks. At the same time it has given them practice in discovering, recording, describing, sharing, and doing a variety of other prewriting activities. Actually, the *process* of this experience can be used with any item; obviously, it is not limited to rocks. Use your imagination! Have fun!

Developing Fluency Through Poetic Dialogue

By Michael Carr
Teacher, Valley Junior High School,
Carlsbad Unified School District;
and Teacher/Consultant, UCI Writing Project

and Erline S. Krebs
Elementary Field Supervisor,
Department of Teacher Education,
Chapman University;
and Teacher/Consultant, UCI Writing Project

The word is alive
The poem is alive
The poet is alive within his poem
and is speaking to us.
If we wish, we may answer him
by weaving our voices into conversations
which create a new kind of poetic dialogue.
In so doing we come to know the poet
and his poem in a special way
and create poems as a result of this dialogue.

by Toby Lurie
from *Conversations and Constructions*[1]

[1]Toby Lurie, *Conversations and Constructions*. San Francisco: 150 Seal Rock Dr., San Francisco, CA 94121, © 1978. Used by permission of the poet.

When you are introducing elementary school students to poetry, it is not enough to give them a model of a haiku, cinquain, or other poetic form and expect them to write. We have found that our students are fearful of expressing themselves freely through poetry. It is evident that they have many preconceived notions about poetry—that it must rhyme, be easy to memorize, have only so many syllables per line, and so forth—and an overall feeling of "I can't do this."

As with any writing assignment, it is necessary to provide students with prewriting activities. In this case we want them to see that writing poetry can be as easy and comfortable as having a conversation with a friend. That is why we focus on the idea of dialoguing with poetry.

We begin by inviting our students to cluster their thoughts, feelings, and attitudes around the word *poetry*, as in Figure 5.

As a group we take a look at the "cluster" and notice what it is saying. Then we discuss some of the myths and fears surrounding poetry. Next, we introduce the concept of dialoguing as a natural way of expressing ourselves, a process we do daily in our conversations with each other. For example, we might say, "Mike, have you noticed the mountains this morning?"

Mike may respond, "You bet. I would love to be skiing right now!" It is as simple as that.

We now have our students respond orally to any line we give them. We tell our students not to "think about" or "figure out" their responses, just express what comes naturally.

Using the same natural process, our students are now invited to participate in a written dialogue. We use Carl Sandburg's "Summer Grass."

Summer Grass[2]

Summer grass aches and whispers.
It wants something; it calls and sings; it pours
out wishes to the overhead stars.
The rain hears; the rain answers; the rain is slow
coming; the rain wets the face of the grass.

By Carl Sandburg

As we read a line of the *frame*, each student copies that line of poetry on a piece of paper and then writes his or her response directly underneath. The following is an example of a fifth grade student's (Jennifer's) response:

Summer grass aches and whispers. (Carl Sandburg's "Summer Grass")
    Rain on the grass and wind blowing. (Jennifer)

It wants something:
    The baby wants a toy.

it calls and sings;
    Birds perching in trees

it pours out wishes
    It is raining wishes

to the overhead stars.
    Twinkling stars up in the air

The rain hears;
    The clouds talk, people hear, the rain falls;

the rain answers;
    The clouds listen;

the rain is slow coming;
    The rain is very slow, it's sprinkling;

the rain wets the face of the grass.
    The grass gets wet, the grass likes water.

By Jennifer Michelle

This process allows for a personal involvement with the poem and transforms the experience of poetry from the dull process of analysis and memorization to the intimate relationship of conversation.

Now the students have an opportunity to share their creations aloud. As we read a line of the frame, a student reads his or her response. We do

Fig. 5. Clustering of Thoughts and Feelings Around *Poetry*

---

[2]"Summer Grass." From *Good Morning, America,* copyright 1928 and renewed 1956 by Carl Sandburg. Reprinted by permission of Harcourt Brace & Company. (Note: Carl Sandburg's poem will work equally well with students at higher grade levels, as will this entire concept.)

this with several students on a one-to-one basis, and then we expand the process to include two or more students in order to form a three- or four-person poem. The following is an example of a two-person dialogue with "Summer Grass":

Summer grass aches and whispers. (Carl Sandburg's "Summer Grass")
Rain on the grass and wind blowing. (Jennifer)
    Summer grass smells good. (Travis)

It wants something:
    The baby wants a toy:
        It is hungry:
it calls and sings;
    birds perching in trees;
        it sings a song;
it pours out wishes
    it is raining wishes
        it pours out your wish
to the overhead stars.
    twinkling stars up in the air.
        looking through a telescope.
The rain hears;
    The clouds talk, people hear, the rain falls;
        People like rain;
the rain answers;
    the clouds listen;
        the rain hears you, the rain listens;
the rain is slow coming;
    the rain is very slow, it's sprinkling;
        it's raining slowly;
the rain wets the face of the grass.
    the grass gets wet, the grass likes water.
        the grass drinks water.

By Jennifer Michelle and Travis Bare

Again, we read Carl Sandburg's frame aloud as Jennifer and Travis read their responses to each line.

As the students experience success and confidence in this process, we now remove the *frame* and introduce the concept of the *silent exchange*. The students select a partner and, together, they participate in a written dialogue with each other. This exercise is done in silence. One student begins and writes a line; the second student responds to that line. They alternate (in silence) until their "poem" is complete. They may illustrate their

paper (still in silence) and place it on a bulletin board in the room. Sharing their poem orally with the class adds a special dimension. The following are two examples of the silent exchange done by fifth grade students:

Hot summer sun is shining.
    Everyone is at the beach.
The waves are talking.
    Are they talking to you?
We go home in the dark, cool wind.
    Are you going to stay home?
The wind is blowing.
    The wind is blowing the trees down.
It is very cold and windy.
    So I sit by the fireplace.
The wind blows the fire out,
    So I light the match and stick it in the fireplace.
I want to sleep by the fireplace.
    I dream about going to the beach again.

By Eleanor Velez and Sara Zampogna

A nice and pretty flower . . .
    It sits in the grass dripping with water.
The grass is wet and green . . .
    We step on the wet green grass.
Unicorns are nice and magicful . . .
    Their horns are gold and pretty.
Pegasus is pretty too . . .
    With white shining wings.
Leaves on a tree are brown and orange . . .
    They lie on the ground in autumn.
The trees have many colors . . .
    Nice colors and gold leaves.

By Jennifer Camia and Becky Pendleton

We have found that by using the prewriting process of dialoguing as a natural extension of conversation, our students develop greater freedom and confidence in both their oral and written expression. The students "come alive" as they discover their own special "poet within." Now they are ready to dialogue with the self and produce poetry that is uniquely their own.

EDITOR'S NOTE: We especially acknowledge the contributions of Travis Bare, Jennifer Camia, Jennifer Michelle, Becky Pendleton, Eleanor Velez, and Sara Zampogna, who were fifth grade students at the Los Alamitos Elementary School when this article was written.

Pattern Writing with Novels for Elementary School Students

By Elizabeth Williams Reeves
Teacher/Consultant, UCI Writing Project

I have found that certain novels provide elementary school students with marvelous springboards for writing experiences. Emulating an author's style and content can be quite simple for students if the literature they read is vivid and motivating. For these reasons I have used *The Adventures of Tom Sawyer* at the fifth grade level to help my students develop written language skills.

In one section of his novel, Mark Twain creates a conversation between Huck Finn and Tom Sawyer regarding the removal of warts. You may recall the scene. On his way to school, Tom comes upon the "juvenile pariah of the village, Huckleberry Finn," carrying a dead cat, and he asks, "Say—what is dead cats good for, Huck?"

"Good for? Cure warts with," Huck replies. Then Tom tries to convince Huck that "spunk-water" is better, but his curiosity about the use of dead cats to cure warts prompts him to ask Huck about the procedure.

Huck replies that you stand by the grave of an evil person "'long about midnight," wait for the devil to come along to take "that feller away," and then, "you heave your cat after 'em and say, 'Devil follow corpse, cat follow devil, warts follow cat, I'm done with ye!' That'll fetch *any* wart," Huck tells Tom.

After my students have read the passages from *Tom Sawyer*, I guide them through directed questioning, to develop their own methods of getting rid of warts. Some possible questions the teacher might ask and expected responses from students for this portion of the prewriting phase follow:

1. Where do you need to go to be cured of warts?
   A dark garage . . . up in a plane . . . haunted house . . . a stranger's kitchen . . . a subterranean lake

2. What time would you need to go?
   Any time . . . midnight . . . three in the morning

3. Who or what should you bring with you?

   No one . . . your baby sister . . . a three-eyed frog . . . a ten-foot snake

4. What other materials should you take?
   Pail . . . shovel . . . matches . . . bag . . . book of cures

5. What would you do once you arrived at the appropriate location?
   Varied responses

6. Is there a chant you would need to say?
   "Wart, wart, off you go, where you vanish we'll never know."

Next, students are given an outline that aids them in structuring their writing. The outline for this particular lesson and a sample of the student writing generated from the exercise follow:

Outline for the Lesson

Though many people promote various means of curing warts, I have one surefire method: _____

_____ .

Certain things are essential: _____

_____ .

First, _____

_____ .

Once there, _____

_____ .

Next, _____

_____ .

Before _____

Sample of Student Writing

Though many people promote various means of curing warts, I have one sure-fire method. Three things are essential: a fat green frog with warts, a bar of soap, and a pond. First, you collect your frog and soap and venture off toward the pond while the sun is high. Once there, expose all your warts to the sun, and begin scrubbing them with the soap. Next, pick up the frog and throw him as far out into the pond as possible. Before he can turn around to look at you, run as fast as you can into the woods. By the time you reach home, your warts should be gone.

Students usually find this kind of patterning experience challenging and fun. It enables me not only to reinforce the literature we are reading with writing but also to teach sequencing and transition skills.

Prewriting in Different Subjects

Prewriting Assignments Across the Curriculum
Science + English = Success

By Jim Lee

English Teacher
Rancho Santa Margarita Intermediate School,
Saddleback Valley Unified School District;
and Teacher/Consultant, UCI Writing Project

It has long been a premise of mine that students can benefit greatly from some sort of prewriting activity. No matter what the assigned topic may be, it is to your advantage as a teacher to get your students' thoughts flowing freely. Then the students need to put the thoughts on paper so that they become workable parts that may be pieced together to form the "perfect" paper that most students believe they should be able to write.

The prewriting activity that I have selected to describe for you is one I used in conjunction with a series of science experiments on a well-known backyard mollusk—the snail. My goal was two-fold: (1) to integrate scientific observation and experimentation with the teaching of composition; and (2) to provide a concrete experience that would enable my students to grasp the abstract concept of aestivation and its application to backyard mollusks. As you may or may not know, *aestivation* is a state of physical inactivity (dormancy or hibernation) that the snails go into when they are deprived of food and water.

I began this activity by giving every student an aestivating snail and instructed my students to examine their respective snails for color, texture, shape, size, and so forth. Then I asked the students to record their observations in clusters, an activity that provided them with a foundation for eventual sentence and paragraph development. (See Figure 1 for an example of the clustering of observations.)

After the students had clustered their thoughts about the aestivating snail, each student put a drop of water on his or her snail's body and watched as it emerged from its shell. The students then clustered their observations of the snails emerging from aestivation, as illustrated in Figure 1.

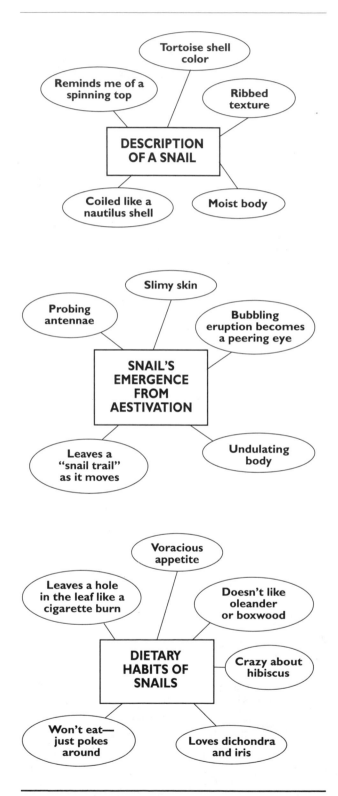

Fig. 1. Clustering the Descriptions and Observations of Snails

The next step in the prewriting activity was to observe snails eating. We gave the snails a variety of leaves that were native to the immediate environment (in other words, whatever can be collected during the morning before the afternoon lesson). The students then recorded in a third set of clusters the snails' dietary habits, as shown in the third part of Figure 1.

From this experimental/sensory prewriting activity, the students orally shared with the rest of the class the results of their clustering. I had all of the information that the students volunteered recorded on the chalkboard and categorized under one of the three headings: Description, Emergence from Aestivation, and Eating Habits. As an example, a class of seventh grade honor students developed the following list of descriptions of aestivating snails:

Basic brown
Coiled like a nautilus shell
Sealed like a tomb
Dead
Tortoise shell color
Bizarre striations
Ribbed texture
Smooth strips with bumps in between
Reminds me of a spinning top
Spirals out like a pinwheel
Intricate pattern fades as it nears the opening
Yellowish tan and dark brown stripes
Looks like a ram's horn from the side
Gross!
Looks like Princess Leah's hair
Has multicolored ribs along the shell
Ribs get farther apart as they move away from the center
Boring
Fragile looking

After a period of sharing observations, the students took the sentence fragments and turned them into simple sentences. Then they shared their sentences, and a lesson on sentence combining evolved from the collected responses, as shown in the following example:

Original Simple Sentences

1. My snail is basically brown.
2. A snail shell is coiled like a nautilus shell.
3. An aestivating snail is sealed like a tomb.

Once your students understand that good writing is a product of systematically acquired skills and that those skills are learned rather than inherited, they will be much more optimistic about becoming good writers.

JIM LEE

4. An aestivating snail looks dead.
5. A snail is colored like a tortoise.
6. A "backyard mollusk" has bizarre striations on its shell.
7. The intricate pattern on a snail shell fades as it nears the opening.
8. A snail shell is fragile.
9. A snail shell spirals out from the center.
10. A snail has a gold, tan, and dark brown shell.
11. The pattern of a snail shell is less impressive toward the opening.

Sentences in Combined Form

1. The snail's coiled shell is fragile.
2. An aestivating snail appears to be dead and is sealed in a fragile tomb made of shell.
3. A snail has a shell with gold, tan, and dark brown striations.
4. A snail shell has an intricate pattern of gold, tan, and dark brown striations that fade to a basic brown as they approach the opening.

These activities covered the spectrum of experiential, oral, and written prewriting and provided my students with a foundation from which they could write a descriptive, narrative, or expository essay.

The following are examples of prompts that were an outgrowth from our experiments:

1. *Descriptive.* Write an account of a day in the life of a snail. Write from the snail's perspective, and include as much specific detail as possible. Incorporate as much factual data as possible to give added credence to your writing. Use as many sensory/descriptive phrases as possible.

2. *Narrative.* Write a story in which you speculate or fantasize about how the snail got its shell.

3. *Expository.* Suppose that the sun is moving closer to the earth each day. Using the theories of natural selection and survival of the fittest, project what physical changes might occur in the snail as it attempts to cope with its changing environment.

As a California Writing Project zealot, I would be remiss if I did not encourage, cajole, and, yes, even beg you to become actively involved in the teaching of composition.

Through the use of prewriting activities and well-designed prompts, you can convince your students that writing, although painful at times, can be exciting, challenging, and rewarding. Once your students understand that good writing is a product of systematically acquired skills and that those skills are learned rather than inherited, they will be much more optimistic about becoming good writers.

Practical Ideas for Prewriting in Different Subjects

A Primary Experience with Snails

By Charrie Hunter

Teacher, Maple Hill Elementary School,
Walnut Valley Unified School District;
and Teacher/Consultant, UCI Writing Project

After seeing a demonstration of Jim Lee's "Science + English = Success" lesson at the 1980 UCI Writing Project Summer Institute, I decided to try his prewriting activities with my first and second graders. They had had many previous writing experiences and were well acquainted with the procedure involved. These children were excited about each writing assignment they were given and were eagerly awaiting the arrivals of their "surprise" animal!

Before starting the lesson, you will need to assemble the following items: 40 aestivating snails, one rock for each child, one margarine container with water in it for each group of children, one large piece of plastic wrap for each child (12 in. x 12 in. [2.5 cm] or larger), and three different kinds of leaves for each child. Note that some snails have problems waking, so you will need some extra snails. Also, if you must make the snails go into aestivation, placing them in a large paper bag seemed to work, as they need a dry environment in which to sleep. My snails were crawling all over the place for about two days until I figured out how to keep their environment dry.

Before you pass out the snails, you need to give a little pep talk about them; otherwise, the children will be hesitant to touch them. I had acquainted myself with some stories about snails and shared the stories with the class. After stimulating the children's curiosity with some sample books and illustrations, I handed each child an aestivating snail. Then I wrote the word *snail* on the chalkboard and drew a circle around it, added the word *aestivating,* and explained its meaning.

I instructed each child to examine his or her snail. As we discussed the snails, I asked about the snail's breathing; its color, texture, shape, and size; and its unpopularity. As the children volunteered their reactions, I added their words to a group cluster on the board. Then we put a drop of water on each snail to wake each one up and passed out the plastic wrap. I continued the cluster with questions like: Where are its eyes? Can it hear? (Clap hands.) What happens if you touch it? I introduced some new words and talked about each one: *tentacles, feelers,* and *foot.* What is the motion of its foot? (The children let their snails crawl up the plastic wrap as they held it up.)

I passed out the rocks and asked more questions. Will it move over or around a rock? Does it leave a trail? What is the trail like? I passed out the leaves to each child and continued with the discussion and cluster. Where is the snail's mouth? Does it have teeth? What kind of leaves does it like and dislike?

By this time the chalkboard was covered with words, and the children were ready to write. I collected all the snails and equipment and passed out a "shape" book to each child. This book has a construction paper cover and back with several sheets of writing paper inside. The book is fastened at the edge, and then the children cut it out (in this case) in the shape of a snail. The class was then told what the topic of their story was. They were to write a story about a day in the life of a snail. We discussed this topic to generate ideas, and then I wrote the rubric on the board. Every story must include (1) what the snail looks like; (2) how it moves; (3) what it does in a day; and (4) how your friends feel about the snail.

At this point, I walked around the room and helped those children who needed help. Each child was allowed as much time as he or she needed to complete the story. Some took several days. I do not have children of this age rewrite because I find that rewriting destroys their fluency. I am continually amazed at their desire to achieve perfection without my requiring it. Once the children understood what good handwriting, punctuation, and capitalization were, they used them.

After everyone had completed his or her shape book, we read each story out loud, considered whether the writer had done everything that was in the rubric, and graded the paper accordingly. The children received a smiley face with hair if they had completed all the tasks or a plain smiley face if they had not. (I always try to make this activity as positive an experience as possible.)

The children in my class loved this "hands-on" writing experience, and the resulting stories were magnificent. One story was published in its entirety in the district newspaper, along with pictures of my class and an article about the California Writing Project.

Science Search—The Write Way

By Patricia Gatlin
Teacher, Cross Timbers Intermediate School,
Mansfield Independent School District, Arlington, Texas;
and Teacher/Consultant, UCI Writing Project

Writing is a great way to stimulate student interest in science because it fits so naturally in the science curriculum. When students complain that science is boring, they are saying that science has no meaning for them; it has nothing to do with their daily lives. If a scientific study is to have meaning, it must relate to something in the students' experiences; it must be a real-life application of a scientific concept. Students may not be particularly interested in the composition and movements of the earth until they feel their houses bouncing around on top of shaky ground. But once they have calmed down, they may find that they are asking, "What's going on here?" or "What's causing this?" Now they have a scientific problem—a question that they are itching to answer—that grew from their unique experiences in the environment. Scientific experiments, though memorable and entertaining, achieve additional meaning for students when they have opportunities to write about the experiments and react to what they observe.

Occasionally, every person has scientific problems of some kind that need to be solved. Many of us might consider it handy information to know how long it takes milk to spoil, just in case the refrigerator breaks down. A good way to begin a science course is to make these kinds of problems the basis for the year's science curriculum. The students develop a giant class cluster by identifying every scientific problem that comes to mind. They classify the cluster of questions in categories that become the units of study, and they recognize that it is necessary for the cluster to remain open-ended in order to accommodate incidental scientific questions that may arise throughout the year.

At the beginning of each unit of study, the science class is divided into smaller study groups, with each group selecting from the unit list a problem that it will study. As the students begin scientific experiments to solve their problems, they find that it is essential to keep journals. The journal, which includes a complete account of each stage of the experiments, is the perfect vehicle for practicing different types of writing. The students write daily in their journals and are encouraged to explore all the domains in writing.

Throughout the study, students must observe carefully the characteristics of their experiments. Acute observation is the key ingredient for successful sensory/descriptive writing. A quick glance will not provide adequate details to describe a particular stage of an experiment. Students must be alert to all the sensory characteristics of the substances used in their experiments. We, their readers, must be able to imagine from the written descriptions the feel, the smell, and the sound, as well as the physical characteristics, of the substances used in the experiments.

The practical/informative mode is the natural style for students to use in reporting the findings of their experiments. However, the analytical/expository style may be more appropriate if stu-

> "Then our job is not to get language into the head of a child. Our job is to get it out."
>
> A TEACHER QUOTED BY OWEN THOMAS

dents are asked to persuade other class members that the results of their experiments provide valid answers to their original questions. There are times when providing such proof is truly a reasonable concern. Analytical writing is also appropriate for students' concluding journal entries. At this point, they should reflect on the complete process of the experiment and decide whether or not (1) they solved the original scientific problem; (2) the study triggered additional questions; (3) other questions were answered incidentally during the experiment; (4) some things surprised, pleased, or disturbed them; and (5) they would follow the same procedures to solve the same problem again.

Using the imaginative/narrative style, students can create a story based on the experiment, tracing their observations from the beginning to the end. They may retell the story, changing one of the variables and drawing a new conclusion, or perhaps retell the story from a different point of view. For example, a student might pretend to be the voice of the moldy bread housed within the petri dish.

Students should be encouraged to explore different formats in their journals. They may choose a poetic format, or they may write a short play for puppets or people. The teacher should encourage class members to write in any way that feels comfortable to them at the time. It is important that they feel good about their writing, because they will be sharing a journal entry with the class during their group's presentations given at the close of each unit. For these presentations, each student will share a writing selection that he or she feels is an example of the most interesting or exciting part of the experiment. During these sharing times, the class can get a glimpse of different ways to approach future scientific problems.

By integrating writing with science, the teacher is providing students with the ideal setting in which to practice decision-making skills, such as identifying cause and effect relationships, drawing conclusions based on evidence, and analyzing possibilities. Writing enables students to extend thinking beyond the basic comprehension level, which is characteristic of questions found in most textbooks. It also links scientific study to the students' outside experiences as they make connections between the principles learned at school and the practicalities of their immediate environments. At the same time, writing about science can appeal to something inside students, as they search for self-understanding and discover their relationships to the universe around them.

Journal Writing Across the Curriculum

By Margaret (Peg) Serences

Former English Department Chairperson, Niguel Hills Junior High School, Capistrano Unified School District; and Teacher/Consultant, UCI Writing Project

During the first UCI Writing Project in the summer of 1978, using journal writing in the classroom was discussed and demonstrated. Speakers stressed that the goal of using this writing approach was fluency. I was intrigued because I am always anxious to find new ways to encourage students to write. Of the varying forms then mentioned—e.g., diary entry, autobiographical sketch, creative writing exercises, learning aid, and idea collecting—I chose to incorporate the creative writing journal format in my seventh and eighth grade curricula. For three days a week, students were asked to write for ten to fifteen minutes on a topic, which was generally teacher-selected. I found this type of journal writing especially productive when I imposed a time limit, and it provided a prewriting stimulus to get my students writing.

In the English classroom I had students keep their journal entries in a special writing folder. After the writing folder contained several writing samples, the students selected one of their favorites to rewrite and develop into a short composition. Working in groups of four (students were allowed to form their own groups), each student would then read the rewritten composition aloud to the other members of the group. I stressed the importance of "hearing" their own words; this proved an excellent tool for catching sentence fragments and run-on sentences. Next, each student graded each of the four compositions, using the response guide that I provided. Finally, I graded all the papers myself, giving a grade for the compositions and a separate grade for the student's ability to grade someone else's work.

Since I had such good results with journal writing in my classes, I began to wonder how this writing approach would work in other disciplines. As chairperson of the English Department, I encouraged teachers in mathematics, music, physical education, science, and social studies to try weekly or biweekly journal writing projects. I stressed that students could write to discover what they had learned about a subject and that teachers could use their students' journals as a way of determining how effectively they were teaching. Several teachers volunteered to initiate journal writing to see whether it would be a useful learning tool. Here are some student writing samples from other curricular areas:

Physical education: Why I like baseball best of all!

I like baseball because . . . it's fun to *try* to hit the little ball and run around the bases. It's exciting to throw the ball to another player to get the runner out. Baseball is a game of skill. It takes lots of practice to be good. You have to have a good coach too. When you're in a league, you can meet people and make friends, learn things, and have fun. Also, if you have a good team, you can win a trophy. When the season is over, you get to keep the hats and the friends too. That is why I like baseball.

Music: Compare three selections of music.

After listening to the three pieces of music, I've decided that they all have a beat of some kind. First let me define beat—pulse. But after listening to the third piece, "Sounds," it seems to be different from the others because the first two seemed to use more instruments that flowed into a steady rhythm. They also had a more defined melody and harmony, so it blended together to create music.

Science: What did you learn from dissecting a frog?

Purpose: Mrs. "B" told us to, so we could learn more about the internal parts of a frog.

Observation: On the frog I cut open, I noticed that the skin is almost like rubber. When we cut open the frog, we saw a layer of muscles, which was gross looking. Then we cut that apart and saw a bunch of yellow intestine-looking things. Mrs. "B" told us it was where she produces the eggs, so we had a girl. Her insides are very clear to see. It was a good study.

Conclusion: I think the frog's insides are clear, easy to observe, and neat.

Drama: How do you express emotions on stage?

I make my emotions on stage by thinking I am really that person. I try to really get into it. I remember how people in real life would act. Before I get on stage, I have to make my emotions first. I try not to be me acting like someone else. I try to be them.

Social studies: What was life like in the Colonies?

Life in the Colonies was pretty good because it was easier to get land here, and in Europe it was hard. It was bad for the slaves because they were bought and sold. It turned gloomy in 1763 because England was in debt in the war, and so they started taxing the Colonies. Then the Colonies got mad at England and the Revolutionary War started, and the Colonies won the war.

With the insights gained from journal writing, several teachers, especially in the area of social studies, began to integrate writing in their respective subject areas. I also noticed the use of essay questions as a replacement for the standard multiple-choice examination. It seems to me that the journal writing assigned in other disciplines reinforced and, therefore, strengthened our English program. At the same time, it enabled students to explore what they thought about a given topic in a way that could never be expressed in a fill-in-the-blank or true-false examination.

Mailbags and Miscellany: Writing in History Classes

By Laurel Corona
Director of OASIS,
University of California, San Diego

Most young people enjoy writing when the assignments are enjoyable and allow them to use their imaginations, their senses of humor, and their growing sensitivity to the life situations of others. The following two class activities promote this kind of pleasure in writing and allow for creative expression outside the English classroom: mailbags from historical sites and miscellany.

Mailbags from Historical Sites

Mailbags from Historical Sites is a class project, but each student is completely responsible for his or her own part of the mail in the bag and for helping create a mailbag as it might have been filled when it left an important historical site. The mail in the bag should represent the writings of as full a range of people in the community as possible, and the destinations of the letters should be as diverse as possible. The purpose of the assignment is to enable the students to sense the ambiance of another place and time and to feel the past as if they were living in it.

In preparation for creating the mailbag, the students should make a list of the people apt to be in a particular place at a particular time. For example, in a Gold Rush town, one might find miners, dance hall girls, preachers and their wives, stable boys, horse thieves, cowboys, teachers, doctors, merchants, and so on. Each of these persons would be living a different life in this town and have a different attitude about being there. For the most part, they would not care about or even be aware of being a part of history. They would be concerned primarily with their daily lives. Each of these people would have different reasons for sending mail.

After developing a large list of people in a Gold Rush town and discussing how each might view life there, the students should then project what kinds of letters each might write and to whom. For instance, a preacher's wife might be miserable and write to tell her mother so. The preacher might be inquiring about inexpensive Bibles. A horse thief about to be hung might write to bid farewell to his true love. After this part of the project has been thoroughly brainstormed, the students should pick the character that interests them the most and then write a letter for the bag. The teacher should encourage the students to adopt a writing style, tone, and point of view appropriate to the character they are writing through.

Some creative student might make a bag at home, or one could be fashioned from a paper sack. The most likely way to display the completed project would be to create a montage in the classroom, perhaps with colored string connecting each letter to the bag. Wall space and grade level would, of course, dictate how such a project would be "published."

Miscellany

Miscellany is a class project that is similar to the one featuring mailbags, but more of the work should be done in small groups. Rather than create the finished products that letters represent, in the miscellany activity the students create the debris of an important historical event. For instance, they might imagine what General Ulysses S. Grant's tent looked like after the deciding battle of the Civil War or what his quarters at Appomattox looked like several days later. As a way of comparing and contrasting the two sides in the war, the class might be divided into a group responsible for creating the miscellany of the Union general's side and a group responsible for the Confederate general's miscellany. Miscellany might consist of battle plans, discarded communiques, drafts of speeches, letters to and from home or the President, and so forth. To create good, verisimilar debris, the students would have to research the subject thoroughly. Because of this, a project of this sort, if expectations are clearly delineated, makes an excellent alternative to a term paper.

Both of the projects described above can be suited to different grade levels and ability levels and also to different subject matter. Although history students would probably benefit most from such activities, teachers of other subjects might also be able to adapt these ideas for their classes. For example, if a science class is learning about Louis Pasteur or Pierre and Marie Curie or Galileo or if an art class is studying Vincent van Gogh or Michelangelo Buonarroti or Pablo Picasso, the miscellany project might be adapted. Similarly, students of Spanish or any other foreign language might create a town and its inhabitants and create a mailbag from that town.

And, teachers, do not let your students have all the fun. Indulge your own fantasies about dance hall girls or cattle rustlers. Willingness to do your own assignments is the single best way to validate them in your students' eyes.

Just a Few Words on Sentence Combining Across the Curriculum

By William Lomax

English Teacher, Benjamin Franklin High School,
Los Angeles Unified School District

Note: **The following is a sample of my address regarding sentence combining to a group of 32 high school teachers from several areas.**

All right, how many of you out there . . . (Is everybody listening?) . . . how many of you have used sentence combining in your classroom in the last, oh, six months? Three, five, six, seven . . . Sir, is your hand up? Okay, eight. That's it? All right, how many of you eight are English teachers? All eight, huh. What about the other, um, 24 of you? What do you teach? History . . . Spanish . . . science . . . government. And how many of you get consistently poor writing from your students? Okay, and how many of you would like to get better writing from your students? It's unanimous again. Well, my friends, let's talk about sentence combining. It may be able to help.

I won't take your time now to go through the research and theory of sentence combining; it's a well-established technique. There are plenty of books available, and it's basically a very simple process. Just ask your local English teacher for a little assistance. I've used sentence combining for several years, and I'm going to describe for you what I think works best.

Sentence combining work should be regular, but never routine. Establish your pattern; then keep it going, but vary it. Have students write the exercises one day; then do them orally the next. Give them as homework, do group work or choral readings, and have competitions between the groups. Use your imagination and sustain a sense of play. Above all, keep at it. After students have learned the basic system, you may spend as little as five minutes a day, three times a week, on sentence combining. It doesn't take much time, but it should be regular and continuous. There is no goal to sentence combining except better writing, so use it

throughout the year. Remember, too, that there are no "wrong" answers in sentence combining, only "better sentence combinations." Help students to see that writing is a process and a skill, not something that is right or wrong.

A single page—five to eight exercises—is enough for one day, once the routine is established, but even that can be varied. I prefer to use at least *two* pages per session. The four basic "signals" used by Frank O'Hare to instruct students (underlining, cross-outs, SOMETHING words, and parentheses) are easily learned, but they are addictive.[1] They are harder to unlearn than to learn. That's why I regularly give one page *with* signals and one page *without* signals *from the beginning*. Start students off with signals with something simple, like this:

> I drove the car onto the freeway.
> I drove the car slowly.

I mean, really simple, right? You won't insult students' intelligence, because you'll steadily increase the difficulty of the exercises—never faster, however, than they can do them correctly. You will be surprised, I suspect, at how fast they will progress to more complex exercises, once the signals are learned.

Now, I think the English teachers here are probably familiar with all the different ways sentence combining can be used—to teach vocabulary, sentence structure, grammar, paragraphing, punctuation, literature—all that "stuff" that goes on in an English classroom.[2] But what about you other teachers? You're all sitting politely, but the muscles in your cheeks are twitching. You're all asking, what's in it for me, right? What's in it is better writing—for *all* classrooms. Just a few minutes ago, you all said that's what you wanted.

Here's the point: *Combining* means more than just putting sentences together. It also means *combining form* and *content*. That is, while you're giving your students writing practice, they are

---

[1]See Frank O'Hare, *Sentence-Combining: Improving Student Writing Without Formal Grammar Instruction.* Urbana, Ill.: National Council of Teachers of English, 1973. Also see Jerry Judd's commentary that appears later in this book.
[2]For further information see William Lomax, "Sentence Combining Across the Curriculum," *California English*, Vol. 16 (November-December, 1980), 18–21.

simultaneously learning *your* subject matter. You teach history, you say? Then give them an exercise like this:

> A man was burned at the stake.
> The man was named Giordano Bruno.
> He was burned in the year 1600.
> He was burned in Rome.

And so on. Now that one is a far cry from the simple little starter we looked at earlier, but it shows where you can go with sentence combining. You science teachers, try this one:

1. Each nerve cell in the body has four major parts.
   One part is the dendrites, which receive messages from other cells.
   One part is the nerve cell body.
   One part is the axon down which the messages pass.
   One part is the synapses, which communicate with other cells.

2. Each axon is surrounded by a sheath of fatty material.
   This fatty material is known as myelin.

3. Myelin does three things.
   Myelin insulates axons so nerve messages are not short-circuited.
   Myelin gives the white matter of the brain its appearance.
   Myelin accounts for the large amounts of fatty cholesterol in the brain.

Those are advanced exercises—your early efforts being much simpler—but I think you can see my point: Students are practicing writing while dealing with the subject matter of *your* course.

Let's face it: Writing has, for some reason, been isolated in English classes. Students do learn to write there, but they don't see that what they learn in English is relevant to other classes—simply because we don't expect it of them. Writing should be taught in every classroom where it is used. No, we English teachers still teach writing as intensively as ever; the primary responsibility is still ours. But if you want better writing from your students, you must teach it for the same reason that an English teacher teaches history with Nathaniel Hawthorne's *The Scarlet Letter* and science with Jack London's short story "To Build a Fire." Sentence combining can help you to do just that without taking time from your own subject matter.

Now, before we take a break, there's time for just a couple of questions. Yes, ma'am, sentence-combining exercises do take time to prepare, but remember that you design them only once. They're good for the rest of your teaching career. Furthermore, there are plenty of books on the market that you may use instead of creating your own. When you do your own, however—especially you non-English teachers—you can match them to your particular course content. I keep nonconsumable class sets of each of my one-page lessons on file in the English office; other teachers can then check them out, use them, and return them for others to use. Students always write exercises on their own paper. Science teachers, get your whole department involved; share the work, and your files will grow quickly. Or ask your English teachers for assistance; they can use your exercises, too. Once your files are established, you'll have a resource that will remain valuable for years to come. And your students will be better writers.

One more word—and this is important—sentence combining is no substitute for a student's original writing. It is just a tool which hones writing ability. Always require students to apply what they learn from sentence combining to their own writing, and give them plenty of opportunity to do that.

Snake in the Grass: An Integrated Approach to Concept Formation

By Carl Babb

Former Science Teacher, Capistrano Valley High School, Capistrano Unified School District; and Instructor, Irvine Valley Community College

and Todd Huck

English Instructor, Rancho Santiago College, Rancho Santiago Community College District; and Teacher/Consultant UCI Writing Project

Picture this:

It is third period. Out on the football field, lined up on the 50-yard line, are ten small groups of students. One member of each group is tensed and ready to run;

some are crouched; some are poised like sprinters in a starting position. All are silent, waiting for the signal. Several yards in front of them, the teacher raises the silver whistle to his lips, inhales slowly, hesitates, and blows. Ten students burst across the line, heads down, eyes on the grass, each stopping suddenly and stooping to snatch a toothpick of red or yellow, blue or green. Now darting a few more steps and taking another plunging stoop, the runners scoop up another toothpick. From the 50-yard line, their teammates scream, cheer, and exhort them to get back across the starting line before the ten-second whistle sounds. All the runners but one cross the line as the whistle shrills. Knowing the rules, the latecomer turns and scatters his gathered toothpicks back across the grassy range in front of his team, while the racers from other teams wrap their collected toothpicks in tape and drop the small bundles into bags held by their teammates.

To the students, this game seems like a cross between a relay race and a treasure hunt, but what they soon discover is that they are experiencing and experimenting with an important scientific concept, the natural phenomenon of protective coloration. Students need no formal prior knowledge about protective coloration to play the game. In fact, it is better if they do not, for the lesson allows students to discover some of the broad dynamics of protective coloration through their own observations and conclusions. As such, this lesson serves as an ideal introduction to this scientific concept.

A large grassy area is needed to conduct the game. Students are divided into roughly ten teams, with approximately three members per team. Teams line up behind a line, leaving at least ten feet between each team. In front of each team, 40 colored toothpicks are randomly distributed in a specified area called a *range*. Each group of toothpicks *must* be made up of ten red, ten yellow, ten green, and ten blue toothpicks. The range should be about ten yards long and three yards wide (see Figure 2). Finally, each team must choose a member to be a *bagger* as well as a racer. The bagger's job is to collect toothpicks gathered during each race, to make sure they are taped together and labeled, and to save them in a bag for use during the next class.

To begin the game, the teacher blows a whistle. The first member of each team has ten seconds to run down the range, picking up as many toothpicks as possible, one toothpick per stoop. When

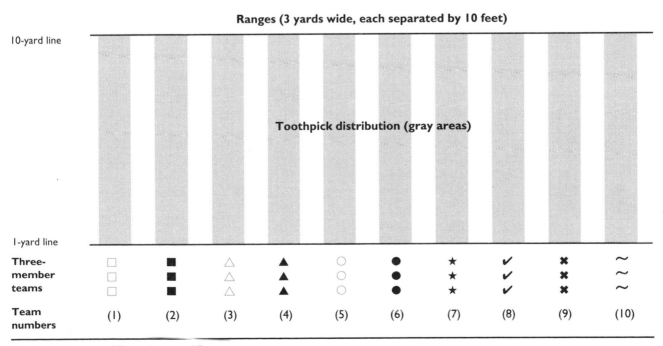

Fig. 2. A Diagram of Team Lines and Ranges

The formation and retention of concepts are deepened and enriched when students are actively involved in their learning.

TODD HUCK

the ten-second whistle blows again, each team member must be back across the starting line; or else he or she must return the collected toothpicks to the range. The players then wrap the gathered toothpicks in a piece of masking tape, label the taped group with the number of the race (Race #1, Race #2, and so forth), and drop the labeled group into the bagger's bag. The procedure of running races and labeling collected toothpicks is repeated until each group member has run three races.

Having played the game, the students are now ready to translate their kinesthetic experience into a carefully considered scientific concept. They will do this, in part, by using writing as a vehicle for discovery. Writing, we know, is not merely a means of recording previously learned information; it is a tool for clarifying and stimulating thinking and for analyzing, interpreting, and speculating about the meaning of gathered data.

Begin the second day's lesson by asking the students to picture this scene:

> Imagine a large, grassy plain. Among the animals that populate this grassy plain are four distinctly colored varieties of snakes. Some are reddish, some yellow, some blue, and some green. The natural predator that preys on these snakes is a large species of hawk. The hawks fly from mountains near the grassy plain, feeding on those snakes that they can find.

Now, ask students to cluster for two minutes about the connections they see between the scenario you have just given them and yesterday's game. When the two minutes are up, take responses from class members about the parallels they have observed and cluster them on the chalkboard. Students are likely to see obvious connections between the game and the scenario;

but if they do not go further in their thinking, ask them to do a *quickwrite* in which they consider which snakes are likely to get eaten most often and which ones might be least often victims of the hawks. You will probably get a consensus that the red and yellow snakes are more likely to be eaten more often than the blue and green snakes. Whatever their speculations, tell the students that they can check out their hypotheses and draw some conclusions about the factors that affect survival of the snakes by tabulating and analyzing the data they collected in yesterday's game.

Students meet in their teams and are given their bag of toothpicks and tables and data sheets (see Figure 3 for a sample). Students fill in Table 1 by counting the toothpicks gathered in each race and tallying the numbers of each color. Next, students total the number of toothpicks of all colors collected during each race and enter this value in the right-hand column. Table 2 simply helps students summarize and consolidate the data from Table 1.

Students now use their finished data sheets to write individual responses to the following data analysis questions. (An interesting option is to have students use their data sheets to generate questions of their own to answer before the teacher provides them with the data analysis questions.)

1. Refer to Table 2.
   a. What happens to the numbers of each toothpick color as you go down the chart?
   b. Why do you think this is so?
2. Refer to the right-hand column on Table 2.
   a. Look at the total number of toothpicks picked up over three sets of races. What happens to these numbers?
   b. Why do you suppose that this is so?

3. a. Which color(s) was (were) picked up most frequently?
   b. Draw a conclusion about why this is so.

4. a. Which colors were picked up least frequently?
   b. Why do you think that this is so?

5. As you picked up toothpicks, was it easier to pick them up if they were clustered close together or scattered far apart, or were they both equally easy to pick up?

6. As more and more toothpicks were removed from the grass, how did this affect the numbers you picked up?

When students finish the questions, have the teams meet, discuss their responses, and compile a set of answers that reflect their best collaborative thinking. Now lead a large group discussion about their answers, considering the kinds of thinking they had to do to get their answers. (An optional activity at this point is to draw a blank Table 3 on the chalkboard and collect the numbers and colors of toothpicks gathered for the sets of races from each of the groups to get classwide totals and averages. Students may then conclude whether data from Table 2 or Table 3 are more accurate and why, whether their small sampling of data from Table 2 showed a trend that was supported by data on Table 3, and how the total number of races influences the accuracy of the data.)

Participation in the game, speculation about its meaning, compilation of data, collaboration with peers, and interpretation of the assembled information all provide prewriting activities that can lead to a variety of writing experiences in different domains. Here are a few sample prompts based on our snakes and hawks scenario:

Analytical/Expository: The color of a snake may be helpful or harmful to its survival. Analyze and draw conclusions about how the color of a snake affects its chances for survival when it is the prey.

- How does the number of snakes in an area affect their chances for survival? Speculate about how it might be advantageous for animals to travel in groups.
- What can you guess or infer about how the color of a snake might affect its chances for survival when it is a predator?
- How might the data be different if the game were played on a red carpet instead of on grass?

Table 1. Toothpicks Collected by One Team Over Nine 10-second Races *(Each team had three participants.)*

Number of race	Number of toothpicks collected, by color				Total toothpicks per race
	Red	Yellow	Green	Blue	
1	//	/	/	/	5
2	/	//	/		4
3	//	//		/	5
4		/	/	/	3
5	/	/	/	//	5
6	/			/	2
7	/	/			2
8		/		/	2
9	/		/	/	3

Table 2. Consolidation of Data from Table 1 into Three Divisions

Number of race	Number of toothpicks collected, by color				Total toothpicks per race
	Red	Yellow	Green	Blue	
Races 1—3	5	5	2	2	14
Races 4—6	2	2	2	5	11
Races 7—9	2	2	1	1	6

Table 3. Average Data Collected per Group, Based on Class Average (n) = (6)

Number of race	Number of toothpicks collected, by color				Total toothpicks per race
	Red	Yellow	Green	Blue	
Races 1—3	6	7	3	4	20
Races 4—6	4	4	2	4	14
Races 7—9	4	3	1	2	10

Fig. 3. Three Tables of Data on Toothpick Experiment

- On the basis of the data you collected, which group of snakes do you think might first become extinct? Why? Speculate on what colors might be found in a group of snakes in a thousand years.

Practical/Informative. Write a snake survival manual. In the manual tell your snake-reader what it should know in order to survive. What should it know if it is brightly colored? If it is colored so that it blends with its environment? What should it consider when choosing the color and number of traveling companions? Are there times of day when it would be safer for it to feed and be active? Depending on its color, is it better for it to move quickly or to remain still when a predator is around? How might its color affect its search for food?

- Write a script for a television nature documentary that describes and explains the fate of a group of snakes over nine days. Use your data table as the basis of your script.

Imaginative/Narrative. Using diary entries, write an imaginary account of a week in the life of either a brightly colored snake or a snake that blends in with its environment. Consider some of these ideas. What might the snake encounter from day to day? What might it notice about the number and color of other snakes in its area over a period of time? What does it think about and experience because of its color? When does it eat? Why? How does its color affect its ability to get food? Does it travel with other snakes? How does it move when it feels threatened?

Students certainly could learn about the scientific concept of protective coloration through a traditional means, such as a lecture, without going through the rigamarole of this game and its attendant activities. However, the quality of an educational experience and the formation and, especially, the retention of concepts that are embodied in it are deepened and enriched when students are actively involved in their learning, when they have a chance to collaborate and share insights, and when writing is integrated across the curriculum as a learning tool for heightening, refining, and clarifying thinking.

Showing, Not Telling

A Training Program for Student Writers

By Rebekah Caplan

Coordinator, English/Language Arts (Kindergarten
Through Grade Twelve),
Oakland Unified School District;
and Teacher/Consultant, Bay Area Writing Project

Year after year we make student writers cringe with the reminder to be specific. We write in margins next to bracketed passages: *Explain, describe.* We extend arrows over words and under words, we circle words, we draw lines through words, and we accompany our hieroglyphics with captions: "What do you mean? Needs more detail; unclear." When we compose essay questions for examinations, we underline the why or why not at the end of the question twice so that our students will realize the importance of that part of the response. Recently, I talked with one teacher who had designed a rubber stamp which bore the words, GIVE AN EXAMPLE, so that he would not have to scribble the phrase again and again.

The assumption behind the Showing, *not* Telling, Training Program is that most students have not been trained to show what they mean. By training, I do not mean the occasional exercises taken from composition textbooks, nor do I mean the experience gained by writing perhaps eight major essays over the course of a year. What I mean by training is the performing of a constant mental warm-up, short and rigorous, which is not unlike the training routines of musicians, dancers, and athletes. Several years ago, while teaching reading and composition in a suburban middle school, I realized the important connection between disciplined practice in the arts and the need

EDITOR'S NOTE: This article is an excerpt from a monograph entitled *Showing Writing: A Training Program to Help Students Be Specific.* Coauthored by Rebekah Caplan and Catherine Keech and reprinted here by permission of the Bay Area Writing Project, 615 University Hall, Room 1040, University of California, Berkeley, CA 94720-1040. See also *Writers in Training: A Guide to Developing a Composition Program,* by Rebekah Caplan. Published by Dale Seymour Publications, P. O. Box 10888, Palo Alto, CA 94303.

> *The difference between the right word and the almost right word is the difference between lightning and the lightning bug.*
>
> **MARK TWAIN**

for it in a writing program. My first students were eighth graders, and not knowing precisely what the junior high school student needed to learn about writing, I experimented for a while.

My Experiment with Eighth Grade Students

For approximately three weeks I assigned my eighth grade students a potpourri of writing exercises and examined their papers carefully for common problems or strengths. I wanted to determine what my students already knew about good writing and how far I might expect to take them. It was not difficult to discover in those first few weeks of my teaching career that although these eighth graders did write with enthusiasm and energy, not many of them wrote with color or sound or texture. In a description of a student's favorite movie, I would read: "It was fantastic because it was so real!" Or the description of a strange person: "He is so weird." Or a description of a friend: "She has the most fantastic personality."

The underlinings proved the earnestness of the students, their sincerity. I attacked these empty descriptions, however, and inscribed in the margins those same suggestions that teachers have used for years. In class I passed out models of rich description—character sketches by John Steinbeck, settings by Mark Twain, abstract ideas by Ray Bradbury. I advised the students, as they scanned the models and glanced back at their own papers, that they needed to be that explicit, that good. That is what writing is all about. I said, "I know that you know what makes a thunderstorm so frightening. I know that you know the same things Mark Twain knew about a thunderstorm. Now what details did he use?" And we would list "the trees swaying" and the sky turning "blue-black" until we had every descriptive word classified on the chalkboard. "And now," I continued, "you describe a beautiful sunset in the same way that Mark Twain described the storm."

The writings from such follow-up assignments were admittedly better; but without the prepping, without fussing and reminding, I could not get students to remember to use specifics naturally. With growing frustration I tried to examine my history as a student writer. I wanted to track down what it had been like for me to write in the eighth grade and what it was like for my students today. I wanted to uncover when it was that I had reached a turning point or gained a sense of discovery about language and expression.

When I tried to recall my own junior high experience, however, I could not remember one assignment, let alone any instruction in writing. What I did remember was signing autograph books and passing notes in class, recording memories in diaries, and signing *slam* books. Those sorts of writings mattered the most. We cared deeply about who was one's friend and who was one's enemy, who was loved, who was hated, who was worthy of secrets, who was not. And as these issues came under judgment, we based our verdict on the degree of someone's good personality. In fact, the supreme compliment paid a friend in an autograph book amounted to "fantastic personality." And it is still so today.

The memory struck me as being significant. The notion that each person has a personality that is separate from looks or dress or wealth is a new thought to the junior high school student. I remember using the same phrase, "a great personality," with fresh, original intentions in diaries and school papers. My friends and I were intrigued by the idea of personality more than any other idea. We were fascinated by people's differences; yet, we could not say exactly what made us like one person and dislike another. Could it be, then, that I was demanding writing that my students were not ready to produce? It seemed crucial to respect their excitement over many of these clichéd discoveries. I had to allow room for naive, exploratory generalizations but, at the same time, challenge them to move beyond simple abstractions and discover what concepts, like personality, were based on—how they derived their meanings from concrete perceptions.

An Examination of My Writing

After examining what motivated my students, I looked at myself as an adult writer. What kinds of things did I strive for? I surely strove for specificity. For years I had kept a journal in which I commented on cycles of personal change. I usually began in a stream-of-consciousness style, listing sensations and noting the details that would explain my perceptions to myself. I wrote often, even if I had nothing to say, in the hope that I would discover something to write about. I believe this ritual of writing regularly developed from my training as a dancer and a pianist. As a young piano student, I practiced daily finger exercises to strengthen manual agility at the keyboard to prepare myself for a Bach concerto. As a young ballerina, I was forced to do leg lifts at the bar for 30 minutes for each lesson; the remaining 15 minutes were devoted to dancing. (How we longed for it to be the other way around!) I notice that beginning artists practice drawing the human body again and again from varying angles, using different materials—charcoals, oils, ink— to capture reality. In the drama classes I attended in college, we began acting lessons with short improvisations that allowed us to experiment with emotions before we rehearsed major scenes for a performance. In all these cases, the learning, the mastering, came more from the practice than from the final presentation.

My Training Program for Student Writers

After drawing these several conclusions about the training of artists, I decided to build into my curriculum a training program for student writers—a program in which I attempted to engrain craft and to make the use of specific detail automatic, habitual, through regular and rigorous practice. I created a writing program that included these coordinating tasks:

1. Practicing two to three times a week the expanding of a general statement into a paragraph

2. Applying the difference between *telling* and *showing* in the revision process
3. Practicing specific ways to select and arrange concrete details in developing an idea or structuring an essay

Next, I will describe the initial phase of my training program.

Since students need the discipline of a regular routine to reinforce the use of concrete details in place of, or in support of, their generalizations, I assign a regular homework challenge: I give them what I call a *telling sentence.* They must expand the thought in that sentence into an entire paragraph which shows rather than tells. They take home sentences like these:

> The room is vacant.
> The jigsaw puzzle was difficult to assemble.
> Lunch period is too short.

They bring back descriptive paragraphs—short or long, but always detailed, and focused on demonstrating the thought expressed in the assigned telling sentence. I challenge students not to use the original statement in the paragraph at all. I ask them to convince me that a room is empty or a puzzle is hard to assemble without once making that claim directly. The challenge is much like one in charades: They have to get an idea across without telling what it is.

To establish the difference between telling and showing, I distribute the following two paragraphs to my students. The first was written by a seventh grader; the second, by novelist E. L. Doctorow. Both passages concern a scene at a bus stop:

Telling:

Each morning I ride the bus to school. I wait along with the other people who ride my bus. Sometimes

> *The chief purpose of words is to convey thoughts, and unless the wavelengths of the words are right, the receiving apparatus will utterly fail to pick up the thoughts.*
>
> **GEORGE OTIS SMITH**

the bus is late and we get angry. Some guys start fights and stuff just to have something to do. I'm always glad when the bus finally comes.

Showing:

A bus arrived. It discharged its passengers, closed its doors with a hiss, and disappeared over the crest of the hill. Not one of the people waiting at the bus stop had attempted to board. One woman wore a sweater that was too small, a long loose skirt, white sweater socks, and house slippers. One man was in his undershirt. Another man wore shoes with the toes cut out, a soiled blue serge jacket and brown pants. There was something wrong with these people. They made faces. A mouth smiled at nothing, and unsmiled, smiled and unsmiled. A head shook in vehement denial. Most of them carried brown paper bags rolled tight against their stomachs.[1]

When asked to distinguish the differences between the two paragraphs, most students respond by saying the second paragraph is better because they can picture the scene more easily. They think the people in paragraph two are "weird, poor, and lonely, " (all *telling* ideas). But this interpretation comes from the pictures (the students' word), pictures of people wearing torn clothing, carrying brown paper bags instead of lunch boxes, and wearing unhappy expressions on their faces. Student writers can easily discern good description. Getting them to write with close detail is not managed as smoothly.

I remind students that the storybooks they read as very young children are filled with colorful illustrations that show the events described on accompanying pages; the writer does not have to describe the lovely red barn with the carved wooden trim, for the picture next to the caption, "The barn was beautiful," reveals that idea. However, in more mature literature, drawings disappear from the pages, and the writer assumes the role of illustrator. Language must be the author's brush and palette. Following such a discussion, I initiate the telling training exercise and explain to students that they will expand one sentence from two to three times a week from telling to showing during the entire course of the semester.

Listed next are sample telling sentences. These sentences are given in no particular order and are not necessarily linked by recurring themes. Sometimes students themselves suggest sentences for successive assignments. By choosing generalizations familiar to students, I increase the likelihood of effective elaboration:

I was pleasantly surprised.
The speaker got our attention.
The pizza tasted good.
The game was a close one.
Saturday is different from Sunday.
Teenagers should have their own telephones.
The jocks think they're cool.
They act older than their age.
Time passed.
Reality set in.

The idea of frequent writing is, of course, nothing new in itself. I know many teachers who have their students "write for ten minutes" the moment they come to class. My writing approach, however, is different in a number of ways. First, many teachers assign topics for elaboration, such as school or family or sports. Although a topic is open-ended and allows more room for creativity, students often spend more time trying to find something to say than they spend in writing the composition. The type of statement I use is similar to the thesis, the controlling sentence of an essay. The generalization supplies the point; the student is given the idea to support. Students are free then to concentrate on experimenting with expressions of that idea. Further, since they are all working on the same idea, they are in a position to compare results—to learn from one another's crafting.

Another departure from other writing warm-ups is that this writing is done at home. Students must come to class with pieces finished and ready to be evaluated. We do not wait ten minutes while they hastily scribble some sort of solution. I want to give them time—if they will use it—to experiment with and think about what they are trying to do.

Importance of Sharing the Writing

Finally, unlike private journals or some free-writing assignments, the exercises are written to be shared. I use the writings in much the same way that a drama instructor uses improvisation as an instructional technique. The daily sentence expansion becomes a framework for practicing and discovering ways of showing ideas. Just as drama

---

[1] E. L. Doctorow, *The Book of Daniel*. New York: Random House, Inc., © 1971, p. 5. Used by permission of the publisher.

In more mature literature, drawings disappear from the pages, and the writer assumes the role of illustrator. Language must be the author's brush and palette.

REBEKAH CAPLAN

students search for ways of expressing ambition or despair by imagining themselves in real-life situations that would evoke these feelings and discovering ranges of bodily and facial expression, my students arrive at ways of showing "empty rooms" or "difficult puzzles" by experimenting with different kinds of language expression. I instruct them very little, preferring that students find their own solutions. But, finally, although the experimenting at home is free, not judged, the practice includes an important element that parallels instruction in acting: the daily public performance. The students know in advance that some papers will be read to the class for analysis and evaluation. However, they do not know which ones. As their papers might be among those I choose (my selections do not fall into a predictable pattern), the students are likely to be prepared.

The *performance* or sharing of improvisational or experimental efforts is an important learning experience for the selected performers and their audience. The first ten minutes of every class session, then, is devoted to oral reading, not writing. I choose between five and seven writing samples, which I read aloud to the class, and as a group we evaluate the density of detail. Where did this writer have success with interesting description? Where were his or her details thin? This is the only time I do not comb the papers for errors in grammar, spelling, and usage, for there is not time. Since we respond exclusively to content, students can give full attention to being specific without the pressure of being grammatically perfect.

I grade each paper immediately as the discussion of that paper concludes. Besides assigning an A, B, or C grade, I quickly write a specific comment made by the group, urging students away from saying only "good showing" about the specific

section that was evidence of good showing: "You show great tension through the expression in his eyes"; "Your verb *conjectured* gives sophistication to his speech." After we respond in this manner, I move on to the next reading. I record a check in my gradebook for those papers not selected for reading. If students do not turn in writings, they do not receive credit. All papers are recorded and handed back before the end of the period, giving the students immediate responses and recognition for their work. At the end of the semester, I average the number of grades a student has earned in the series of assignments.

Advantages to Using a Training Exercise

There are five major advantages to using such a daily training exercise with its follow-up sharing and discussion:

1. *Students write almost every other day.* I do not, however, assign sentences on the eve of an examination day, on days major assignments are due, or on holidays.
2. *I am freed from having to grade an entire set of papers each night, yet I provide an immediate evaluation.* If a student is disappointed because a particular writing was not selected, I invite him or her to share it with me after class. Generally, a student wants to share when he or she has written a good paragraph and wants me to enter a grade for this particular one, which I am glad to do. Sharing may also occur when a student is unsure of his or her solution and wants help.
3. *Students who are selected to perform hear useful comments immediately.* They do not have to wait a week to receive responses and constructive criticisms. The other students learn from the process of specifying weaknesses as

well as strengths of work and from hearing suggestions given to the performing students by peers and teachers.

4. *Students learn new developmental techniques and linguistic patterns from each other.* Students assimilate new ideas for specificity by regularly hearing other students' writing. In addition, they often internalize the linguistic patterns of other students either consciously or unconsciously. This process is similar to assimilating the speech patterns of a person with a different accent. After close association with this person, we may tune our speech to the inflections of an attractive or entertaining accent. I believe it is often easier for students to learn from other students who write well than from professional writers whose solutions may be out of the student's range.

5. *Students write for a specific audience.* They write with the expectation that classmates may hear their compositions the following day. Therefore, they usually put more effort into their writing than they would have given if the compositions were intended for their private journals or for a teacher's evaluation.

A selection of writing samples follows. Two students, a remedial freshman and a college-bound sophomore, show growth and change over a two-week time span. Their writings illustrate two important results of the training practice:

1. Students write more either because they are finding it easier to generate more writing or because they are working harder on the assignments (or both).
2. Students gain control over a wider range of techniques.

From the telling sentence, *The new students were lonely,* the freshman wrote the following at the beginning of the two-week time period:

> It was the first day of school and there were two new students, Dick and Dan, who had moved over the summer. They were brothers and this was a new city and school which they had come to, and in this school they would have to make friends because neither of them knew anybody or anyone.

As you will note, the freshman's writing is composed entirely of generalities (telling sentences).

The writer explains the cause of the loneliness—a new city, new school, absence of old friends—but unless he shows us his new surroundings, unfamiliar faces, and different customs to support those reasons, he will do little to convince us. Perhaps if he could contrast "playing pool with the gang at Old Mike's Pizza Parlor" to the "eyes avoiding his unfamiliar face in the study hall," the reader might appreciate the realities of "new city, new school, new friends." Here is the same freshman student's writing two weeks later; the daily sentence was *The crossword puzzle was difficult to solve:*

> The sixth row down got me stuck. It was plain to tell that this crossword puzzle was rough. The puzzle, as it was, was made for a 12th grade level, and it made me feel as if I was in the 6th grade level. Intellectual words were included, such as "the square root" of 1,091,056 in four digits and others. The next one was a five-letter word for philodendron, which was "plant" to my surprise. I, as a normal person, had a very hard time trying to figure out what an Australian green citrus fruit was with four spaces. Instinctively I gave up the whole game, as it was too frustrating to cope with.

The freshman's selection illustrates his improvement in generating examples. The writer introduces his subject by *telling* that the puzzle was tough, but he immediately proves his claim with a series of illustrations: twelfth grade level versus sixth grade level, intellectual words like *square root*, unfamiliar plants and fruits that call for specialized knowledge. His writing is more enjoyable to read because of the examples he added. Notice also that his paragraph is longer, but he does not ramble or leave the point.

At the beginning of the two-week period, the sophomore responded to the daily sentence: *The room was vacant,* by writing this:

> The next show didn't start for another hour. As I repositioned the spotlight in the upper balcony, the squeaks of the rusty screws seemed to echo throughout the desolate building. I walked down the aluminum stairs that resounded with the sound of rain beating on a tin roof throughout the auditorium. I then opened the curtains to the large, lonely stage which looked dark and forbidding. As I put up the sets and decorated the stage, I guess it would seem to anyone walking in, that the room was very much

alive with color and objects. But to me, even the set and decorated auditorium looked bare.

In the first half of the paragraph, this student carefully constructs detail. Like many students trying to master a skill, he concentrates intensely at first, very mindful of his task. However, there comes a point when, losing his fervor, he reverts to telling. With the sentence, "I then opened the curtains . . . ," he abandons his use of specifics, relying instead on vague adjectives like "dark and forbidding," or on general nouns such as "color and objects."

Within two weeks this student increased his observational skills considerably. In addition, he was able to sustain the use of vivid details throughout a much longer piece of writing. With the telling sentence, *The roller coaster was the scariest ride at the fair*, as a prompt, he wrote:

> As I stood in line, I gazed up at the gigantic steel tracks that looped around three times. The thunderous roar of the roller coaster sounded like a thunder cloud that had sunk into my ears and suddenly exploded. The wild screams of terror shot through me like a bolt of lightning and made my fingers tingle with fear. Soon I heard the roar of the roller coaster cease. As the line started to move forward, I heard the clicking of the turnstile move closer and closer. Finally, I got onto the loading deck and with a shaking hand gave the attendant my ticket.

> It seemed like I barely got seated when I felt a jolt which signified the beginning of the ride. While the roller coaster edged up the large track, I kept pulling my seatbelt tighter and tighter until it felt like I was cutting off all circulation from the waist down. At the crest of the hill, I caught a glimpse of the quiet town which lay before me and gave me a feeling of peace and serenity. Suddenly my eyes felt like they were pushed all the way back into my head, and the town

> *I don't start a novel or a play saying, "I'll write about such and such." I start with an idea and then find out what I'm writing about.*
>
> **WILLIAM INGE**

> had become a blur. All I could see was a mass of steel curving this way and that as the roller coaster turned upside down. I was squeezing the safety bar so tight that my fingers seemed to be embedded in the metal. I could see the landing deck, and I let out a deep breath that had been held inside ever since the first drop. As the roller coaster came to a halt, I felt weak and emotionally drained. When I stepped off onto the deck, I teetered a bit to the left, but caught my balance quickly when I saw my friends waiting for me at the exit gate. I tried to look "normal," while trying to convince them in a weak voice that, "Oh, it was nothing."

Even though he makes general claims—"I felt weak and emotionally drained"—he remembers to support his feeling with specific evidence: "When I stepped off onto the deck, I teetered a bit to the left. . . ." Or, as he tries to look "normal," he proves this with dialogue: "Oh, it was nothing." This student puts himself in the experience every step of the narration. Two weeks earlier, he could not sustain such a practice.

To summarize, the practice of showing, not telling, through regular sentence expansions provides a framework in which students can experiment and discover ways of showing ideas. It is a time for self-exploration in the attempt to attach meaning to experience; it is also a time for increasing fluency and creating a style and voice.

Practical Ideas for Training Students to Show, Not Tell

Preparing for Showing, Not Telling, Through Share Days

By Michael Carr

Teacher, Valley Junior High School,
Carlsbad Unified School District;
and Teacher/Consultant, UCI Writing Project

Rebekah Caplan's showing, not telling, technique can be taught effectively in kindergarten and first grade. But because many of the students may be nonreaders or nonwriters, they will need some oral preparation. *Share Days* make wonderful prewriting experiences for children who are making the transition from speaking to writing.

Essentially, Share Days are an updated version of show and tell. A child brings an object to share to class, but the object must be hidden from view in a bag or box. When it is his or her turn, the child comes to the front of the class, puts the item in our share box, and proceeds to describe it by answering these questions:

What is its shape?
What is its color?
What is its texture?
What is it made of?
What do you do with it?
Who uses it?
What is it like? Can you compare it to anything else?

After the child describes his or her object by answering the questions cited above, selected students get three tries to guess what the item is. See how you do on this example:

The item is round.
The colors are white and gold.
It's hard and smooth.
It's made of rubber.
You throw the item.
People use it.
It's like a flying saucer.

If you guessed a Frisbee, you are right. When the item has been guessed correctly, or all tries have been exhausted, the child can take the item out of the share box to show the class.

Using this process, children in my class are able to construct orally the elements of a showing paragraph by describing rather than telling. This activity not only increases their oral fluency but also prepares them for writing. Moreover, at the same time that they are getting practice in speaking and, by extension, writing, they are also building problem-solving skills.

Preparing Junior High School Students for Showing, Not Telling

By Marie Filardo

Former Teacher, Serrano Intermediate School, and
De Portola Elementary School,
Saddleback Valley Unified School District;
and Teacher/Consultant, UCI Writing Project

Every September a new wave of students registers for intermediate school all decked out in their designer clothes and speaking a uniform language. Everything is "awesome," "radical," and "mega." Conformity abounds. Unfortunately, the accepted labels in their speech infiltrate their writing, and I know I am in for countless papers filled with stilted, lifeless, abstract images.

As an intermediate school teacher aware of the social impact on writing, my initial step in preparing students for showing, not telling, is to make them aware of the consequences of labeling. In my first assignment I ask my students to write a letter to a friend in which they recall a memorable place, person, or event that they encountered last summer. The following samples indicate the extent to which labeling occurs in their writing:

Dear Kim,

I remember when we went skin diving at Shaw's Cove. It was rad.

Dear Tom,

Jim and I went surfing in Laguna. We caught some really gnarly waves.

Dear Michelle,

My family and I went on the log ride at Knott's Berry Farm. It was awesome.

Dear Collette,

Friday we all went to Dodger Stadium. We got a bunch of autographs. I wish you could have gone. It was spastic.

Dear Heather,

Our vacation in Hawaii was mega bucks but we had a blast.

Dear Sandy,

I had the most funnest summer. I went to a friend's house and played so many fun games. I stayed there really late and had the most funnest time.

After collecting the letters, I read them and underline the labeling words. In class the following day, we work in pairs. I ask partners to question what they envision when they hear a labeled word and to jot down specific details of their impressions. During a session of questioning, students realize quickly that what was awesome to one student might not have been imagined by the other. In comparing notes, they see that each individual has conjured up a different image of the labeling word. An awesome day at the beach may prove to be a peaceful, lazy day for Tom; while, to John, it may mean surfing in waves 12 feet high. When individual groups have had sufficient time to review several labeling words, I call the class together and provide a list, such as the following, on which I ask the students to identify words that may be interpreted differently.

In follow-up lessons we review labeling phrases and labeling paragraphs. In an attempt to have students become cognizant of labeling words in their daily lives, I post a chart on which we record labels as they crop up in daily discussions.

To counteract the unproductive cycle of labeling that permeates both thinking and writing skills, we need to identify labeling as being generic and non-

Identifying Labels[1]

Instructions: Find every label word in the list below and indicate it by printing "L" beside it.

deafening	green	sexy
threadbare	fantastic	hateful
ugly	malodorous	fabulous
moss-covered	frayed	sturdy
close-cropped	bumpy	great
boring	unlikable	wonderful
awful	immoral	upturned
slow-moving	sharp-featured	awesome
curly	sweaty	bug-eyed
lovely	foul-mouthed	horrible
splotchy	adorable	ragged
capable	timid	purple
blue-and-white	fetid	right
checked	amazing	exciting
pug-nosed	looming	obese
cautious	wild-eyed	leathery
respectable		

definitive, a statement of opinion rather than fact, subjective rather than objective. Once the students are aware of labels and their effect on writing, we concentrate on replacing labels with words that are less abstract. It becomes our goal to replace a label with concrete images that can easily be perceived by our senses. For example, the awesome log ride at Knott's Berry Farm becomes a slow-ascending, winding, jarring, fast-descending, or splashing ride. This process of replacing labels with concrete, explicit vocabulary focuses the students' attention on the pleasure of communicating more clearly. Indefinite words are transformed into clear images.

Once students are made aware of the pitfalls of labeling, it is necessary to provide them with the skills needed to further the attributes of showing rather than telling. These skills may include:

---

[1]This is part of a list from Gene Stanford and Marie Smith's *A Guidebook for Teaching Creative Writing.* Newton, Mass.: Allyn & Bacon, Inc., © 1981, p. 4. Used by permission of the authors.

1. Vocabulary
2. Metaphors and similes
3. Techniques in imagery
4. Sentence structure
5. Paragraph form

From evaluating my students' writing over a period of time, I am convinced that the progression of showing in their writing was directly proportional to the writing skills taught. This fact furthered my sense that it is essential to prepare students for *showing* before assigning descriptive, showing, not telling, paragraphs.

Here is a sample of writing produced after a lesson on the use of similes in replacing labels:

> Finding my way to class was like running in a marathon and not knowing where the finish line was. While I was finding my classes, I had a picture in my mind of myself as a mouse quickly running so I wouldn't get stepped on. I felt very relieved at the end of the day, sort of like an experienced adult who has been working at a job for many years. After the second half of the day, I was pretty relaxed and not tense anymore. I had great fun that first day at Serrano. It was like a day at an amusement park.

The following writing sample was generated after a combination of vocabulary, metaphors and similes, and sentence structure skills were taught:

> The dark, brown-haired boy came and sat next to me with disdain. When he sat down, he looked as if he was about to throw his books at me with a great deal of strength. As the day went on, my head felt like it was being pounded on while I worried about whether or not he was going to hit me. At lunch he would act very indomitable, like a boulder making its way through other rocks to get his food. Even worse, he acted like his brain was as small as a sunflower seed. He, trying to think, is worse than a pig trying to sing. Sometimes he would try to be funny. None of his jokes were very good. But, you would have to laugh or he would pound you on the head as if you were a nail and he were the hammer. So, if he tells you a joke, for your sake, laugh your head off or he'll knock it off.

Finally, this was a sample of writing taken after all five previously mentioned skills were taught:

My Mother the Worker

Even before the sun rises, my mother does, and she is already busy executing her daily tasks. She begins her day by preparing breakfast for our family. Perfectly browned toast and creamy orange juice greet our taste buds every morning soon after we have awakened. While I am at school, every inch of our house is pampered by her delicate touch. Our floor seems to glitter as if it were gold. The plants in our home are radiant with health. As you get close to them, tiny droplets of water seem to be covering each leaf like a thin skin. Mom takes special care to spray each plant twice a day. After almost seven hours of work, she takes time out of her busy schedule to come and pick me up from school. I hope that someday I can be just like my mother.

My students still would not be caught dead in anything but their designer clothes. And everything they talk about is as awesome as ever. But, in writing, after careful preparation and guidance, they are showing, not telling.

Integrating Clustering and Showing, Not Telling

By Carol Booth Olson
Director, UCI Writing Project

I have had good luck with using clustering as a way to introduce and generate ideas about a concept, character, event, or experience and showing, not telling, as an organizational device for logically developing and supporting those ideas in well-detailed, descriptive paragraphs. In a sense, clustering becomes a prewriting activity that culminates in a showing, not telling, writing assignment.

Provided below is an experiential exercise I use to help students enhance descriptive writing skills. The exercise is based on the integration of clustering and showing, not telling.

Lesson Plan for Clustering and Showing, Not Telling, About Blindness

Provide an introduction to descriptive writing prior to this exercise. Activities can include:

- Lecture/discussion on concrete versus abstract diction
- Examination of professional and student models to discover what makes writing vivid
- Presentation of color slides that students respond to with "I see," "I hear," "I smell," "I taste," and "I feel" statements
- Visualization to music

The activities above focus primarily on the visual in descriptive writing. The following exercise enables students to tap their other senses.

Step 1: Orientation

Ask each student in the class to pick a partner. Explain that every class member will have an opportunity to experience blindness as well as to become a guide for a blind person. As you are passing out one blindfold to each pair, ask the students to choose which role—guide or blind person—they prefer to assume first. Once the students have selected their respective roles, the guide should assist his or her partner in putting on the blindfold.

It is the guide's responsibility to lead the blind person out of the classroom and to provide him or her with a sensory experience, which should involve exposure to some or all of the following: smell, texture, taste, the experience of ascending and descending, the feeling of an open space versus a closed-in space, and changing temperatures. No conversation should take place during this excursion. However, students can communicate through body language. After approximately five to ten minutes, the students should stop, switch roles, and continue their walk.

Step 2: Prewriting Exercise

When the students return to the classroom, print the word BLIND on the chalkboard. Ask the students to put this word in the center of a blank piece of paper and cluster in a circle around the stimulus word (in single words and short phrases) all of the images, associations, and feelings that come to mind when they think of being blind. After about five minutes, ask each person to share orally one of his or her cluster words or phrases. As the students volunteer their thoughts, you can ask other students whether they identify with the feelings expressed or whether they have different reactions to add. Record all of these responses in a composite cluster on the board, as shown in Figure 1.

Step 3: Writing

After the clustering and discussion period, elicit one main idea or feeling about blindness that the group seemed to share. Then create a telling sentence (a general, declarative statement)

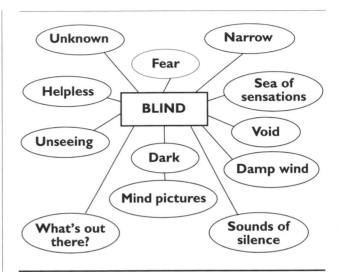

Fig. 1. Clustering of Images and Feelings of Being Blind

which expresses that idea in a specific context students can illustrate. For example, if the predominant class response to the sensation of blindness was fear of the unknown, you might write a sentence like this on the chalkboard: "The blind woman was terrified of unfamiliar places." Draw the students' attention to this sentence. Ask them if they were to write a paragraph showing a blind woman who was terrified of unfamiliar places, what details would they use to:

1. Indicate that the woman was blind.
2. Make it clear that she was in an unfamiliar place.
3. Let the reader know how frightened she was.

Once they have discussed various ways to describe the telling sentence, ask the students to write one or more paragraphs that show how it feels to be a blind person in an unfamiliar place. They can use "The blind woman was terrified of unfamiliar places" as their topic sentence, but encourage them to illustrate this sentence through vivid, sensory details. Allow 20 to 30 minutes for writing.

Step 4: Sharing and Rewriting

Explain to the students that if they have written a vivid, well-detailed descriptive paragraph, they should no longer need their topic sentence. Without the topic sentence, the supporting paragraph should communicate effectively that the blind woman was terrified of unfamiliar places. Ask students to cross out their topic sentence and exchange papers with a friend. Working together, the two should answer the following questions: Does the paragraph communicate the message effectively without the topic sentence? In other words, can it stand alone? If not, what descriptive phrases and sensory details are necessary to show that the blind woman was terrified of unfamiliar places? Provide the class with at least one model of a well-written paper that is rich in showing writing.

Here is an example:

Telling sentence:

The blind woman was terrified of unfamiliar places.

Showing paragraphs:

She cautiously hobbled down the street, her white cane carefully tapping out the steps before her, sensing the ridges and rhythms of each concrete square. She could hear the blaring of midday traffic and the cursing of angry cab drivers and feel the crushing weight of the sound reverberating off tall buildings. Each step was an effort—a venture into the unknown. When would it end? A feeling of nausea welled up in her stomach, and beads of sweat appeared on her brow.

Suddenly, her cane missed a beat, and she stumbled off the curb. Car tires screeched in front of her and obscenities filled the air. An arm reached out to steady her. "Thank you," she mumbled as she collected herself and tried to blend back into the waiting crowd. Closing . . . it was all closing in. She could feel herself shrinking into the pavement.

"Pardon me, miss," a concerned voice said. "Can I help you across the street?"

Oh, dear, she thought, her chest beginning to tighten as she suppressed the sobs, all I need is for someone to be kind.

He could feel her stiffen as he gripped the back of her elbow and guided her across the street. When they reached the other side, she dismissed him with a "thank you" and appeared to be debating something. Curiously enough, she then reached for the walk button on the streetlight as if to head back in the direction she came from. From a block away, he caught a glimpse of her over her his shoulder. Statue-like, she was still standing exactly where he had left her—frozen in indecision.

Allow in-class time for rewriting and a second round of sharing with a partner. Have students polish and edit this draft so that it may be turned in for evaluation.

I like this particular assignment because it starts with a prewriting experience the students can draw on to write about. The clustering exercise that follows is a right-brain activity that helps students express their feelings and generate content. This logically leads into the showing, not telling, lesson where using concrete, sensory detail to create a picture and communicate emotions is stressed. Since descriptive writing is the most concrete writing domain and the easiest for most students to create, the lesson focuses on fluency—getting the language to say what the students mean. Later experiences, such as clustering and showing, not telling, about literary characters, will build a bridge from sensory/descriptive and imaginative/ narrative into more analytical/expository writing.

Using Cooperative Learning to Facilitate Writing

Using Structures to Promote Cooperative Learning in Writing

By Jeanne M. Stone
Cooperative Learning Consultant;
and Teacher/Consultant, UCI Writing Project

and Spencer S. Kagan
Former Professor of Psychology, UC Riverside;
Director, Kagan Cooperative Learning

Once upon a time, as all fairy tales start, there was a teacher who loved to teach writing. She did not have a wicked stepparent to thwart her means of enjoyment, only a sense that there had to be an easier way to teach writing. One day her fairy godmother heard her lamentations and told her about the UCI Writing Project. From the day her application was accepted, it seemed like a match made in heaven; and the teacher lived happily ever after, teaching writing through the stages of the writing process and enjoying every minute of it.

Then one day this teacher attended a training session in the structural approach to Cooperative Learning. She immediately saw the connection between the communicative processes involved in the writing process and Cooperative Learning. With these two instructional ideas interwoven in her classroom teaching strategies, she lived even more happily ever after.

Teachers use basic Cooperative Learning structures in all stages of the writing process to involve the students with each other and with their writing. When teachers use Cooperative Learning to teach writing, they can facilitate the interactive stages of the writing process: prewriting, responding, evaluating, and publishing. Rather than being lectured to by the teacher, students within their teams discuss at length the topic at hand, collect ideas, share writing to receive feedback, develop editing skills, and share the finished writing with the whole class. Using the Structural Approach to Cooperative Learning, the teacher fosters fluency, rethinking of content and form, and publishing of

> *Teachers use basic Cooperative Learning structures in all stages of the writing process to involve the students with each other and with their writing.*
>
> SPENCER S. KAGAN

the final piece of writing through student-to-student interaction.

Cooperative Learning and the Writing Process

Cooperative Learning structures used throughout the stages of the writing process provide teachers with a wealth of ideas and instructional strategies. In practice, a writing lesson can follow from one Cooperative Learning structure to another, from stage to stage, creating a multistructural lesson. The following writing lesson, based on *The Three Billy Goats Gruff*, shows how Cooperative Learning structures can be used during each stage of the writing process. The objective of this lesson is for students to create new ways of dealing with the troll and then to rewrite the ending of the story.

Throughout the following lesson only a thumbnail description of the Cooperative Learning structure used is given. During each stage of the writing process, a structure (or structures) illustrates the use of Cooperative Learning. Each structure has its own domain of usefulness and can be used in various stages throughout the writing process. For a detailed description of the structures, and their usefulness in the writing process, see Spencer Kagan's *Cooperative Learning*[1] and Jeanne Stone's *Cooperative Learning and Language Arts: A Multi-Structural Approach*.[2]

Example of a Writing Lesson Using Cooperative Learning

The section that follows contains a discussion of how to integrate the structures from Cooperative

Learning with the seven stages of the writing process: prewriting, writing, responding, revising, editing, evaluating, and publishing.

Prewriting

Students begin their prewriting with Team Discussion (working in teams of four members) to talk about bullies and create a definition of a bully. Each team records its definition, which a representative from each team shares with the rest of the class. Students continue the activity by using Paired Reading to review *The Three Billy Goats Gruff*. In Paired Reading two students share a copy of the story and read alternate paragraphs. When the students have finished reading, they use Team Discussion to define the billy goats' problem.

Students participate in a Team Interview to "meet" the characters and explore their feelings about the bully under the bridge. In this activity each team member becomes one of the characters in the story: the smallest billy goat, the middle billy goat, the largest billy goat, and the troll. In turn, each character stands up to be interviewed, in his or her role, by the other team members.

Using Roundtable, the students create a list of ways to get past the troll. Students pass a paper and pencil around the team so that each team member, in turn, records an idea for getting past the troll. Through Roundtable all students participate, and different viewpoints are shared. The students who may have a richer background on the Roundtable topic can help the others.

Writing

Students begin the actual writing by reviewing the list the team created and selecting an alternative solution to the problem of the troll (bully). The students then "Fastwrite" to record their new

[1]Spencer S. Kagan, *Cooperative Learning.* San Juan Capistrano, Calif.: Kagan Cooperative Learning, 1992.
[2]Jeanne M. Stone, *Cooperative Learning and Language Arts: A Multi-Structural Approach.* San Juan Capistrano, Calif.: Kagan Cooperative Learning, 1992.

Cooperative Learning and the Writing Process

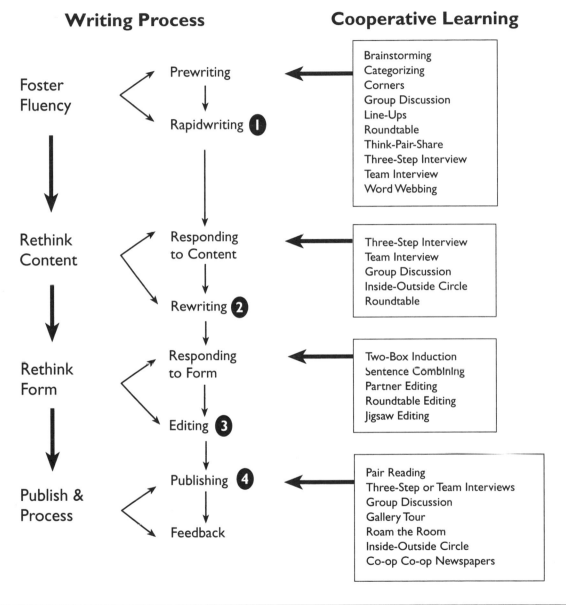

Writing Process   **Cooperative Learning**

Foster Fluency

Prewriting

Rapidwriting ❶

Brainstorming
Categorizing
Corners
Group Discussion
Line-Ups
Roundtable
Think-Pair-Share
Three-Step Interview
Team Interview
Word Webbing

Rethink Content

Responding to Content

Rewriting ❷

Three-Step Interview
Team Interview
Group Discussion
Inside-Outside Circle
Roundtable

Rethink Form

Responding to Form

Editing ❸

Two-Box Induction
Sentence Combining
Partner Editing
Roundtable Editing
Jigsaw Editing

Publish & Process

Publishing ❹

Feedback

Pair Reading
Three-Step or Team Interviews
Group Discussion
Gallery Tour
Roam the Room
Inside-Outside Circle
Co-op Co-op Newspapers

❶ = Notes, Letters, Journals, Stories, Lists, Narrations, Logs, Descriptions, Biography, Autobiography, Poems, Dialogue . . .
❷ = Show don't tell, Appealing to senses, Point of view, Emphasis, Audience, Foreshadowing, Momentum, Character Development . .
❸ = Colorful adjectives, Complete sentences, Word choice, Alliteration, Rhyme, Meter, Concrete detail, Verb agreement,
  Organization, Proofreading, Sentence Combining, Topic Sentences. . .
❹ = Mail, Modem, Read, Bind, Illustrate, Post, Perform, Gift wrap. . .

The source for this chart is Spencer Kagan and Laurie Robertson, *Cooperative Learning: Coop Across the Curriculum*. San Juan Capistrano, Calif.: Kagan Cooperative Learning, 1993. p. Language Arts: 3. © Spencer Kagan, Kagan Cooperative Learning. Reprinted by permission of the publisher.

endings fluently. They write what they think should happen, without worrying about organization or correctness, a process that encourages fluency.

Next, using Three-Step Interview, students practice presenting their writing to an audience. During the first step of Three-Step Interview, students, working in teams of four, pair up to interview each other. One student reads his or her writing while the other listens and asks questions from the viewpoint of the intended audience; for example, a parent, fellow student, or friend. Next, the students reverse roles. Finally, each student shares with the team the essence of the partner's writing. On the basis of how the other students react, students then rewrite or add to the fastwrite to create a new ending for the story.

Responding

Structuring a time for responding in the classroom increases students' success. A whole-class sharing session using student writing presented on an overhead projector or chart paper models responding for the class. "Gambits" (open-ended, model phrases) can be provided to guide students in making appropriate responses.

After students have finished writing their new endings to *The Three Billy Goats Gruff*, each team member is given three response handouts. Using Simultaneous Roundtable, team members pass the four story endings around the team. Each student reads the new ending in front of him or her and then writes statements, questions, or suggestions on a "Response Sheet" handout. The story ending is then passed to the person on the left. The Simultaneous Roundtable is completed when the team members have read and responded to each of their teammates' writings. The writings and the responses are then returned to the writer for review.

Revising

Throughout the writing process students continually reread and make changes. After the students have finished their writing and received responses from others, they look at the writing as a whole and answer such questions as:

Does my writing say what I want it to?
Did people understand what I wanted them to "see"?
Do I need to add more details?

Does my writing communicate to the correct audience?
Does my writing successfully meet its purpose?

Cooperative Learning structures help students to develop techniques that address such ideas as organization, sentence structure (sentence combining and sentence expansion), word choice, clarity, and emphasis. The instructional part of the writing lesson may occur before students begin the writing process or while they are revising their papers.

Two-Box Induction is one structure that can be used to develop the concepts students need when they are revising their papers. For example, if the teacher noted that short, choppy sentences occurred throughout the students' writing, a lesson on sentence combining could become a part of the writing lesson. To use Two-Box Induction, the teacher designates two boxes as Box 1 and Box 2 and adds an item to each box (using examples from students' papers is recommended):

Box 1 : There were three billy goats. They were on the hill.
Box 2 : There were three billy goats on the hill.

The teacher asks the class members to think about the differences between the sentences in the boxes. Students pair up with another student and discuss their answers. As more simple sentences are added to Box 1 and more combined sentences are added to Box 2, the teacher can use Think-Pair-Share for students to process the information. Students *think* about their responses, *pair* to discuss them with a partner, and then *share* them, in some way, with the class. As students learn the rules for adding sentences to the boxes, they add items to Box 1 and Box 2 rather than give the rules. This process continues until all students have had a chance to contribute sentences. Each team then develops a definition of combined and simple sentences and discusses the uses of each.

Editing

During the editing stage of the writing process, students look at correctness. Teachers refer to mechanics and grammar skills taught previously. Students can work cooperatively to edit their work and provide support for each other. Because

Gambits for Responding

Pointing

I like the part when you said . . .

I liked the words . . .

. . . and . . . stuck in my mind after you finished reading your writing.

I didn't understand . . .

I wanted to know more about . . .

Summarizing

I think the main point of your writing is . . .

To me your story says . . .

To me the word . . . , summarizes your writing.

Telling

When you said . . . , it made me think of . . .

I felt . . . when you read your story.

I wondered . . . when you said . . .

I saw . . . in my mind when you were reading . . . part of your writing.

Source: Jeanne M. Stone, *Cooperative Learning and Language Arts: A Multi-Structural Approach.* San Juan Capistrano, Calif.: Kagan Cooperative Learning, 1992, p. 1:9. © 1992 by Kagan Cooperative Learning. Reprinted by permission of the publisher.

Response Sheet

Writer's name _____

What did you like best about this paper? What made it hold your attention?

_____
_____
_____
_____
_____

What questions do you have? What is confusing or unclear to you?

_____
_____
_____
_____
_____

What would you like to know more about? What needs more detail?

_____
_____
_____
_____
_____

How would you rate this story on a scale of 1 (low) to 4 (high)? If you give a rating of 1 or 2, tell what you think would make the story better.

_____
_____
_____
_____
_____

As students engage in a variety of cooperative learning activities—many focusing on various types of problem solving—they build critical thinking skills.

JEANNE M. STONE

students need to learn to edit their own writing, cooperative activities will not always be used.

As students enter the editing stage of the lesson, the teacher reviews the necessary conventions that students need. Numbered Heads Together is the Cooperative Learning structure used to check for understanding and to help develop mastery of a specific skill. In Numbered Heads Together the students number off from one to four within each team. The teacher then asks a high-consensus question (one with specific, identifiable answers) and tells the students to "put your heads together" and make sure that everyone on the team knows the answer. The teacher calls number one, two, three, or four; and all students with that number raise their hands or stand and respond.

Numbered Heads Together contrasts with a competitive whole-class question-and-answer period in that (1) all students can participate; (2) everyone is accountable for having an answer; and (3) the students with the right answers are appreciated rather than looked down on because they help their teammates prepare to answer the question, thus building positive interdependence.

Partner Editing allows students to edit their own writing while being coached by a teammate. In Partner Editing, partner 1 reads for errors in his or her own paper while partner 2 coaches. Then partner 2 reads his or her own paper, while partner 1 coaches. Working in pairs, students coach each other, while editing their own writing for punctuation, capitalization, and spelling. This coaching occurs in three rounds:

1. *Punctuation Round.* Partner 1 reads his or her writing orally, listens for, and then marks with a period or comma the pauses that he or she "hears." Acting as a coach, partner 2 stops

partner 1 when he or she reads past a pause, or punctuation, in the writing. When partner 1 finishes, the roles are reversed.

2. *Capitalization Round.* Using the same procedure as in round 1, the students each, one at a time, read orally through their own writing, checking for correct capitalization.

3. *Spelling Round.* When students check a paper for spelling, it is best to Backwards Read. Students read their own papers, starting at the last word, and touching each word, as they check the spelling, word-by-word, backwards to the beginning of the paper. When a student is unsure of a word, he or she circles it and continues. After both partners have checked their own papers with Backwards Read, they trade papers and read their partner's paper the same way. After finishing checking for spelling errors, students use dictionaries, each other, or the teacher to correct and verify the spelling of circled words.

Evaluating

Evaluating offers final feedback to the students. Their story endings can be shared with other students or the "audience," whose members make comments, ask questions, or do both. Gallery Tour and Roam-the-Room adapt well to sharing finished pieces of writing. In Gallery Tour each team's finished story endings are posted in one place. Next to each story ending, a blank sheet of paper (comment sheet) is mounted for the other teams to record comments or questions or both about the story ending. Starting in front of their own writing, the team members travel, in turn, to each team's posted writings. After reading each team's story endings, students record comments, questions, or both on the comment sheets.

In Roam-the-Room the story endings with comment sheets are mounted throughout the classroom. The students randomly wander throughout the room, reading the story endings, reacting on the comment sheets, and then returning to their seats to compare their reactions to the different story endings with their teammates.

Publishing

A finished piece of writing can be published by being charted, posted, illustrated, mailed, or included in a newspaper or magazine. A quick way to allow students to present their story endings to the other students is to use Inside-Outside Circle. In this activity students form two concentric circles with the inside circle facing out and the outside circle facing in. A student in one circle reads the story endings to the student across from him or her and that student responds. The students then change roles. After both students have read, each student makes a quarter turn to the right. After the teacher gives a direction ("Walk to the third person."), the students rotate around the circle, face a new partner, and again read their story endings to each other. The teacher continues to give directions so that students share their story endings with a number of different students.

Integrating Language Arts Curriculum Through Cooperative Learning

The writing process occurs as just one part of an integrated language arts program. Without adding more to the curriculum, the structural approach naturally enhances the listening and speaking components of a language arts program. Moreover, as students engage in a variety of cooperative learning activities—many focusing on various types of problem solving—they build critical thinking skills. One additional and essential plus of Cooperative Learning is that it fosters social development. Through Cooperative Learning, the writing process becomes not only a cognitive but also an affective enterprise.

Practical Ideas for Using Cooperative Learning to Facilitate Writing

Cooperative Writing for Little Ones (Kindergarten Through Second Grade)

By Lorna Curran
ABC Unified School District;
and Teacher/Consultant, UCI Writing Project

You use the writing process and Cooperative Learning in kindergarten? *Yes* is my emphatic answer. The writing process works as well for

EDITOR'S NOTE: We are grateful to Kagan Cooperative Learning for permission to reprint this lesson from *Cooperative Learning Lessons for Little Ones: Language Arts Edition* (1993) by Lorna Curran. © 1993 by Kagan Cooperative Learning. For further information, write Kagan Cooperative Learning, 27134 Paseo Espada, Suite 302, San Juan Capistrano, CA 92675.

kindergarten and young primary students as it does for older students. But the process is done orally, with pictures, with invented spelling (the students write letters and marks that they can use to read back the information), or with the teacher's assistance in doing the written portion. Students working in groups of two, three, or four have greatly increased opportunities to speak and to become involved listeners. Research studies show that students need many opportunities to listen and speak before they can become fluent readers and writers. Therefore, I like a high percentage of the ideas my students develop and retain to be the outgrowth from group projects.

In kindergarten and first grade, many of the students need guidance in emerging from the "working side by side" stage to the "working together" stage. Cooperative Learning helps them develop interpersonal skills. I have found that having students focus on one social skill at a time is particularly effective. During a lesson they learn or review how a certain social skill looks and sounds, they practice using the skill, they give each other feedback on how well they used that skill, and they may take time to think about how they can perform that social skill more easily the next time they work together.

I decided to include Lesson 33, "Talking Trees," from my book *Cooperative Learning Lessons for Little Ones: Language Arts Edition* in *Practical Ideas for Teaching Writing as a Process* because that lesson models the brainstorming/clustering process and also shows the process for doing shared writing of a sentence or sentences depending on the ability of the students in the groups.[1] The lesson is designed for first and second graders. At the end of the lesson is a section that includes adaptations for kindergarten students, with whom the language experience approach is used. In this version of the lesson, the teacher writes down the dictated sentences that the group has agreed on.

The social skill we practice in "Talking Trees" is happy talk. This activity involves the development of a repertoire of positive statements that students say to each other as they work together. Use of these statements is called happy talk because of the positive contributions each individual makes toward the team effort. Sample happy talk statements from my kindergarten class are included on the class standards chart that appears in the next column.

Either the teacher adds statements the students think of or the class members could compose and

---

[1] Lorna Curran, "Talking Trees," in *Cooperative Learning Lessons for Little Ones: Language Arts Edition*. San Juan Capistrano, Calif.: Kagan Cooperative Learning, 1993, pp. 33:1–33:5.

Standards

Active Listening

Look at the speaker.
Listen to what is said.
Have your hands in your lap.

Happy Talk

I like your coloring.
Nice job
Pretty coloring
Super duper job
I like how you stay in the lines.
That's a very good job.

Everyone Participates

Right to pass

post their own statements that are appropriate for their team projects.

"Talking Trees," then, has a dual objective—the development of interpersonal skills and language arts skills. Working together, while practicing happy talk (providing encouraging and complimentary statements) to foster team spirit and cooperation, students create an alphabet tree that contains a message for the president of the United States. The steps of this lesson are provided in the material that follows. At the end of the lesson is a section of adaptations that tailor the lesson to the needs of kindergarten students.

Lesson 33

Talking Trees

GRADE LEVEL
1–2 (Adaptations for kindergarten appear at the end of the lesson.)

TYPE OF LESSON
Writing Skills: Sentence writing

MAIN STRUCTURES
Cooperative Project
Teams Share
Roundtable
Rotating Reporters

COGNITIVE OBJECTIVE
Students work together to create a tree with a sentence containing a message for the president.

SOCIAL-SKILL OBJECTIVE
Happy Talk

MATERIALS
The materials needed for this activity are listed as follows:

- *The Alphabet Tree* by Leo Lionni
- Ditto sheets of leaves
- Pens or pencils to write words
- Large paper for the tree
- Crayons, scissors, glue

Background Information

Students have heard or read the story *The Alphabet Tree* by Leo Lionni. The class has discussed who the president is, what his job is, and some important issues to write to him about.

Procedures

The steps of this lesson are provided in this section.

1. **Give an overview of the lesson:** "Your team is going to make an alphabet tree with a message for the president. Your team will think of a message, write the words for the message on some leaves, cut out the leaves, and glue them onto a tree you draw. While you work together, you will use happy talk to compliment each other on nice things that are said and done." Show students the sample tree provided at the end of the lesson.

2. **Present ideas for happy talk:** "Because you are to use happy talk while you make the alphabet tree, let's think of some compliments you could give each other as you work together." Write down the suggestions the students make that may be similar to these: "That's a good idea." "Good message." "Good cutting." "That's neat writing." "That's a terrific tree we made!"

3. **Create a message:** Students meet in teams of four members each. Tell the class: "Your team will think of several messages that could be sent to the president. Choose the one your team likes best. Say it together several times so you won't forget your sentence. Remember to use happy talk."

4. **Check for use of happy talk during Teams Share:** Give the teams a minute to decide whether they used happy talk. Have the

CURRAN'S COMMENTS

"I usually run off extra leaves because some groups finish early and can use their extra time making additional pieces which they can add to their project. I call this a 'Sponge Activity' because the extra cutting soaks up their extra time. Sometimes in this activity, a fast team will create an additional sentence to use up their extra leaves."

teams that did so share one of their statements with the team next to them. Remind the teams to continue using happy talk and to try to use some different happy talk statements.

5. **Prepare for the alphabet tree:** The team members number off so that each member has a number. The team is given a large piece of background paper, crayons, and a bottle of glue. Each team member receives a strip of four leaves, a pair of scissors, and a pencil.

6. **Write the sentence, using Roundtable:** The team members decide which sentence they want on their tree. "Now your team will share the responsibility of writing the sentence by having person number one write the first word of the sentence on one of the leaves, person number two will write the second word of the sentence on one of the leaves, and so on until all the words of the sentence are written on the leaves. You may consult with each other to decide on the spelling of the word before the person responsible writes the word. There may be enough words in the sentence so that some of the people on the team may have more than one leaf with a word on it. Then continue cutting out all your leaves. If your team has time to cut out extra leaves, more will be available. I'll be listening for happy talk." As the students work, walk around listening and writing down happy talk statements that you hear.

7. **Construct the tree:** "Your team now needs to make the tree. First, share drawing the sky, a tree trunk, and branches. Then arrange the leaves on the tree. Be sure the words are in the right order so that the sentence can be read. Then everyone helps glue the leaves onto the tree. I am hearing a lot of happy talk. Keep up the good job."

8. **Recall the use of happy talk:** Pass out a happy talk card to each team. "Your team will have about five minutes to remember and write down at least two happy talk statements your team used. Then person number two will read the statements to another team when I give the silent signal."

9. **Have rotating reporters share happy talk statements**: Give the silent signal. Let the team members know which team they are to visit to share happy talk statements. "Would person number two from each team now go to the team assigned to you and read two of your team's happy talk statements. Then hand the happy talk card to person number three on that team. Person number three, raise your hand so that we know who you are."

10. **Evaluate the use of happy talk:** "If your team heard two happy talk statements, person number three will draw a happy face at the bottom of the happy talk card. Give the card back to person number two from the other team so that he or she can

take it back to the team." Count the number of happy faces written on the cards and praise or reward the class for use of happy statements.

11. **Have the teams share alphabet trees:** The teams pair up to show their trees and read their sentences to each other.

12. **Debrief the lesson with group discussion:** Find out how the teams felt about the lesson by having the members discuss among themselves the following questions:

   - What did you enjoy about making the team tree?
   - How could your team members work even better next time?
   - Can you think of another good message to write on a tree?
   - How did it feel when your team members used happy talk?
   - How did you feel about using happy talk?

Adaptations for Kindergarten Students

The following procedures show how the preceding lesson can be adapted for kindergartners:

   - Kindergarten students will think of several messages they would like to send to the president.
   - They agree on one message that they would like to send.
   - They cut out the leaves and glue them onto the tree.
   - When the tree is complete, the teacher writes the team's message on it.
   - Instead of writing down the team's happy talk statements, person number three writes a happy face on the card if the team can remember two happy talk statements they used.
   - Kindergarten trees are shared in front of the class, and the teacher reads the message.

Other Applications

Students may send happy talk statements to others by creating:

   - A tree with a message for the principal
   - A tree with a message for a character in a storybook
   - A praising tree with a happy message for the members of another team

Extensions

Extensions of this activity are listed as follows:

   - Students write stories that tell what happened when the president received the alphabet tree.
   - Teams plan and act out a skit that shows the president receiving the alphabet tree.
   - The students decide what the president should do when he receives each of the messages.
   - Have the students watch news broadcasts for current issues that would be appropriate to use for an alphabet tree message.

Variations

Variations of this activity are listed as follows:[2]

   - For younger students the teachers visit teams and write the message while they cut out the leaves.
   - For younger students the teacher writes the sentence and cuts it apart. The students assemble the sentence on the tree.
   - Older students write a longer message by putting several trees, each containing a sentence, in their picture.
   - Rotating reporters read the tree message. Each student is a reporter once, each to a different team.

---

[2]Choose activities that would be appropriate for the ability level and interests of your students.

The Alphabet Tree

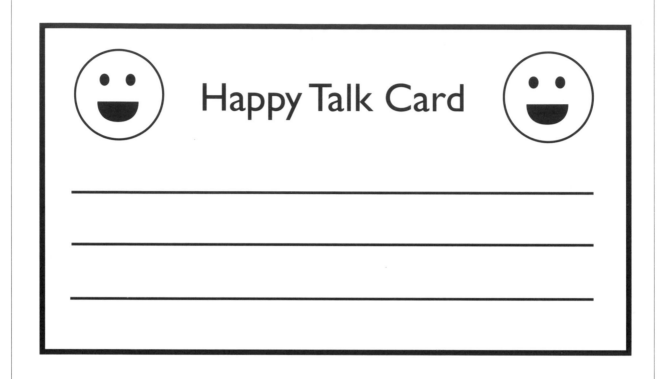

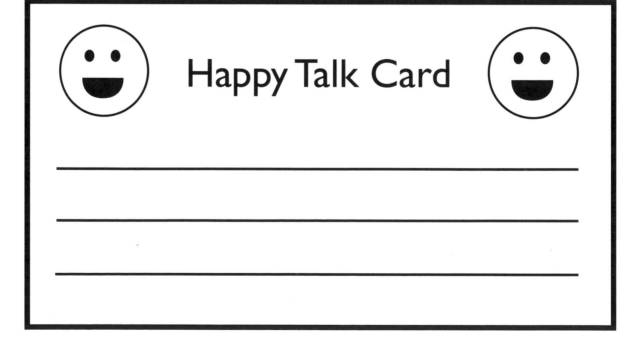

Fable Writing:
A Lesson from Aesop . . .
and Spencer Kagan

By Linda Bautista-Pappert

Teacher, Linda Vista Elementary School,
Saddleback Valley Unified School District;
and Teacher/Consultant, UCI Writing Project

Among the most important principles of Cooperative Learning are that students should experience growth in academic and social skills and that quality time should be provided to discuss this growth and its process in both areas. With these dual goals in mind, I have adopted ideas and activities from Spencer Kagan's book *Cooperative Learning* for use in my elementary-level language arts program.[1] Additional goals are to foster the critical thinking skills of my students at the synthesis level described in Bloom's *Taxonomy* by having them formulate and compose an original fable and learn to cooperate in groups by collaborating on a group fable as preparation for creating an individual fable. This lesson, which can be taught in one week, combines a variety of Cooperative Learning structures, social skills, and roles that can be adapted to suit various grade levels and to meet the needs of special students. The steps of the Cooperative Learning portion of this lesson are described in the rest of this article.

Prewriting

The steps in the prewriting process are listed as follows:

1. Students should be seated in groups of five. If random seating in groups is preferred, a lineup can be done by counting heads (the students number off from one through five) to determine where students will sit. These groups will be called home teams (HT). Before explaining the directions of the

---

EDITOR'S NOTE: More information on the synthesis level described in Bloom's Taxonomy appears in Taxonomy of Educational Objectives. Handbook I: Cognitive Domain. Edited by Benjamin S. Bloom. New York: David McKay Company, Inc., 1956, pp. 166–67. See also the section on "Blooming Worksheets," which appears in Spencer S. Kagan, Cooperative Learning. San Juan Capistrano, Calif.: Kagan Cooperative Learning, 1993.

[1] Spencer S. Kagan, *Cooperative Learning*. San Juan Capistrano, Calif.: Kagan Cooperative Learning, 1993.

Cooperative Learning task, the teacher introduces a social skill to be practiced such as being positive. A chart like the one following can grow out of a discussion about what the teacher may see or hear when the social skill is being practiced.

Social Skill: Being Positive

See	Hear
• Heads nodding • Sitting in a close circle • Smiles	• Words such as "Good," "I like the way you _____," "Nice job," and so forth • Laughter, and so forth

2. Write the phrase *sour grapes* on the board, and ask students what comes to mind when they see or hear these words. Their responses may be recorded as a cluster. A sample cluster might look like Figure 1.

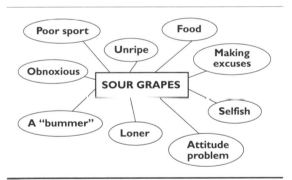

Fig. I. Clustering of *Sour Grapes*

3. Ask whether anyone knows where the phrase *sour grapes* originated. Give background information about Aesop, the Greek storyteller, and share the fable "The Fox and the Grapes."

4. Ask students to share what they already know about fables or can infer from the fable they just heard, and record their information on the board. Introduce and discuss the following elements if they have not been noted:

• Fables are short.
• The main characters in the fables are usually animals with human qualities. (*Note:* The concept of personification may need to be introduced and discussed.)
• Fables provide a lesson, a moral, or advice, usually at the end.

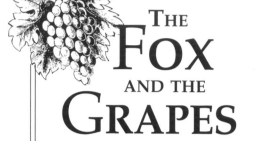

THE FOX AND THE GRAPES

One hot summer's day a Fox was strolling through an orchard, when he saw a bunch of ripe grapes hanging on a vine trained over a lofty branch. "Just the thing to quench my thirst," said the Fox.

Stepping back a few paces, the Fox jumped high in the air, but just missed the grapes. Turning around, he jumped up with all his strength, but once again missed. Again and again he tried to reach the luscious grapes. Finally he became so hot and so tired that he gave up. Walking away with his nose in the air, the Fox said, "I don't want those grapes, I am sure they are sour."

It is easy to despise what you cannot obtain.[2]

[2]*Aesop's Fables.* Edited by Michael Hague. New York: Henry Holt and Company, Inc., 1985, p. 21. From *Aesop's Fables.* Selected and illustrated by Michael Hague. Edited text copyright ©1985 by Henry Holt and Company, Inc. Reprinted by permission of Henry Holt and Company, Inc.

- Fables are structured around three or four main events supported by descriptive details.

5. Read aloud "The Fox and the Grapes" once again, and explain how to structure visually the sequence of events and descriptive details of the story by using a mapping technique. Have students help map the sequence and generate ideas about the moral or lesson in this fable. A sample map might look like Figure 2.

6. Have each HT count heads again to form expert teams (ET), with the same number of students in each group (five); and have these teams move to their numbered table or area. For example, all number ones move to Table 1. (This activity is called a jigsaw.) Pass out one copy of a different fable to each ET and enough paper for each member. Allow ETs enough time for choosing a reader to read the fable to the team, for each member to map out the main events and descriptive details of the fable, and for members to share their maps with one another. Before having the ETs

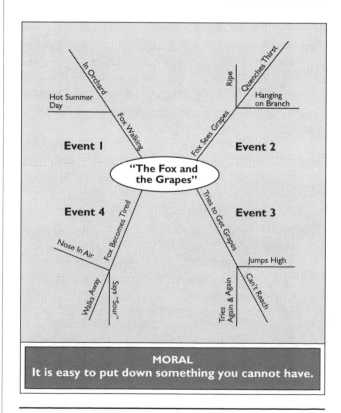

Fig. 2. Mapping Technique for "The Fox and the Grapes"

disband to return to their HTs, ask each member of the group to make one positive statement about the group's interaction as a way to reinforce the social skill.

7. Have the HT members decide who will perform the following roles and responsibilities for their group: a recorder (to record their responses); a reporter (the spokesperson for the group); a timekeeper (to keep track of the time); and a manager (to keep the team on task). One other important role is that of encourager (to keep the discussion positive). In a storytelling fashion have each member of the HTs share the fable learned in the ETs, using maps to help them remember the main events and details. HT members should add to their list of characteristics of fables any additional features that surface during their discussion.

The Prompt

Present HTs with the following prompt:

Use a moral of your choice to write a group fable. Incorporate the following characteristics of a fable: It is short; contains three or four main events supported by descriptive details; centers on characters who are animals with human qualities; and concludes with a lesson, a moral, or advice.

Precomposing

The steps in the precomposing process are listed as follows:

8. Before the students begin writing fables in their groups, return to the board and cluster names of animals that might be characters in a fable. Add qualities and character traits for a few of them. A sample cluster might look like Figure 3.

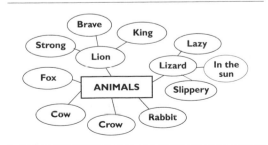

Fig. 3. Clustering of *Animals*

9. Next, the HTs will need to select a maxim or moral and determine which animal characters will relate best to their moral. Using chart or butcher paper, each HT can make an animal cluster that can be shared with the entire class, taped on the classroom walls for students to read, or both. Groups can determine their own maxim or moral or choose from a list provided by the teacher such as the following:

- A villain may disguise himself, but he will not deceive the wise.
- It is easy to propose impossible solutions.
- It is possible to have too much of a good thing.
- Slow and steady wins the race.
- Do not pretend to be something that you are not.
- Precious things are for those who prize them.
- Little friends may prove to be great friends.
- Look before you leap.
- He who plays the fool should not be surprised if he misses the prize.
- Do not trust flatterers.

10. Once the HTs have developed their maxim or moral and animal characters, they can decide on a possible sequence of events and the supporting details, using the map shown in Figure 4.

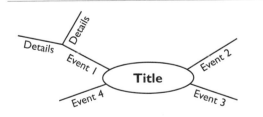

Fig. 4. Map of Events and Supporting Details

Writing

The steps in the writing process are listed as follows:

11. Students can now collaborate on their fable. They can each contribute through a small-group discussion and composing

session, with one person serving as the recorder; or they can write their story round-robin style. In this activity paper and a pen or pencil are passed around the circle, and each member contributes a line until the story is complete. As the students generate their stories, encourage them to keep their maxim or moral in mind as well as their maps showing the sequence of events.

12. Once the HTs have generated a draft of their story, turn their attention back to "The Fox and the Grapes." Ask them to fill in descriptive words from the fable, as shown in Figure 5.

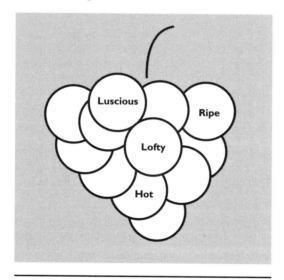

Fig. 5. Descriptive Words

Then ask each group member to add one descriptive word to his or her own fable. To reinforce the social skill, ask group members to say what they like about each other's added words.

13. When the groups' fables have been written, allow HTs time to discuss the following evaluation questions within their groups:

   a. Did your team complete the task assigned? Why (how) or why not?
   b. Did you successfully practice the social skill? How or why not?
   c. What worked well for your group? What did not?
   d. Did you have any problems or concerns? Were they solved? How or why not?

Sharing

The sharing process is described as follows:

14. Each student in the HT will have to copy the fable before the sharing session begins. The teacher will also need to record all of the maxims or morals used by the students—either on the chalkboard or on butcher paper. Once the maxims or morals are displayed where everyone can see them, each student should fold his or her paper so that the maxim or moral of the fable does not show.

   Students should now return to their ET and share their group's fable. After reading the fable aloud, the reader will serve as his or her own recorder and ask and record the answer to the questions on the "Fable Response Sheet." The roles of taskmaster, timekeeper, monitor, and encourager should rotate as papers are being shared.

Revising

The revising process is described as follows:

15. ETs will then return to their HTs. Members of the HT will compare notes and make changes or additions to their fables accordingly.

Additional Activities

Depending on the inclinations of the teacher and the class, the groups' fables can be edited and published in a class anthology, or each group can perform them in Reader's Theater style. I prefer not to take group fable writing to the evaluation stage. Rather, I use it as a prewriting activity leading toward each student's creation of an individual fable. But before moving on to the individual writing tasks, I ask each child to bring this portion of the lesson to closure by writing for five minutes about the most positive aspect of their experience with group fable writing. I find that the children love working together in Cooperative Learning groups and that the practice in the social skill—being positive—transfers to other class activities. Equally important, each student's fable will be enhanced by the influence of group learning and practice.

Fable Response Sheet

Does this fable begin with a good title? Yes _____ No _____

Suggestion: _____

_____

Is this fable structured around three or four main events? Yes _____ No _____

These events and details can be "mapped" as follows:

Suggestion: _____

_____

Do the animal characters in this fable have human qualities?

Yes _____ No _____ Some examples are _____

_____

Suggestion: _____

_____

Does this fable have many uses of descriptive words and details?

Yes _____ No _____ Some examples are _____

_____

Suggestion: _____

_____

What do you think is the moral of this fable? _____

_____

Suggestion: _____

_____

What did you like best about this fable? _____

_____

Any additional comments? _____

_____

_____

Implementing Cooperative Learning in a Native American Classroom

By Reba McLaughlin

Former English Teacher, Sherman Indian High School;
and Teacher/Consultant, UCI Writing Project

I believe that the only way to implement Cooperative Learning effectively in a classroom is to experience the activities first yourself through in-service training. I had an opportunity to do just that early in 1989 when the Western Association of Schools and Colleges (WASC) team and curriculum consultants began working with staff from Sherman Indian High School, a residential boarding school accommodating students from approximately 77 different tribes.

Some persons suggested that intertribal conflicts and rivalry would defeat any effort to get students working cooperatively and interactively. I did not accept that notion for a moment. I had already made some progress toward increasing students' participation in my classroom. However, the students' prevailing behavior was to fill out ditto sheets at their seats or to fall asleep in class.

Perhaps my desire to increase students' participation in classroom activities convinced the interviewers and Carol Booth Olson, Director of the UCI Writing Project, to include me in the 1989 Summer Institute; or maybe the statement "I need help" did the trick. For whatever reason I was accepted, the experience provided the tools necessary for me to proceed.

The excellent presentation on Cooperative Learning structures by Russell Frank, a UCI Writing Project Teacher/Consultant, and the activities from the UCI Writing Project itself served as a model, enabling me to implement Cooperative Learning and interactive learning in my classroom.

Assisted by a few of my more responsive students, whose cooperation I had been cultivating, I began to establish Cooperative Learning writing groups. The steps are as follows:

1. I created groups of five to six students, using their reading scores to ensure an academically heterogeneous mix (reading levels ranged from the fourth grade to the twelfth grade). I took care to place at least one strong reader/writer in each group. I did not consider representation in each group according to tribes but, rather, left that mix to chance.

2. I asked members to choose a group name. I gave little direction at first; but when I noticed the increasing frustration, I suggested that group members combine their names to form a group name, choosing things they had in common, or create a name that would reflect their combined personality traits. Now that I have had experience with one cooperative learning-oriented class, I can share the names chosen by that class as a model for next year's students.

3. I then asked each group to design a poster that would highlight their group's name and reflect images and symbols associated with it. The poster for one of my groups, "Sacred Feelings," is included as Figure 6.

4. Groups then posed for a photograph that we put in the center of each poster. Students were shy about this activity at first. But once the members of one group had pasted their

Fig. 6. Portion of Poster "Sacred Feelings"

photo and hung their poster on the wall, others were excited to follow.

5. Next, I chose and trained one group to model a writing group for the class. (They were terrific!)

6. After breaking the ice with the modeling of a writing group, I asked each group to appoint a recorder, provided them with a set of criteria with which to critique their first pieces of writing, and set the peer group process in motion.

7. I gave individual grades for the writing but a group grade for the sharing as a way to encourage positive group dynamics.

I have only just begun to use Cooperative Learning, but because of its immediate benefits, I initiated cooperative reading groups and the development of a book of Indian stories that we wrote and compiled for Native American students in elementary and intermediate schools. Learning in my classroom became more interactively based, and I saw students from a diverse mix of tribes working cooperatively side by side. But, rather than speak for my students, I'll let them speak for themselves regarding Cooperative Learning:

I think we learn more in a group. Our communication skills really improved.

FRANK S.

More people generate more ideas. . . . We learn from each other.

OLETHA L.

Everybody gets involved in what we do. . . . It's more fun.

MIKE H.

You can get a better idea of what you are learning about through another person's outlook. You're not only helping yourself but others too.

LARRY Q.

It gives students a chance to speak out. . . . Five brains are better than one.

MIKE J.

We learn better when we get everyone's opinions. . . . We put them all together and get an intellectual answer. . . . We learn from each other. I like working in groups.

HOPE C.

More than 85 percent of the students preferred Cooperative Learning to seat work, and I'm 100 percent convinced that Cooperative Learning is effective.

Fostering Peer Response Groups Through Cooperative Learning

By Russell Frank

Principal, Altimira Middle School,
Sonoma Valley Unified School District;
and Teacher/Consultant, UCI Writing Project

In the sixth grade I experienced the magic of responses from peers. Mr. Pierce, my teacher, read a student's parody of Ian Fleming's James Bond, Agent 007, and Goldfinger entitled "Yellow Pinky." I vividly remember the convulsed laughter and tears as we enjoyed the story. I can only guess at the author's pride and perhaps surprise as he witnessed our responses. I also remember wanting to write as well as he and wanting to share my work with my peers.

I was lucky enough to have had many opportunities to experience the joy of responses from peers—of having an effect, of making a difference. However, I have also experienced the fear of inadequacy—of laying open one's private thoughts to acquaintances or even to strangers. Both experiences convinced me of the value and vulnerableness of sharing.

Years later, as a teacher, I tried peer response groups (PRGs) in my classroom. Students in groups of four or five read their own texts aloud and shared responses. I discovered that students lacked (1) skill in responding meaningfully to student-generated texts; and (2) the interpersonal and group skills that often keep groups together. These problems were often frustrating for my students and me. Therefore, I grew to appreciate the complex factors affecting successful PRGs.

I knew I wanted to help students create what Donald Graves calls a "community of writers," through which students expand their literacy in an environment where they value and respect each

Peer response groups are a powerful way for students to help each other become more caring, perceptive, and literate.

RUSSELL FRANK

other as authors with important, interesting life experiences to be shared through reading, writing, listening, and talking. Developing this community required combining literacy skills and interpersonal, cooperative skills.

Ideas from the Writing Project helped me to develop literacy, especially writing and response skills. Peter Elbow's ideas for sharing writing in *Writing Without Teachers;* Mary Kay Healy's approaches for building peer response groups shared at the UCI Writing Project Summer Institute; and Rebekah Caplan's ideas for teaching descriptive/narrative ("show, not tell") writing in her book, *Writers in Training,* helped create this part of the community.[1]

Activities that helped bond students were missing in many early attempts at implementing PRGs. Fortunately, I discovered that Cooperative Learning can help create the positive climate necessary to establish a community of writers. By integrating concepts from Cooperative Learning and from the Writing Project, I found that successful PRGs provide students with:

- The fun of real-life audience response and connection
- Response which leads to rethinking and revision
- Opportunities to learn from the writing strategies and approaches of peers
- A more developed sense of others' points of view

Developing successful PRGs involves coaching students to assume new attitudes and responsibilities. The process cannot be accomplished in a

couple of weeks. It involves several chronological steps:

1. Building a classroom climate
2. Grouping students in teams or response groups
3. Building teams by structuring activities that build positive interdependence among team members
4. Teaching, modeling, and coaching writing/ response skills[2]

Building a Classroom Climate

Building a classroom climate helps establish a cooperative, friendly "our class" attitude among the students and between the students and teachers. This attitude helps lead toward the "community of writers." Climate-building activities can be as simple as having students bring in their baby pictures and asking peers to identify the owners. (Another example of a climate-building activity is a people-search, in which students list information about themselves; for example, favorite food or television show, number of brothers or sisters, or type of pets.) Students then search for people in class with similar characteristics. Students whose interests are similar sign each other's list.[3]

For the random-grouping activities described in the next paragraph, it is helpful to have students generate a list of unique facts about themselves; for example, winning an award or traveling to an

---

[1]These publications are cited in the "Selected References" section.

[2]The following books have helped me develop approaches to building positive classroom climate and group interaction: Spencer Kagan, *Cooperative Learning.* San Juan Capistrano, Calif.: Kagan Cooperative Learning, 1992; and Roger Johnson and David Johnson, *Learning Together and Learning Alone.* Englewood Cliffs, N.J.: Prentice Hall, Inc., 1987.

[3]The preceding footnote lists publications by Spencer Kagan and Roger and David Johnson that contain descriptions of many climate-building activities.

exotic place. Students may turn these lists into art objects, such as mandalas or personal coats of arms, and use them to share information about themselves.

Random grouping can be used as a climate builder, especially at the beginning of the year. The teacher randomly deals each student a playing card (from ace to eight) that corresponds to eight numbered tables in the class. Students take their mandalas or coats of arms and go to their assigned tables where they meet the three others in their group. Teammates pair off, introduce themselves to each other, and talk about a unique or amusing fact about themselves that is illustrated in their artwork. The process of interviewing a partner is repeated twice until all four group members have talked to each other. Then each person tries to recall the others' names and facts. Partners help each other until every partner can recite the name and fact.

Random regrouping and doing other climate builders regularly for several weeks help students develop networks of acquaintances until they know almost everyone in the class. Periodic climate-building throughout the year helps maintain an "our class" attitude.

Organizing Successful Peer Response Groups

Random grouping is quick and easy to implement, but it can leave teams imbalanced by gender, ethnicity, ability, or citizenship. For this reason I usually avoid keeping a random group together for long. Sharing and responding to peers' writing can be a difficult challenge—one that requires sensitivity and trust. Because of this challenge, and so that students may work with a range of peers, I believe that PRGs should be carefully structured according to students' academic abilities, ethnicity, gender, leadership abilities, and social skills.

Typically, PRGs are heterogeneously structured. Teachers may wish to wait several weeks before assigning students to PRGs, so that climate-building activities can help to create networks of acquaintances and the teacher can have a clearer idea about students' abilities and student cliques. The criteria one sets up (ability, gender, leadership, or ethnicity) should be flexible. For example, if a good reason exists to create an all-girls group or to put two or more members of an ethnic group together, a teacher should consider it.

I assign students to their PRGs in a way that, to many students, *appears* to be random. While students are working quietly, I deal each one a playing card that corresponds to his or her assigned table. Then, at once, students gather their material, turn over their card, and go to their assigned tables as if they were doing random teaming. Each student finds out his or her partner's first and last names and something fun about that person. By this time the students may already know their teammates because of previous contacts. To help unify each team, the teacher directs the students in team building.

Preparing for Team Building

Team building nurtures a sense of team identity and mutual support among a group of students. This activity is a crucial part of creating successful PRGs.

"Create a Story" exemplifies a round-robin team builder that encourages all partners to collaborate in creating a story. As one paper and one pencil are passed around the group, each person adds one word at a time to create a story based on a phrase or sentence, such as "Joe Cool left school." The interaction sparks laughter and draws the team together physically, emotionally, and mentally. Stories are then read aloud to the class. In a variation of this activity, each person writes as many words as possible in five to ten seconds. When time is called, the paper is passed to the next partner and so forth until classroom time or the story ends.

Building a Team's Identity

One goal of team building is to create a positive, original team name that represents what the partners have in common. This act symbolizes the team's coming together and forming positive interdependence. Several team-building activities help to foster this unity.

Partners interview each other in pairs to discover information. The interview could include some teacher-directed questions, such as what animal or machine would they be if they had to and why they would choose it. After the interviews partners introduce each other and take notes on the introductions. When the interviews are completed, a circle is drawn on construction paper; and partners write all common facts in the middle of the circle. All facts that are unique to specific individuals are written outside the circle.

On the basis of the information written inside the circle, the team creates a positive name that represents something that all team members share in common—a name with which both students and teachers can be comfortable. For example, a team which discovered that all the members liked going to the movies and chose birds as their animals might choose "Flying Movie Fans."

Students create team banners on manila folders with the team's name in fancy letters, a team photo or logo, and the team members' signatures. The banner is hung on a coat hanger over the table whenever teams are working on cooperative projects.

Teaching Response Skills

While climate building and team building create cohesive classes and teams, teachers also help develop students' response skills. Rebekah Caplan's "showing, not telling," strategy is an effective point of departure for introducing and practicing response skills. This strategy moves students away from their overreliance on vague, overly general, and commonplace discourse, which she calls "telling," toward specific, original, figurative, and sensory-based discourse, which she calls "showing."

To introduce the first "show, not tell," writing assignment, I role-play a bored student amusing himself during a lecture that a volunteer "teacher" delivers from a book. When the role play is finished, students share what they have observed and heard. I draw a circle on the board as if we are going to cluster ideas, but I leave the center empty and ask the class members what they have observed. Some observations are specific: "slouched in your seat"; "tapped a pencil on the desk like you were drumming." Others are more general (telling): "You flirted"; "You wrote a note." When these telling statements are being shared, the teacher writes them in red and asks questions that invite the student to "show" the concept more or to develop the idea. How did you know I was flirting? What did the note say? Finally, the class agrees that

these observations show or illustrate boredom. *Boredom* is written in the center circle of the cluster. Then I give the students the telling sentence: "The kid was bored" and ask them to show it in a descriptive paragraph.[4] When the students have completed the assignment, I randomly read aloud four or five student pieces, modeling three basic responses to the writing. Although a wealth of responses to these assignments are possible, teachers, for simplicity's sake, initially may want to limit the modeling to three responses:

1. I like . . . (a specific word, phrase, sentence) . . . because . . . (specific reason).
2. I want to know more about (something in the piece).
3. Ask questions.

When teachers introduce, model, and coach students in these basic responses, students are less likely to give vague statements such as "I liked it because it was good." To make the responses more meaningful, students are coached to identify particularly effective texts and give reasons for their effectiveness. For example, "I liked 'tapped a pencil like a drummer' because I could hear a rhythmic sound" is a more specific and meaningful response.

I also emphasize that a controlling and nonsupportive response, such as "You need to write more details," violates the spirit of the "community of writers." Few of us like to be told what to do, especially with our creative works. Changing a directive response to a question improves the tone of interaction; for example, "What do you mean by flirting?" or "How could you show flirting?" facilitates discussion and revision better than does a statement such as, "You need to show more details about flirting." (Consistent modeling and coaching will enable students to resist the intial impulse toward directive or controlling responses and to turn them into questions that provoke more thought and development.)

As students become more sophisticated response partners, teachers may wish to model other types of responses, such as the following:

---

[4]A more detailed version of this lesson appears in "Bobby B. Bored" in *Thinking/Writing: Fostering Critical Thinking Through Writing.* Edited by Carol Booth Olson. New York: HarperCollins College, 1992, pp. 55–68.

- This piece made me feel . . .
- This piece reminds me of . . .
- This piece is like (a color, another story, a movie) because . . .

To develop their writing and response skills, students write assignments based on two or three telling statements per week. For example:

The room was a mess.

He (or she) looked scared.

Homeless people need help.

Recording Responses

An important rationale for PRGs is the potential for encouraging student revision. A great discussion of student writing in a PRG does not necessarily lead to revision. One way of increasing the likelihood that responses from students will be a springboard for revision (aside from teaching students about options for revision) is to demonstrate how to record their responses on their rough drafts. This record helps preserve possibilities for revision. It also becomes a kind of transcript, giving the teacher feedback on the quality of the group's interaction.

To demonstrate the recording of responses, the teacher places a transparency of anonymous student writing on the overhead projector and models the following process to the class while students write responses on a photocopy of the material shown from the projector. Eventually, all PRGs follow this four-step procedure on their own:

1. The teacher who assumes the role of the text's author reads the text aloud, enabling the students to hear the text as they follow along. (The incongruity between what is read aloud and what is on the page often leads an author to self-revision and self-editing.)
2. The class silently *re*reads the text. A second silent reading often deepens understanding of the text.
3. The class responds, and the teacher records the responses on the transparency. For example, a student may say, "I liked when the author said, 'tapped his pencil on the table like a drummer,' because I could hear the tapping sound." The teacher may underline the phrase, draw an arrow to the margin,

and write the reason why the student liked it: "I could hear the tapping sound." Meanwhile, each student also records the responses and questions on his or her copy of the text. Since PRGs are often used to help students revise, the teacher may want to remind students that they may forget what was said; but they have a written record to help guide revision.

4. The teacher (acting as author) asks questions about the text. When writers finish their texts, they often have questions about weak or strong parts or whether a particular part was clear. For example, an author might ask: "What came to your mind when I wrote . . . ?"

At the end of the discussion, the transparency and the students' copies should be full of meaningful, useful questions and responses.

Introducing Roles in Response Groups

During the process of building class climate, teams, and response skills, teachers may also want to introduce, model, and coach students in how to assume roles that help groups function smoothly. By assuming one of four roles within the PRG—taskmaster, gatekeeper, monitor, or timer—each partner becomes responsible for monitoring an aspect of group dynamics. A discussion of these roles appears in the sections that follow.

Taskmaster

Any group can get off task. The taskmaster knows the directions for completing the task and politely directs the group members' attention to it when they become distracted. Modeling polite redirection of a group is important. A good taskmaster:

- Knows the directions (See the previously mentioned four-step procedure.)
- Says things like, "We're getting off task. . . . We should be doing . . . " at the right times
- Has good eye contact and body language

Gatekeeper

The gatekeeper monitors participation and makes sure that everyone has an opportunity to respond. Active response partners sometimes dominate discussions. They should be acknowledged for their contributions, but attention should eventually be shifted to quiet partners who are

By building a cooperative classroom climate, developing carefully organized teams, helping teams develop cohesiveness and identity, and teaching social skills, peer response groups are a powerful way for students to help each other become more caring, perceptive, and literate.

RUSSELL FRANK

encouraged, but not required, to give responses. Good gatekeepers:

- Maintain good eye contact with all group members.
- Are aware of who is participating and who is not.
- Say such things as "We haven't heard from Tiffany yet. What do you think, Tiffany?" or "Thanks (for your suggestions), Carlos, but what do the others think?"

Monitor

Student authors receiving responses to their writing often enjoy the interactions so much that they forget to record responses on their drafts. The monitor politely reminds authors to record the responses so the feedback will not be lost.

Timekeeper

A timekeeper in each group helps prevent the group from spending too much time on one text and not enough time on another. In a 50-minute class with four texts to share, each person will have about 12 to 15 minutes of response time. A time-keeper helps the group move forward equitably and frees the teacher from clock-watching.

Determining When to Introduce Roles

Teachers may want to introduce, describe, model, and coach the roles before students begin working in their PRGs to provide plenty of time for them to practice each role. An ideal time to intro-duce and practice gatekeeping comes when teams practice responses to students' texts. The monitor may be introduced after the teacher has demon-strated how to record responses. The role of the timekeeper may be saved for last because it re-quires the least amount of coaching.

Teachers also facilitate the learning of roles by recognizing good examples of this activity in class

and by providing students with time to talk about the group process and the effect of the roles on it. Teachers may also provide a laminated card to each partner describing the roles to which they are assigned; that is, how the role looks and sounds.

Monitoring Peer Response Groups

I send the peer response groups (PRGs) to the corners of the room or into the hallway to help minimize noise. Students sit so that the author is reading her or his duplicated copy (use carbon paper stapled between two sheets) of the text aloud as one teammate follows along with the author. At the same time two other teammates follow the original text. Each student is assigned or volunteers for a role and is given a card that describes the role's responsibilities. Roles can be rotated within the group during the period, or they may be kept for the entire period. The PRG follows the four-step procedure for each text as each author records responses to his or her text on the author's copy.

During response time the teacher observes group dynamics and writes notes, listing the characteristics of groups that are functioning well and giving the reasons. The teacher periodically tells teams how the members are doing. The teacher may wish to assign points or a grade based on these observations. An excellent way to monitor groups, especially toward the end of the period, is to ask to see one partner's paper and evaluate it for meaningful, useful responses and questions from the team.

Reflecting on the Group's Effectiveness

At the end of the period, it is important to ask the teams to reflect on the effectiveness of their group's interaction. Students may be asked to write their responses to or to talk to each other about the following questions:

- How often did each person perform his or her role?
- Which role helped the group to work well?
- Which responses were the most helpful?
- In which ways can the group's members improve the way they worked?

The teacher can also share his or her observations based on the monitoring of a response group.

Grading Students

Depending on the class and teacher's inclination, the group dynamics within a PRG and the quality of responses can be graded; each partner in a group receives the same grade. Depending on the assignment and the student's skills, texts shared in class may be revised and brought back to the class for a final edit-around for spelling and punctuation before being submitted for individual evaluation.

Inevitably, I have found that students extend, enrich, and clarify their final drafts because of the responses received in their PRG. This activity makes reading those final drafts much more rewarding.

But what I find even more rewarding than the improved writing is the process—standing back and watching 35 or more students, oblivious to my presence, having fun reading, sharing, and discussing writing. That process did not always happen; Cooperative Learning helped make it happen. By building a cooperative classroom climate, developing carefully organized teams, helping teams develop cohesiveness and identity, and teaching social skills, peer response groups are a powerful way for students to help each other become more caring, perceptive, and literate.

Writing

Developing a Sense of Audience, or Who Am I Really Writing This Paper For?

By Mary K. Healy
Director, English Credential Program
UC Berkeley School of Education;
and Associate Director, Research and Evaluation,
Puente Project

Simply stated, having a developed sense of audience on the student writers' part means that as students write, they have images of the intended readers of their writing flickering— consciously or unconsciously—around in the background. To the degree that these images are sharply delineated in the writers' minds, student writers will select details and develop their pieces of writing, anxious always that their known readers' expectations be fulfilled.

Students who have developed beyond the point where writing is more of an exercise in physical dexterity than an exercise in composing thoughts on a piece of paper can tell what their teachers will look for when reading and evaluating their papers. For some teachers, neatness really counts—no ink blots or crumpled papers are allowed. For others, mechanical accuracy is primary—periods where they belong, capital letters signaling sentence beginnings, and commas accurately placed and not scattered like confetti to make an interesting, albeit illogical, design. To still other teachers, what counts is what happened from the first to the last draft—what changes were made, what tightening and expanding, what diction—in sum, what evidence there is of a mind at work revising, reseeing. There are a legion of other teachers' priorities—from sophisticated vocabulary choices and syntax to the students' adherence to injunctions, such as never starting a sentence with the

EDITOR'S NOTE: For further information on the concept of audience in writing, see Mary K. Healy's monograph, *Using Student Writing Response Groups in the Classroom,* which was published in 1980 by the Bay Area Writing Project, Education Business Office, 615 University Hall, Room 1040, University of California, Berkeley, CA 94720-1040.

Audience
(writing)

word *and*. Whatever the constructs may be through which the teacher views the students' papers, it is certain that the students will understand what they are as soon as enough marked writing has been returned. And the students will know the real nature of their audience—and be fairly accurate in describing the teacher's values—regardless of how the teacher describes orally what he or she values. Students can do this because they make their generalizations about what is important to the teacher on the basis of hard evidence: the grades and final comments they get on their papers.

The task of developing a sense of audience is, in fact, a misnomer. After a few years in school, student writers already have a sense of audience, even though they might look at you blankly and mumble something like "We don't do that in here" if asked for which audience they are writing. A more accurate description of the task for the thoughtful teacher of writing might be described as expanding the students' sense of audience to encompass a wider range of responsive readers. And a major step in this expansion is simply to provide audiences for the students' writing beyond that of a conscientious proofreader and evaluator.

In the landmark study *The Development of Writing Abilities (11–18)*, James Britton and his colleagues in England outlined a broad spectrum of the possible audiences that students might meet in the writing situations in their schools. In their research sample Mr. Britton and his colleagues used this range of audiences as one of the characteristics by which they categorized over 2,000 student papers from subjects across the curriculum. As the researchers put it, ". . . one important dimension of development in writing ability is the growth of a sense of audience, the growth of the ability to make adjustments and choices in writing which take account of the audience for whom the writing is intended."[1] The main categories which the researchers used and the percentage of papers falling into each category are shown in the accompanying table, which is reproduced here from *The Development of Writing Abilities (11–18)*.

It is evident from the research James Britton and his colleagues conducted that the ever-present audience for the writing done in most classrooms is the teacher-as-examiner. This audience can make itself manifest in many ways: a single letter grade for overall quality; split letter grades, one each for content and mechanics; a written critique of the piece, outlining the strengths and weaknesses of the style, organization, structure, or mechanics; a written response to the piece, featuring the reader's involvement with the content and raising questions of clarity and development. However, in all of these instances, the emphasis is still on the evaluation of a final product.

Just as writing for an audience of teacher-as-examiner is the most prevalent in schools today, writing for self is the least prevalent. Yet the self as audience is crucial to young writers' development

Table Distribution of audience categories*
(n = 2,104)

Categories	Percent
Child to self	0.5
Child to trusted adult	1.6
Teacher-learner dialogue	38.8
Pupil to teacher, particular relationship	1.0
Pupil to examiner	48.7
Expert to known laymen	0.0
Child to peer group	0.1
Group member to working group	0.2
Writer to his readers	1.8
Child to trusted adult/teacher-learner dialogue	0.6
Teacher-learner dialogue/pupil to examiner	4.0
Teacher-learner dialogue/writer to his readers	1.0
Miscellaneous	1.7

[1] Reprinted, by permission, from James Britton and others, *The Development of Writing Abilities (11–18)* (Schools Council Research Studies). Houndmills Basingstoke, Hampshire: Macmillan Education Ltd., 1975, p. 58. Also reprinted, by permission, from Thomas Nelson Ltd., Walton-on-Thames, Surrey, England.

*This table is reproduced here, by permission, from James Britton and others, *The Development of Writing Abilities (11–18)* (Schools Council Research Studies). Houndmills Basingstoke, Hampshire: Macmillan Education, Ltd., 1975, p. 130. Also reproduced, by permission, from Thomas Nelson Ltd., Walton-on-Thames, Surrey, England.

> *A poem . . . begins as a lump in the throat, a sense of wrong, a homesickness, a lovesickness. . . .*
> *It finds the thought, and the thought finds the words.*
>
> **ROBERT FROST**

because it allows students to discover how the act of writing can be functional for them in the day-to-day life of the school. Keeping logs or journals of reactions to class events, to books or films or TV programs, and to chapters in a textbook can be a valuable first step in making personal sense of new information. Writing to work out new ideas, to raise questions, and to find out what one understands enables students to see that writing can be of direct benefit to them both in their initial development of a new subject matter and as preparation for the more formal, extensive writing required in their courses. Because students have an extended record of their own emerging opinions and understandings, they have themselves as resources when it comes to developing and shaping an essay or a final report. The teacher can encourage this type of writing by providing models of subject-matter journals or logs, by setting aside class time for this writing, by allowing credit toward the final grade for completion of such writing, and by allowing students to keep their logs handy during the writing of tests or essays in class.

One of the next steps a teacher may take to expand student writers' sense of audience beyond that of writing for teacher-as-examiner or for the self is to begin to respond to the students' writing at stages earlier than the final draft. This response can take the form of comments written on a first draft, which provide the writer with a sense of a real reader's initial reaction. These comments may be questions: "How old were you when this happened?" "What did the room look like?" "How did she feel when you said that?" These questions indicate to the writer that the reader is interested in what is going on and wants more information. Or the comments may take the form of an anecdotal response: "The same thing happened to me when I was in high school." "I remember being terrified of water also." Such comments let the writer know that the reader has made a connection with the piece, and the feedback is very important. Another form these comments might take is that of responsive coaching: "Why not leave out the parts about the journey to camp and concentrate on that frightening first night?" "I need more specific details here about conditions in the camp to understand how the rebellion started." All of these responses and their thousands of variations enable the writer to visualize better the effect of the words on a reader. Giving such responses on early drafts allows the writer to make revisions—to work on the piece in progress, not after the writing has been completed, polished, and handed in.

Responses from the teacher like those mentioned previously might be classified in James Britton's audience terminology as teacher as "trusted adult" or as "partner in dialogue." Either audience is certainly necessary before the teacher assumes the traditional role of examiner.

Beyond the variations of teacher as audience, many others can profitably be addressed in classroom writing. Students can write for their peers—either fellow students in their classes or those in other classes or other schools. The key point here is that this writing be genuinely addressed to an audience that will, indeed, read and respond to the writing. Only through this genuine response, with all the attendant confusions and misunderstandings, can a real sense of audience develop. For example, juniors in high school can write to incoming freshmen and describe the school and offer suggestions on how to succeed. In this case, it is crucial that real incoming freshmen read those letters and write back. The whole point is lost if the teacher asks the juniors to write as if they were writing to incoming freshmen and then reads and evaluates the papers herself. For in that case what the teacher has done is set up a double image; the real teacher audience is superimposed on the "imaginary" freshman audience, and the writer's job then becomes doubly difficult. For the sake of an evaluation, the student must imagine what the teacher thinks one should say to incoming freshmen and how the teacher would like it said. It is not surprising that writing of this kind often sounds strained and false; it is almost inevitable when students are placed in an artificial situation in which they are asked to satisfy two different audiences at once. And in addition to the double image difficulty, the student is being asked to perform, in James Britton's words, a "dummy run," a practice exercise instead of a piece of real communication.

There is little reason for relying completely on "dummy runs" when there are so many genuine situations that call for real writing. What follows is a listing of possible contexts in which students can write for audiences beyond the classroom teacher:

Writing for Other Students

1. An exchange of letters between classes. The topic may be a book both classes have read, a film they have both seen, or a reaction to some contemporary issue.
2. An exchange between classes of profiles written about people in the community. This exchange could take place before the final drafts were written so the revisions could incorporate the readers' questions.
3. Notes written to absent classmates explaining what went on in class so the students will come back prepared.
4. Booklets or stories written for younger children and "tried out" on them by the writers in the younger children's classroom.

Writing for People in the Outside World

1. Letters written to authors of works read in class, in which the students discuss points that had arisen during class discussion. Similar letters can be written to film writers or directors.

2. Actual letters of application for part-time jobs.
3. Letters to the editor of local newspapers or magazines in which the student writers discuss topics of interest to students.
4. Oral histories, transcribed and shaped by the students and presented in a booklet for distribution or purchase through some community organization.
5. Stories, poems, or essays for the school literary magazine.
6. Argumentative or persuasive essays on contemporary topics sent to a local political or civic organization.
7. Entries written for writing contests of any kind.

These are only a few of the many possible audiences for students' writing. All of them demand that the writers think about their audience's uniqueness and shape their writing accordingly. The teacher can be of enormous assistance here by showing students how to analyze whom they are writing for. This can be done either by giving exercises in the whole class in which the general characteristics of a known audience are listed on the chalkboard or by asking specific questions about the intended audience of each student who is already working on an initial draft. Questions such as "How much does your audience know about the subject?" or "How formal do you think you have to be in word choice?" subtly remind students that there is no one way to write anything. Rather, the craft of writing demands that students pick the best way in this particular case for this particular audience. And, over time, with thoughtful nurturing from responsive teachers, this sense of an audience's needs will become automatic—as automatic, we hope, as beginning a sentence with a capital letter and ending it, eventually, with a period or a question mark or an exclamation point!

Practical Ideas for Developing a Sense of Audience

An Exercise to Introduce the Concept of Audience to Students and Teachers

By Lynda Chittenden

Teacher, Old Mill School,
Mill Valley Elementary School District;
and Teacher/Consultant, Bay Area Writing Project

The following is a guided fantasy that successfully communicates the concept of audience. Many teachers have used this exercise both in in-service workshops and in the classroom.

First, ask your group to take out a scrap of paper. Tell them this writing will not be turned in or shared without each writer's approval. Ask each member of the group to select a place where, right now, he or she would rather be. Even the most dedicated teacher or student has a fantasy place that he or she periodically escapes to. Ask all members of the group to close their eyes and imagine themselves in their fantasy land.

Pause awhile; then, speaking slowly, ask the members of the group to visualize themselves in their fantasy lands. What is their position? Are they standing, sitting, lying down? After a few moments, ask them to be receptive to the tactile sensations that are part of being there. What is the weather like? What smells might they also be aware of ? What are the sounds that are very much a part of this place? Allow a few more moments for each individual's fantasy to grow.

Encouraging the group members to imagine and believe that they are compulsive recorders who wish to capture this moment so as to be able to relive it later, ask them to begin a diary that will do just that. (See a sample in paragraph number 1 in the next column.)

After four to five minutes, state that you know this piece is unfinished, but skipping a few lines and, remaining in this place, ask them to begin a letter to Mom, or some other loved one, in which they tell the person about this place. (See paragraph number 2.)

After three to four minutes, acknowledge that this letter is also unfinished but, skipping down a few more lines, ask them to begin writing a memo to their principal or superintendent in which they request funds to subsidize their being in this place and which justifies the released time necessary for them to be there. (See paragraph number 3.)

At the end of three to four minutes, ask for volunteers to share the results of their guided excursion to a special place and to talk about what they noticed in their own writing as they did this exercise. Participants are often surprised to discover how much impact audience has on style. When writing for themselves (paragraph number 1), they tend to be very descriptive and detailed. Concentrating on sense impressions, they, in effect, paint pictures of their memories with words. Many of them become so absorbed in writing that when you call them to a halt and switch audiences, they get slightly annoyed. In paragraph number 2, addressed to Mom or a friend, they often assume a more conversational tone and do much more telling than showing. Sentence length is reduced as rich detailed descriptions are omitted from the writing. Finally, in paragraph number 3, the letter to the principal, they become very formal, and the "voice" in the writing is much more distant. Much less is likely to be written during this part of the exercise because the audience sometimes can inhibit fluency. A sample of an unedited exercise that a UCI Writing Project teacher shared with the group will illustrate these general points:

1. A moss green sea turtle glides lazily by, and a huge rainbow striped parrot fish in hues of lime green, turquoise, and tangerine slowly weaves its way through the filtered light. I can hear my breathing through the snorkle as I float upon the surface of the salty ocean, my back broiling in the sun and turning a deep

> *For teachers and students alike, the guided imagery exercise is an experiential introduction to the concept of audience.*
>
> **LYNDA CHITTENDEN**

shade of crimson. I must appear to the inhabitants of this estuary an ungainly creature—lumbering about in the tranquil waters of Xel Ha. How pleasant it is to float weightlessly in their watery kingdom.

2. Dear Mom:

Michael and I took a trip to a natural aquarium of sorts called Xel Ha today that was truly fantastic! This is an estuary where the river meets the Caribbean. The whole area is enclosed by a coral reef that keeps the sharks out—thank goodness. Anyway, we went snorkling and saw some of the most amazing fish. The colors were just fantastic! One fish I saw was all the colors of the rainbow. Orange wasn't orange but tangerine. It was really unbelievable.

3. To: Dr. Barrow

I have enjoyed my vacation in Cancun immensely and see many possibilities for offering a unit of study on this area. I'd like to stay on a bit longer to investigate all the educational possibilities further. I'm sure I could design a class that would benefit my students. I'm planning to take many slides for illustrated lectures on: the natural aquarium at Xel Ha, the Mayan ruins at Tulume, the windy island of Isle Mujeres, etc. I hope you'll be as excited about my idea as I am . . . .

For teachers and students alike, the guided imagery exercise is an experiential introduction to the concept of audience. It makes what could be just an abstract idea tangible and concrete and creates a positive awareness of audience in future writing assignments.

Writing for a Live Audience

By Anita Freedman

Former Teacher, Fairhaven Elementary School,
Orange Unified School District;
and Teacher/Consultant, UCI Writing Project

One easy way to provide a live audience for your class is to have your students write for children in the lower grades. I begin to help generate ideas for writing by showing the class my "Mouse Collection." I have a large box filled with discarded story display figures: mice outfitted to play tennis, baseball, or golf; to play cards; to clean house; or to stitch up the American flag. I take out one figure and we discuss possible stories about it, stories which younger children would enjoy. "What could we name him or her?" "Think of a problem he or she might have." "How could it be solved?" I write the students' suggestions on the chalkboard, and, from them, we develop a story.

Then everyone gets a chance to pick out a mouse. I have several duplicates, so there are no hassles. As the students write their stories, I walk around the room, making suggestions, serving as a word bank for those who need a walking dictionary, and offering story ideas for those students who get stuck.

When the stories are finished, I use either whole-class or small-group evaluations. Generally, I stay out of the discussion and let the class decide whether or not the stories meet the criteria of sustaining interest, clarity, and appropriateness for the chosen grade level. Students may ask such questions as these: Is it interesting? Is it clear? Who would enjoy it? My students do a truly fine job of evaluating, and they give succinct comments. I have heard them dismiss wandering writers with "That's too long for little kids." They motivate the author to go back and tighten his or her efforts. Sometimes boys are told "That's too scary," so they omit the dripping blood.

Peer groups are also efficient at assigning papers to the correct grade level: "Kindergartners'd love that." "Yours is kinda grown-up; you'd better send it to the third grade."

After the stories are written and evaluated, we set up a schedule for each student to read his or her story and to show his or her mouse to children in a lower grade. Teachers of the primary grades will welcome this activity when it is arranged in advance. Even though our school is very small, my 30 or more children are all given this opportunity to read their work to small groups. As a special reward I let my authors display their figures on their desks for the rest of the day.

Everyone basks in the obvious approval of the audience. Some receive letters! It is always a huge success, and I see a great improvement in my students' ability to put words on paper and to structure a story.

Pen Pal Clubs

By Virginia Bergquist

Teacher, Meadow Park Elementary School,
Irvine Unified Shool District;
and Teacher/Consultant, UCI Writing Project

Starting a pen pal club at your school or in your classroom is a great way of changing the audience for your children, promoting writing in the practical/informative domain, and opening the door for writing across the curriculum.

Students may communicate through letters or through a telecommunications network. In September of each school year, the Scholastic Book Club provides teachers with material that contains information on pen pals. This service is free. For more information, write to the Scholastic Book Club, Inc., 2931 E. McCarty, Jefferson City, MO 65102-7503. Students with the equipment and financial resources may exchange messages

through the National Geographic Society's Kids Network, an international telecommunications network. Fees are charged for the initial costs of this service and for telecommunications time. For more information, write to the National Geographic Society, Kid's Network, 17th and M Streets, NW, Washington, DC 20036.

Once the students begin communicating, post a map in the classroom. Use map pins and string to indicate where each student has a pen pal. Children can keep a scrapbook of the letters and small items (stamps, menus, napkins, postcards, photos, artwork, or recipes) that they have exchanged with their pen pal.

You may also wish to have students do research on the state or country of the pen pal. They may write a saturation report, learn songs from the country or state, order travel brochures, and locate and display books that pertain to their pen pal's home. The possibilities are endless.

You might have one of your students who has artistic talent design special stationery, which can be duplicated, or you may wish to have each student design his or her own stationery. This is a great motivation for writing more letters.

Writing to "Dear Abby"

By Karen Walden

Teacher, Sunkist School,
Anaheim Elementary School District;
and Teacher/Consultant, UCI Writing Project

I became uncomfortable and almost indifferent about using textbooks as the sole source for the written communication of ideas to students in my classroom last year. Daily, I felt the nearly impossible struggle of making appropriate, meaningful connections with those remote, impersonal messages found in textbook selections. That material written from writer to unknown audience caused such a feeling of indirect involvement in me and in my students that it became more and more difficult to justify basing my lessons on the textbook selections.

One day I brought a newspaper into the classroom. I hoped that the fact that the paper had been published that day would make the nature and the purpose for the writing more immediate. As we reviewed and discussed the various sections in the newspaper, students began to demonstrate increased interest in the writing. Those articles to a then known audience began to take on meaning.

As we extended our exploration of the newspaper, the children discovered a column that elicited an even more personal response—Dear Abby. Their enthusiasm prompted my weekly initiation of role playing in the class. For the next few weeks, I decided to become a Dear Abby of sorts, providing my students with a new audience to write to. They wrote small, anonymous messages on folded pieces of paper and placed them in a collection box. I then attempted to provide suitable answers to real problems. Each Monday morning eager faces lined up outside the door to receive a handout of questions and responses for our "Dear Abby" session. I was truly pleased with the trust that began to develop.

In the weeks that followed, students offered additional comments to my responses, oftentimes posing solutions far more appropriate than mine. Thus, I began gradually to relinquish my role to secretly chosen "Abbys" or "Alberts" and to reassume my previous capacity as full-time teacher. What a success! Additional questionmakers began to emerge in the class. Students felt less inhibited about identifying themselves when they wanted or needed answers. The range of topics began to broaden. We discussed the validity of school rules, difficult relationships with siblings, inadequate allowances, the effects of drugs and smoking, consequences of shoplifting, and pending love affairs—just to mention a few. As our chosen expert responded to a particular problem, classmates listened attentively. They displayed unquestionable tolerance of her or his opinions. Differing

points of view were both respected and appreciated. Our expert's literary skills in actual interpretation and editing also naturally emerged, as some of the written questions required revising for clarity.

The experience in writing to a real audience was most rewarding. It provided not only motivation for written communication but also fostered meaningful relationships among class members.

I Think We Need to Write a Substitute's Manual

By Lynda Chittenden
Teacher, Old Mill School,
Mill Valley Elementary School District;
and Teacher/Consultant, Bay Area Writing Project

The self-contained elementary school classroom provides many opportunities for children to write to a real audience and for a specific purpose: a job description book that specifies exactly how each clean-up job must be performed at the end of the day or a list of adopted rules for those physical education games that are a continual source of argument.

Early in the school year, I plot to create in my fifth grade classroom the circumstances that result in a wildly successful project. I am rarely absent in September. However, on the first rainy day in October, I take a planned day off and spend it in bed reading a trashy novel. On returning to class the next day, I am assaulted by a predictable barrage of complaints: "Don't you *ever* get that terrible person again!" "She wouldn't even let us read at the rug!" "I only missed three problems, but she made me do the whole page over."

I listen to these laments with great seriousness, which encourages even more verbalized outrage. With furrowed brow and in a concerned voice, I say, "This is terrible. Our class is so special and different that it must be very difficult for a stranger to try to understand how we work. I think we need to write a substitute's manual!"

With that prewriting exercise accomplished, we get to work. First, we brainstorm all the necessary ingredients for such a book. From those suggestions we write on the chalkboard a list that will become the manual's contents: the class meeting, the day's schedule, the class standards, terrible tasks, learning logs, math time, writing groups, group response, literature, physical education, clean-up, and so forth.

Last year, instead of the experienced authoritarian matron, the class had as its first substitute a young person who allowed herself to be completely overwhelmed by a majority of rowdy boys. The next day when we were brainstorming, someone made the appropriate suggestion that we also include a chapter of advice, including the following:

1. You must expect some persons to change their names at roll call and sometimes drop pencils at math time, *but* don't let that offend you.
2. At the class meeting, if the class is out of hand, don't leave the chairperson to do all the work. Help the chairperson contain the class!
3. When you come into the room, you should expect everyone to be seated at the rug unless people are turning in homework.

This year we began the substitute's manual with some more direct talk about expectations:

> We expect you to be patient with us and we'll try to be patient with you. Sometimes things that seem easy for you are hard for us, and we don't want a lecture about how simple it is. We expect you to be a teacher, not a parent or friend. You should expect us to do our best work, although sometimes we forget and fool around.

Once we agree that we have thought of everything a substitute teacher needs to know about our class, we decide who will write what. Knowing that the best writers always volunteer first, I start with the most important beginning chapters of the book. "Who wants to do expectations?" The two or three students who raise their hands get that assignment. "Who wants to write the advice section?" Those with raised hands then have their assignment. If at the end of the list, some students do not have assignments, they may do the illustrations; for example, a picture of a boy out picking up trash in the yard—a "terrible task" consequence of breaking a class standard.

Once the first drafts are completed, the students meet in their writing groups to determine what must be done to make these important pieces of writing clear and completely understandable to a substitute teacher. The final drafts are then written and handed to a small committee that puts them together, numbers the pages, prepares the contents page, and binds the manual with a front and a back cover.

When the manual is completed, we have much more than an aid for the next substitute teacher. Through a seemingly subtle process, the necessary structure and expectations of the class have been clarified for everyone.

Learning Logs

By Mindy Moffatt

English and History Teacher,
White Hill Middle School, Ross Valley School District;
and Teacher/Consultant, UCI Writing Project

If your students could *freewrite* (à la Peter Elbow) about what they had gleaned during the school day, what do you imagine they would write? As a middle school teacher, I also wondered. What would their perceptions of the day be? The idea of writing in a learning log intrigued me enough to try it.

Starting from the first day of the school year and every day thereafter, students were instructed to write during the last ten minutes "about the day" and to date each entry. Students earned credit for each day's notation. I collected their logs once a week, staggering the collection day so that I would have 30 logs a day to review instead of 180 a week. Each class period had a regular day of the week when the logs were due. I was surprised that reviewing each day's logs took only 20 to 30 minutes, depending on how many quick comments I wrote.

Imagine my reaction when I read Pam's log of the first week:

> 9/9/85: I'm in English class right now (unfortunately). The teacher wants us to write this stupid, dumb, and absolutely boring paragraph. Well, anyway, I'm going to learn in this class—but I also have to because the teacher will probably yell my brains out if I just sit

here. I hate this class. I really think it's stupid because it's not like I'm going to grow up and tell my kids to do this.

I hadn't quite prepared myself for such an honest reflection. But I persevered through her accounts:

9/10/85: Well, today I'm in English again! No—I don't want to be but have to be! Well, today we were supposed to be doing a talk about the stupid paper I wrote about yesterday, but the teacher sent me and Michelle out of class because we didn't have the paper, and it was in our locker and she wouldn't let us go get it. This is boring!

9/11/85: Today we got together in groups and discussed things about ourselves. I met some people today that are in our group. I guess it's gonna be cool. Three more minutes until the bell. I have to go home! I'm dying of starvation. I'm getting pretty proud of myself because today I made a friend that was my worst enemy for two years. Bye Bye.

9/12/85: Well, I've got three minutes to tell you everything I have to. I feel fine about my writing. My writing makes me feel good because I write down what I feel, think, and believe, so if people don't like it, that's ok, because it's me and they don't have to be me.

9/13/85: We write in the learning logs so we can write down what we feel, think, and believe. I like the learning logs because we can write down what we want to. There's nothing really I don't like about learning logs.

Reading Pam's account of her first week in the eighth grade made me believe in both the cognitive and affective values of learning logs. This activity provides insight for a teacher to keep in touch with the development of students. I enjoyed writing supportive, positive comments to students; "I feel this way, too!" "I'm impressed!" "Thanks for sharing this."

The students were anxious to get their logs back; not only did they look for my remarks, but also they reread their entries to see what they had written the week before. With some middle school students, it often seemed as if a lifetime had passed during the week. They remembered the captured moments, the exercises in class, and the trials and tribulations that they had survived.

After the first week, when students began to trust writing in their logs, I gave them more specific prompts:

Write first about everything you did in class; then tell your reactions and feelings about the activities.

We had read-around groups that helped us with our paper in punctuation and spelling. If I didn't have them, I'd be lost like a needle in a haystack.

Greg Hughes

I got a good start on my draft about Renee. Debbie really gave me some great suggestions on how to spice up my draft.

Kevin Donovan

This was interesting to have other people besides teachers tell you honestly what they think about your writing. . . . I learned how to help other people without giving away the answer.

Heather White

Today we proofread each of our papers. It was kind of fun reading other people's papers and correcting them.

Nico Dourbetas

Today we started to proofread other students' material. I think that it helps me as much as the student I proofread for.

Russell Clark

I had fun working on my paper today. We talked about it and discussed what I could do to fix it.

Eric Degenhart

The class got noisy and Ms. Moffatt almost gave the whole class a detention.

Eric Degenhart

Today, We Noticed things that were
very Interesting and
very Different. I
    Learned that
people Live and
    Listen according to
their Lifestyles and sometimes
their Status.

Chris May

What is something you want to know more about?

I like writing. I would like to learn more about science fiction writing.

Brady White

I'm a person who is especially interested in new ideas and would like to learn.

Deborah Wissink

I knew within a week where certain students needed my assistance; I did not have to wait until later in the quarter to discover that someone was having trouble.

What do you like about our class?

I do like working in groups because they give opinions and help you with what you are doing.

Sheila Nora

It makes me feel good when I think of something to write. . . . I like it because it lets my mind do the writing.

Sean Ciechomski

I like learning logs because you can tell the teacher how you feel about things.

Jason Bumcrot

It's fun writing in learning logs because you search for and gather your thoughts in a short period of time.

Russell Clark

What don't you like about learning logs or our class?

Sometimes I don't like learning logs because there is either nothing to write about or not enough time.

Rex Huang

I don't like the learning logs but as long as we have to do them, I might as well try and make it fun.

Anthony Lawson

If your parents had been watching this class through a one-way mirror, what would they have seen? Explain to them what you were doing.

If my parents were here . . . they would have seen us in groups talking and commenting about each other's papers which makes it look like we were passing notes or something.

Rex Huang

If my mom or dad were observing our class today, they'd be pleased cuz we got a lot of work done. . . . I'm proud of myself, and I'm sure my parents would be too!

Stefanie Takii

If my parents were observing this class, they would infer that we were a rowdy, unsupervised, uncontrolled class, but in a way independent because even though we were talking a lot, we were also working at the same time.

Michael Lietzow

I was learning a great deal about my students' learning processes. Their feelings were validated when I discussed their responses with the whole class. For example, Chris May wrote, "My writing makes me feel good in a way that everybody in the class will probably respect me for it."

When I shared an insight from a log, the students' learning became more personalized, and my teaching became more focused.

> *Learning logs provide insight for a teacher to keep in touch with the development of students.*
>
> **MINDY MOFFATT**

Reading their learning logs was an activity I looked forward to, especially after a difficult day. The students' entries were all I needed to remind me of my reasons for becoming a teacher. "This is Ms. Moffatt's learning class," wrote Tashawna Donaldson.

"It gives us a chance to use our brains," said Chuck White. I felt that I had time to adjust my goals and plans so that I could continue to teach students, not just content.

So many enlightening responses appeared in the logs that I made a bulletin board of their disclosures. I noted particularly valuable phrases, allowing students to edit their "freewrite" comments for display. Students valued the log entries more when this postwriting step was added. "I want one of my quotes to go on the board, but I can't think of anything good enough to write," noted Tod Grossman.

Parents also appreciated the learning logs. They were pleased and entertained to see such insight from the students. During conferences with parents the logs became a concrete basis for them to understand a student's perspective regarding goals and expectations of the class. Parents saw that students were learning how to learn, and I was rewarded when parents expressed that they wished their English classes had been like this. They valued the writing and supported the effort.

Students were not the only writers at the end of the class period. I joined them by writing in my own log and allowed them to read my entries. Through this sharing of my own trials and tribulations, I found myself facing the same challenge as they—trusting one's audience. Having ten minutes of "quiet writing time" at the end of each class was immensely therapeutic, especially in a middle school schedule of seven daily periods. We were all more prepared to meet the challenges of our next classes after such closure.

Regardless of the subject matter or the ability levels of students, spending the last few minutes of class writing learning logs allows teachers and students to harvest memories, trust, smiles, and knowledge. As Stefanie Hill explained, "It kind of makes me feel good to know that I'm helping people with using my knowledge and putting it together with theirs to make our writing better." We are learning how to learn with logs.

Telecommunications: A Powerful Tool for Facilitating Writing to a Distant Audience

By Steven Pinney

Former Teacher, TeWinkle Middle School Sixth Grade CORE Newport-Mesa Unified School District; and Teacher/Consultant, UCI Writing Project

"Would you hand me the thesaurus?"

"Does community have one or two m's?"

"I want them to think I know how to write a decent letter."

Having students write to an unknown and geographically distant audience can be a powerful incentive and teaching tool. By arranging for an audience of students in a classroom from another county, state, or, if possible, country, the teacher can maximize the writers' opportunities to "own" their writing. The audience reviewing students' writing through a telecommunications network exerts a powerful influence on students

because the reviewers are unknown. When young authors begin to write, they inevitably want to know who will read their work. When students learn that the peer group reviewing their work will not be from their classroom, they tend to focus more keenly on their final product, which they want to present positively. Writing for another student in their classroom, their teacher, or their parents pales in comparison with having another student in a classroom linked by telecommunications as the audience.

Using Telecommunications

"Do you consider this the best you have done?"

"Well, I've checked the spelling of all the words and compared this final draft with my original plan. . . . Yes, . . . this is my best. I'm ready for you to send it to the class in Placerville now."

While most teachers might feel that they can easily address the issue of a writer's audience within their own classrooms, the technical aspect of making connections beyond their school site may seem overwhelming. This situation is changing slowly as increasing numbers of schools are incorporating instruction using computers and word processors into their curriculum plans. Expanding the use of computers, either in laboratories or in individual classrooms, makes this wider audience more accessible to the mainstream classroom.

With telecommunications as a tool for learning, the teacher is a true facilitator as young authors write to a distant audience. The teacher becomes a resource, providing students with support during the writing process.

Students can complete a variety of individually inspired or teacher-directed writing activities. Once material has been recorded with a word processor, the first step has been taken. To be transmitted, the piece does not need to be rewritten in another form. Students can complete their assignment individually, work with the teacher to complete a collaboratively written piece, or work in cooperative writing teams. This article contains a two-page sample of the writing projects planned for the kids2kids network, which I founded several years ago.

Writing Projects

The *kids2kids Writing Circle* offers your class a real writing audience. Here is a sample of writing projects planned for the coming school year:

No Place Like Home - students research their family, their neighborhood and their school to gather information for a letter introducing themselves to students in their matched class. The article chosen as best from each class will be included in a special edition of the network student newsletter.

Report of Information

The Great Pumpkin Letter Writing Campaign -
students write friendly letters sharing a remembered frightening moment. Other network students respond from the point-of-view of this great benevolent character offering solace and historical facts of this special time of year.

Autobiographical Incident

Tell It Like It Was - students from one
class interview older family members asking about childhood holiday memories. Essays are then written in class and sent to sister classes for a response.

First Hand Biography Sketch

Round Robin - a classic team writing assignment receives technical support. Using telecommunications, three classrooms work together to build an exciting three-chapter short story.

Short Story

Special Report - students speak out on environmental issues in a variety of formats for a special edition of the student network newsletter: *The Electronic Express.*

Report Of Information,
Speculation About Effect

Superior Toy, Inc. - student teams write business letters requesting products or services of a company called Superior Toy, Inc. Other students **are** Superior Toy customer service agents and respond.

Problem/Solution

Writers' Anthology - semester magazine of student work in a variety of writing genres. Published twice each year, this collection represents the best of the writing posted electronically throughout the fall and spring.

Join Us !

Within the classroom, access to computers, a phone line, and a modem makes the successful connection possible. Those technical tools are common in the business world but less so in education. Accessing a school phone line might seem difficult, yet increasing numbers of administrators realize that having students' work read by a distant audience has learning value for reluctant writers. Administrators may become receptive to controlled access to school phone lines when teachers take the time to address issues of cost and management. Each year, more classrooms are accessing local and national telecommunications networks and reaping the benefits from communicating with a distant audience.

Once the students' writing has been completed and the technical tools have been set up, the teacher needs to locate viable educational networks. Many teachers who use technology have learned that use of telecommunications works best in the classroom when the teacher directs the activities. Programs available through local and national networks offer classrooms expanded opportunities for writing to an audience and provide activities that address varied modes of writing. Enhancements that teachers have brought to the use of telecommunications in the classroom include calendars for writing activities published months in advance, substantive writing directions, and technical assistance.

Waiting for Responses

"Do you know if she received my letter?"
"I'm worried. Do you think he'll write right back?"
"I sure wish I would hear from them."

Most young writers hastily assume that a response takes just a few hours to complete. However, under the direction of the teacher from the matched class, developing a meaningful response requires following the steps of the writing process. When the originating authors understand the need for patience while the writing process is being completed, they appreciate the energy involved in their own writing as well as that of the student preparing a response. The student wrote a real letter to a real person who needs time to write a real response.

By building a writing curriculum in which students have access to an authentic though distant audience through telecommunications, a teacher maximizes the power a colleague's students bring to the writing instruction. This activity helps the teacher facilitate a powerful and complete writing process within his or her own class and brings a wonderful quality to the work of young authors: the enjoyment of writing to a real audience.

Steven Pinney died in April, 1993, because of complications arising from pneumonia. He will be greatly missed by his students at TeWinkle Middle School and at Chapman University; by his colleagues at TeWinkle, Chapman, and the UCI Writing Project; and by all those teachers affiliated with Computer Using Educators (CUE). In May, 1993, Steven was posthumously awarded the Gold Disk Award, the highest honor that CUE bestows.

Teaching Writing in the Culturally and Linguistically Diverse Classroom

English Learners and Writing: Responding to Linguistic Diversity

By Robin Scarcella

Director, English-as-a-Second-Language Program, University of California, Irvine

ncreasing numbers of nonnative English-speaking students, here referred to as *English learners*, are enrolling in classes in which full proficiency in English is often assumed.[1] These students have often received special language instruction designed to (1) help them become proficient in English; (2) enable them to participate in the core curriculum; and (3) promote their positive self-image and cross-cultural understanding. However, when they have acquired an advanced level of English proficiency and progress to mainstream instruction, they still need an instructional program to promote their continued development of English-language proficiency. Although writing instruction is only one aspect of that program, it can play an important role since effective writing instruction for English learners can help them gain the academic writing abilities that they need to be admitted to institutions of higher education as well as to succeed in the job market. As is often argued, skill in writing can open the way to success in our society. English learners with effective English writing abilities can succeed in the United States more easily than English learners without those abilities. This article addresses the teaching of writing in the core curriculum to English learners who have acquired advanced levels of English proficiency but who still lack native-like writing skills. It is intended for elementary school and high school teachers.[2]

---

[1]Many terms have been used to describe these students; for example, English-as-a-second-language (ESL) students, limited-English-proficient (LEP) students, and culturally diverse students. In this paper the term *English learners* is used. They are defined as "children whose language background is other than English."

[2]These issues are discussed further in "Building Bilingual Instruction: Putting the Pieces Together," *BEOUTREACH*, Vol. 3, No. 1 (February, 1992), 6–8. (*BEOUTREACH* is published by the Bilingual Education Office, California Department of Education.)

English learners with effective English writing abilities can succeed in the United States more easily than English learners without those abilities.

ROBIN SCARCELLA

For all writing instructors whose students speak English as a second language, knowledge about linguistic diversity is not a matter of political liberalism but rather a necessity. What are the most effective ways to teach diverse populations of English learners? In response to that question, this article contains a discussion of some general pedagogical guidelines that can be adapted for teaching writing to English learners and some ways of adapting teaching practices to provide individualized instruction for those students.

Guidelines for Teaching English Learners

The material that follows contains guidelines for effective ways to teach writing to English learners:

GUIDELINE I

Respect students' home languages and cultures.

Too often, our students feel that their cultures and languages are not valued in their classrooms. The goal in writing programs for English learners is to teach standard English writing, not to replace students' first languages and dialects with standard English. Ideally, we want to build on the students' culturally rich experiences. The goal is not to make students monolingual in standard English; rather, it is to help them acquire standard English in addition to their first language or dialect. To accomplish this goal, we must learn about the students' linguistic and literary traditions and incorporate them into the curriculum. Consider, for instance, the rich literary traditions of Korean students, whose country has a 24-hour *dial-a-poem* telephone service. Young children in Korea are encouraged to keep daily diaries and to enter literary contests. Poetry readings and contests are held during school picnics. Incorporating some of these Korean traditions into the regular curriculum could increase the self-esteem of Korean-

American students while simultaneously facilitating their English writing development.

GUIDELINE 2

Give students lots of comprehensible English input.

Stephen Krashen's research indicates that a sufficient quantity of comprehensible English input tailored to the current English proficiency levels of the students aids their overall English-language development. He suggests that a level of English appropriate for the students, one that is neither too difficult nor too easy, facilitates English language acquisition. According to Stephen Krashen, when students receive English input that they do not understand, their English language development does not proceed smoothly.[3] Perhaps this outcome explains why one of my nonnative English writing students complained bitterly about his high school English class. This student claimed that he did not understand what was going on in the class because the teacher talked only about *Shake Spear.*

Several ways can be used to increase the amount of comprehensible English that students receive in class. Familiar, predictable input is often the most comprehensible. Preview questions or warm-up activities inform English learners of the topic of the lessons. Visual aids—pictures, diagrams, charts, gestures, and items from the outside world—also aid students' comprehension. Focusing on the students' own experiences helps learners understand the input.

Another way of helping students understand writing lessons is by relating topics and activities to one another throughout the instruction. D. Scott Enright and Mary Lou McCloskey

---

[3]See Stephen Krashen. *Insights and Inquiries.* Hayward, Calif.: Alemany Press, 1985.

suggest "integrating a series of related topics using speaking, listening, reading and writing activities. In their unit entitled Rain Makes Applesauce, designed for second through fifth graders, students participate in a variety of activities, including science, math, literature, art, field trips, and cooking 'centered on the theme of apples.'"[4] Similarly, Stephen Krashen encourages teachers to use a series of related topics and activities so that English learners have additional opportunities to understand the input.[5]

Simply talking to students individually provides them with comprehensible spoken English. When teachers interact one-on-one with students, the teachers' English can be tailored to the proficiency levels of the students; and the students' difficulties in understanding the teachers can be determined. Although it is possible for teachers to remind themselves to speak slowly and clearly, teacher-centered lessons almost always prevent instructors from accurately tailoring their language to the students' English proficiency levels. When students can react individually to teachers' comments, using such expressions as "Hm?" and "I don't understand that word," teachers find it easier to know which parts of their conversations students cannot follow.

Because students cannot always be provided with one-on-one interaction, they must be encouraged to converse with one another. Peer tutoring, read-arounds, and cooperative learning activities can provide learners with ideal input for language development since those activities foster the kind of interaction that allows students to use and develop their existing communicative potential as listeners, speakers, readers, and writers.[6] However, teachers need to be aware of the type and quality of language input that students receive when they interact with one another. For example, if during peer editing, revision, or brainstorming sessions, English learners are paired only with other English learners who speak varieties of immigrant English rather than standard English, the sessions may not help them to make significant progress in acquiring standard English writing skills. They may acquire new vocabulary words and structures from their peers, but many of those words and structures may be characteristics of immigrant English varieties rather than of standard English. Students must be helped to develop the conversational skills needed to interact effectively so that they can obtain comprehensible English input. For example, they can be taught such conversational management skills as asking questions when they do not understand and encouraging everyone in their group to contribute.

Often, students understand the teacher's spoken English quite well. One bilingual researcher, Jim Cummins, argues that many English learners acquire conversational skills in their first few years in the United States but fail to acquire the ability to communicate in academic situations in which they cannot guess the meaning of the language they read or hear from the context.[7] As a result, English learners have greater difficulty understanding academic English than informal, spoken English and often struggle with the reading materials given to them.

To make sense of the classroom reading material, English learners need to draw on several kinds of culture-specific knowledge. They have not had the same experiences as those of their native English-speaking peers. They need additional information about the reading assignments to understand them. Prereading assignments and explanations (which include the use of pictures and realia and which develop concepts, vocabulary, and structures used in the reading) all help to build students' comprehension of the reading.

---

[4] D. Scott Enright and Mary Lou McCloskey, *Integrating English: Developing English Language and Literacy in the Multilingual Classroom.* Reading, Mass.: Addison-Wesley Publishing Co., Inc., 1988, p. 281. Reprinted from Robin Scarcella, *Teaching Language Minority Students in the Multicultural Classroom.* Englewood Cliffs, N.J.: Prentice-Hall, Inc., 1990, p. 79. Reprinted by permission of Prentice-Hall, Inc.
[5] See Stephen Krashen and Tracy Terrell, *The Natural Approach.* New York: Pergamon Press, 1983.
[6] See Spencer S. Kagan, *Cooperative Learning* San Juan Capistrano, Calif.: Kagan Cooperative Learning, 1992, which contains a discussion of cooperative learning and activities for cooperative learning in the classroom.

[7] Robin Scarcella, *Teaching Language Minority Students in the Multicultural Classroom.* Englewood Cliffs, N.J.: Prentice Hall, Inc., 1990, p. 102.

Books such as the classics have been abridged and simplified to make them more accessible to English learners. Easy reading for pleasure, including the reading of comic books, seems to ease the path for English learners who later want to read more difficult material. The reduced length, larger print, pictures, and illustrations of easy-to-read materials make them comprehensible to English learners who lack English proficiency.

However, if students are to develop proficiency in academic English, they must be exposed to reading materials that are more difficult to read than simplified readers. Students need to read academic texts—essays, articles, and books—that are not usually simplified for nonnative English speakers. *Narrow reading* helps students to understand such academic material. When students read *narrowly*, that is, read many materials on a related topic or materials written by one author, their English proficiency improves because they are repeatedly exposed to similar vocabulary and grammatical structures. Using this method, students have multiple opportunities to acquire English words and structures.[8]

GUIDELINE 3

Check to make sure that the students understand.

Many ways exist to ensure that students understand the English used in their lessons. Asking students whether they understand the instruction is often ineffective. They are often embarrassed to admit not understanding. Head nods in many Asian countries mean "We are following you," not "We understand what you say." No one likes being spotlighted (singled out in front of the classroom and asked to perform before others), least of all English learners who lack English proficiency. Yet many ways exist to get students to display their understanding without embarrassing them. A quick true-or-false quiz may be helpful. Students can also act out a story or perform the actions in the story as they reread it a second time. They can retell,

summarize, or analyze the reading material; discuss it with a group; illustrate it; or use it to complete a different task. Students with even very limited English proficiency can be asked to respond chorally or individually to *yes/no* or *either/or* questions or to give one-word answers to general questions. Students with more advanced English proficiency will need to be challenged so that they are encouraged to use their English in more sophisticated ways.

GUIDELINE 4

Encourage students to use language purposefully.

Exposing learners to comprehensible input in the writing classroom is not enough. For example, they can be given the right type of comprehensible reading material; but to get them to learn from it, teachers need to have them interact meaningfully with it and to use it in their writing. Encouraging students to convey real messages (such as an invitation or a complaint) to real audiences (such as peers or political leaders) helps students to understand the significance of writing. When English learners begin to use English to accomplish goals that they themselves see as important, they realize that English is not just a series of word lists or grammar forms but a living language for communication. Moreover, when they are engaged in sustained meaningful communication related to their own personal interests, they feel that their efforts to write are worthwhile. This in turn helps learners to develop positive attitudes about writing.

GUIDELINE 5

Provide writing tasks at the appropriate level for English learners.

The kinds of writing English learners do greatly affect their language and writing development. It is important to provide English writing assignments that are a little beyond the current English proficiency levels of the students.[9] If students are given tasks that are too easy, they are not challenged and do not learn

---

[8]Scarcella, *Teaching Language Minority Students,* p. 86.

[9]See Stephen Krashen, *The Input Hypothesis: Issues and Implications.* New York: Longman, 1985.

new skills. Yet too often the demands made on students to write beyond their English proficiency levels are too harsh. If students have to use too many new vocabulary words and grammatical structures in an activity, they may spend too much time consciously trying to string sentences together or translating from their first languages. In the end they may become frustrated and even feel themselves driven to plagiarize. For instance, an English learner was asked to write a book report on a sophisticated novel. He knew he did not have the ability to complete the task. So he fabricated the entire report and titled it "Catch Her in the Right."

For many students the alternative to plagiarizing is carrying out a difficult writing assignment in their own garbled, ungrammatical English. If they are given no feedback on their writing, they may come to believe that their poorly formed sentences constitute correct standard academic English. This situation actually happened to one of my own students. Only when I showed him that *firstable* was not in a dictionary was he convinced that *firstable* was not an English word!

A good rule of thumb to follow when deciding on writing tasks is to have the students write what they can comprehend and say. An exact fit between a student's English proficiency level and the writing task is improbable. Both the content and the genre of the material contribute to the difficulty of the task. The easiest content for English learners is related to their everyday activities, such as those with their families and in their neighborhoods. Culturally familiar topics are also easier for students to write about. Students more easily complete tasks that are personally interesting and that they would do outside the classroom than tasks that they consider irrelevant. For instance, tasks such as ranking which equipment to take camping may interest students who are avid campers but may have little relevance for students who hate camping.

GUIDELINE 6
Allow students to choose their own writing topics and tasks.

This practice enhances the development of students' ability to write in a second language because choice is a critical component of writing. Allowing students to choose topics and tasks in which they are interested motivates them to elaborate on their ideas, clarify their thoughts, revise their texts, and perfect their writing.

English language learners come from distinct cultural backgrounds and have distinct interests and needs. Some students need to write in personal genres—including notes, telegrams, postcards, diaries, and informal letters—while others need to write in institutional genres—including summaries, reports, and essays. All benefit from writing about their personal experiences. Tasks focused on the students' personal experiences are the easiest ones for English learners because they can readily relate to them. One of my Latino students was delighted to describe her experiences learning to write Spanish in a public school in Michoacán. After describing her past education, she lamented, "Sometimes I feel my life experiences are not important here in United States. I'm happy you want to know about me."

GUIDELINE 7
Provide comprehensible, constructive feedback.

English learners need different types of feedback on their written work than do native English writers. English learners need to know alternative ways of using language, vocabulary items, grammatical structures, and specific transition words that increase the cohesion of their essays. Developing students' sense of audience awareness is not enough; English learners need to know how to vary their language appropriately to appeal to diverse audiences. Similarly, those students need to know which level of language to use to display formality and informality. They need to know the rhetorical structures and language associated with different genres such as the narrative, short story, and persuasive essay. Giving English learners the precise language they need to compose entire sections of their writings can be helpful. In general, the more comprehensible, constructive feedback that students receive, the better. This statement does not mean that teachers need to put masses of red ink on the papers of English learners. Comments can be discussed during conferences and editing sessions, and students can be individually coached.

GUIDELINE 8

Grade fairly.

In conjunction with this guideline, teachers need to reward and acknowledge students' efforts while simultaneously avoiding culturally biased writing tests that show what students cannot do rather than reveal their strengths. Students need honest information about their progress. To ensure fair grading, teachers can create writing tasks that bias for the best (elicit the best sample of the students' writing).[10] Teachers may need to give intermediate and advanced English learners one grade for grammar and another for content and organization. Students who are just beginning to acquire English will need more encouragement and positive feedback. Although teachers may be tempted to cushion the efforts of English learners, at no time should they be led to believe that they have acquired perfect standard English when in fact they have not yet acquired a high level of proficiency in standard English.

GUIDELINE 9

Build a climate of trust in which students feel free to try out new linguistic behaviors.

Teachers need to lower their students' anxieties by inviting, but not demanding, students' participation and by creating rules of etiquette for the classroom such as "No put-downs," "Help others," and "Listen carefully."

Affect is important in language development. *Affect* refers to the learner's affective characteristics, such as motivation, attitudes, anxiety, self-esteem, cooperation, competition, and learning styles and strategies. In the writing classroom, teachers must pay close attention to these characteristics of learners so that activities can be designed and tailored to meet learners' needs. A lack of knowledge about students' affective characteristics may cause writing

instruction to fail. Unless learners feel comfortable writing in class, they will not enjoy the experience. To create writing situations that lessen students' anxiety, teachers need to begin with writing tasks at levels appropriate for the students and also occasionally to provide easier tasks that give opportunities for all students to attain success. In this way teachers can help the students enjoy using English to strengthen their positive feelings about the language and to discover new meanings.

Individualized Instruction for English Learners

This section contains a discussion of ways to provide individualized instruction to English learners. An impressive diversity of English learners are enrolled in California classrooms. Among those students are at least three groups:

1. Recent immigrants who can read and write well in their first languages (These students have an important advantage over the other two groups; their previous schooling fosters skill development in English.)
2. Recent arrivals who find writing in academic contexts painful (These students are illiterate in their first languages and have had little or no previous schooling. They have acquired some English conversational skills, but in academic contexts they are unable to communicate effectively in writing.)
3. English learners who are fluent in a variety of nonstandard English forms (These students fill their pages easily, but the writing is not academically acceptable. The students have lived in the United States for a lengthy period, some for as long as five years, and they are often unable to relate to the immigrant experiences of others.)

The students come from many different educational traditions and cultural backgrounds. Observations of their speech and writing reveal that they have acquired different levels of English proficiency in each of the four language skill areas—listening, speaking, reading, and writing. They follow diverse patterns of acculturation. Some spent many months eagerly preparing for their life in the United States, while many others were forced to come here by their parents. Some hear a

---

[10]Scarcella, *Teaching Language Minority Students*, p. 158.

lot of English outside school; others hear none at all; and yet others hear only nonstandard varieties of English.

All students can benefit from the rich experiences and literary traditions of recent arrivals who have been educated in their own countries and are literate in their first languages. Some of these recent arrivals may transfer first-language writing skills into their second language. For example, some Korean learners might avoid writing thesis statements since avoiding the statement of theses in some types of Korean writing is conventional and preferred. Similarly, some Latino learners might hold different expectations of their audience. For instance, unlike some European-American learners, they might expect their audience to appreciate descriptive language—even in expository essays. However, first-language transfer does not occur wholesale. It interacts with other variables—such as age, proficiency level in English, degree of acculturation, and writing proficiency in the students' first language. Not surprisingly, the more experience the learners have in writing about specific topics in particular genres, the more English writing proficiency they gain. Recent arrivals are sometimes unable to write in specific genres because they simply lack the experience.[11]

Immigrants who are illiterate in their first languages and who have had little previous schooling have their own rich cultural traditions that can be appreciated in their classrooms, too. These students will need to learn the written symbol system of English. Increased emphasis will need to be made on the English alphabet, the formation of letters, the patterns of spelling, and the stylistic conventions of English (including capitalization and punctuation). Before moving on to more difficult levels, these students will need time for their initial language skills to mature. In addition, they will need encouragement and many successful experiences using the language during short and frequent easy-writing assignments.

Students who have lived here for a long time, some for as long as five years, and who show signs of beginning to acquire a nonstandard variety of English need to be given much exposure to standard English input inside the classroom. Teachers must not think that students in this group have mastered standard English because they know English slang and converse fluently. Feedback about their progress in English is especially critical. The students must not be allowed to think that they know standard written English when they do not.

Today's writing instructors need to respond to linguistic as well as to cultural diversity. English learners have different language learning experiences, and teachers need to become sensitive to those experiences. Becoming sensitive to and learning about the educational traditions and cultural backgrounds of linguistically diverse students is not impossible for teachers but imperative.

---

[11]Robin Scarcella and Rebecca Oxford, *The Tapestry of Language Learning: The Individual in the Communicative Classroom*. Boston: Heinle and Heinle, 1991, p. 122.

Practical Ideas for Teaching Writing in the Culturally and Linguistically Diverse Classroom

The Missing Piece: Enhancing Self-Esteem Through Exposure to Culturally Diverse Literature

By Pamela W. Jones

MacArthur Elementary School,
Long Beach Unified School District;
and Teacher/Consultant, UCI Writing Project

I believe that the self-esteem of culturally diverse students is greatly enhanced when students are allowed and encouraged to examine literature from the perspective of their cultures. This idea comes from a personal experience and from Jawanza Kunjufu, author and educational consultant, who says specifically that:

> African American children need to be given a frame of reference that is consistent with their culture. Our children should analyze images, literature, history, [and so forth] from an African frame of reference.[1]

This idea provides a "missing piece" for me and possibly for many of today's culturally diverse students who may miss the opportunity to become avid readers, critical thinkers, and fluent writers.

I am reminded of my high school years, when I attended an integrated school staffed by a faculty that was 99 percent white. The academic project for all college-bound students was the senior theme, a 30-page research paper consisting of a biography of an American author and critiques of at least five of the author's books. Prior to this experience, I had lived for 11 years in a totally African American community and had attended a grammar school where the history and traditions of the culture

were integrated into the curriculum. I was well steeped in my culture. Additionally, the civil rights and black awareness movements were on the rise; therefore, I automatically considered prominent African American authors for my senior theme.

After considering Lorraine Hansberry, Booker T. Washington, and Richard Wright, I decided on Langston Hughes, because he had been a college classmate of my father and had published more than five books. I cannot believe my naivete at that time. I should have realized that no African American authors would be on the English Department's recommended list. When I asked if I could research the author of my choice, the teacher replied, "Oh, no, we are doing only the classics." So, I settled for Willa Cather and immersed myself in *The Lost Lady* and *My Antonia*. Although Willa Cather seemed to lack relevance for me, I persevered in order to get that grade—meaningful education or not.

Needless to say, that experience did not enhance my self-esteem. But I am excited about the possibilities that the current educational reform movement, particularly in California, offers culturally diverse students. As I look through the *Model Curriculum Standards*, the works of James Baldwin, Richard Wright, Ralph Ellison, Maya Angelou, Alice Walker, and, yes, Langston Hughes are on the list of "Recommended Reading for a Core and Extended Literature Program."[2] Furthermore, I am also encouraged to see the following statement in the *Model Curriculum Standards*:

> Because the diversity of the American society should be reflected in the literature program that students encounter, it is important that excellent writing by authors from racial and ethnic minority groups be sought out and included. This should be done deliberately and with care at each grade level.[3]

---

[1] Jawanza Kunjufu, *Developing Positive Self-Images and Discipline in Black Children*. Chicago: African American Images, 1984, p. vii.

[2] *Model Curriculum Standards, Grades Nine Through Twelve.* Sacramento: California Department of Education, 1985.
[3] *Model Curriculum Standards*, p. E-40.

I take this statement as an invitation to teachers to expand and enrich their existing literature curriculum with works by authors from diverse cultures and ethnic backgrounds.

Through integrating core literature and emphasizing critical thinking and the writing process, students have greater opportunities to go into, through, and beyond culturally diverse literature. Students are invited to get "into" a piece of literature by sharing, verbally or in writing, personal experiences that build a bridge between their lives and the book's theme. They are taught to go "through" the story by exploring their knowledge; sharing what they understand; applying what they learn; and not only analyzing the elements of setting, characters' goals, conflicts, events, and solutions but also offering their responses to those elements. Finally, they are encouraged to go "beyond" the literature as they create and evaluate their own experiences based on similar themes and issues that are indicative of their culture and heritage.

Surely, such an approach can greatly enhance students' self-esteem and increase the number of avid readers, critical thinkers, and fluent writers from diverse cultural backgrounds.

Literature for Culturally Diverse Students, Kindergarten Through Grade Eight

This list of publications provides examples and sources of literature relevant to the experiences of students from diverse cultures.

Baylor, Byrd. *Hawk, I'm Your Brother*. New York: Macmillan Children's Book Group, 1986. (P)*

Coerr, Eleanor. *Sadako and the Thousand Paper Cranes*. New York: Dell Publishing Company, Inc., 1977. (P)

Ets, Marie Hall. *Gilberto and the Wind*. New York: Puffin Books, 1978. (P)

Flournoy, Valerie. *The Patchwork Quilt*. New York: Dial Books for Young Readers, 1985.

Haskins, Jim. *One More River to Cross: Twelve Black Americans*. New York: Scholastic, Inc., 1992.

Hoffman, Mary. *Amazing Grace*. New York: Dial Books for Young Readers, 1991. (P)

Levine, Ellen. *I Hate English!* New York: Scholastic, Inc., 1989.

Levine, Ellen. *If Your Name Was Changed at Ellis Island*. New York: Scholastic, Inc., 1992. (P)

Lord, Bette Bao. *In the Year of the Boar and Jackie Robinson*. New York: HarperCollins Children's Books, 1984.

Mathis, Sharon Bell. *The Hundred-Penny Box*. New York: Viking Children's Books, 1975. (P)

Mendez, Phil. *The Black Snowman*. New York: Scholastic, Inc., 1989. (P)

Miles, Miska. *Annie and the Old One*. New York: Little, Brown and Co., 1972. (P)

Mohr, Nicholasa. *Felita*. New York: Dial Books for Young Readers, 1979.

Polacco, Patricia. *Chicken Sunday*. New York: Putnam Publishing Group, 1992. (P)

Read to Me: Recommended Literature for Children Ages Two Through Seven. Sacramento: California Department of Education, 1992. (P)

Readings in Spanish Literature, Kindergarten Through Grade Eight. Sacramento: California Department of Education, 1991.

Recommended Readings in Literature, Kindergarten Through Grade Eight. Sacramento: California Department of Education, 1990.

Steptoe, John. *Mufaro's Beautiful Daughters: An African Tale*. New York: Lothrop, Lee and Shepard Books, 1987. (P)

Steptoe, John. *The Story of Jumping Mouse*. New York: Lothrop, Lee and Shepard Books, 1984. (P)

Surat, Michele Maria. *Angel Child, Dragon Child*. Madison, N.J.: Raintree Steck-Vaughn Publishers, 1983. (P)

Tate, Eleanora E. *Thank You, Dr. Martin Luther King, Jr.* New York: Bantam Books, Inc., 1992.

Taylor, Mildred D. *The Friendship and The Gold Cadillac*. New York: Bantam Books, Inc., 1989.

Taylor, Mildred D. *Mississippi Bridge*. New York: Dial Books, 1990.

Trotter, Tamera, and Joycelyn Allen. *Talking Justice: Six Hundred Two Ways to Build and Promote Racial Harmony*. Saratoga, Calif.: R & E Publishers, Inc., 1993.

Yashima, Taro. *Crow Boy*. New York: Puffin Books, 1976. (P)

---

*Publications marked (P) are mainly for primary grades.
EDITOR'S NOTE: Several of the publications in this list are available from more than one publisher.

A Literature Unit of Study About Vietnamese Children

By Lea Kiapos

Teacher, Morningside Elementary School,
Garden Grove Unified School District;
and Teacher/Consultant, South Basin Writing Project

Angel Child, Dragon Child by Michele Maria Surat is a story about a young girl who has just come to the United States from Vietnam and does not like her new school or her classmates. She especially misses her mother, who had to remain in Vietnam because the family could not afford to pay for her and all the children to come to the United States. Since approximately 70 percent of my students are Vietnamese, I thought this story would elicit a lot of response. I was right! Not only was the response positive and enthusiastic, but the discussion the book generated was among the liveliest, most personal, and most touching that I have ever facilitated.

With most of the stories I use for units of study, I follow a similar format: a prereading stimulus; information about the author and, if applicable, the illustrator; reading; postreading questions at the literal, interpretive, and evaluative levels; and engagement activities.

The entire unit of study may take as little as one class period or as long as two or three days to complete.

Prereading

Show the book to the students, tell them the title, and ask them what they think the story will be about. Ask, too, where they think the story takes place.

About the Author

Michele Maria Surat is a writer and a high school teacher in Richmond, Virginia. She was inspired to write this story to promote understanding between Vietnamese children and their American classmates after hearing a tearfully shared story from one of her students.

Reading

Read the story aloud, taking time to let the children look carefully at the illustrations.

Postreading Questions

These questions are all oral discussion questions presented to the whole group:

1. Why did the children laugh at Hoa?
2. How do you feel when other children laugh at you?
3. What is an Angel Child?
4. What is a Dragon Child?
5. Do you think the principal had a good solution to the problems Hoa and Raymond were having? Tell why or why not.
6. What made Hoa change her mind about telling Raymond her story?
7. How do you think Raymond felt when Hoa told him why she kept a picture of her mother?
8. Describe what you think a Vietnamese fair would be like. What kinds of games or activities would be included?

Engagement Activities

It is not necessary or recommended to do all of the activities listed. Pick those that you feel most comfortable working with and that you think will motivate your students. Be sure to discuss any chosen activity with the whole group so that all students will succeed with the assignment. This procedure helps not only the ESL student but also the reluctant writer and gives all the students plenty of ideas to work with.

1. Students respond to the question: What makes you have an angel face and a dragon face? They use story paper to draw a picture of both, and they write a description of each. The following frame may be helpful:

   When I have an angel face, it is because
   When I have a dragon face, it is because

2. Students write individual miniautobiographies that include their name, place of birth, and when and how they came to the United States (or how their ancestors came to live in the United States if the students were born here). Photographs or illustrations may be included.

3. Students write a brief description of their first day at school. This event can be described as a positive or a negative experience. Papers are

read aloud to the class or shared in small groups.

4. Students brainstorm as a class (or in small groups) about how their experiences during their first day of school could have been better and what could be done to help other new students.

5. Students research the origins of their first names. They can ask their parents why they were given their name and what it means or symbolizes.

6. Students discuss special "at-home" names. If students are willing to share their names, ask them how and why they were given a pet name and what it means.

7. Students write and illustrate a description of the traditional school clothes worn by children in their country of origin. American children can ask their parents, or grandparents, what they had to wear when they first went to school and then write and illustrate a description of those clothes.

8. Students plan a classroom cultural fair. Each student brings in items from his or her culture to be shared, such as food, traditional clothing, toys, items sold to tourists, and photographs. Parents may be invited not only to attend but also to become active participants by wearing traditional clothes, explaining some of the traditions, and describing some of the foods and the occasions during which special meals would be served.

I found that reading *Angel Child, Dragon Child* to my class validated the experiences of my Vietnamese students and enhanced their self-esteem. Equally important, the book gave them a chance to open up and to tell their own stories about leaving Vietnam and arriving as strangers in a new country and a new school. As in the story the non-Asian students in my class gained an awareness of the trials their newly arrived peers had endured. Students mutually respected and accepted each other.

My Name, My Self

By Brenda Borron

Instructor, Irvine Valley College,
Saddleback Community College District

> *"My name is Hue, but you can call me Helen."*
>
> *"My name is Truong, but you can call me Nick."*
>
> *"My name is Dung (yoong) on the roll, but I changed it to Karen."*
>
> *"My name is Rafael, but call me Ralph."*
>
> *"My name is . . . My self."*

When I first read "My Name," by Sandra Cisneros in *The House on Mango Street*, a chord resounded, and I began thinking of my name and my self. How has my name made me what I am? And how have I made my name me?

Then I thought of my students: the *Hues*, the *Truongs*, the *Dungs*, the *Rafaels*, the *Marisols*, the *Guadalupes*, and the *Refugios*. I thought about my students —about their names, their cultures, and our classrooms. And as I thought about these things, I became disturbed.

In Aharon Megged's short story, "The Name," Grandfather Zisskind says to his grandchildren:

> "I'll tell you what ties are. . . . Ties are remembrance! Do you understand? The Russian is linked to his people because he remembers his ancestors. He is called Ivan, his father was called Ivan and his grandfather was called Ivan, back to the first generation. And no Russian has said: From today onwards I shall not be called Ivan because my fathers and my fathers' fathers were called that; I am the first of a new Russian nation which has nothing at all to do with the Ivans. Do you understand? . . .
>
> "And you—you're ashamed to give your son the name Mendele lest it remind you that there were Jews who were called by that name. You believe that his

name should be wiped off the face of the earth. That not a trace of it should remain . . .

"O children, children you don't know what you're doing . . . You're finishing off the work which the enemies of Israel began. They took the bodies away from the world, and you—the name and the memory . . . No continuation, no evidence, no memorial and no name. Not a trace . . ."[1]

"They took the bodies . . . and you—the name and the memory. . . ." By changing our students' names—arbitrarily, accidentally, or even at their request—I believe that we as teachers are taking away their cultures and identities. Conversely, in acknowledging and valuing our students' names, we also acknowledge and value our students and, in turn, their cultures and their values.

After some reflection, I began collecting literature in which name was central to character or theme. As I looked, I tried to find literature from diverse cultures, literature that reflects the diverse cultures of my students. Then I began my lesson.

Steps in the Name Lesson

1. Ask volunteers to tell stories about their names.
2. Have students create a coat of arms for their names and their cultures.
3. Have students investigate how their parents chose the students' names and what those names mean in the family and culture.
4. Have students compile a "The Name I Share" chart for the names they share with famous people, family members, people at school, people in history, and characters in literature.
5. Read literary selections focusing on names; for example:
   a. "The Name" by Aharon Megged
   b. "Major, Major" from *Catch Twenty-Two* by Joseph Heller
   c. The Kizzy section of *Roots* by Alex Haley
   d. Selections from *This Boy's Life: A Memoir* by Tobias Wolff
   e. *Knots on a Counting Rope* by Bill Martin, Jr., and John Archambault
   f. "My Name" from *The House on Mango Street* by Sandra Cisneros
6. Have students research magazine articles on names and naming.
7. Have students locate their names in dictionaries of names and other sources such as *The Lives of the Saints*.
8. Have students write a personal essay on the relationship between their names and their personalities and cultures.
9. Have students share and revise their essays.
10. Have students give speeches about their essays on their names.

As students explore their names, they also explore themselves. Parichat Smittipatana describes what she learned about herself and her culture as she wrote about her name.

Flower from God
By Parichat Smittipatana

Parichat is like silk, a very nice gentle sound which just flows through your mouth. If you pronounce it right, *Parichat* sounds very pretty. It's not too hard, just three simple syllables. You pronounce *Par* like a pear that you eat, *ri* with a short *i*, and then *chat* like chart without the *r*. My name means "flower from God" in Thailand. Also it is the name of a flower whose sweet scent you can smell only in the morning. Most people present these flowers to the monks because of their meaning and their sweet smell. The monks allow only this flower to decorate their temples. The flower represents a virgin with its sweet smell and the purity of a lady with its white petals.

It is a tradition in Thailand, that when a baby is born, its name is given by the monks. It is said that the monks know what we're going to be like in the future; therefore, they know the best names for us. But my parents weren't going to settle for just any name the monks thought up. My dad wanted to call me "Little Brat" because he knew I was going to be spoiled. My mom wanted to call me "Little Angel" because I was a cute baby. They couldn't decide, so they went to the monks.

When I was born, I weighed seven-and-a-half pounds, so my parents brought seven-and-a-half pounds of parichat flowers for the monks when they brought me to the monks to be named. That is how I got my name *Parichat*, as pure as a baby.

I was born in the Chinese year of the ox; that sounds dangerous and wild, but I think it fits me

---

[1] Aharon Megged, "The Name." Translated by Minna Givton. In *Israeli Stories*. Edited by Joel Blocker. New York: Schocken Books, Inc., 1962, p. 102. © 1962 by Schocken Books Inc. Reprinted by permission of the author.

better than "flower from God." I should be sweet, nice, polite, and lady-like, but I'm not.

I don't know why my name was so hard to pick; even my nickname was a problem. My dad wanted to call me "Cherry" because when I was born, our cherry tree gave its first fruit. It was small like me, and red, like my fat cheeks. My mom wanted to call me "Nonk" which means "Little Sister" because I have three older sisters and one older brother. So it was both names for me. I call myself "Little Sister," and everybody else calls me "Little Sister Cherry." When I turned thirteen years old "Cherry" began to sound childish to me, so I changed my nickname to "Sherrie" because it sounded more mature, yet it was still easier for people who can't pronounce my real name to say than "Parichat."

I used to want to change my name to "Patricia" because I'm an American citizen now. I thought I would like to have an American name it wouldn't take everybody ten minutes to say. Doing things like an American—like eating steaks and salads, dressing American, and speaking English—makes me homesick sometimes. I want to speak Thai, which I can no longer remember. The Thai culture and traditions have made me think twice about changing my name. *Parichat* is unique, one-of-a-kind, and it lets me know that part of me is still Thai.

Getting Off Track: Core Literature for All Students

By Mifanwy Patricia Kaiser

English Teacher and Department Chair, Costa Mesa High School, Newport-Mesa Unified School District; and Teacher/Consultant, UCI Writing Project

and Michelle Lindfors

English Teacher, Costa Mesa High School, Newport-Mesa Unified School District; and Teacher/Consultant, UCI Writing Project

What educator would argue with this quotation from Robert Maynard Hutchins: "The best education for the best is the best education for the many"? The concept of equality in education is not only universally ascribed to but also perhaps most easily dealt with when left on the level of warm, fuzzy adages. The issue of tracking versus detracking is controversial. Regardless of whether

the students labeled remedial are scheduled into classes geared toward a homogeneous ability level or are scheduled into the same classes as the students labeled advanced, they should all be taught a challenging curriculum. Remedial students should *not* be subjected to a monotonous stream of work sheets or grammar lessons.

When teachers talk about placing students, the teachers of advanced placement (AP) or honors students almost never talk about what their students *cannot* do. The students are spoken of in terms of what they *can* do. Conversely, when teachers talk about remedial students, they discuss and place those students according to what they *cannot* do but rarely talk about what their students *can* do. Labeling students advanced, honors, remedial, special education, or non-English proficient/limited-English proficient (NEP/LEP) invites teachers to expect no more or no less than the label conveys.

Recent research studies have shown that almost all heterogeneously grouped students make academic gains. A couple of years ago, we decided to see how well Hutchins' theory worked. What follows is the story of what happened when high school students in remedial and advanced placement classes were taught the same literature lessons. We told the students nothing of the meaning of any of the literature we studied but allowed them to negotiate meaning through reader-response activities and collaboration. Results from our project not only confirm Hutchins' theory but also suggest that the impact of this approach on students' self-esteem can be phenomenal.

Like all good things, this project evolved serendipitously. During the summer of 1986, we attended the California Literature Project Institute, where we were charged with designing a literature unit for our students. Patricia developed one for her class, composed of ninth through twelfth grade students with specific learning needs such as those provided for in the resource specialist program, special education, and ESL; and Michelle developed one for her advanced placement seniors. Never one to shy away from a challenge, Patricia wrote a lesson to teach her so-called remedial students the difficult poem "The Hollow Men" by T. S. Eliot.

In the fall, before beginning Joseph Conrad's *Heart of Darkness,* Michelle borrowed Patricia's unit on "The Hollow Men" because both works have similar themes. The *Model Curriculum Standards* encourages teachers to adopt core literature for all students.[1] Our school was highly tracked, and the remedial English curriculum was, to say the least, very different from that for regular or advanced students. In spite of this disparity, when Michelle borrowed Patricia's lesson to use with her AP students, neither of us thought of the ramifications. But after we had taught the lesson and informally compared the final essays from both classes, we were nothing short of amazed at the similarities between the classes in the responses to the meaning of the work. Patricia's students may not have had the same command of words as Michelle's, but they were just as capable of understanding T. S. Eliot, thinking critically, and writing about "The Hollow Men" without the teacher explicating the poem for them. The results achieved from our students' writing are an eloquent argument for getting off track and for allowing *all* students access to a challenging curriculum.

A ninth grade student with a fifth grade reading score wrote as follows:

> I think the peom "The Hollow Men" means, men are walking around kind of not caring what's going on in life. The men's lives are just a meaningless wandering around the world. In stanza on Mr. Elliot talks about scarecrows. Mr. Elliot was trying to say that scarecrows are hollow because they do not have a heart or feelings toward anybody or anything. In stanza two Mr. Elliot is trying to say that they do not have any eyes, so they can not see. The scarecrow is wearing diguises. In stanza three Mr. Elliot is talking about lips that do not kiss and stone images. What he means by stone images that the hollow men are seeing shadows and lips that don't kiss, you show love when you kiss and lips when you do not kiss you are not showing love. In stanza four Mr. Elliot is talking about hollow men that are groping and avoiding speech. What Mr. Elliot means by groping and avoiding speech is when someone is groping they can not see, so the men can not see that they are hollow inside. They are trying to avoid speech so they will not have to show there feelings or love towards anybody. Stanza five means that life is meaningless if you do not have faith in yourself.

[1]*Model Curriculum Standards, Grades Nine Through Twelve.* Sacramento: California Department of Education, 1985.

This first draft is, of course, unedited. In keeping with the writing process, the student cleaned up his errors for the final paper.

An LEP student from Patricia's class who had been in America for only two years wrote the following:

> In the poems, the hollow men were the stuffed men. They are quiet and meaningless, gesture without motion. The hollow men were dreaming of the death's in the twilight kingdom, and their were the hollow valley were they avoid speech and sightless. The death's causes by the shadow of the scarecrow, the scarecrow is hollow, had no feeling, blind, and helpless. To be hollow men mean quiet, meaningless, and gesture without motion.

In comparison are excerpts from two of Michelle's AP students. The first one states that:

> T. S. Eliot's poem, "The Hollow Men," contains a potent series of haunting images in which he analyzes the rather futile existence of a race that has lost it's humanistic qualities. Eliot pictures mankind suspended in an emotional vacuum, void of faith or animation. His people are numb, their surroundings are depressing (to say the least), and their lives are meaningless. In such a world, Eliot shows us that man ceases to exist.

And another follows:

> T. S. Eliot, in his melancholy poem, "The Hollow Men," describes men who have lost faith in themselves, in other men, and in a supreme being. They have become only empty, soul-less shells. The men described by T. S. Eliot in his poem, "The Hollow Men," are hollow both literally and symbolically. The literal hollowness is suggested by the poet's comparison of the men with scarecrows. Because the men lack faith, their souls as well as their bodies are symbolically hollow.

Both of Michelle's AP students cited the same images from the poem as Patricia's students had; and although the AP students expressed themselves more eloquently, all papers contain remarkably similar statements of meaning. This discovery excited us, and we began to talk about pursuing other collaborative lessons between the classes. That year our students also studied Nathaniel Hawthorne's *The Scarlet Letter* and Arthur Miller's *Death of a Salesman.*

Of course, teaching a complex poem like "The

The self-esteem of all students is reinforced when they realize that they . . . have something important to talk or write about when studying difficult curriculum.

MIFANWY PATRICIA KAISER AND MICHELLE LINDFORS

Hollow Men" to any group of students involves more than xeroxing the poem and assigning an essay. All our lessons grew out of reader-response theory, which allows for many distinct and even contradictory interpretations of the literature. A delicate balance exists between encouraging each reader to create his or her own personal meaning and asking the students to collaborate on discovering meaning. In keeping with the reader-response theory, we focused less on formalistic concerns, such as literary terminology or structure, and more on generating personal response and meaning.

The unit on "The Hollow Men" began by having students visualize the word *hollow* and list things that can be hollow. Next, we told the students the title of the poem and asked them to quickwrite their descriptions of hollow men. (A quickwrite is a brief response, prompted by a teacher, to a topic.) After each step in the lesson, students shared and collaborated on their ideas. After we had read the poem aloud and distributed copies, the students answered in their journals several open-ended questions adapted from Robert Probst's reader-response questions. (See "Dialogue with a Text," which appears elsewhere in this publication.) Then the class was divided into five groups, each of which focused on one of the sections in the poem. The task for all the groups was to create a title reflecting the meaning of the section, to defend their choice by citing evidence from each stanza, and prepare a dramatic reading of the stanza for the rest of the class. After the students had thought, written, and talked about the poem, we asked them to write an essay explaining the meaning.

After this activity we decided to tackle a longer work, *The Scarlet Letter.* Michelle's students read the entire novel, including the introductory section, "The Custom-House"; but Patricia devised a budget tour for her students. This technique has proven successful in teaching difficult literature to less-prepared students. Students read a shortened version of the *original* work of art, not an easier version written by someone removed from the classroom. The *teacher* decides which material in the original work is not necessary for students to be able to comprehend the work of art. The beauty of the budget tour is that the student still uses the original work and is not singled out as needing the abridged version. The same activities to make the work meaningful that are used in studying the full-length sections are employed: reader-response activities, visualization, journal entries, scripting, understanding vocabulary in context, writing to learn, and jigsaw dramatic reading.

Although students read slightly different versions of *The Scarlet Letter*, the activities for both classes were the same. The students did interpretive drawings to show their understanding of the initial scene in which Hester is forced to stand on the scaffold in shame. They also wrote a series of interior monologues in which they pretended to be various characters (Hester, Dimmesdale, Chillingworth, or Pearl) during each of the four scaffold scenes. The students were asked to write interior monologues to demonstrate their grasp of the events and the meanings in the novel.

Another activity featured the writing of show, not tell, paragraphs about the characters, a technique we learned and refined with Rebekah Caplan at the UCI Writing Project Summer Institute. (See "A Training Program for Student Writers" by Rebekah Caplan, which appears elsewhere in this publication.) We made an interesting discovery with this activity. The following is a show, not tell, paragraph that one of Patricia's LEP students wrote about Pearl after he had read chapter six of the novel:

> She unfriendly. She had to live along and she had only mother she never take and look some children She aspect was imbued with a Spell of the infinite

variety in one child the were many the children comperehend. She Smart so understanding child. the most people hate there looked at her. She make something right a mean people make all the children in this town eerie her then. She Don't have a friendy.

You will agree that the paragraph is almost unintelligible and that perhaps this student should not be working with *The Scarlet Letter*. However, when the student was asked to draw what he understood from listening to the reading of the chapter in which Hester stands on the scaffold in shame, notice how much information he understands, as shown in the illustration below.

Hester is standing with the child, a rosebush is beside the prison, the sun is shining, and people are jeering at Hester.

At the conclusion of our study, we gave our students a variety of essay topics to choose from. Having been trained in the stages of the writing process as a part of the Writing Project, we guided our students through the writing of several drafts, allowing plenty of time for peer response and revision.

When the student was asked to draw what he understood from listening to the reading of the chapter in which Hester stands on the scaffold in shame, notice how much information he understands.

Hester is standing with the child, a rosebush is beside the prison, the sun is shining, and people are jeering at Hester.

In one of the essay topics, the students were asked to identify who they thought was the greatest sinner in the novel. And again we received papers with remarkably similar ideas. We got varied responses: some thought Dimmesdale was the greatest sinner, and some thought Chillingworth was.

Excerpts from students' writing about Arthur Dimmesdale, first from Patricia's students and then from Michelle's follow:

> Arthur's sin is the greatest of the three because he didn't ask God to forgive him . . . His sin was also the greatest because he was untrue to himself and to others. An example of this is that in his sermon, he didn't come right out an tell the townspeople of his sin. He made it seem like everything was fine, when it wasn't.
>
> Then he watched her take her punishment and he did not tell the town's people he was the father. He was a leader and his responsibility was to preach about sin and guilt and while he was doing this he was actually lying to the towns people and himself and because of that and his guilt he put himself through a Hell on earth.

* * *

> "To the untrue man, the whole universe is false,—it is impalpable—it shrinks to nothing within his grasp" (p. 134). Nathaniel Hawthorne's *The Scarlet Letter* conveys the concept that those who lack honesty and truthfulness will suffer because of the falsehoods that their lives represent. Arthur Dimmsdale, a representative of God with basically good morals and intentions, succumbs to the worldly sin of adultery with Hester Prynne. Hester faces the ignominious ridicule of the townspeople, while the "man of God" conceals his guilt under the guise of his prestigious calling. The minister feels a deep sense of sorrow, and he suffers greatly from his tragic weakness, which is his inability to acknowledge his guilt in public. Additionally, Dimmesdale's Puritan values lead the minister to rationalize with himself concerning the importance of his position. He, therefore, compounds the original sin by adding dishonesty and hypocrisy.

Students' responses about Roger Chillingworth appear next. The first excerpt is from Patricia's student, followed by one from Michelle's:

> Rodgers sin was torcher and attented murder, and I feel that would be a greater sin than to have an afair.

When Roger sinned he sinned, out of hateridness and he planned on taking someones life. In my eyes I feel that Rodgers sin was the greatest sin and that there was nothing wrong with an afair out of wedlock.

*   *   *

The last of Hawthorne's sinners presented in his novel is Chillingworth. Hester's husband, the man supposedly the most wronged and sinned against, becomes the worst sinner. The mode of revenge he takes upon Dimmesdale is truly evil. So evil in Hawthorne's eyes, that his descriptions of Chillingworth often refer to Satan . . . . Chillingworth's sin is worse than that of Hester and Dimmesdale because theirs was merely a sin of passion, whereas his is utterly evil.

In the spring we decided to bring our classes together for a unit on Arthur Miller's *Death of a Salesman*, since our classrooms were next to each other and our classes were scheduled at the same time. All of the activities for this unit were done with the students in groups of four, two from Michelle's and two from Patricia's class.

We first asked our students to conduct an interview with their parents. We gave them questions that focused on the parent-child relationships and the American dream—themes that we wanted to pursue during our study of this tragedy. The students could tape or write the responses. We then presented a minilecture on the definition of tragedy and the tragic hero. Next, we distributed a list of homework questions designed to get students to think about the play, had the groups discuss them, and present their findings. The groups also adopted a character to analyze orally and in writing. After we had finished reading the play, we had the students come to school one evening to view the film and eat popcorn. By far the most popular project, aside from the eating of doughnuts on the final day, was the making of collages. The groups selected one of the themes from the play (illusion versus reality, fulfilled versus unfulfilled dreams, the American dream, or parent-child relationships) to portray in a collage.

The culminating writing project was an essay in which the students compared the characters in *Death of a Salesman* to those in either *The Scarlet Letter* or *Oedipus Rex*. And, again, we quote from students' papers, first from Patricia's student and then from Michelle's.

Bif Loman is a tragic hero because he doesn't live up to what is expected of him by his father and this causes him much shame. He suffers as, he doesn't really know what his dreams for himself really are. But when he finds his dream his father has trouble accepting and understanding it, the fact that both he and his father are just a dime a dozen is hard for willy to accept. Bif stands up for what he believes by finally being honest with his family, I feel that he wanted to do this for a long time but he had to go through the shame and suffering first!

*   *   *

Biff's act of shame or horror was his refusal to face reality after discovering his father's affair. He gave up on life, and continued to live in an dillusion. His lack of happiness and inability to hold down a job provoked and prolonged his suffering. He gained self-knowledge upon realizing the phony life he had been living. He was trying to be something he wasn't: a leader, a success. "I am not a leader of men, Willy, and neither are you" (p. 1342). His affirmation comes as a result of the recognition of his insatiable desire to conform to his father's image of him.

What did we learn from this classroom research? Our initial reservations about the hows and whys of tracking were reinforced. Patricia's students deserved and could handle a challenging curriculum; Michelle's more reserved students blossomed when they were not overshadowed by their more vocal classmates. NEP/LEP students perceive much more aurally than they can process into writing, and they can handle challenging works of literature. And, it goes without saying, the self-esteem of *all* students is reinforced when they realize that they do, in fact, have something important to talk and write about when studying difficult curriculum, whether it be in kindergarten or college.

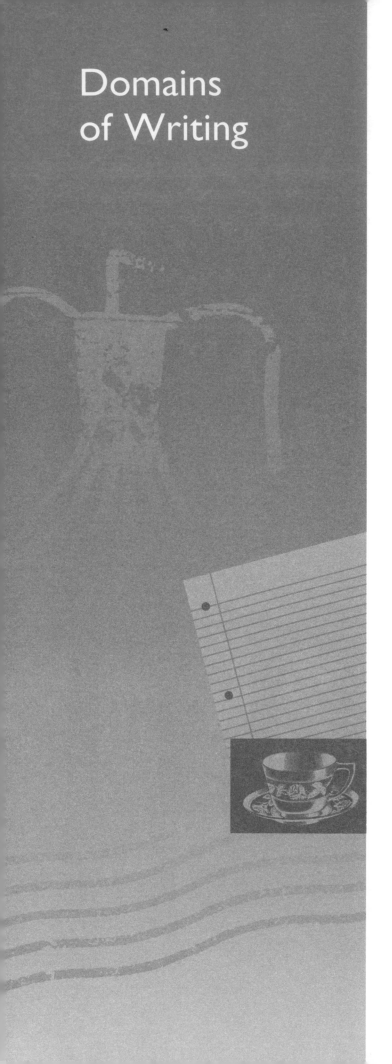

Domains of Writing

Teaching the Domains of Writing

By Nancy McHugh

Former Director, Writing Competencies,
Los Angeles Unified School District

Dividing the "universe of discourse" into domains is not new. Traditionally, there have been at least three domains in the curriculum: descriptive, narrative, and expository writing. However, until recently, the widespread practice had been for teachers in the elementary grades to concentrate on *creative* writing (mainly imaginative/narrative writing) and for teachers in the secondary grades to emphasize expository writing almost to the exclusion of other domains.

The Los Angeles Unified School District reintroduced the broad concept of domains in writing in 1976 when it printed and distributed a description of its composition program and suggested four domains: sensory/descriptive, imaginative/ narrative, practical/informative, and analytical/ expository. Several theories were behind this move. One was that students do better in one domain than in another; therefore, the curriculum should have balance to provide equal opportunity for success for all students, regardless of their abilities, and plans for careers or continuing education. Another theory was that, although the domains are not totally discrete (indeed, they often blend one into the other), each has a place in writing/thinking development; and all are necessary for competent writing. With the most difficult expository task, a person probably uses all four domains to develop a theme. Another theory for using the four domains was that, although any mode can probably be used in any domain (poem as description, as narrative, as information, as analysis), working in separate domains encourages the teacher to use a wide variety of modes and audiences. A teacher may plan lessons exclusive to one domain at a time (a domain as a unit) and explore the variety of modes within that domain (sensory/descriptive domain: journal entries, tone poems, informal essays, letters, monologues, and so forth); or a teacher may choose to work with a theme or an experience and move from domain to domain and mode to mode crafting communication for a variety of audiences and purposes. Preplanning is essential, even though the teacher may choose to follow up an in-class lead and deviate from the plans occasionally.

Description of the Four Domains of Writing

The four domains are categories for defining somewhat exclusive purposes of writing. Part of writing competence is having a clear concept of the intent for the writing, including audience, and being able to organize in the mode (form) that best fits that intention. In the early grades the teacher may want to select the mode best suited for the domain and writing task. In the upper grades the teacher may want to encourage students to select the mode that seems most reasonable, perhaps providing a variety from which to choose. For example, after a prewriting exercise of listening to a record, the students may want to express their feelings about the experience. They will be using the sensory/descriptive domain. The students may be assigned a word poem or a paragraph, or they may be asked to express their feelings, and a number of ways might be suggested: Dear Diary, a word poem, haiku, a letter to a friend, and so forth.

The easiest of the four domains in writing is sensory/descriptive because it deals with the concrete. In this domain a student tries to present a picture in words, one so vivid that the reader or listener can recapture many of the same perceptions and feelings that the writer has had. The writer draws on all the senses to capture this picture of a person, place, or object. In this domain student writers must focus and sharpen their powers of perception and ability to choose precise words.

A second domain is imaginative/narrative (creative) writing in which the writer's main intent is to tell a story—sometimes real, sometimes imaginary. The forms may range widely, but the main idea is to tell what happens. In this domain student writers build on the first domain in that they must put descriptive detail into a time/order frame. Students learn ordering, transition, balance, suspense, climax, beginnings, and endings. This domain requires students to become more adept in using verb forms.

In the third domain, practical/informative, students are required to provide clear information; often the writing in this domain takes the form of what might be considered social and business correspondence; for example, letters, memorandums, directions, and notes. The main intent is for the writer to present information without much analysis or explanation. Working in this domain, students learn to give attention to detail, accuracy, clarity and appropriateness of tone, and mastery of forms like the letter.

A fourth domain is analytical/expository, which is the most difficult because it is the most abstract. In this domain the intention is to analyze, explain, persuade, and influence. The writers tell why and how about a subject. They borrow from the other three domains to make their points, and they emphasize organization and development.

Intent and Suggested Modes of Each Domain

The chart on page 116 identifies the intent of each domain and suggests possible modes of writing within the domains.

Note that the same prewriting experience may be used as the stimulus for a variety of exercises in the domains. For example, after popping corn, one may describe in a variety of modes, explain the process, write advertisements, explain popcorn's origin in a folk tale, analyze the various uses of popcorn, or attack or defend it as a food.

A Plan to Introduce the Domains of Writing

Depending on your students' needs and the objectives of your course, you may want to spend from a few days to several weeks on each of the four domains. Provided below is a five-day plan to introduce the domains of writing to your students:

Objectives: Students will be able to awaken their senses, use clustering to elicit language, produce metaphoric description, create poetic forms, fashion commercials/advertisements, form interview questions, vary sentences, write exposition.

Materials and equipment: Popcorn or other suitable sense stimulus, paper and pen, chalkboard, overhead projector.

Sensory/ Descriptive	Imaginative/ Narrative	Practical/ Informative	Analytical/ Expository
Intent: to describe in vivid sensory detail; to express individual feelings	**Intent: to tell what happens, real or imaginary; to put in a time sequence**	**Intent: to present basic information clearly**	**Intent: to explain, analyze, persuade**
Possible modes:	*Possible modes:*	*Possible modes:*	*Possible modes:*
• Journal entry	• Anecdotes	• Postcard message	• Single paragraph/ topic sentence plus support
• Diary entry	• Limericks	• Friendly notes of various kinds (invitation, thank you, acknowledgment of gift, and so forth)	• Editorial
• Personal letter	• Diary entries (fictional and real)		• Little theme (three paragraphs)
• Personal essay	• Captions to cartoons, pictures	• Lecture/class notes	• Letter to editor
• Poem (haiku, diamante,[1] cinquain, catalogue, prose poem, acrostic, and many others)	• Dialogues	• Memorandum	• Speech
	• Monologues	• Directions/steps in a process	• Dialogue to persuade
• Monologue	• Scripts	• Self-evaluation statements	• Reviews and reports
• Dialogue	• Capsule stories (outline for plot or reconstruction of a cartoon strip)	• Commercials	• Poems (to persuade or analyze, make analogies)
• Advertising copy		• News report	• Multiparagraph themes (describe/ conclude; narrate/ conclude; analyze/ conclude; analyze/ persuade; define, classify, defend a judgment, interpret literature)
• Character sketches	• Biographical and autobiographical sketches	• Accident report	
	• Vignettes	• Business letters (complaint, order, request for information, and so forth)	
[1]A diamante is a seven-line poem written in the shape of a diamond. The form of the poem is as follows: one noun, two adjectives, three participles, four words that form a phrase, three participles, two adjectives, and one noun.	• Short stories	• Application	• Library/research paper
	• Folk tales	• Summary	
	• Myths	• Precis	
	• Allegories	• Scientific abstract	
	• Ballads and other poetic forms (story emphasis)	• Encyclopedia paragraphs	

4 Domains
Writing

> *Part of writing competence is having a clear concept of the intent for the writing, including audience, and being able to organize in the mode (form) that best fits that intention.*
>
> NANCY McHUGH

Prewriting: Popcorn (if possible, popped in class) is sampled by students, who examine it minutely and cluster all of their responses. Students share clusters (in groups, orally, on chalkboard). These experiences and ideas form the basis for later writing. (For more suggestions on using popcorn in a prewriting exercise, see Sue Rader Willett's practical idea, which appears in "The Process" section of this book, and the section of the book entitled "Clustering: A Prewriting Process.")

Composing skills: Students write two or three of their cluster ideas in complete sentences and check each other's work. The teacher shows them how to transform these sentences into metaphoric statements: The popcorn is white = The popcorn is as white as cotton puffs. The teacher also reviews the form for a diamante or cinquain. Subsequent to later assignments, the teacher reviews the format and special rules for a commercial or advertisement, a descriptive essay, an interview, and an expository essay.

Writing Task 1: (Differentiated) Choose one or more of the following to try:

1. Write another of your cluster ideas as a metaphoric statement.
2. Write several of your ideas in metaphoric statements, and put them together to form a catalogue poem.
3. Write a cinquain or diamante, including one of your metaphors in it.

Editing and evaluation: Students share their work in pairs or small groups, making suggestions for revision or corrections. The focus is on "help" and "appreciation," not "criticism."

Extension activities:[2] (To be used over the next three or four days, depending on the nature of the class):

---

[2]These activities were based on ideas provided by Kathy Schultheis, Cadre II, Writing Competence Project, Carver Junior High School, Los Angeles Unified School District.

Sensory/Descriptive

1. Expand your original clustered ideas into a multiparagraph sensory/description. Describe popcorn before, during, and after popping it. Try to involve as many senses as possible in your description. Try to include a few metaphors as well.

   NOTE: The teacher may present a sentence combining exercise as a composing skill prior to this exercise or the next. Make your writing so vivid that your reader can see, smell, hear, and taste the popcorn.

Imaginative/Narrative

2. Think of a memory associated with popcorn. It could involve sitting in a movie theater or stringing popcorn on a Christmas tree or whatever event comes to mind. Remember where you were, who you were with, and how you felt. Then, write a narrative account of your popcorn memory.

Practical/Informative

3. Create a set of instructions for how to make popcorn. Make your step-by-step process so clear that a reader following your directions will be able to make popcorn.

Analytical/Expository

4. Persuade a friend either to eat the movie-theater style popcorn, which is drenched in calories, or to try one of the new light-calorie varieties. Anticipate that your readers may prefer the other style of popcorn, and give logical reasons to overcome objections they might have. Write your persuasive paper in the form of a friendly letter and use a tone suited to your audience.

Writing Assignments in Each Domain

The following are descriptions of writing assignments that are specifically focused on each of the four domains. You may use these as points of departure to develop your own lesson plans.

Sensory/Descriptive Domain

Observing and Organizing Details

OBJECTIVES

1. Students will be able to sharpen their senses and deepen their sensitivities to sensory impressions.
2. Students will be able to write vivid, specific, creative sentences.
3. Students will be able to use figurative language.
4. Students will be able to write effective, coherent, organized descriptions.

MATERIALS

1. Holiday cards
2. Paintings or photographs

PREWRITING ACTIVITIES

1. The teacher will present several greeting cards and ask each student to select a card.
2. The students will look carefully at the picture on their cards and concentrate on remembering as many details as they can.
3. Each student will cluster as many details of his or her picture as possible in one minute without looking at the picture.
4. The students will write titles for their pictures based on the details they have created.
5. The teacher will help students to state in a sentence the main impression that they received from the picture and ask them to develop it with the specific details from the cluster.

COMPOSING SKILLS

1. Make use of descriptive words. Describe sensations of feeling, hearing, seeing, smelling, or tasting.

   Copy each adjective and after each write at least one noun that completes a picture.

   Example: *Blazing fire, blazing furnace, blazing sun*

bitter	dazzling	roaring	sharp
buzzing	gritty	rough	tart
clanging	moist	rushing	whizzing

2. Use words as nouns and adjectives. Write one sentence using the word as a noun and another as an adjective.

   Example: *Flower*

   Noun—My favorite *flower* is the lilac.

   Adjective—Dad exhibits lilacs in the *flower* show.

fruit	house	guest	tree	egg
silver	winter	song	program	dress

3. Make a comparison: Compare things which are not really alike, recognizing one similarity between two basically unlike objects or ideas.

   a. Students will work in small groups of three or four. They will examine all the cards and identify at least a major impression and the details which evoke it for each card.
   b. The cards will be circulated until each group gets a new set to work with.
   c. As students view cards, they will respond by pointing out similarities they see between the object illustrated and something else.
   d. Students write a simile or metaphor about a holiday card.

4. Review elements of complete sentences.

WRITING TASK

Write an interesting paragraph in which you discuss your painting or photograph in close detail. Try to make the reader (your audience is a pen pal) see your painting or picture as vividly as possible and feel what you feel for it. You should write complete sentences and also vary your sentence structure to create interest.

EDITING PLANS

Students exchange papers and read them aloud in small groups. They will make needed corrections.

EVALUATION

Teacher selects examples and duplicates them. Students are to underline the phrase(s) expressing the main impression in each paragraph and to discuss whether or not there are enough supporting details and whether any of the details do not support the main idea.

EXTENSION ACTIVITIES

Students create their own greeting cards and write a poem based on their experience with sensory impressions: haiku, acrostic verse, or starters.

Imaginative/Narrative Domain

Point of View

OBJECTIVE

Students will be able to narrate an imaginary experience using the voice of a person.

MATERIALS

Chapter Three in John Steinbeck's *The Grapes of Wrath*, a chapter devoted entirely to a turtle that makes a torturous crossing of a main highway, during which it is flipped like tiddledywinks after a pickup truck runs over the edge of its shell

PREWRITING ACTIVITIES

1. Using cartoons, pictures, poems, and so forth about turtles, make observations and discuss turtles.
2. Read orally Chapter Three of *The Grapes of Wrath.*
3. Discuss the changes that would have to be made in the story if it were told from a different point of view; e.g., the turtle's.
4. Discuss possible points of view.

WRITING TASK/COMPOSING SKILLS

First, choose one of the following to cross a highway as the turtle had to do:

blind man	chicken	snake
puppy	child	boy scout and old lady
drunk	tarantula	a person or animal of your choosing

Then choose one of the following to come down the highway and confront the one you chose above:

Hell's Angels	pickup truck
Marine Corps Band	a group or vehicle of
moving van	your choosing

Then, using the voice of one of the participants, describe the trip across the highway.

EXTENSION ACTIVITIES/EVALUATION

With sound effects record the good papers on tape.

EVALUATION

Teacher reads final drafts holistically. (See the "Evaluation" section of this book for a discussion of holistic scoring.)

EXTENSION ACTIVITIES

Those who wish may read their stories to the entire class.

Practical/Informative Domain

Balloon Experiment

OBJECTIVES

1. Students will be able to address postcards.
2. Students will be able to write simple, clear, and concise directions.
3. Students will be able to use map and measuring skills.
4. Students will be able to draw logical conclusions from given facts.
5. Students will experience a "space" launching.

MATERIALS

1. Postcards, pens, stamps
2. Maps of California

3. Balloons (ordinary rubber balloons), string
4. Helium

PREWRITING ACTIVITIES

1. Class discusses space launchings, lighter-than-air aircraft, the properties of gases, and the properties of helium.
2. Students are each assigned to bring to school a postcard and stamp. Further, they are told that if they fulfill the assignment, a surprise will await them.
3. At the next class meeting, the surprise, the balloon experiment, is revealed and discussed.

COMPOSING SKILLS

1. The teacher presents instructions on how to address a postcard.
2. The teacher reviews sentence and paragraph structure.
3. The teacher reviews the development of a paragraph by successive steps.
4. The teacher reviews the necessity to write clear and complete sentences.
5. The teacher stresses the necessity to use correct forms in addressing and writing postcards.

WRITING TASK

Write your address in the proper space on the postcard, and put a postage stamp on the card. Using an appropriate salutation, write a message on the postcard to the person who will find it. In your message, tell this person that you are doing an experiment for your physical science class; therefore, you are requesting that this person first write on the postcard the names of the city and cross streets where the postcard was found and, secondly, to drop the postcard in the nearest mailbox. Use an appropriate complimentary close and sign your name.

EDITING PLANS

Teacher will edit the rough drafts of the messages (before the messages are written on the postcards).

EVALUATION

Using a rubric, the student and then the teacher will evaluate the completed postcard. (See the "Evaluation" section of this book for suggestions.)

EXTENSION ACTIVITIES

Punch holes in the postcards and fill the balloons with helium. Then attach two or three helium-filled balloons to the postcards. A month later, most of the postcards should have been returned, depending on climatic factors. Then compile a list of the places where the postcards were found. The students are assigned to locate these places on the map, to measure the distance each balloon traveled, and perhaps to write a complete report of the experiment.

Analytical/Expository Domain

A Letter to Throckmorton (U. S. History)

OBJECTIVES

1. Students will be able to formulate explanations and a rationale for the American Revolution.
2. Students will be able to organize a friendly letter.
3. Students will be able to develop logical sequence in written arguments.
4. Students will be able to analyze historic events from the perspective of the eighteenth century.

MATERIALS

1. Any good U. S. history textbook
2. Copy of fictitious letter from a former teenage classmate in England

PREWRITING ACTIVITIES

With readings, discussions, and lectures, the teacher and students explore in depth the causes and events of the Revolutionary War period.

COMPOSING SKILLS

The teacher and students review the form for a friendly letter.

WRITING TASK

Pretend you are a young person in the colonies about 1776, just after the Declaration of Independence was issued. You still remember your good friend, Throckmorton Algire, with whom you went to school in London before you and your parents came to the New World. Throckmorton has written to you that he is surprised that the colonies are now in open rebellion against King George; Throckmorton is sure it is treason. And he is confused about the reasons why such a rebellion developed. In a recent letter to you, he asked you these questions: "Do you think such a treasonous thing as the Declaration of Independence is defensible?" and "Who will win this war?"

Read Throckmorton's letter carefully and write back to him.

Keep in mind that Throckmorton gets news from a great distance and that his letter indicates that almost everyone in England thinks of the "patriots" as traitors. You will need to explain carefully and logically how the current rebellion developed. You should include facts and your own opinion to help your friend understand both the sequence of events and the prevailing colonial spirit.

EDITING PLANS

Students may check each other's letters for facts, tone, and letter form.

EVALUATION

Teacher develops a rubric for correctness of letter form, logicalness and completeness of both facts and concepts, and perception of the prevailing sentiments of eighteenth century America.

EXTENSION ACTIVITIES

Without identifying writers, teacher chooses especially effective and ineffective letters and reads them to the class (ineffective first). Then the class votes on whether or not their views would have been changed if they had been Throckmorton. If possible, the teacher should read letters from a different class to avoid embarrassment of authors.

Providing students with practice in all four domains of writing will enable them to hone specific writing skills (use of concrete diction and figurative language, sequencing, transition, construction of a logical argument, and so forth) and make them aware of their options as writers. Then, in the future, the students can consciously integrate elements from the different domains to suit their purpose and audience.

Practical Ideas for Teaching the Domains of Writing

Expanding the Different Domains of Writing

By Julie Simpson

English Teacher, Sunny Hills High School,
Fullerton Joint Union High School District;
and Teacher/Consultant, UCI Writing Project

In designing the first direct writing assessment, California educators chose a paradigm of domains of writing based on James Moffett's *Active Voice: A Writing Program Across the Curriculum.*[1] Acknowledging that one kind of writing uses rhetorical devices from other types, the developers of the writing assessments selected 11 specific types of writing to be tested, dividing them into eight types at grade eight and eight at grade ten.

Chart A, "Writing Types," on the next page identifies 11 types of writing and demonstrates how they overlap the four general domains that Nancy McHugh described in her article titled "Teaching the Domains of Writing."

All types of writing use descriptive techniques—either to create vivid sensory details that paint a picture in words or to report information clearly and with accurate detail. Thus, it is important to sequence activities to provide a variety of writing lessons and to present a scaffold of writing instruction to facilitate skill building and carryover of concepts from one kind of writing to another.

Chart B, "Suggested Writing Topics," points out some of the overlapping features between and among types and suggests some writing topics for a variety of classroom projects. Topics are included for a literature lesson on *Little Red Riding Hood*, an exercise on reading maps, and a U.S. history lesson on the Clay Compromise of 1850.

The scaffolding for the activities in a literature lesson for *Little Red Riding Hood* appears in Chart C, "Scaffolding."

Because writing is also a part of the mathematics standards, students should be provided with a variety of writing experiences at various levels of instruction in mathematics. Open-ended questions probably fit most readily into these categories: Report of Information, Problem Solution, and Interpretation. Working to create mathematics situations to write about, a teacher might try to:

- Give a problem to a student to explain over the telephone to a friend. (Report of Information)
- Ask students to write a set of step-by-step instructions for drawing a geometric figure. (Report of Information)
- Ask students to create a real-life mathematics problem (buying something on credit or figuring measurements to build something). They write the information as a word problem, write the formula for solving it, and write an explanation of how to arrive at the solution. (Problem Solution)
- Present a word problem that requires students to make inferences to solve. Students write an explanation of what they have to know to be able to solve the problem. (Interpretation)

Providing students with practice in all types of writing within various content areas will expand their writing repertoire and help them to see how learning is integrated.

EDITOR'S NOTE: The domains in this article were from the California Learning Assessment System (CLAS), which developed and drew on projects and advice from members of the California Writing Projects and California Literature Projects.

[1]James Moffett. *Active Voice: A Writing Program Across the Curriculum* (Second edition). Portsmouth, N.H.: Boynton Cook Publishers, Inc., 1992.

Los Angeles Unified School District's **Domains of Writing**	Story	Autobiographical Incident	Firsthand Biography Sketch	Observational Writing	Report of Information	Problem Solution	Speculation	Interpretation	Reflection	Controversial Issue	Evaluation
Sensory/Descriptive											
• Use vivid sensory detail.	X	X	X	X	X				X	X	X
• Portray individual perspective.	X	X	X	X			X	X	X	X	
Imaginative/Narrative											
• Tell what happens.	X	X	X	X	X						
• Order events in a time sequence.	X	X	X	X	X				X		
Practical/Informative											
• Report information clearly.			X	X	X	X	X	X		X	X
• Provide accurate details.			X	X	X	X	X	X		X	X
Analytical/Expository											
• Explain clearly.						X	X	X	X	X	X
• Persuade.						X	X	X	X	X	X
• Analyze.						X	X	X	X	X	X

Chart A. Writing Types

Chart B. Suggested Writing Topics

Type	Features	Little Red Riding Hood *topics*	*Map-reading topics*	*Clay Compromise topics*
Story	Narrate a well-told story of a particular incident in the writer's life: • Use first-person point of view. • Use vivid sensory details to portray the incident. • Include people moving, speaking, and acting. • Order events logically. • Create tension to sustain interest. • Include significance to writer.	Retell the story of *Little Red Riding Hood* from the grandmother's point of view.		
Autobiographical Incident	Narrate a fictional event and provide: • A clear beginning, middle, and end • Conflict that motivates a character into action • Character development from dialogue, action, and comments from others • Vivid sensory detail to establish tone, setting, and motivation • Plot elements that fit together logically, even in fantasy • A story that has a logical turning point, or climax	Write about an incident when you learned that the world is not as ideal as you had assumed. Write the story of this incident and your feelings as the events unfolded.	Describe an incident when you became lost trying to get somewhere. Write the story of that incident and your feelings as the events unfolded.	Write about an incident when you had to compromise. Include enough details to show what the problem was and how the compromise solved the problem.
Firsthand Biographical Sketch	Portray a particular personality and physical traits through incidents and description: • Show the person through action, dialogue, and comments from others. • Use vivid sensory details. • Select details to show the writer's attitude toward the subject (not just a catalogue of statistics). • Tie incidents and description together logically.	Write a sketch of one of your grandparents who is special to you. Include several incidents to show your reader what is special about this person. Be sure to let the reader know why this person is important in your life.		
Observational Writing	Re-create accurately a scene or situation that the writer observed as a bystander: • Present the recalled situation in a specific time and place. • Observe details vividly, enabling the reader to see through the writer's eyes. • Focus on the other subject, although the scene is presented from the writer's perspective. • Disclose significance or impact of the scene explicitly or implicitly.	Some people try to be something they are not just to get their own way (a "wolf"). Write about an incident you observed but were not directly involved in when someone did something phony to get his or her way.		

Chart B. Suggested Writing Topics (Continued)

Type	Features	Little Red Riding Hood topics	Map-reading topics	Clay Compromise topics
Report of Information	Arrange and report information clearly and logically: • Control details from a clear perspective. • Describe with physical detail. • Use a variety of means to elaborate on a mass of factual information. • Offer details in logical order. • Establish a tone of authority.	Write a news article that reports the incident between Little Red Riding Hood, the wolf, and Grandma. Be sure to include a headline.	Explain a set of directions clearly enough to get a friend without a map from one place to another. He or she does not want to have to ask again for help.	Define *compromise*. Explain the compromises that were involved in Clay's Compromise.
Problem Solution	Identify a problem, propose a solution, and convince the reader to accept the proposition: • Describe the problem clearly enough to establish its need for solution. • Present (directly or indirectly) several alternatives. • Analyze why the proposed solution is the most plausible one. • Order the argument logically. • Establish an authoritative, convincing tone.	Plan an updated film of *Little Red Riding Hood*, choosing between science fiction, a monster fantasy, a punk opera, or a musical from the 1950s. Consider each alternative, choose the one that will sell the best, and write a presentation arguing for your choice.		Imagine you are a senator in 1850, representing Kentucky. What forces would sway you in favor of Clay's Compromise? What would lead you to oppose that plan? How would you vote?
Speculation	Present a plausible explanation for either the causes or effects of a given situation: • Define the situation under speculation clearly. • Explain possible causes or outcomes in detail and in logical order. • Persuade the reader that the argument is plausible. • Speak with authority, even though the speculation is tentative.	What would have happened if Little Red Riding Hood had arrived at her grandmother's house before the wolf? Base your speculation on inferences you can make from the story.	Traffic north on the 55 freeway is always backed up in the afternoon. Analyze the map of Orange County, California, and what you know about traffic patterns to explain why this phenomenon occurs.	What might have happened if Calhoun had won his argument with Clay? How do you think his ideas would have affected Clay's Compromise? Would it have brought the country closer to Civil War?
Interpretation	Analyze the meaning of a concept: • Introduce the idea with adequate context for the reader to follow, that will clearly control all the arguments to be presented. • State a thesis clearly. • Select details that support and develop the thesis. • Choose details from a text or from experience. • Show how the details relate to the thesis. • Convince the reader that the idea is plausible. • Order ideas logically.	Little Red Riding Hood said she "would never more pick flowers in the wood or listen to a wolf." Analyze what this sentence symbolizes about the story.	From what you know about the location and environment of the Town Center in Costa Mesa, California, analyze why it was a logical place to build the Orange County Music Center.	Study a political cartoon from 1850 and interpret its meaning.

		Chart B. Suggested Writing Topics (Continued)		
Type	Features	Little Red Riding Hood topics	Map-reading topics	Clay Compromise topics
Reflection	Reflect on the meaning a specific idea, object, or event might have on the world in microcosm: • Clearly explain the idea, object, or event that occasions the reflecting. • Turn the concrete situation over, exploring it clearly to find an abstraction it may represent. • Show the writer's process of wondering, probing, and thinking. • Come to a new or deeper awareness about the original idea. • Establish a clear, comfortable, personal voice.	The story illustrates the adage "Never talk to strangers." What does it say about us that we have created this slogan? Reflect on what you can learn about the human condition from this idea.	Reflect on what you can learn about humanity from looking at its highways. Think about the advent and development of freeways in southern California. What do our freeways say about us?	
Controversial Issue	Present a clear, convincing stand on an issue: • Describe the issue clearly. • Defend the stand with logical reasons supported by examples. • Show how the reasons support the position. • Present arguments against the opposition. • Order arguments logically.	In a sense Little Red Riding Hood learns not to take risks. What are your views on taking risks? Assuming your reader may not agree, state your opinion and support it convincingly.	Mass rapid transit for southern California is controversial. State your opinion about this issue. Assuming that your reader may not agree, present your argument and support you idea convincingly.	Imagine you are a senator representing Kentucky in 1850 and debating a senator from New York over the Clay Compromise. How would you persuade the Northern senator to agree with your position on the issue?
Evaluation	Judge the validity of a topic or subject: • Assert a clear judgment that controls the paper. • Establish clear criteria for judgment. • Argue and provide convincing details. • Order ideas logically. • Present an authoritative, convincing tone.	Other versions of Little Red Riding Hood have the grandmother escaping to find a hunter to kill the wolf before it attacks the child. Which version should be taught as part of our American culture?	Should the Corona del Mar Freeway in Orange County be extended from the San Diego Freeway through the Wild Life Preserve and Laguna Canyon and back to the San Diego Freeway? State your judgment and support it convincingly.	To what extent should compromise influence politicians' decisions?

Chart C. Scaffolding

Prewriting for *Little Red Riding Hood*

The steps for prewriting are as follows:

1. Summarize the incidents in the plot. (Report of Information)

2. Draw conclusions from incidents in the plot; for example, Little Red Riding Hood is an innocent young girl, and so forth. (Thinking skill for drawing conclusions about significance and preparing for evaluation, speculation, or interpretation)

3. Quickwrite: What might happen if Little Red Riding Hood had arrived at grandmother's house before the wolf? (Speculation about Effects)

4. Discuss how these new changes would affect the plot. (Thinking for Speculation)

5. Quickwrite: What would an updated version of *Little Red Riding Hood* contain if it were done as (choose one): a. science fiction? b. monster/fantasy? c. punk opera? d. a musical from the 1950s? (A plan for a story)

6. Develop your plan into an actual story. (Story)

7. Think of a movie you have really liked. What made the movie good? List the features of a good movie. (Preparation for Evaluation)

8. Take your lists of conclusions and features of a good movie (items two and seven) and fit them together with your story. What elements does your story contain that keep it close to the original story of Red Riding Hood as well as make it a possible hit movie? What would you add to make your story into a good movie? (Thinking skills for Problem Solution, Evaluation, and Speculation about Effects)

9. List the reasons your story could become a box-office hit as a film. (Thinking skills for Problem Solution, Evaluation, Speculation about Effects)

10. In a mental dialogue, argue your idea with someone who has a different one. (Thinking skills for Problem Solution, Evaluation)

Writing

Before students write, they are given a writing situation that provides background for their assignment and directions for writing that explain the concepts to be developed.

Writing situation. Assume that you are a filmmaker under a contract to make an updated film version of *Little Red Riding Hood*. The producer is considering science fiction, monster/fantasy, punk opera, or a musical from the 1950s. He or she wants to be sure that the film will be a box-office hit. He or she has asked you to investigate the possibilities for the story and to recommend the best film version to make.

Directions for writing. Write a presentation to the film producer arguing for your choice of the kind of film to be made from *Little Red Riding Hood*. Show that you have considered each of the alternatives and that your choice will become a box-office hit.

Specific Activities for Teaching the Domains of Writing in the Elementary Grades

By Mary Turner
Principal, Rolling Hills Elementary School,
Fullerton Elementary School District;
and Teacher/Consultant, UCI Writing Project

and Rich Blough
Principal, Ethel Dwyer Middle School,
Huntington Beach City School District

We developed the following continuum of writing activities to make the domains of writing meaningful to elementary classroom teachers. Using the Los Angeles Unified School District's model as a point of reference, we created a graduated list of specific examples of writing skills for each of the domains, kindergarten through grade six. We found that a detailed

sequence of this kind encouraged teachers to include lessons in all of the domains rather than to concentrate on one or two modes of expression.

We found that a detailed sequence of this kind encouraged teachers to include lessons in all of the domains.

MARY TURNER AND RICH BLOUGH

Activities for **Kindergartners** in the Domains of Writing

Sensory/Descriptive	Imaginative/Narrative	Practical/Informative	Analytical/Expository
• Tells about experiences in the five sensory areas of seeing, hearing, tasting, touching, and smelling • Uses words to describe colors • Uses words to describe shapes and sizes • Begins to use words that describe people and animals and their characteristics • Begins to use language to identify sounds and noises • Begins to use language to designate location	• Begins to identify and participate orally in simple nursery rhymes, chants, limericks, and jingles • Begins to dictate stories • Begins to create fanciful characters • Begins to tell stories in own words • Begins to create simple stories • Begins to create imaginary animals	• Dictates notes • Dictates simple stories about experiences • Dictates signs, labels, and captions • Dictates invitations • Dictates greetings • Identifies own name	• Begins to tell about a series of pictures • Begins to summarize a story • Begins to explain an incident or event

Activities for **First Graders** in the Domains of Writing

Sensory/Descriptive	Imaginative/Narrative	Practical/Informative	Analytical/Expository
• Uses descriptive language to tell about experiences and impressions for each of the five senses: seeing, hearing, tasting, touching, and smelling	• Begins to identify and to create simple rhymes, chants, limericks, and jingles	• Writes letters of the alphabet	• Begins to organize a series of pictures in sequence
• Uses specific language relating to colors	• Begins to dictate and write experiences and stories	• Begins to dictate and write own name	• Begins to organize a series of sentences in a logical sequence
• Uses specific language to describe sizes and shapes	• Begins to dictate and write words for simple songs	• Begins to write simple notes	• Begins to categorize items
• Begins to use language of comparison	• Begins to create characters, lifelike or fanciful, and to dictate or write stories about them	• Begins to write invitations	• Begins to collect information
• Uses specific words to describe people and animals, their characteristics, and their actions	• Begins to dictate endings for stories	• Begins to write signs, labels, and captions	• Begins to summarize a story in appropriate sequence
• Uses language that describes sounds and noises	• Begins to dictate and write original stories	• Begins to dictate and write friendly letters, using simplified letter format	• Becomes aware of and begins to use a variety of sentence types or patterns in dictating and beginning writing
• Uses language to designate location	• Begins to describe imaginary animals	• Begins to dictate and write simple greetings	• Begins to write one- and two-sentence accounts of an experience
	• Begins to use personification in dictating or writing a story	• Begins to write one or two facts about an event or special interest	

Activities for **Second Graders** in the Domains of Writing

Sensory/Descriptive	**Imaginative/Narrative**	**Practical/Informative**	**Analytical/Expository**
• Expands use of specific words that relate to the sensory impressions • Expands use of language relating to colors • Expands use of words in describing sizes and shapes • Increases use of vocabulary in describing location • Expands use of comparative language • Uses language of contrasts • Expands use of language to describe people and animals, their characteristics, and their actions	• Writes endings for stories • Writes simple summary of story heard • Writes new endings for familiar stories • Writes about imaginary animals, people, and objects • Begins to use personification in writing original stories • Dictates and writes new endings for limericks and poems	• Writes own name and the names of others in manuscript letter forms • Writes simple notes • Writes invitations • Writes signs, labels, and phrases for captions • Writes simple friendly letters and greetings • Writes lists • Writes one or more facts about an event or area of interest	• Writes one or more sentences about a picture or series of pictures • Sorts and lists items in two categories • Collects and organizes information • Summarizes a story in sequence • Uses more than one kind of sentence in writing about an event or experience • Writes two or more sentences about a single idea, event, or experience

Activities for **Third Graders** in the Domains of Writing

Sensory/Descriptive

- Writes about experiences and impressions in the areas of each of the five senses
- Uses specific language to describe colors and shades of colors
- Uses specific language to describe sizes and shapes in writing
- Continues to expand use of comparative language
- Expands use of contrastive language
- Selects and uses words to describe emotions

Imaginative/Narrative

- Writes simple rhymes
- Writes new endings for limericks, poems, and chants
- Begins to write haiku and other forms of poetry
- Writes original fairy tales and tall tales
- Begins to keep a class diary
- Begins to keep a personal diary
- Rewrites in own words fairy tales, tall tales, myths, fables, and folktales
- Composes original fairy tales, fables, and tall tales
- Writes simple lyrics for songs
- Adds episodes to stories
- Begins to write short plays
- Writes a new plot for a familiar story
- Lists things that objects would say if they could talk

Practical/Informative

- Writes invitations and greetings
- Writes signs, labels, and sentences for captions
- Writes titles for stories
- Writes personal letters and notes
- Writes addresses and return addresses on envelopes and postcards
- Begins to write reports
- Records telephone messages
- Fills in application for library card
- Begins to prepare book reviews
- Begins to chart information
- Prepares group reports

Analytical/Expository

- Writes about events in sequence of ideas
- Begins to write articles for class newspaper
- Begins to collect facts on a selected topic and writes an explanation using them
- Begins to select and use exact words in writing a description
- Begins to write simple dialogues about events
- Begins to write simple explanations
- Begins to use outline form in writing explanations
- Begins to use paragraphs in writing when interpreting a sequence of pictures, explaining a picture, or describing a happening

Activities for **Fourth Graders** in the Domains of Writing

Sensory/Descriptive	Imaginative/Narrative	Practical/Informative	Analytical/Expository
• Expands use of vocabulary relating to sensory impressions	• Creates and writes rhymes	• Writes friendly letters	• Writes an account of an experience or event in sequence
• Expands use of language relating to colors and shades of colors	• Writes original riddles, limericks, and chants	• Writes simple business letters	• Arranges a series of facts and writes them in chronological order
• Expands use of language relating to sizes and shapes	• Writes haiku and other forms of poetry	• Writes original invitations and greetings	• Selects and uses specific words in writing a description or explanation
• Adds to vocabulary of contrastive language	• Composes and writes original myths and legends	• Writes addresses and return addresses on envelopes and postcards	• Writes an account of an event from a simple outline
• Begins to write personal sketches	• Writes puppet plays and vignettes	• Writes short reports	• Writes simple explanations
• Selects and creates specific words to describe emotions	• Writes original stories	• Records telephone messages containing one or more facts	• Uses outline as basis for writing explanation
	• Writes original lyrics for known songs	• Charts information	• Develops and writes a paragraph as a unit with a main idea and supporting facts
	• Creates new names for known things	• Writes simple news articles of one or more sentences	• Begins to expand ideas in written form
		• Fills in various forms, such as library card application and front of test answer sheet	
		• Writes sentences for news items on bulletin board	
		• Writes individual report	

Activities for **Fifth Graders** in the Domains of Writing

Sensory/Descriptive	**Imaginative/Narrative**	**Practical/Informative**	**Analytical/Expository**

Sensory/Descriptive

- Creates sensory images through word choices
- Creates language relating to colors and shades of colors
- Creates language relating to sizes and shapes
- Extends use of vocabulary of contrast
- Writes personal sketches
- Begins to write biographies and autobiographies
- Identifies, selects, and uses synonyms, antonyms, homonyms, and homographs

Imaginative/Narrative

- Creates and writes rhymes in more than one pattern
- Writes original riddles, limericks, chants, and poems
- Writes haiku, cinquains, and other forms of poetry
- Begins to write ballads
- Begins to write a log
- Writes simple dialogue
- Writes simple short plays and vignettes
- Continues to write original myths and legends
- Writes interpretations of old sayings
- Writes original songs
- Expands known stories
- Writes original stories
- Writes poems about historical events and others based on scientific topics

Practical/Informative

- Writes friendly letters of more than one paragraph
- Writes business letters
- Writes invitations, greetings, acceptances, thank-you notes, and congratulations
- Takes and records telephone messages
- Writes directions and recipes
- Records and organizes notes
- Writes reports based on interviews
- Writes more than one kind of newspaper article
- Fills in various forms
- Writes reports based on reading and on spoken reports by others
- Writes simple announcements and explanations

Analytical/Expository

- Writes a paragraph account of a sequence of events
- Writes directions with increasing precision in selection of vocabulary
- Selects and uses exact words in writing an explanation or description
- Uses transition words, phrases, and sentences
- Uses outline as basis for writing
- Expands ideas
- Develops and writes one or more paragraphs as units, each paragraph having a main idea

Activities for **Sixth Graders** in the Domains of Writing

Sensory/Descriptive	Imaginative/Narrative	Practical/Informative	Analytical/Expository
• Writes personal sketches	• Writes rhymes in a variety of patterns	• Writes friendly letters and business letters using proper format	• Writes more than one paragraph in an account of an event or experience, a description of a favorite food or sport, or an explanation of how something works
• Writes to express feelings and actions	• Increases ability to write original riddles, limericks, chants, and poems	• Writes invitations, acceptances, thank-you notes, and letters of congratulations	• Expands use of transition words, phrases, and sentences in writing an explanation
• Writes personal essays	• Writes short stories	• Records telephone messages with exact facts	• Uses supporting facts in writing a report
• Creates sensory images through choice of words	• Writes biographies	• Writes directions, recipes, and steps in making a product	• Takes notes, organizes them, and expands them for a report
• Writes and creates images through use of language comparisons of many kinds of things	• Writes an autobiography	• Takes and organizes notes	• Uses outline form in writing
• Writes factual descriptions in imaginative ways using descriptive and specific language	• Writes various kinds of poetry	• Writes reports based on facts	• Writes opinion supporting a point of view
• Writes descriptions of characters	• Writes ballads	• Writes reports based on spoken reports, interviews, and readings	• Writes persuasive papers
• Uses and writes with synonyms, antonyms, homographs, and words with multiple meanings	• Writes and keeps a diary	• Writes a variety of news articles	• Writes comparisons to clarify meaning
• Creates word pictures through choices of words	• Writes and keeps a log	• Writes comparisons	• Writes contrasts in sentences and paragraphs
	• Creates and writes original dialogue	• Writes opinion based on facts	• Analyzes characters and events
	• Creates and writes plays and vignettes	• Writes concise titles and captions	• Develops ideas in depth
	• Creates and writes original folktales and tall tales	• Writes simple original commercials for original products or existing products for television time slots	
	• Creates and writes original myths and legends	• Writes weather reports	
	• Writes conversations	• Writes editorials	
	• Writes new twists for old sayings	• Uses reference sources, including bibliographies	
	• Writes interpretations of figurative language		
	• Writes continuing stories		
	• Writes original scripts for films and filmstrips		
	• Rewrites stories into scripts for films and filmstrips		
	• Writes poetry and stories on historical and scientific topics		

Using Visual Stimuli to Motivate Reluctant Writers and to Foster Descriptive Writing Skills

By Sue Rader Willett

English Teacher, Capistrano Valley High School,
Capistrano Unified School District;
and Teacher/Consultant, UCI Writing Project

Motivating reluctant students to write is one of the toughest challenges facing any teacher. Often, we blame the problem on previous instructors, poor self-images, television, inadequate funding, boring textbooks, and (sometimes) ourselves. The problem seems to be perennial, but it is not without its solutions. I have found that using concrete visual stimuli in writing assignments seems to motivate and stimulate students to begin writing.

The following lesson on beginning descriptive writing works well with students of wide-ranging abilities and grade levels. I have employed it with great success in seventh through twelfth grade English classes, but I foresee no difficulty in adapting it for students in the primary and upper elementary grades.

Lesson: I See, I Hear, I Smell, I Feel, I Taste

Supplies needed: Slide projector, screen, slides of interest to students. (I have used slides of scenic vacation spots, local places of interest, common neighborhood and household scenes, master artworks, and historical sites. Many can be purchased at parks or museums or through publications such as *Arizona Highways*.[1])

Set the stage: Explain to your students that they will become sensory guides to their classmates and that they are responsible for constructing vivid images for each other. Emphasize the importance of using an accurate vocabulary that focuses on the senses. To help my students, I have planned vocabulary lessons of sensory/descriptive words. For example, I have shown my students a box of 64 crayons to remind them of the variations in shade and intensity of color. They often forget about magenta, teal blue, and chartreuse.

[1]*Arizona Highways* is published monthly by the Arizona Department of Transportation, 2039 West Lewis Avenue, Phoenix, AZ 85009.

Take a quiet moment to tune the students into their present environment. Have them stop to listen to all the different sounds in the room, feel the temperature, look carefully at the carpet, and so forth. When you feel that the class is ready to begin the exercise, turn out the lights and project the first slide on a screen that all can see.

Slide one: Ask for volunteers to describe the scene in front of them as if they were there. One at a time, students will begin to explain what they sense by prefacing their statements with, "I see . . . , I hear . . . , I smell . . . , I feel . . . , I taste . . . ." (You may wish to omit the sense of taste, but do not ignore it completely for later assignments.)

Give immediate positive reinforcement to those who use specific and vivid language to create the scene. Tell them exactly what you find effective: "The word *mahogany* describes accurately the color of the leather saddle . . . I get a strong feeling of the sun warming your shoulders . . . ."

When you and your students believe that you are ready to proceed, ask for a few students (two to five), who act as imagery guides, to continue looking at the screen while the other students put their heads on their desks and cover their eyes.

Slide two: Project another slide on the screen, and ask the guides to begin constructing the scene for the other "blind" class members. One by one, the guides tell the others exactly what they see, hear, smell, feel, and taste. It is important to keep the comments quickly paced to increase interest and motivation.

The "blind" students may then ask the guides questions for more specific information: "How close is the tree to the rock? What shade of blue is the sky? What else would I hear?" Stop the students from asking questions when you believe that sufficient descriptions have been provided.

All the students may then look up to see the slide. Ask the students whether they had imagined the scene as it really appears and, if not, what did they see differently and why? Emphasize the strengths of the descriptions of the student guides but also tactfully suggest how they could have improved their descriptions. This is the natural time to discuss descriptive techniques that lead to effective writing.

You may wish to reinforce the following:

1. Organization, order, unifying factors
   a. Top to bottom and bottom to top
   b. Side to side

c. Diagonally

d. Out to focal point or in to focal point

e. Tracing the light source

f. Near to far or far to near

2. Word choice

   a. Vividness

   b. Accuracy

3. Comparison and contrast

   a. Metaphor

   b. Simile

4. Originality

   a. Avoiding clichés

   b. Using a fresh approach

   c. Creating an apt mood or impression

5. Full sensory involvement

   a. Sight (shape, light, color, texture)

   b. Sound (pitch, volume, intensity, rate)

   c. Taste (sweet or sour, texture, temperature)

   d. Touch (texture, temperature, weight)

   e. Smell (often linked to taste)

Continue the oral practice until the students are confident with their skills and are ready to stop. (Do not "slide" them to death!)

Begin to write: Ease into the writing practice by assigning students to write individual phrases or sentences rather than to say them aloud to the class. After the majority of the students finish writing their descriptions, encourage them to share their best sentences with the class. Continue to reinforce good techniques.

Variations of this exercise may include clustering or making lists of words or phrases. Homework may involve continuing the writing practice by having students use magazine pictures or snapshots as motivators.

This practice is designed to lead your student writers into developing effective paragraphs and compositions. Longer papers may be developed, with entire paragraphs unified by one of the five senses. The writing may also be integrated into assignments of narration, saturation reporting, journal writing, impression cataloguing, poetry, expository essays, letter writing, speech writing, and so forth.

As you begin to motivate your students to write by using slides and photographs as motivators, you will develop your own techniques to charm that reluctant writer into action. Then, believe it or not, one day you may even hear, "May we do some more of that fun writing today?"

Guided Imagery in the Sensory/Descriptive and Imaginative/Narrative Domains

By Dale Sprowl

Former English Teacher, Irvine High School,
Irvine Unified School District;
and Teacher/Consultant, UCI Writing Project

Guided imagery, a technique that enables students to tap their creative imagination and visual thinking skills, motivates students to write fluently in the sensory/descriptive and imaginative/narrative domains. "A Walk Through the Forest" is an exercise in guided imagery that I have used with students in a ninth grade basic level class, and it is outlined below. However, the lesson could be adapted to any other grade or ability level. The role of the teacher in this exercise is as a guide to help students create pictures in their minds. Once they have formulated these mental images, it is easy for them to translate the images into descriptive or narrative passages.

A Walk Through the Forest

Day 1—Prewriting exercise: Turn off the lights and ask the students to close their eyes and relax. Read the following story slowly, pausing between sentences, to give the students time to develop images. Take 10 to 15 minutes for this.

> Picture yourself in a forest. You are walking through the forest on a path. As you walk, you see a person. You exchange glances with the person, but then the person leaves. You continue walking and you come to a body of water. You cross the body of water. You begin walking on the path again. Soon, you find a cup. You pick it up, look closely at it, and put it down. You continue walking until the path leads you to a fence. On the other side of the fence, you see a house. You go through the fence and into the house. Inside is a table. Something is on the table. As you are looking at it, you see the person you met in the forest.

As you are relating this story, you may want to add questions such as, "What does the forest smell like?" or "What is the weather like?" or "What is the texture of the water like?" Try not to limit the students' images by using only *he* for the person or by adding a handle to the cup. If it is left open to the student, he or she will be able to create a more vivid picture.

After telling your students the story, turn on the lights and ask them to share what they saw on their walks through the forest. Be sure to ask for specific descriptions of items—such as the cup, the house, the table— and list on the chalkboard the various perceptions your students had. Then ask them to retrace their journey in writing. Allow 20 to 30 minutes for this exercise.

Day 2—Read three to five papers aloud and ask the class to discuss the techniques the writers used to convey the pictures in their minds. Reinforce sensory details, similes, metaphors, alliteration, or fine word choice. If the students were vague in their writing ("I saw a body of water."), elicit and list on the chalkboard possible bodies of water. Then ask specific questions about size, color, texture, surroundings, and so forth. Have the students reread their drafts and clarify hazy images.

Day 3—Read three to five more stories aloud and discuss them as you did on day 2. Ask the students to extend their stories by adding dialogue. Discuss natural places for dialogue to fit in the story. If necessary, teach dialogue form. Continue writing.

Day 4—Break down into peer response groups. Each person reads his or her paper to the group. Then each person in the group makes three positive comments about how the writer conveyed the images ("I like the way you used detail to . . . " or "One phrase I liked in your paper was . . . "), and each person makes one helpful suggestion ("One part that was hard for me to visualize was . . . ").

Rewrite according to the comments. Make sure all items mentioned in the story are described in detail and in sequence.

Day 5—Papers are due. Read three to five papers orally. Discuss vividness of detail, sequence of events, and literary terms that apply (plot, character, conflict, setting, point of view, and theme).

"A Walk Through the Forest" is just one of many guided imagery exercises that can be used to stimulate fluency and enhance both descriptive and narrative writing skills. Try this particular prewriting experience as a trial case, and then develop your own guided imagery frames to suit the objectives of your class.

How to Carve a Pumpkin— A Writing Exercise in the Practical/Informative Domain

By Michael Carr

Teacher, Valley Junior High School, Carlsbad Unified School District; and Teacher/Consultant, UCI Writing Project

Holidays can serve as a springboard to a wealth of activities in all of the domains of writing. When I taught (kindergarten and grade one), Halloween provided a great opportunity to introduce practical/informative writing in which the objective is to present information clearly, systematically, and sequentially.

For this lesson I brought to class two pumpkins and a knife and proceeded to discuss "How to Carve a Pumpkin" with my 25 children. I asked the class what we needed to do first; and, after much discussion, we decided we needed a pumpkin. Since most of my class consisted of nonreaders, we used symbols to represent the words and later added the words. Following their directions, I put the sequence given below on the chalkboard:

1. **Get a**
2. **Get a** **to draw with**
3. **Draw**
4. **Draw a**
5. **Draw a**
6. **Get a**
7. **Cut out a**
8. **Take out the**
9. **Cut out the**
10. **Cut out a**
11. **Cut out a**
12. **Put on the**
13. **Cook the**
14. **Happy Halloween!**

Then, to verify the accurateness of our sequence, I demonstrated each step on our class pumpkin.

After printing the process on the chalkboard and carving a model Halloween pumpkin, I transferred the data to packets of 14 pages of ditto masters—one for each step—leaving room for the children to draw pictures to illustrate the directions. When all the children had completed their booklets, they were able to follow their own directions and carve a pumpkin at home. Parents can cook the pumpkin seeds.[1]

The main objective for me in this writing exercise was to give the children a problem-solving activity that involved group discussion, sequencing, clarity, and fun! In addition, they learned the words that corresponded to their pumpkin-carving symbols.

How to Do "How To"

By Greta Nagel

Teacher, Rio Vista Elementary School,
Placentia Unified School District;
and Teacher/Consultant, UCI Writing Project

Students in our classes ride across campus on horses, set up model trains that whiz around the classroom, encourage dogs to do tricks, and cast trout flies across the basketball court. They cook and serve fancy hors d'oeuvres, set up mock theaters and roller coaster rides, and toss bowling balls across the carpet. They do these and many more things as part of the "How To" project.

"How To" is a unit of research and practical/informative written/oral work that is based on the students' hobbies. Each student does work that is related to his or her favorite hobby during eight to ten weeks of language class time. The project has four phases: (1) the basic written report; (2) the oral report and hobby fair; (3) extra written activities; and (4) follow-up activities.

My colleague Terry Kristiansen and I designed the "How To" activities in 1973 for students in grades four through eight. That year, the project won the "Promising Practices Award" that was

offered by our school district, the Placentia Unified School District. Over the years, students have worked on "How To" in our classes and in classes of other district teachers who like the idea. Former students return years later and talk about the hard work and the fun that they had. High school teachers have mentioned that they are able to adapt "How To" ideas to their students' needs. It has been, indeed, a promising practice.

Tips on the "How To" Project

In order for the activities of the lengthy project to be effective, we believe that these tips should help:

1. Work on the unit during a time when students have already had some introduction to research tasks and to various types of writing. Otherwise, plan to do a great amount of intermittent modeling and practice as you proceed through the activities.

2. At least two weeks prior to starting the unit, announce that each student needs to choose a hobby. (Note: We have always allowed students to think of sports as a hobby.) Not only does this allow students to form a mind-set, but it also permits you to check on the appropriateness of the topic and the availability of the materials. A topic like "How to Collect Smurfs" is difficult to research and hard to demonstrate. It is probably best left alone. A topic like "How to Collect Baseball Cards" can, on the other hand, be researched well if prior contacts are made with stores and organizations. Giving a two-week notice can also provide students with time to locate other people who practice the hobby and who can serve as valuable research aides.

3. We always provide at least one piece of research material for each student. He or she must obtain two or more additional resources. The public libraries (children's sections) have been very accommodating in lending groups of books on special teacher loans, mainly because the choices are so varied and the supply of any one type of book will not be exhausted.

4. Plan to model activities for your students; show clearly the expectations that you have for their work. Terry Kristiansen and I share

---

[1]Recipe for parents:
   1. Wash and salt seeds.
   2. Cook for an hour to an hour and a half at 250° F.
   3. Turn seeds over (at halfway point).

the hobby of cross-country skiing. We both brought in our outfits and equipment, and we demonstrated how we would write and do the various activities related to our hobby. We also designed posters (related to x-c skiing) that helped remind students of the basic sections of the report. We used these posters to decorate the classroom walls during the duration of "How To" work.

5. Do not forget to ask students whether or not you may save drafts of their work, samples of both the good and the average. They serve as excellent models for future classes.

6. Another tip is to set up a workable management system for handling the large volume of rough and final drafts that will come your way. Evaluate as you go along; do not wait until the end of the project. The threat of misplacing papers led me to set up a system of mailing envelopes. One envelope per activity is labeled and has a class list grid stapled to the front. Papers are checked in, and scores are recorded on the fronts of the envelopes, not in a separate grade book. At the end of the unit, I glue two sheets together, matching class list entries, and I have a complete permanent record.

7. A final tip: Keep a camera handy. The nature of this project makes it highly motivating; it is tied to students' senses of relevancy. They are proud to share their expertise in subjects usually not touched by the school's curriculum, and they are interested in one another's hobbies. They also enjoy bringing in their equipment and products for their oral reports and for the hobby fair. Snapshots and slides enhance those special moments—the boy with his king snake wrapped around his neck, the girl roller-skating backward across the classroom linoleum, the boy on his dirt bike by the chalkboard. Admittedly, excitement about the "fun" times helps students to plow through the great amount of writing. A spoonful of sugar . . .

The Written Report

The first phase of the project, the written report, requires skills in research, note taking, outlining,

and the writing of rough and final drafts. There are six segments in the written report. For fifth and sixth graders, the usual lengths produced have been:

1. *History*—one or two handwritten pages: a narrative.
2. *Steps*—five to ten pages: Lists and drawings form just a part of a narrative piece that explains in great detail how to learn and do the hobby.
3. *Famous person*—one or two pages: a narrative about a person or animal that is related to the hobby. Some students have written about persons with an obvious tie-in to their hobby: Charles Schulz, Jesse Owens, Ringo Starr, and Margaret Bourke-White (photography). Others have used persons with an indirect relationship: Benjamin Franklin (philatelist), Teddy Roosevelt (stuffed animals), and Elizabeth Taylor (horses). Research strategies have sometimes included writing to famous people.
4. *Powers and pitfalls*—one or two pages: a narrative or a sentence chart that notes the good aspects and rewards of the hobby as opposed to the things that can go wrong, the dangers, and the costs. In this segment the student writer explains how to avoid or overcome the pitfalls.
5. *Interesting experience*—one or two pages: a personal account of an experience with the hobby, such as "The First Time I Rode Colossus," "My First Tornado," "The Day I Won the Third Grade Art Contest," or "A Bad Luck Day Trading Baseball Cards."
6. *Interview*—two to five (or more) pages following a narrative, then question-and-answer format (à la "Q & A" in the *Los Angeles Times*'s magazine): Students seek face-to-face contacts with neighbors, shop owners, or local instructors. Telephone contacts are allowed when it is not possible for the students to meet a "local authority." Students often use tape recorders but are nevertheless expected to do written versions.

Oral Report and Hobby Fair

Once the written reports have been completed, oral reports are scheduled; and students are allowed 15-minute time slots in which to tell about and demonstrate their hobbies. We have their fellow students complete evaluation score cards at the end of each report, noting points for each of the segments: (1) catchy opening; (2) how to; (3) audio-visuals; (4) eye contact; (5) loudness; and (6) appropriate time. Each speaker is expected to start with a "catchy" opening. Some examples are:

> "I have a real catchy hobby." (fishing)
> "This hobby will keep you in stitches." (sewing)
> "My hobby is a real hit." (baseball)

Minidemonstrations are also required. Students show how to hinge stamps for album placement, to tie flies, and to do knots for macrame pieces. They also show how to do ski turns, to fix a bicycle chain, and to sink a difficult putt.

When the class finishes giving oral reports, we hold a hobby fair and invite parents and other students to come. All class members set up booths where they display equipment and give minitalks to passersby during "milling" time. Several chosen speakers give their full oral reports at designated times. (Peer selection of honored speakers seems to work well.) If the room is large, several speakers may talk at once to their own audiences clustered near them. It is possible for two, or even three, shifts of speakers to talk, with their report times alternated with milling time for fair visitors. All students display their written reports.

Extra Written Activities

The extra activities are all creative in nature. Students enjoy these tasks and come up with delightful results. They write new words to old tunes ("Art of My Heart"). Using magazine advertisements, they practice the ploys of advertising copy and format ("Strong, adventuresome people collect stamps."). With graphs and lists, students present and analyze the results of popularity surveys and questionnaires ("From these five choices, more people selected roller-skating."). Complete with costumes and props, students entice new hobbyists from their "television studio" ("You'll just love learning to cook!"). With poems, often humorous, they proclaim positive and negative aspects of hobbies ("breathing, panting, gasping along"). Using home movies, the students show the details of "How To" ("Here's my dad

guarding our basketball net."). Through an original piano solo, a student musician expresses the joy of playing the piano.

Follow-up Activities as Final Phase

Once the students' notebooks are compiled, one last phase of the project is possible. The follow-up activities are evaluative and analytical tasks that require the students to take a close look at the practical/informative "How To" experience. As students look back, they are pleased to have polished their skills in oral/written expression as they polished their skills with their hobbies.

Teaching Practical/Informative Writing Through Novels

By Elizabeth Williams Reeves
Teacher/Consultant, UCI Writing Project

Novels for adolescents provide excellent vehicles for teaching writing in a variety of domains. Characterizations and settings lend themselves to sensory/descriptive writing; story plot and embellishments and adaptations of a plot are appropriate for imaginative/narrative writing; analyses of characters and authors' styles and content are suitable for analytical/expository writing. Because it is often viewed as a somewhat mundane, uncreative domain, practical/informative writing is frequently ignored. But the content of a novel often provides motivational material for practical/informative writing.

One practical/informative lesson that I have particularly enjoyed is based on a portion of *The Hobbit* that describes a barrel ride. In it, Bilbo, the hobbit, and his dwarf friends ride down a river in barrels in an attempt to escape from the Wood-elves:

> . . . first one barrel and then another rumbled to the dark opening and was pushed over into the cold water some feet below. Some were barrels really empty, some were tubs neatly packed with a dwarf each; but down they all went, one after another, with many a clash and a bump, thudding on top of ones below, smacking into the water, jostling against the

Novels for adolescents provide excellent vehicles for teaching writing in a variety of domains.

ELIZABETH WILLIAMS REEVES

walls of the tunnel, knocking into one another, and bobbing away down the current.[1]

After students have read the complete section of *The Hobbit* in which this account appears, I ask them to write practical/informative instructions to a novice on how to go barrel riding. During prewriting, discussion questions should focus on the sequence of steps needed to ride in a barrel. For example, I ask the students to consider what would be the first thing to tell a person who is about to go barrel riding—then the second, the third, and so forth. I stress that their instructions must be clear and well organized so that the reader can follow them easily.

Practical/informative writing developed through the use of novels can be most inventive. An example of a fifth grader's description of the barrel ride follows:

> If you are going to ride a barrel down a river, you must take certain steps. First, find a barrel big enough for you. Empty out contents, if any. Then wash the smell out. Lift or cut the lid off the barrel. Then cut air holes on top of the barrel—about seven holes an inch wide. Now, get inside the barrel. Have someone help you get packed with straw or anything soft. Brace yourself. You might get bumped a little. Put the lid back on. Someone will push you off into a river or stream. Don't panic. Stay calm. Don't rock too much, and keep your air holes up. Last, but not least, wait for someone to get you out.

This barrel riding exercise not only reinforces the sequencing skills necessary for "how to" writing but also enhances critical thinking ability.

---

[1] From *The Hobbit* (p. 177) by J. R. R. Tolkien. Copyright © 1966 by J. R. R. Tolkien. Reprinted by permission of Houghton Mifflin Company. All rights reserved. Also reprinted by permission of George Allen & Unwin, now Unwin Hyman, an imprint of HarperCollins Publishers Limited, London.

In order to write precise barrel riding instructions, the students must read and evaluate the text carefully, determine which details are essential, organize those details or steps, and compose an account that incorporates what they know of barrel riding with what they surmise a rider would need to know. In addition, because they are writing for a person who is about to embark on a barrel ride, their sense of audience is strengthened.

Welcome to the New World!

By Laurie Opfell

Former English Teacher, Irvine High School; and Teacher/Consultant, UCI Writing Project

I have had remarkable success in my eighth grade English class with my "Welcome to the New World" assignment, which is outlined below. This project taps each of the four domains of writing; reinforces peer group interaction; and integrates writing, speaking, and drawing activities. It also enables me to introduce relevant works of literature, such as Jonathan Swift's *Gulliver's Travels*, William Golding's *Lord of the Flies*, and so forth. The enthusiasm generated by the assignment has been extremely high, and the level of cooperation in the classroom has improved greatly. I give my students the following instructions for the lesson:

> Welcome to the New World. In the next few weeks you will be involved in creating your own utopia or "imaginary or ideal world." You will be graded on the completeness of two individual assignments, all group assignments, and the quality of your work. However, the most important aspect of the grade will be how you combine imagination, creativity, and

innovation with the basic requirements. The objective of the project is for you to clarify and use your values, wishes, ideals, knowledge, and talents to create a personal and group statement about what you want and hope for in life.

The assignments described below are for each person in the group to do. They will be assigned over many days:

Assignment 1

A. Although you are extremely wealthy, you and your friends are tired of the rat race and decide to get away. You decide to buy an island, but before seeing the real estate agent, you each:

1. Write down a preferred location.
2. List four to six things you want your island to include; for example, beaches, mountains, and so forth.

B. Now, compare your lists and decide on a group location and a list that includes everyone's desired features.

C. You are now ready to see your agent. She has just the place and shows you some slides.

1. Sketch out a few practice shapes for a map of your island, decide on one (or a combination), and draw the outline on a large sheet of paper.
2. Now, divide your island into equal portions so each group member has a section.
3. Agree on a symbol for each of the features on your group's list; for example, mountains ⋀⋀, lakes ⌇⌇⌇, beaches ⌒⌒, and so forth. Each person is responsible for filling in his or her section with the features that are appealing.
4. Be sure you also include a scale of miles, directions, symbols for roads, cities (if there are any), rivers, and so forth.
5. Decide how all major services (mechanics, food supply, health care, and so forth) will be handled, and set up a location for them.

    Now, go back over what you have noted and write it into a well-organized, descriptive one to one and one-half page piece. Share it with at least two people in your group, and get some suggestions for revision before you write your final draft.

Assignment 2

A. You now need to decide on the values that will be the controlling ideals of your island's government. Make a list:

1. Helpfulness?

2. Equal power?
3. Freedom?

B. Now, share your list with your group members. As you read it to them, explain why you think each item is important. Make a group list of everything you all agree on.

Assignment 3

Since you have unlimited money, you need to start thinking about the home you will build. Take about 15 minutes to brainstorm, and then start writing about your ideal home. What would it look like? How many rooms? What type of furniture? Colors? Building materials? View? Landscaping?

Now, go back over what you have sketched and write it into a well-organized, descriptive one to one and one-half page piece. Share it with at least two people in your group, and get some suggestions for revision before you write your final draft.

The next assignments are individual. You must select any two of the options listed below, all of which involve some critical thinking and creative writing:

1. *Constitution.* Write up your group's values or rules of living into some sort of document. (Look at the U.S. Bill of Rights for an example.) Make it beautiful, official looking, and one to one and one-half pages long. Include a statement of your philosophy.
2. *Architecture.* What types of design are likely to be seen on your island? Do they stand out? Blend in with the environment? Are they energy self-sufficient? Beautiful? Modern? Old fashioned? Draw four or five different buildings, and write a paragraph explaining each structure's best features.
3. *Clothing.* How do people dress on your island? Design four or five possible outfits that adapt to the environment. Make them as crazy, practical, or comfortable as you want. Draw a picture of each one and write a paragraph explaining it.
4. *Foods.* What are the island's staples? Interview all persons and get a list of their ten favorite foods. Design a restaurant menu that features everybody's favorite foods. Describe the foods and illustrate the menu with magazine pictures. (You might want to think up some original specialties.)
5. *Recreation.* What are the major forms of recreation? Interview all persons and find out what they want included. Then design a park that includes each item. Try to come up with at least

three original sports or ideas that can be enjoyed only on your island. Illustrate and explain the new sports, and draw a picture of the park on a separate sheet of construction paper.

6. *Flora.* Your island is the home of many different plants, but in addition to the usual varieties, you have several exotic types of trees and flowers. Illustrate and describe three of them, and also include your island's environmental protection policy.

7. *Fauna.* Your island includes some well-known animals as well as a few that have yet to be discovered. Describe four or five of these rare species and write a paragraph explaining each one.

8. *Travel agent. You* are in charge of designing a brochure that advertises your island. Include a small map that mentions important or beautiful places, and add photographs from magazines accompanied by flowing descriptions. Make it the ~ foldout kind. Neatness and layout are very important.

9. *Culture director.* What do the people on your island do to improve their lives? Interview the members of your group to discover their educational and artistic pursuits. Design and illustrate a cultural center and make a program of activities; for example, theater, movies, music, mime, computers, science, and so forth.

10. *Production manager.* On the final day of the project, you will present your island to the rest of the class. There will be only one chance to do this, so only responsible persons need apply. You will need:

    a. A specific knowledge of all important aspects of the island
    b. Good speaking ability
    c. Slides or visuals to use for illustrations
    d. Two or three music selections to play as background music

    Write a five- to ten-minute presentation that coordinates all of the above. Consult the clothes designer and wear a suggested outfit. You will be graded on your organization and how well you capture our interest.

11. *Editor.* The group grade depends on you because you will compile all of the individual articles into a guide to your island. Proofread the articles for errors in correctness. Everyone should hand his or her rough draft in to you. Underline spelling, punctuation, and grammati-

cal errors. Pay special attention to sentence structure. If you have any doubts about fragments or run-on sentences, consult with me or a parent. Return the edited drafts to their authors for correction. Final drafts must be written neatly in ink or typed and must be done on your own time. As the editor, you are in charge of collecting the articles, compiling all of the them in a folder, and preparing a table of contents.

Congratulations on the creation of your own personal utopia.

Exploring the Domains with an Extraterrestrial

By Todd Huck

English Instructor, Rancho Santiago College, Rancho Santiago Community College District; and Teacher/Consultant UCI Writing Project

When I was a middle school teacher, students in my classes sharpened their sensory/descriptive skills by creating vivid, precise word pictures of outer space creatures. As part of the assignment, they shared their otherworldly visions with their classmates, who provided feedback, both in words and in pictures, as to the clarity and precision of their depictions. The writers, in turn, used the feedback to tighten and clarify their written descriptions. It proved to be one of those no-lose assignments. The students enjoyed both the writing and the artwork involved. (Never once did a student say to me, "I'm sorry. I just can't write about a space creature.") I was happy not only because the students responded well to the assignment but also because it addressed an important writing issue on my instructional agenda: the need for students to revise their papers for greater specificity and clarity. Nonetheless, after a summer stint at the University of California Irvine (UCI) Writing Project, I realized the assignment had other possibilities: The creation of an extraterrestrial led very naturally to writing in domains other than the sensory/descriptive, and its value as a subject for writing could be extended and enriched.

The Original Assignment

Here is a brief overview of the original sensory/descriptive assignment. Then I will suggest how it might lead to writing in the other domains.

Designing Your Own Extraterrestrial

Prewriting

1. Students define *extraterrestrial*. Can they think of other words that have the same root? Of other names for extraterrestrials?
2. Cluster on the chalkboard the names of all the outer space creatures students can think of from films, books, and television.
3. Ask students to invent categories for some of the creatures clustered on the chalkboard. For example, they might say that some of them are robots, some look like humans, or that some are good while others are evil.
4. Give them these categories suggested by a professor who has taken hundreds of phone calls from people who think they have seen outer space creatures:

   Human (indistinguishable from humans)
   Humanoid (having body parts analogous to humans)
   Animalistic
   Robotic
   Exotic (having bizarre anatomical features)
   Apparitional (ghostlike)

   See how many of the creatures in the group cluster they can fit into one of these categories.

5. Cluster on the chalkboard the features of one well-known extraterrestrial, such as E.T. Press them for precise details on size, shapes, colors, textures, and proportions. (For suggestions on clustering, see the "Prewriting" section of this book.)
6. Have the class members create a creature on the chalkboard. As they call out the creature's features, you draw them on the chalkboard. Make students be specific in their oral language as to the size, shape, number, and proportion of features they suggest.
7. Having discussed and described a variety of extraterrestrials, tell students that they are now going to visualize an alien that no one has ever seen before.
8. Take them through the following guided imagery:

Guided Imagery

Close your eyes. Imagine that it is a cool, clear night. The stars burn brightly in the sky, and you are in a quiet, beautiful setting. It might be at the beach, in the mountains, or in the desert. Picture that setting. You are there with friends or family, but at this moment you have decided to be alone; and you have gone for a walk away from the group. As you walk, you realize that it has been some time since you have been able to hear the distant voices of your friends and family. You pause for a moment to enjoy the still beauty of the night. Suddenly, you hear a sound. What is it? What does it sound like? You walk around a huge rock, and there you see it— an extraterrestrial. You are surprisingly calm and unafraid. The creature seems interested in you, and it is likewise calm and friendly. You have at least a full minute to study the creature.

- What does it look like?
- What kind of an extraterrestrial is it?
- What is its size? Shape? Weight? Coloration?
- What type of body covering does it have?
- Does its body have a variety of textures?
- What kind of limbs or appendages does it have? How many?
- How does it move? By what means does it move?
- Can it take in food? How?
- Does it make a noise? What kind of noise? How does it make this noise?
- Does it have any particular smell?
- Does it have a head?
- Does it have eyes?
- A smelling apparatus (a nose)?
- Auditory adaptions (ears)?
- Does it have any extrasensory capabilities?

After you have had a good look at it, it turns away and vanishes into the night! You realize that since you are the only one who has seen this creature, you are the only one who can describe it.

9. Cluster the features of your creature.

Prompt. Describe the extraterrestrial you encountered in as much specific, vivid detail as possible. Your description should be so clear and detailed that a classmate can draw a reasonably accurate picture of your creature just from reading your description.

Writing and Drawing. Students use their clusters to write descriptions of their creatures. When they have finished, each should draw a picture of the imagined creature. If they add features to the drawing that are not in the written sketch, they must also add them to the writing.

Sharing

1. After putting their drawings away, students exchange their written descriptions with peer partners.
2. Peer partners read the descriptions they have received.
3. Each peer partner then writes on a blank piece of paper a positive comment about some feature of the piece she or he has just read.

4. On the other side of the blank piece of paper, each peer partner will make a drawing of the creature she or he has read about, basing it as closely as possible on the written description.

5. Peer partners return to the writers the original pieces of writing accompanied by their comments and their drawings.

6. Writers take out their sketches and compare them and their writings with the sketches from their peer partners.

7. The writers determine where their partner's sketch differs from theirs or does not portray the creature as they saw it. They go back to their text and determine where and how to make their text clearer and more specific.

Revising. Revision takes place based on the pictorial and written feedback the writer has received and analyzed. Writers make the additions, deletions, substitutions, and rearrangements necessary to ensure that their pieces are more specific, vivid, and precise.

Editing. Students will edit their papers for the conventions of English which the teacher values and has taught for this assignment.

Evaluating. In part your evaluation of the piece should be based on the number of clear, vivid details the writer has provided. You may also wish to consider other elements that you may have taught, such as the creation of details that appeal to other senses, logical organization, and the use of the conventions of standard English.

Postwriting. Student writings and drawings make great classroom displays.

Springboard for Other Writing

Once students have completed the sensory description of the extraterrestrial, this assignment may profitably serve as a springboard for other types of writing. Here are some suggestions for prompts that enrich the extraterrestrial experience and extend it into other domains:

Sensory/Descriptive. Describe the experience with the extraterrestrial from the point of view of the creature itself. Write a sensory description of yourself (the terrestrial) as the extraterrestrial sees you. Remember, an extraterrestrial may perceive things about you that you do not see (or smell, hear, taste, or touch).

Imaginative/Narrative. Opportunities for storytelling about this creature are endless. Here are just a few ideas:

- Have the creature tell the story of what life is like on its own planet.

- Write a monologue from the point of view of the extraterrestrial in which you tell why the creature came to earth. You might also tell of the journey itself and relate at least two specific incidents that happened along the way. Likewise, you might have the creature explain when and why it intends to leave the earth, where it is going next, and what it expects to encounter.

- Write a diary of the creature's stay here on earth.

- Tell the story of how you helped the extraterrestrial get out of a difficult situation here on earth, or of how the extraterrestrial helped you.

Practical/Informative. Analyze three of your creature's basic needs (food, rest, an occasional back rub to keep its heart beating, and so forth). Design a step-by-step informative guide in list form for the care and feeding of your extraterrestrial. Present the steps in logical, sequential order; and describe all the special equipment and material needed for the proper care of your creature.

Write a letter to your mother or father in which you try to persuade your parent to let you keep the extraterrestrial.

Analytical/Expository. From the point of view of the extraterrestrial, write a report to the creatures on your planet in which you analyze and draw conclusions about some feature you have observed here on earth (cars, telephones, human clothing, and so forth). Your report can follow simple expository form: introduction, body, and conclusion.

In expository form write a "scientific" paper which analyzes and draws conclusions about the functions of three anatomical or behavioral features of your extraterrestrial.

Again, in a scientific paper, speculate about how some of your creature's physical features were geared or adapted to the environment on the creature's home planet. What characteristics of the environment helped shape the features you see in your creature?

Exploring the domains with an extraterrestrial can be a profitable, entertaining, and broadening experience for students. Generating extended writing assignments focused on a central topic, the extraterrestrial, will allow students to concentrate on how various domains of writing differ in form, construction, and organization. Once these skills are practiced and internalized, students should be able to develop and elaborate on ideas related to any central subject.

Writing the Saturation Report

Using Fictional Techniques for Nonfiction Writing

By Ruby Bernstein
English Teacher, Northgate High School,
Mt. Diablo Unified School District;
and Teacher/Consultant, Bay Area Writing Project

By using saturation reporting, you can encourage students to write about real events, people, places, and new experiences that they can observe firsthand. When you employ this technique, you ask your students to make all the sophisticated choices professional writers make: which points of view to use; which details and dialogue to include; which research, if any, to pursue; and, finally, how to structure the nonfiction experience.

Tom Wolfe, contemporary essayist, coined the term "new journalism" (saturation reporting) when he discovered in the 1960s that newspaper and magazine nonfiction journalists had borrowed fiction writers' techniques for preparing their feature stories. Today, examples of new journalism can be collected from the daily press, *The New Yorker*, Sunday magazine sections of major newspapers, and monthly magazines.

Giving students opportunities to practice observing, interviewing, separating fact from opinion, and using the library will result in better saturation reporting when the major assignment is made. These prewriting activities are particularly helpful in sharpening the students' focus in their writing. It is also helpful to have them brainstorm and ask lots of questions before they leave the classroom to carry out their prewriting activities, and it is equally helpful to have them share their experiences and pieces of their reports after they have made their observations or conducted their interviews.

My own experience with saturation reporting occurred several years ago at a summer writing class for teachers at the University of California, Berkeley, taught by Jim Gray, Director of the Bay Area Writing Project, at that time. I had been making daily trips to a weight-loss clinic, one of those advertised in the daily newspaper. The 30-day experience lent itself to saturation reporting, especially since I had reservations about the weight-reduction method, and my intent was to be a modern-day muckraker.

My purposes for writing, my underlying theses, were (1) to show that taking shots for weight loss was harmful to one's health; (2) to affirm that this particular clinic was directed by professionals with questionable credentials; and (3) to point out to my readers that the public generally wants quick solutions to problems, such as obesity, which may have taken years to develop.

After I had brainstormed my ideas for the paper with my six-member writing group, my paper's scenario took the shape shown in Figure 1.

The scenes surrounding my experiences with the weight-loss clinic, which were described separately, were put in final order, as indicated by the letters A through G in Figure 1. Hopefully, the

total effect of this collage of scenes achieved my purposes.

After this experience with saturation reporting, I enthusiastically brought the assignment to my class. In my junior/senior composition elective course, which is one semester long, the saturation report became the major assignment, culminating the first quarter's work. Among the topics my students chose to saturate themselves with were revisiting junior high school, fast-food jobs, the senior prom ritual, department store dressing room gossip, cruising the Main, the school orchestra's bus trip to Modesto, riding on Bay Area Rapid Transit, bartending at a publisher's cocktail party, the local hangout after a football game, the final week of rehearsals for a community play. The possibilities for writing were limited only by time and sometimes transportation.

Saturation reporting lends itself to cooperative learning. Recently, my juniors, more than 60

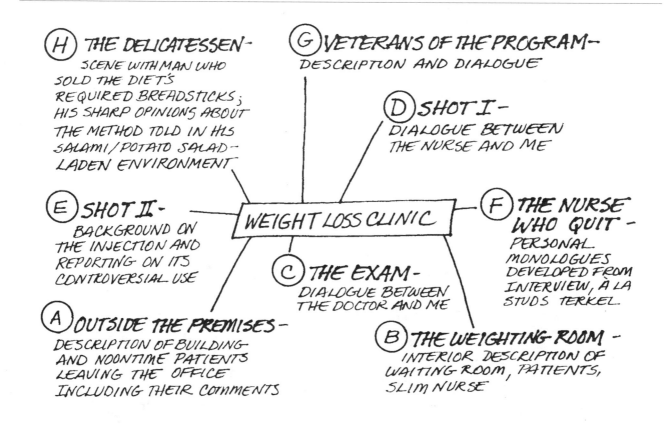

Fig. 1. Brainstorming of Observations for Saturation Reporting

Giving students opportunities to practice observing, interviewing, separating fact from opinion, and using the library will result in better saturation reporting.

RUBY BERNSTEIN

students, contributed to a many-faceted assignment: "Walnut Creek, California—American Dream City." They used many writing modes and research techniques to examine the city's history and landmarks, the flight to the suburbs, commuting, their schools, weekend hangouts, and so forth.

Provided below is a list of the features of a saturation report that I share with my students before they select a topic:

Saturation Reporting

Features—A "saturation" report involves:

1. Writing about some place, some group, or some individual that you know well or can get to know well firsthand. You "saturate" yourself with your subject.
2. Writing a nonfiction article, using fictional techniques. There will be scenes, characters and characterizations, dialogue, and a subtle, rather than overt, statement.
3. The appeal of information and facts. You are writing nonfiction, and the reader will want to "know" about your subject; in short, be sensitive to this thirst for facts on the part of your reader.
4. Author identification. Your point of view can be quite flexible. You can be an active participant in the action; you can remove yourself; or you can come in and then move out.
5. Microcosm. You are focusing on some particular subject, but in so doing you are saying something more. As you capture an isolated segment of today's world, you say something about the total world.
6. Implication. Much of what you attempt to "say" in your article (because of your use of fictional techniques) will be said through implication—through dialogue and through your manipulation of details.

7. Reporting. You will observe your subject with a keen eye. You will note interesting "overheard" conversations. You might want to interview someone.
8. Form. You might write your article in pieces—conversations, descriptions, interviews, facts—and then piece it together, finding the best form for your subject (time sequence and so forth). A "patchwork"— working sections together with no transition—can be quite acceptable.
9. Choice of subject. You can pick some subject from the present or recreate some subject from your past.

Saturation Report—Triple Credit Paper

This paper will bring together some of the techniques you have practiced this quarter: use of descriptive detail, dialogue, narrative, close observation. For the saturation report you may do one of the following:

1. Teach or be taught a task.
2. Visit a place.
3. Capture an event.
4. Vividly describe a person.
5. Show your job in action.

No matter what you do, you will need to bring in an abundance of notes in which you have recorded your feelings, your detailed observations, conversations that you have heard, people you have spoken to, and descriptions. After all your visiting, looking, and listening, bring your notes in (more than you need, please), focus on your subject, and then write. Remember that your paper should make some kind of statement about lesson, place, event, person, or job. That statement may be stated or unstated as your material demands.

I also hand out a three-week schedule so that every student knows at what point in the writing process he or she should be on any given day.

Time Schedule for This Project

NOTE: Prior to the first week, students will have had experiences with showing writing, James Moffett's sensory reporting, ordering details, writing descriptions, and interviewing.

WEEK 1

Monday	Introduce saturation reporting. Read Tom Wolfe's *The New Journalism*—scene-by-scene construction, use of detail, point of view, use of dialogue.[1]
Tuesday	Read student examples. Read more of Tom Wolfe's explanations.
Wednesday	What are you going to write about? Check topic with teacher. Get your assignment for the on-campus group saturation report. Bring lunch to class today because you will be working during the lunch period.
Thursday	During the class period write your description of the campus scene.
Friday	Read and discuss the group's report. Use student models.

WEEK 2

Monday	Work with clauses.
Tuesday	Work with tightening.

[1]Tom Wolfe and E. W. Johnson, *The New Journalism*. New York: Harper & Row Pubs., Inc., 1973.

Wednesday	Notes are due.
Thursday— Friday	Confer with teacher. Bring complete notes. We will discuss your focus, including underlying ideas and point of view. While conferences are in progress, complete the exercises in parallel structure, sentence combining, and clauses. Key will be available.

WEEK 3

Monday	Every student brings page one of report to share.
Tuesday	Write in class.
Wednesday	Completed rough drafts are due at the beginning of the period for peer evaluation and assistance.
Thursday	Bridge to the essay.
Friday	**Your finished paper is due.**

Saturation reporting can be adapted to grade and ability levels and to locale. Whether the students are asked to write a description of a scene, an interview, or multiple scenes, or whether they are responsible only for collecting facts with their tape recorders that their classmates will transcribe and edit with them, the finished product will be writing that the students will be proud they have done and that you will enjoy reading.

Practical Ideas for Assigning the Saturation Report

Preparing Students to Write the Saturation Report

By Carol Booth Olson
Director, UCI Writing Project

The saturation report is one of the most popular writing assignments I give to students in my first-year composition class. Because the students choose their own topics, they almost always get *into* their subject. Moreover, they are challenged to come up with unique approaches to communicating factual information in an almost cinematic style. The task of capturing an actual person, place, or event and bringing the subject to life through fictional techniques will naturally lead students to blend the sensory/descriptive, imaginative/ narrative, practical/informative, and analytical/ expository domains of writing.

To ensure that students put the most into and get the most from their saturation reports, I take the students through a sequence of steps that will prepare the students to select a topic, organize their ideas, and write their papers. The sequence is as follows:

- *Step 1.* Explain to students several weeks in advance (so they have some "think time") that they will have opportunities to immerse themselves in a person, place, or event and bring their subject to life by presenting factual information, scene by scene, using description, characterization, dialogue, and so forth. Pass out the list of key features of a saturation report, as outlined by Ruby Bernstein at the beginning of this section. (*Note:* You may want to encourage elementary school students to select a place or event for their first attempt at creating a saturation report since capturing a person is a more difficult task to undertake.)

- *Step 2.* Provide students with a model of a saturation report and a list of criteria on which their papers will be evaluated. (*Note:* The rubric should be created by each teacher to fit his or her objectives and classroom situation.) I usually begin by reading a paper to the class that I wrote about shopping at the swap meet just before Christmas. Then I pass out a student model, such as "Just Another Painless Test" by Adrianne Abbott, an eighth grade student at Thurston Middle School in Laguna Beach, so that students can get a feel for how one of their peers approached this assignment. I included Adrianne's paper here in its entirety because it is a well-written saturation report that conveys the "you are there" feeling very effectively.

Just Another Painless Test

"I'll help you up," my mom said as she lifted my arm with one hand and balanced my neck with the other. I dragged myself into a sitting position and realized we had already arrived at the hospital.

The hospital building was a light shade of brown. There were windows placed all around the building, but the drapes were closed, so I couldn't see in. As we neared the air conditioned waiting room, the automatic doors opened. In contrast to the drab exterior of the hospital, the waiting room was mainly red, blue, and yellow. Walls were decorated with pictures of giraffes and elephants and other animals. One picture had the alphabet scattered all over it.

The room had a scent of sick people. It was a sour, dirty smell. I thought I even smelled antiseptic. When I walked past certain people, the aroma of Ben-Gay filled my nostrils.

A small section was blocked off. This area had games for all of the kids who were waiting to play with. On the floor were Legos, colored wooden blocks, and picture books. I saw two little boys playing with big trucks, a skinny little girl trying to dress a Barbie doll, and a mother and her children engaged in putting the pieces of a puzzle together.

My mom led me across the dark blue carpet in search of a place to sit down. We found a couple of red cushioned chairs with wooden arms. As I gratefully slouched into one, I heard a child scream for its mom. Across the way I noticed a tiny little baby. The haggard woman holding the baby must have seen me staring because she said, "He is so small because he is five months premature. He has to come here every other day for I.V. until he is a normal size." As she laid him down gently it looked like he would break. His hands were so small they looked like doll's hands. His feet were no longer than a matchbook. His whole body was so tiny. It wasn't bigger than a teddy bear.

I leaned on my mom's shoulder and thought about what was happening. I had never had to go to the hospital before, but I had some kind of sickness and I didn't know what was going to happen to me. I was scared. With these thoughts, I hugged my blanket that I brought with me from home.

It seemed like we had been waiting for an eternity when a voice finally called, "Adrianne Abbott!" The nurse at the big white door was beckoning me. She was young and short with dark brown hair woven into a braid, and she was wearing a white medium length nurse's uniform with beige mushroom shoes. My mom told me to follow her. I got up, squeezed my mom's hand, said good-bye to the lady across from me, and followed the nurse through the door.

I was motioned into another room which was small and very simple. It had plain white walls, two soft blue chairs and a small counter with some

> *My experience has been that the saturation report brings out the best in student writers. I always look forward to reading them because they are as diverse as one's students are— interesting, educational, and well crafted.*
>
> **CAROL BOOTH OLSON**

light blue cupboards above it. The bed against the wall was a light cream color and had white paper rolled out on it.

The doctor came in and said, "Well now, Adrianne, I hear you're not feeling too well. What seems to be the problem?"

I responded, "I can't move my neck, and I can't eat or drink because I have lots of sores in my mouth. My neck is all swollen, and it looks like I have a golf ball on the left side."

The doctor gently pressed two fingers on each side of my neck. He told me to open my mouth, and he looked inside.

"I'll have to do some tests on you, Adrianne," he said.

I braced myself for the pain, but, to my surprise, none of the tests hurt. He took my blood pressure, a urine sample, and x-rays of my back and neck. I began to calm down, but then he called my mom into the room, and he finally said, "Adrianne, you're going to have to stay in the hospital awhile so that I can do some more tests."

I didn't know what to think. I couldn't believe this was happening to me. My mom's eyes got all red, and she asked, "How long will she have to stay in the hospital?"

"It's hard to tell at this point. I will be able to tell you more about her sickness after I run some more tests," is all he would tell us. With that he walked out of the room.

After waiting for what seemed like an hour, a young nurse assisted me into a wheelchair, led me into a big elevator, and pushed number four. The number immediately lit up, and the elevator moved softly upward. When we got out, the nurse wheeled me down a long hallway. As we passed rooms, I peered inside and saw kids of all ages, colors, sizes, and shapes; some sitting in their rooms looking sick and helpless, others watching a movie or visiting with friends, and some yakking away on the telephone.

The nurse made an unexpected turn into a cold,

gray room. I was led to a bed opposite a girl in her early teens. Above my bed was a big shelf that held a red telephone. There was a large window next to my bed, but I didn't have that great a view. All I could see were an Arby's and a busy street with cars driving from one destination to another. Beside my bed was a cold metal nightstand with a gold colored bucket containing a white and blue poka-dotted nightgown. The nurse advised me to put it on.

I told my mom, "Just sit down while I change. I will be right back." I reached over and picked up my nightgown. As my feet hit the cold, gray tile floor, my knees felt weak, and I could barely walk because it made my neck and back hurt. I felt crippled and helpless. I didn't want to be helpless because I enjoyed doing stuff for myself. I changed, and when I returned to my nightstand, I glanced at my mom and observed her in conversation with my doctor.

Both of them had very serious looks on their faces.

I climbed in between the white sheets and waited for the doctor to say something. Finally, he came over with my mom to my bed and said sternly, "In a few minutes, I would like you to have a spinal tap."

"Fine," is all I said. He told me a nurse would come in and take me to the room where I was supposed to go for the test. All I thought was that it was going to be just another painless test like the ones I'd had earlier.

Immediately after the doctor left the room, the same young nurse came back in with a squeaky, blue and black wheelchair that looked at least ten years old or more, and we were off. As I was wheeled into the room that felt as cold as a refrigerator, I saw a woman who looked like she was draped in a white sheet. In reality, it was her uniform.

The room had an unusual aroma. It smelled like a dentist office, but with more of a medicine scent.

The smell made my stomach churn. I tried to inhale through my mouth and exhale out of my nose so that I wouldn't get the awful smell in my nostrils.

The doctor told me to climb up on the bed that had uncomfortable paper spread out over it. I inched up out of my wheelchair, and the cordial nurse helped me onto the rocklike bed that was at least four feet high. I glanced over and noticed my mom sitting on the edge of her seat with an anguished look on her face.

"Adrianne," the doctor said, "I need you to roll over on your side, honey." He squished me into a ball and had the nurse and my mom hold me in that position. He lifted the back of my shirt very gently, and I asked, "Will it hurt?"

"It will hurt some but just remember not to move at all. It's very important to stay still."

The nurse handed the doctor a needle the size of a new pencil. My mouth dropped open when I saw how huge it was. I felt numb. I couldn't move any part of my body. I wanted to yell at him to stop, but I couldn't get the words that were on the tip of my stiff tongue out of my dry mouth. I wanted to faint or at least seize the needle from the doctor and thrust it into him so he would know how scary it was. Instead, I clutched my mom's cold hand.

I felt a sharp poke in my back right by my spine. It actually felt like I was being stabbed in the back with a sharp knife or an icepick. I got a chill from my head all the way down to my toes. I was so terrorized I didn't even have time to think. He pulled the razor-sharp needle out and placed a small bandage where the needle had been. I turned over and lay on my stomach. I still had a little sting in my back, but I was ecstatic because it was over—at least for the time being, anyway.

_____

I went back to my room with my mom and immediately fell asleep. When I awoke, the doctor was talking with her.

"How are you feeling, Adrianne?" the doctor asked.

"I'm really sore," I said. "I thought that the spinal tap was going to be just another painless test, but it wasn't."

"Well unfortunately, the spinal tap didn't give us much information. It did tell us that your spine won't be affected by whatever you have. I'm still not sure what is wrong with you. It could either be limphatic meningitis or just a virus. You will have

to stay a few weeks to a month so that we can find out what's wrong with you and cure it."

As I heard this news, I immediately pictured that long needle, the stabbing pain, the knot in the pit of my stomach and I winced. I couldn't believe that the test didn't give him much information. I was furious, but I didn't say how furious I was. Instead I asked, "Will there be any more tests?"

"Yes, there will be more tests but they won't be as painful as the spinal tap," the doctor assured me.

After two and a half weeks in the hospital and lots of I.V. and other medicines, I was better. My glands slowly went back to their normal size, and I was able to eat again.

The doctor came to the conclusion that it must have been just a virus and that it might come back. You can bet that I am praying real hard that it doesn't.

Adrianne Abbott
Thurston Middle School
Laguna Beach Unified School District

- *Step 3.* Once students have a clear idea of what the saturation report entails, ask them to brainstorm about the people, places, and events they could write about and to place the names on a chart like the following:

People	Places	Events

Then have them put a *GI* next to the topics they are *genuinely interested* in and an *MC* beside the topics they are *mildly curious* about. After eliminating all the MCs from their lists, students can set priorities for their GIs and select the most promising topic.

- *Step 4.* Enable/require students to begin planning early by asking them to write a one-page abstract that explains what their topic is, why they selected it, and how they intend to go about getting the information they need. Review these abstracts while students are sharing their ideas and getting feedback from their peer groups. Meet with any students who still need to narrow their focus.

- *Step 5.* The students are now ready to go out and observe their person, place, or event. Encourage them to record everything they hear, see, touch, smell, taste, and so on and to note their impressions and reactions. Allow a week for the information-generating stage of the process. (You may find the accompanying chart helpful for showing your students how the data they collect can relate to the domains of writing. Teachers in kindergarten through grade six might want to help students practice recording impressions by taking the class to a common location and having them fill out a sample chart with a partner.)

Sensory/Descriptive	*Imaginative/Narrative*
RECORD: Sights, smells, tastes, textures, sounds, action words, atmosphere words, character description	*RECORD:* Dialogue, time frame, ideas for scenes, transition words, dramatic effects, mood
Practical/Informative	*Analytical/Expository*
RECORD: Historical background, interesting facts and statistics, "how to" information, interview questions, and responses	*RECORD:* First impressions, reactions, afterthoughts, opinions, judgments, criticisms

- *Step 6.* When students come back to class with their notes, help them to organize their ideas by asking them to think of themselves as photographers or cinematographers. If they were filming this, what kind of camera angles would they use? What focus? What kind of lighting? How often would they change the scene? Then show them Ruby Bernstein's cluster of her exposé of weight-loss clinics (Figure 1) and ask them to create a scene-by-scene cluster of their report. Walk around the room to review these and offer suggestions.
- *Step 7.* Finally, to make sure that the students are off to a good start, have them write their opening scene and bring copies to class for

sharing. Jenee Gossard's read-around technique (in the "Sharing/Responding" section of this book) works particularly well for bringing to the students' attention papers that look particularly promising. These papers can be read aloud to the whole group (in addition to being read silently by all) and discussed in terms of their special merits. Students can then go back to their own papers with a fresh perspective on their own writing, some new ideas gained from seeing other students' work, and the motivation of writing for their peers.

Even with all this preparation, some students will still write flawed saturation reports, but those students will be in the minority. My experience has been that the saturation report brings out the best in student writers. I always look forward to reading them because they are as diverse as one's students are—interesting, educational, and well crafted.

The Add-on Saturation Report

By Linda Bowe
Teacher, Evergreen Elementary School, Walnut Valley Unified School District; and Teacher/Consultant, UCI Writing Project

Saturation reporting is a natural outgrowth of a writing exercise I use in my second grade classroom: writing add-on books. This five-day writing experience helps students develop complete, detailed stories, each with a beginning, a middle, and an end. Once familiar with the add-on technique (described below), students can write saturation reports in any unit of study. Science and social studies are particularly appropriate. Reports can easily be done with science lessons on the following subjects: fruit flies, tadpoles, snails, tide pools, earthworms, or any similar subject that generates student interest and investigation.

My science unit on silkworms has provided an excellent opportunity for students to use the knowledge they have acquired through the enjoyable process of storywriting. Following intense weeks of observation and discussion as the silkworms hatch, grow, molt, spin, emerge as moths, lay eggs, and die, the students become thoroughly immersed in the life cycle of the silkworm. At this point they are very capable of writing about the experience.

Students may take one of two approaches in writing their add-on saturation reports. They can describe a different life cycle of the silkworm each day, or they can concentrate on one cycle and write daily about a different aspect. Limiting the daily topic helps students to focus on the subject and to produce more descriptive pieces of writing than they might otherwise produce.

In a more creative vein, the students can fantasize and write imaginative stories about pet silkworms. The following format works well for this assignment:

Day 1: The students describe the silkworm's character.

Day 2: They describe the silkworm's habitat.

Day 3: They put the silkworm in an exciting situation that involves some kind of problem or conflict.

Day 4: They propose a solution to the problem or a resolution to the conflict.

Day 5: They tell about the feelings of the silkworm after its exciting experience.

Using this day-by-day add-on technique, the students develop an ongoing story in which they integrate factual information and imaginative ideas. Often, students become so involved in the study of their silkworms that they choose to write their stories from the first-person point of view.

Once the students have prepared a draft of their add-on saturation reports, they can revise them and put their final versions in booklets made of brightly colored construction paper. They should also be encouraged to illustrate what they wrote. Students love to share their newfound knowledge with their classmates, parents, or community members at an open house. (For other suggested postwriting activities, see page 24 of the *Handbook for Planning an Effective Writing Program.*)

I have found that once students write an add-on saturation report by blending science with creative writing, their enthusiasm for classroom study in all curricular areas grows, as does their desire to communicate what they have learned to an audience.

Point of View in Writing

A Lesson on Point of View . . . That Works

By Carol Booth Olson
Director, UCI Writing Project

To make the concept of point of view comprehensible to students, I include a writing assignment in my composition class that enables each student to become a literary character and to speak through that character's voice. The emphasis of the lesson is twofold. First, it provides an experiential "learn-by-doing" approach to improving writing skills. As James Britton, a British researcher on writing, points out in *The Development of Writing Abilities (11–18)*, when writing becomes a genuine mode of learning instead of just a vehicle for showing what one has already learned, there is more opportunity for the student to discover his or her own personal voice as a writer.[1] Second, this kind of assignment fosters critical reading skills because the student must think deeply about a piece of literature in order to assume the point of view of one of the characters.

Although the lesson described below was originally designed for community college students, the concept and the strategies can be easily adapted to any grade level and work of literature. To begin, I introduce the following aspects of point of view: *who* (first person, third person, omniscient narrator, and stream-of-consciousness narration); *when* (past, present, future, and flashback); and *where* (from a distant perspective, in the midst of the action, from beyond the grave, and so forth). I then ask the students to read John Steinbeck's novella *Of Mice and Men*. This book works well for a variety of reasons. Since the majority of my students do not read for pleasure and need to be encouraged to discover the value of a good book, the brevity and pacing of *Of Mice and Men* is attractive for an initial reading and writing assignment. The universal themes of the novella are also readily accessible and lend themselves to a class

---

[1] James Britton and others, *The Development of Writing Abilities (11—18)* (Schools Council Research Studies). Houndmills Basingstoke, Hampshire: Macmillan Education Ltd., 1975.

discussion that everyone can contribute to. Finally, the authorial voice that John Steinbeck uses to set the stage for his drama is quite distinct from the dialogue in which his main characters, two itinerant farmhands, speak for themselves—revealing their hopes and dreams, frustrations and limitations.

Because of my exposure to the California and National Writing Projects, I am a believer in teaching writing as a process and, whenever possible, structure my assignments in such a way as to include instruction and "think time" for each stage of composition: prewriting, writing, sharing/ responding, rewriting, editing, and evaluating. As a prewriting exercise for my lesson on point of view, I use Gabriele Rico's clustering technique to generate ideas for discussion. (See Dr. Rico's description of clustering that appears earlier in this publication.)

During the clustering session, the instructor writes a stimulus word on the chalkboard and asks students to make free associations to conjure up words, images, and phrases in bubbles around that stimulus word. These clusters are then used as a basis from which to create short paragraphs about the designated topic. For this particular prewriting exercise, I ask the students to take ten minutes to jot down anything that comes to mind in relation to Lennie and George, the protagonists in *Of Mice and Men*. We share these associations as a group and develop clusters, such as the one shown in Figure 1. Then, rather than asking students to write freely, using their clusters as a point of departure, I try to elicit one sentence from our discussion, such as, "Lennie's mind is not right," which students must illustrate in a paragraph using Rebekah Caplan's

strategy of "showing, not telling" (see Rebekah Caplan's section earlier in this book); that is, of showing Lennie's mental infirmity rather than directly telling about it, as in the sample that follows:

Lennie's mind is not right.

Towering over all like a giant, ignorant of his strength, Lennie crushes the life out of the objects of his affection like so many paper dolls. And then he looks at George, helplessly, questioningly, burning with shame because he has done another bad thing and terrified that there will be no more soft, fuzzy creatures to fondle. He's kind of like those puppies he smothers with love—filled with need, anxious to please, obedient to his master. George just shakes his head and wonders what's to become of them. "Tell me again about the rabbits!" The broken record is stuck on the same groove. Lennie smiles dreamily as the nightmare unfolds—oblivious to all but the pretty picture in his head.

We follow the same procedure of sharing cluster words about George, although more emphasis is now placed on comparing and contrasting the two characters. But when it comes time to show that "George is his brother's keeper," I ask the students to write their paragraphs as monologues from George's point of view, as was done in this example:

He ain't smart but he's a worker, old Lennie is. He can do anything once you tell him how. Sometimes he makes me so mad, I just tell him to jump in the lake. But he does it. Pathetic! How can you deal with a guy like that? I know I'd probably be better off without him. Trouble is, I think I'd probably miss him, crazy as it sounds. And I'd always be wonderin what kinda trouble he was gettin into with no one to get him out of it. I guess we gotta stick together.

Having established this foundation for writing, I give the students the following assignment:

At the conclusion of *Of Mice and Men*, Slim leads George away from the river and up towards the highway, reassuring him that he had to kill Lennie; there was no way out. Imagine that Slim and George head into town for some stiff drinks and deep conversation. Please begin your paper at this point. *Writing assignment:* In George's words explain to Slim why *you* killed Lennie. Remember that you must *become* George to write this paper. You are limited to his vocabulary, his perspective on life, and his level of

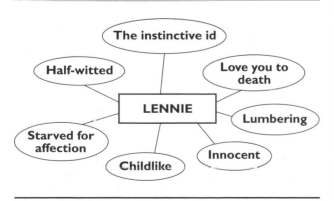

Fig. 1. Clustering of *Lennie* from *Of Mice and Men*

To make the concept of point of view comprehensible to students, I include a writing assignment in my composition class that enables each student to become a literary character and to speak through that character's voice.

CAROL BOOTH OLSON

sensitivity. In your dialogue suggest either directly or indirectly: what Lennie meant to you, what significance the dream of the land and the farmhouse has or had for you, and your perception of what life will be like without Lennie.

To clarify what is expected of the student on this assignment, I hand out a two-page scoring guide based on a 1 to 9 holistic scale that outlines the characteristics of a successful and unsuccessful paper:

9—8 This paper is clearly superior—well written, coherent, clearly organized, and insightful. A 9—8 paper does most or all of the following well:

- Maintains a clear point of view; i.e., speaks through George's voice and sees through George's eyes.
- Portrays George in a manner that is consistent with John Steinbeck's depiction of him.
- Shows insight into George's character and into the main themes Steinbeck presents in the novella.
- Responds to the questions of why you killed Lennie, what he meant to you, what significance the dream of the land and the farmhouse has or had for you, and what you think life will be like without Lennie.
- Displays the writer's own voice through the description that is external to George's and Slim's dialogue (such as establishing setting).
- Uses descriptive, precise, and appropriate diction.
- Handles dialogue effectively.
- Varies sentence structure and length for effect.
- Uses the conventions of written English (spelling, punctuation, grammar, complete

sentence structure, proper format for using dialogue, and so forth) correctly. (*Note*: Grammar may be violated and slang words used in this case in the dialogue portions of your paper.)

7 This paper is a thinner version of the 9—8 paper. It is still impressive and interesting but less well handled in terms of point of view, organization, or diction. The 7 paper is also apt to offer less insight into George's character and into Steinbeck's main themes.

6—5 These scores apply to papers that are less well handled than the 7, 8, or 9 paper. A 6—5 paper may be less insightful, more loosely organized, or less comprehensible to the reader. A 6—5 paper will exhibit some or all of the following:

- Speaks through George's voice but is not entirely clear in terms of the message conveyed.
- Portrays George in a manner that is generally consistent with Steinbeck's depiction of him but in such a way that the character does not sound real.
- Responds directly to why *you* killed Lennie but only touches on the other three subquestions.
- Tends to say the obvious and does not display any special insight into the characters.
- Displays little or none of the writer's voice through description of setting.
- Uses less descriptive, precise, or appropriate diction than in the 7, 8, or 9 paper.
- Handles dialogue less effectively than the 7, 8, or 9 paper. (The dialogue may either drag or be too sketchy.)
- Uses little or no variation in sentence structure and length.

- Contains some problems with the conventions of written English but none that seriously impairs the message.

4—3 These scores apply to papers that follow the general idea of the writing assignment but that are weak in thought, language facility, or the conventions of written English. A 4—3 paper exhibits some or all of the following:

- Speaks through George's voice only intermittently or not at all. Who is speaking may be unclear.
- Portrays George in a manner that is inconsistent with Steinbeck's depiction.
- Fails to respond to the four questions posed in the writing assignment.
- Displays very little insight into Steinbeck's characters or main themes.
- Uses overly general diction not suited to George's character.
- Uses dialogue ineffectively or not at all.
- Presents the purpose of paper unclearly.
- Contains little or no differentiation between style and sentence patterns in the "George portion" of the paper and in the writer's description of setting. Contains serious problems in the conventions of written English that impair the author's message.

2—1 These papers:

- Fail to speak through George's voice.
- Neglect the four questions posed in the writing assignment.
- Have superficial and/or fragmented and cloudy content.
- Indicate that the writer has misunderstood or perhaps has not read the book.
- Contain serious problems in the conventions of written English.

Note: An extremely well-written paper in terms of the conventions of written English may receive a point higher from the scorer than it would on the basis of content alone. A paper that is strong or satisfactory in content but that has serious problems in the conventions of written English should be docked up to two points, depending on the nature and frequency of the errors committed.

I give students one week to write rough drafts of their point of view papers and ask them to bring four photocopies of their work to class for discussion. I then allow one class session for students to meet in their groups to make critiques, read their papers aloud, get feedback from their group members, and make notes for revision. Early in the semester I train my students to use the following techniques adapted from Peter Elbow's *Writing Without Teachers* (see Peter Elbow's section that appears later in this book):

- Pointing to the words—trying to remember key words or phrases that seem strong or weak
- Summarizing the writing—summarizing the piece of writing in a single sentence or choosing one word that captures it to help the writer determine whether the message he or she intended comes across clearly
- Telling the writer what happened—describing the thoughts and feelings that come to mind as the writer shares his or her work

I also stress that students should be descriptive rather that evaluative in their remarks, and I remind the class that there is no right and wrong in writing—only what communicates and what does not. While students are sharing their papers, I call them up one by one and offer my comments and suggestions.

The revised paper is to be scored in class the following week. Using the scoring guide I provided, members of writing groups must score the papers, come to a group consensus, and fill out an evaluation sheet for papers written by four students from another writing group. The papers are then handed in to me for my score (which I average with theirs) and my written feedback.

I was particularly impressed with the quality of the papers that were turned in for this assignment. The students demonstrated a clear grasp of point of view, a depth of feeling for the character whose voice they were assuming, and an overall understanding of John Steinbeck's underlying themes. Ultimately, I feel that this lesson positively affected future papers, because it not only made students more aware of point of view in literature, but it also increased their recognition of their own voices as writers. A sample of a student paper written by Charles Wrightson, who was in my English 1A class at Irvine Valley College, follows:

George Speaks

The sun had fallen through the soft, dusty haze when they finally reached Soledad. Slim let the other farmhands come along but told them to leave George and him alone. They went to Suzy's Place, their boots kicking up little dust clouds and scraping on the gravel at the side of the rutted old road.

Suzy met them at the door and looked them up and down. But before she could say anything, Slim said softly, "The boys can do what they want. Me an' George want a quiet table alone."

After reading Slim's face and tone, she looked at George, lowered her eyes, and slowly nodded her head with its lovely blond curls. She led the way to the side table, brought a whiskey bottle and two shot glasses, and left after a slow look at Slim.

It seemed that George had sat there for hours, slumped, looking deep into the dark grain of the wood table for an answer. All he saw was the gun shaking in his nerveless hand, Lennie's head exploding from the impact, his body twitching as it fell over, and the blood pool beginning to grow like water from a slow spring.

"I been lookin' after Lennie my whole life," he finally whispered, still staring into the table.

Slim poured two shots of whiskey and handed George one. George downed it and felt like throwing up but kept it down because he needed not to think for awhile.

"You done all you could, George," Slim softly said. "All you could."

As he looked into Slim's eyes of steel, George felt the shock starting to leave him, but anger was welling up: "I had to shoot 'im! I had no choice. I couldn't let 'im alone for a minute. That bastard Curley was just waitin' to string 'im up."

George grabbed another shot of whiskey and downed it, trying to calm his nerves: "He was jus' like a big kid, but so strong an' he didn't know what he was doin! I couldn't let 'im go on like that."

George felt his eyes begin to burn, but he wasn't going to cry in front of Slim. So, he kept talking: "That poor kid couldn't a' been mean if it meant his life! Poor kid."

Again, George downed the refilled glass. Slim didn't say anything—just poured another and another. George kept talking. He felt like telling Slim everything. Without Lennie, there was no secret to be kept.

"I kept tellin' 'im about a place—a beautiful, green place all our own. At first it was jus' to keep 'im in line, ya know; but he'd get me talkin' and dreamin' and soon I'd start to ask myself, 'Why not? We could do it.' Oh, I knowed it probably wouldn't never of happened, but it was all that kep' us goin'."

George stopped, feeling the burning in his eyes again, thinking about living without Lennie. Lonely. Just drifting from place to place—with no friends. Terribly lonely.

"Yeah, all we had . . . ," he said, "except each other. Now I ain't even got him no more."

"What you gonna do now, George?" Slim asked.

"Don' know, Slim, I jus' don' know. He was all I had. But I had to shoot 'im. You see that, don' you Slim?"

Without responding, Slim stood up, deciding it was time to leave. "Come on, George, we'd better be gettin' back," he urged.

Slowly wavering, George got to his feet. He was pretty drunk, but his head was clear: "I guess I'll work the month out an' then move on, Slim."

Slim looked at George for a minute, put his arm out to brace his friend, and helped him outside. "I guess that's best, George," he agreed. They moved out into the deep night with the rich smell of barley on the dry, whispering breeze and headed down the dusty road.

Practical Ideas for Teaching Point of View

A Seventh Grade Approach to Point of View

By Marie Filardo

Former English Teacher, Serrano Intermediate School
and De Portla Elementary School,
Saddleback Valley Unified School District;
and Teacher/Consultant, UCI Writing Project

Point of view is one of the most difficult techniques of fine writing to teach seventh graders. To simplify teaching the technique, I take a two-step approach. First, I assign my students a novel entitled *A Special Gift* by Marcia L. Simon, which I ask them to summarize. The ability to summarize is not just a reading skill but a critical thinking skill. According to Edward Fry, Director of the Reading Center and Professor at Rutgers University, summarizing is more than merely finding the main idea; it also involves the production of a message, a concise statement that is spoken or written. For most seventh graders, summarizing is the mere reproduction of a story. I attempt to teach them to internalize thoughts and emotions evoked by the author and to generate new ideas.

A Special Gift is the story of a teenage boy named Peter who is torn between two talents. He is an excellent basketball player as well as an excellent ballet dancer. At first, ballet is something Peter does as a young boy simply because he accompanies his sister to lessons. As Peter matures and becomes more sensitive to the feelings of others, he realizes his sister's enjoyment of the art is readily approved of, whereas his is not only disapproved of, but frowned on. Nevertheless, he pursues his love for dancing, insisting that the strenuous exercises enhance his basketball performance. His dad is thrilled with the prospect of his son's becoming the school's star basketball player but has difficulty accepting the fact that he enjoys ballet. Peter finds himself torn between winning his dad's admiration and bearing his rejection. Peter is also aware that he has kept his dancing a secret from his friends and classmates. When his

father's friend, Pearson, discovers Peter's talent for ballet, he calls his enjoyment of dancing "weird." Peter realizes the horror facing him if and when his double life should be revealed.

As the story unfolds, Peter is chosen to dance in the *Nutcracker* ballet. He admits that he is thrilled with the opportunity, finally sensing how much dancing really means to him. All of Peter's difficulties become compounded when basketball season overlaps with ballet season. Rehearsals for the games and performances are scheduled for the same times, and Peter is caught in a dilemma. He must come to terms with himself, his values, and his friendships.

After we have summarized the story orally, I ask my students to embark on step two, the critical thinking stage, which has as its ultimate goal the production of a written statement. When students are fully immersed in the plot and characters of the story, I ask them to employ Gabriele Rico's technique of clustering. (See Dr. Rico's description of clustering as a prewriting process, which appears earlier in this book.) As Dr. Rico points out, clustering is a visual, nonlinear development of ideas. It helps the students find and generate ideas. It is the discovery or brainstorming stage of writing sometimes labeled prewriting. Given a nucleus word, the writer is asked to associate satellite words. Later, the writer discovers structure in these thoughts. In this lesson we use clustering to focus on Peter's problems. The intent is to have the students project themselves into Peter's mind and to brainstorm about his dilemma, using Peter's voice.

To do this activity successfully, the students must adhere to the issue at hand; i.e., how Peter feels. I emphasize that their success depends on how well they get into Peter's mind. The writers must be objective and unbiased in their reactions. They must be willing to suspend their own thoughts and feelings and to refrain from judging Peter. Instead they must think as Peter thinks. They must strive to sense the emotional turmoil that Peter is experiencing. The physical movements Peter engages in must be as realistic to the students as are Peter's mental and emotional states. Given the word *dancing* as a nucleus word, we arrive at a cluster, as shown in Figure 2.

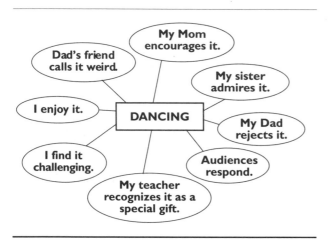

Fig. 2. Clustering *Dancing* from *A Special Gift*

Then I present a scene from the book to use as a springboard for the students' writing. It is one in which Peter has given in to his father's pressure to play basketball when he should have been attending an important rehearsal for the ballet. Because he plays poorly, his coach yells at him, and then he hurts his ankle. He uses the accident as an excuse to leave the game and rush to the rehearsal. While hectically changing clothes in his dad's car, he feels frustration and resentment. Marcia Simon writes:

> He was angry with his father for making him go to the game, and angry with the coach for scolding him. Most of all he was angry with himself—for agreeing to play in the game in the first place when he should have been at the ballet rehearsal, for playing like a clumsy idiot, and for leaving the game to go to ballet when any kid in his right mind would have wanted to stay at the game and help his team win.[1]

Using this scene as a point of departure, I give my students the following prompt:

> Imagine you are Peter riding in your dad's car. You have just returned from a humiliating game, which you did not want to play in the first place. You were manipulated by your dad, your coach, your team members, classmates, and friends. You are furious because no one has shown any regard for your

feelings or rights as an individual. You are tired of being ignored. You love your father and want him to understand that you are a young adult capable of making intelligent decisions. Prove that you are your own person. Convince your father that you have reviewed all the pros and cons before making this decision to quit the team and dance. You know beyond a shadow of a doubt that playing basketball will make you a hero, whereas dancing will make you a laughing stock.

A Special Gift is especially geared to junior high school students who are beginning both the school year and an examination of themselves and their place in the world. Writing about Peter's decision allows these students to examine the importance of being themselves—even if it is at the expense of fitting in. This book also provides them with the opportunity to explore the challenges, decisions, and difficulties of growing up, as viewed from the standpoint of a young person. Remaining anonymous allows young students to express their innermost feelings without the burden of repercussions from their peers.

A Parent's Point of View

By Dale Sprowl

Former English Teacher, Irvine High School, Irvine Unified School District; and Teacher/Consultant, UCI Writing Project

To teach point of view, I use "Charles," a very short story by Shirley Jackson, which tells of a young boy's conflicts in his first days of kindergarten. Narrated from his mother's point of view, the story unfolds as her son, Laurie, comes home each day to tell his family about another boy, Charles, who causes persistent trouble at school. In the course of the story, Charles becomes less naughty and more congenial and productive at school. Curious to find out who Charles's parents are, the mother attends a P.T.A. meeting only to find that there is no Charles in the class and, thus, that her son has been talking about himself.

After I have read the story aloud to my low-ability-level ninth grade students, we discuss Laurie's motivation in creating Charles, his transi-

---

[1]Marcia L. Simon, *A Special Gift*. New York: Harcourt Brace Jovanovich, Inc., 1978, p. 65. © 1978 by Marcia L. Simon; reprinted by permission of the author.

tion into becoming a cooperative member of the class, clues the author gives of what the mother will discover, and the mother's point of view. Then the discussion moves away from the short story to the students' own experiences. I ask questions about the students' feelings on the first day of school, about conflicts with teachers, and about saying, "I have a friend who _____," to test a parent's reaction to a predicament. Why do we try to protect our parents from who we truly are? We discuss the need for acceptance.

After the discussion I give the writing assignment. I have the students write a letter to themselves from either their mother's or father's point of view. The students write the letters to themselves ("Dear Sean") and sign it from one of their parents ("Love, Mom"). I explain the proper format for a friendly letter and write criteria for the letter on the chalkboard.

The students responded well after they had completed the prewriting exercises of reading and discussing. Their responses, however, indicated that they perceived their parents as critical and rule conscious: "P.S. Clean your room." "Please don't forget to clean your room, make your bed, take the trash out, and stay in the house until everyone comes home." Fewer responses contained affection and acceptance. This outcome helped me to understand my students and their perception of authority. They were motivated to write by the switch in point of view (and perhaps, they felt power in becoming a parent). A lesson plan on my "point of view" assignment follows:

Suggested Lesson Plan on Point of View
(Ninth grade English, one to two days in class)

First—Read Shirley Jackson's short story "Charles."

Second—Discuss the story.
1. Why did the boy create Charles?
2. How did the boy grow as the story progressed?
3. What clues did the author give of how the story would end?
4. What is point of view? (Teach this concept if the students cannot derive a good definition.)
5. From whose point of view was the story written?
6. What is the mother's point of view toward Charles's behavior?

7. How did the author use the mother's point of view?

Third—Discuss the students' personal experiences.
1. How do you feel about starting school, a new job, or summer camp?
2. What conflicts do you have with teachers?
3. Have you ever covered up by creating a "friend" to blame for something you did that was wrong? Do you test your friends' or your parents' reactions before you tell the truth?
4. What is acceptance? Why does it motivate us?

Fourth—Teach the friendly letter form.

Fifth—Present the written assignment.
1. Pretend you are either your mother or your father.
2. Write a letter to yourself from one of your parents' points of view.
3. Use the proper friendly letter format.

Sixth—Read five or six papers aloud to the class, and make comments about what was effective in the writing.

Suggested follow-up activities:
1. Discuss how the students perceive their parents.
2. Discuss insights the students may have about their parents after experiencing their point of view.
   a. What do you do that annoys your parents?
   b. What do you do that worries your parents?
   c. How can you please your parents?
   d. Do you feel accepted by your parents?
   e. How can you help your parents to understand your point of view?
3. Have the students give the letter they wrote to their parents, and ask them to respond, taking the student's point of view.

On the whole this has been a successful assignment for me because my students have been motivated to write fluently, to learn the letter form, and to experience the point of view of another person and to describe it in their writing.

The choice of a point of view is the initial act of a culture.

JOSE ORTEGA Y GASSET

The New Kid

By Mark Reardon

Director of Education and Training, The Learning Forum;
and Teacher/Consultant, UCI Writing Project

One way to approach point of view is through an eyewitness account. I use the short story, "The New Kid," by Murray Heyert, focusing on the event where the main character, Marty, and the new kid are forced into a fight by their peers.

Prior to reading the selection, students, who are formed into groups, cluster the word *bully*, focusing on motives, attitudes, and personality traits. These clusters are shared by each group's spokesperson as I write the ideas on butcher paper, which can be referred to later.

Knowing the power of creative dramatics, I involve the students in improvisations as the next step in prewriting. Volunteers are solicited to participate in the following sketches:

- Students gathered around a locker as a person walks by and slams the locker door shut
- A school lunch line when someone cuts in
- A private game in which a person steals the ball
- A person or persons who will not let someone be part of a game or group

As these improvisations unfold, I freeze the actions and ask the characters to tell what they are thinking and feeling. These words are added to a "Thinking-Feeling" list.

At this point, I share this portion of the prompt with my students: "We will be reading a story about a bully in a situation you may find to be familiar. As we read the short story, you will be looking closely at the characters' actions, feelings, and thoughts, much as we have done with these improvisations."

To help the students identify immediately with the characters of the story, especially with the characters' actions, feelings, and thoughts, I lead my class through two guided imagery journal writings as part of the precomposing stage. The first guided imagery has the students recall a time when they were bullied:

- Recall a time when you were bullied or picked on by someone who was perhaps older, stronger, or smarter. This experience should stand out clearly in your mind. It may have happened at school, in class, in a line, in a store, or on a street.
- Now that you have this experience in your mind, recall specific details, such as the place, time, sounds, and so forth.
- Remember the person's words, tone of voice, facial expressions, attitude, the look in his or her eyes, and so forth.
- Repeat the entire episode in your mind.
- Now, focus on your feelings. Remember how your nerves, heart, and skin felt. Recall your thoughts. Perhaps you spoke aloud. Hear what you said.
- Now, recall the entire episode once again in your mind.

As if the incident were a journal entry, have students write about the time they were bullied. When the students are finished, have them make a list of their feelings during and after the experience and of their reactions, both emotional and physical. Here is an example:

Feelings		Reactions	
During	*After*	*Emotional*	*Physical*
scared	embarrassed	cried	knot in stomach
nervous	threatened	yelled	tense
		swore	

Have students share their journal entry with the class.

In the second guided imagery, I have my students recall a time when they were the bullies:

- Recall a time when you were a bully, when you picked on or intimidated someone because you were tougher, smarter, or older. This should be an experience that stands out clearly in your mind.
- Now that you have remembered that experience, recall the setting—place, time, and sounds. Hear what people were saying; see what they were doing.
- Listen to what you said, your tone of voice. Think about your attitude.
- See what you did.
- Replay the entire episode in your mind.
- Now, focus on your feelings. Remember what you did.
- Remember what your body felt like, your heart, your nerves. Focus on how the experience made you feel. Recall your thoughts.
- Now, replay the entire episode once again in your mind.

One way to approach point of view is through an eyewitness account based on a familiar situation.

MARK REARDON

As if this experience were a journal entry, have students write about it. When they are finished, have them make lists as before. Have students also share this experience with the class.

Up to this point the students have been writing from the first-person point of view. To help them move from that standpoint to third-person observation, I assign the following showing, not telling, sentence: "The person was a bully." They are to include the person's actions, attitudes, and feelings, creating a half to three-quarter page vivid description that leads the reader to conclude that the person was indeed a bully.

Before reading the selection, I share the remainder of the prompt with the students:

> After reading the short story "The New Kid," you will re-create the bully incident that occurred between the main character, Marty, and the new kid. You will want to create an accurate account of what happened by being precise, vivid, and detailed so that someone who has never read the story will have a clear picture of the incident. By not being directly involved, you are in a good position to understand why this person did what he or she did. After re-creating this incident, tell the reader why you think Marty did what he did. Include what Marty was possibly thinking and feeling. Finally, tell your reader what you learned from observing the incident.

We read the story in three parts, with close reading for actions, attitudes, feelings, and traits of each of the characters: Marty, Eddie and the boys, and the new kid. We use an observation sheet (see the illustration on the next page), with each of the characters listed as a major category. Subcategories of actions, attitudes, feelings, and traits are listed for each. We read the first three pages, focusing on Marty and Eddie and the boys. Through the next

three pages, we look for additional material on Marty and Eddie and the boys and begin, with the introduction of the new kid, to fill in words for this category. The remaining pages reveal the incident between Marty and the new kid. We add to the observation chart, especially noting feelings and actions to help students better understand why the characters did what they did.

After reviewing the prompt, the students write an eyewitness account of the incident between Marty and the new kid. They write from a third-person point of view in the first part of their paper as they describe the incident. Then they move into first-person reaction during the second part of their paper when telling why they think Marty did what he did, and they reflect on what they learned from observing the incident.

One to two class days are given to write the first draft. One day is given for students to share those drafts with their response groups. Members of each group complete a response sheet that includes *what, why,* and *how* sections. (See the "Sharing/Responding" section of this book for suggestions on writing-response groups.) Students write specific descriptive responses to the writer's description of the event *(what),* the writer's reason for Marty's action *(why),* and their perceptions of how the incident affected the writer *(how).*

I provide time in class for revision and encourage students to make use of the comments on their response sheets and to pay careful attention to the specifics of the prompt. I also use this day to work with individual students.

Before the papers are turned in for my evaluation, students form into read-around groups and evaluate papers, using a holistic scoring guide like the one that follows:

Observation Sheet for "The New Kid"

Reader/Writer _____

Observations											
of Marty				of Eddie and the boys				of the New Kid			
Actions	Attitudes	Feelings	Traits	Actions	Attitudes	Feelings	Traits	Actions	Attitudes	Feelings	Traits

Primary Trait Scoring

3 A 3 paper clearly and logically describes the event, explains why the writer thinks the persons did what they did, and considers the significance of this event for the writer. It:

- Re-creates an accurate account of the bully incident between Marty and the new kid, using vivid, precise description
- Gives reasons for Marty's actions based on his possible thoughts and feelings
- Responds with an evaluation of what the writer learned from observing the event

2 A 2 paper contains all the features of a 3 paper, but it is not as strong in details. It gives reasons for Marty's actions, but it is weak in supporting them with examples of Marty's possible thoughts and feelings.

1 A 1 paper is missing the basic features needed for an eyewitness account. It lacks description, reasons for actions, or a personal response to the event.

Secondary Trait Scoring

2 A 2 paper follows conventions of proper grammar and syntax, margins, paragraph structure, spelling, capitalization, and end punctuation.

1 A 1 paper has minor errors in the conventions named previously.

0 A 0 paper has gross errors in the previously listed conventions.

Basing an eyewitness account on a familiar situation, such as a peer-induced fight, proves very motivating. Students identify easily with the characters, adding to their depth and insight as they move from third-person observation to first-person reaction.

If there were an art of writing, it would be nothing more or less than the art of feeling, the art of seeing, the art of hearing, the art of using all the senses.

REMY DE GOURMONT

When Clay Sings: A Point-of-View Lesson Integrating Art, Writing, History, and Literature

By Erline S. Krebs

Elementary Field Supervisor,
Department of Teacher Education,
Chapman University;
and Teacher/Consultant, UCI Writing Project

and Mindy Moffatt

English and History Teacher,
White Hill Middle School, Ross Valley School District;
and Teacher/Consultant, UCI Writing Project

Clay *can* sing. By assuming the clay's point of view, a writer can share its voice as it sings its story.

We wanted the students to write about their lives and what is important to them, but we knew from experience how superficial this type of writing can be. We needed to have our students break out of their left-brain, evaluative "parent" voice in order to tap the free thoughts of the right-brain "child" within. We wanted the students to reach within and to express themselves from a metaphoric place.

Byrd Baylor's book *When Clay Sings* sang to us. This delightful prose poem communicates the heritage of the ancient, strong, brown Southwest desert people, from which emerged events that still sing today through pieces of their clay pottery.

To create the mood for this point-of-view piece of writing, we read *When Clay Sings* to our students. Then the class members make a cluster about what they remember from the text, as shown in Figure 3.

During this step of the lesson, we encourage students to reflect on all aspects of the clay pottery, such as its creator and its colors, designs, shapes, and uses.

Once students' knowledge about ancient pottery has been established through the clustering process, we weave in the connection of this newly acquired information with the students' lives. Ancient pottery was most often used as containers. When students are asked to look around the

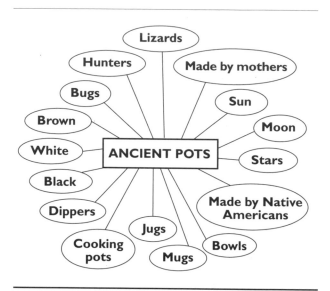

Fig. 3. Clustering of *Ancient Pots*

classroom to identify containers, everyone becomes enlightened. Lunch bags contain food, desks contain school materials, books contain words and ideas, pockets contain secrets, stomachs contain food, and the room contains us all. As students glance thoughtfully around the classroom, they can identify and find many different types of containers in their immediate environment.

At this point homework is assigned to bridge the similarities between ancient and present life. Students are instructed to find a container that no one else might think of, and they are to bring it in for sharing with the class on the following day. We have found that every student can succeed with this specific assignment. Acting as facilitators, teachers should encourage and assist unprepared students in finding a unique contribution: shoes contain feet, heads contain brains, fingernails contain dirt, and the playground contains children at recess.

After the students have shared their ideas, the next step is for each student to connect with voices from the inner "child." The students make this connection by physically creating containers or clay pieces, using any clay medium available. (We have at various times used play dough, and ceramic clay.) This kinesthetic connection is essential. We encourage students to explore all the possibilities of the clay as they push, pull, mold, roll, and knead it.

To move the activity further into a metaphoric mode, we play Native American flute music recorded on cassette tapes. (A list of titles and sources of Native American flute music appears at the end of this article.) Within this atmosphere we notice that the students' conversations dwindle as their individual clay pieces take shape.

Once the clay pieces have been created, we ask our students to think of what is important in their lives. Almost always, students' perceptions include intrinsic as well as materialistic values. They jot down ideas and then select the three *most* important ones. Students must then design a symbol for each of their three selections; for example, figures holding hands to represent their family, the sun and trees to symbolize the outdoors, and animals to glorify their favorite cartoon heroes. Using paints or etching tools, students transfer their designs onto their clay pieces.

Once the pots have been formed and decorated with the students' symbols, we give the class the following writing prompt:

> If this clay object were to sing about itself, what would it say? You will write about the pot and the life of the person who made it as if you were the pot. Imagine you are the pot. Describe yourself—your colors, shape, and design. What are you used for? Tell about the person who made you, basing your description on the three designs that show what is important in his or her life right now. Communicate to others about the person who made you.

Allow students at least 15 minutes of class time to begin writing.

The next step in this process is sharing. Model for students how to listen and look for stories in their pots. Ask questions such as: What do you see? From the shape, designs, and so forth of the pot, what can you tell about the person who made it? What does this clay "sing" to you?

By looking and listening to the small voice in the clay piece, partners share their perceptions of the songs the clay sings. Once a partner has listened to the song from the clay and told its story to the maker, the maker responds to the interpretation. The maker may either read the piece of writing or respond to his or her partner's verbal interpretation of the song in the clay. Students may revise their writing on the basis of this interactive sharing.

Students tell us that this lesson makes it easy for them to write about themselves. We observe how effortlessly the writing seems to flow. The fluency and depth of feeling and expression become apparent as students write about themselves and their lives. Writing from the pot's point of view

> *The student must think deeply about a piece of literature in order to assume the point of view of one of the characters.*
>
> CAROL BOOTH OLSON

creates a distance that allows students to see more discriminately and tap into the metaphors of their lives. A truly rich depth of expression emerges.

And we discovered in our students' writings that their clay could, indeed, sing.

Sources of Native American Flute Music

Titles of musical works appropriate for activities presented in this article and available on cassette tapes are listed as follows:

Kater, Peter, and R. Carlos Nakai. *Migration*. Boulder, Colo.: Silver Wave Records, n.d. (The address for Silver Wave Records is P.O. Box 7943, Boulder, CO 80306.)

Nakai, R. Carlos. *Changes*. Phoenix, Ariz.: Canyon Records Productions, Inc., 1983. (Native American flute music) (The address for Canyon Records Productions, Inc., is 4143 N. 16th St., Phoenix, AZ 85016.)

Nakai, R. Carlos. *Earth Spirit*. Phoenix, Ariz.: Canyon Records Productions, Inc., n.d. (Native American flute music)

Nakai, R. Carlos, and William Eaton. *Carry the Gift*. Phoenix, Ariz.: Canyon Records Productions, Inc., n.d. (Music performed by R. Carlos Nakai on flute and William Eaton on guitar and harp and guitar and lyre)

Rainer, John, Jr. *Songs of the Indian Flute*. Globe, Ariz.: John Rainer, Jr., n.d. (To obtain information about this cassette, one may write to John Rainer, Jr., P.O. Box 890, Globe, AZ 85502-0890.)

Writing the I-Search Paper

The Reawakening of Curiosity: Research Papers as Hunting Stories

By Ken Macrorie
Professor Emeritus of English,
Western Michigan University

An I-Search is a hunting (with emotion and common sense) for the answer to a question that a student cannot put aside. An I-Search paper is the story of that search told in the voice students most commonly use when they are thinking and communicating with family and friends. In writing the I-Search paper, students do not have to be told to avoid "Engfish," the strained, pretentious language they mistakenly think will impress the teacher. They are in the search themselves. They are conducting it, and it is designed to be useful to them. The I-Search paper is not an exercise in being pseudo-objective.

In 1980 the book *Searching Writing*, for high school and college students, was published. In a later edition it was titled *The I-Search Paper*.[1] Hundreds of teachers have told me that the I-Search papers meant more to their students than any others they did and were written with more flow and power. Now several middle school teachers and a publisher have suggested that I write a manual for middle and elementary schools about I-Searching. Apparently, *The I-Search Paper* had influenced teachers who wanted their students to do more than acquaint themselves with the forms of footnotes and bibliographies and carry out a sham act of "research." We all know that many traditionally assigned papers were cut-and-paste jobs, unwitting pushes toward plagiarism. And boring, boring, boring for everyone involved.

After seeing several experiments in using the I-Search idea in middle schools and elementary schools, I have lately been asking myself whether

---

[1] Ken Macrorie, *The I-Search Paper* (Revised edition). Portsmouth, N.H.: Boynton Cook Publishers, Inc., 1988.

or not students at those levels are ready to profit from I-Searching. I am writing to you educators in the hope that you might help me answer that question.

Steps in Writing the I-Search Paper

The I-Search as I conceive it is a rebellious, self-contradictory, absolutely necessary four-step program. The steps to be taken by a student searcher follow:

1. Begin by locating a real itch that needs scratching right now.
2. Tell a small group of your classmates why you are writing this paper. If they do not think the topic arises from a real, felt need, defend yourself. If their response is negative, maybe you will want to look for another search question. Ask them for names of experts you might talk to before you read any printed matter.
3. Start searching. Keep notes of what you do. Record your interviews with experts either by writing notes or tape-recording the conversations.
4. Tell what you learned from the search, or did not learn. A search that failed to answer your question may be as exciting and valuable as one that succeeded.

You can divide your paper into four sections: (1) what I am searching for and why; (2) what I know and do not know about my question right now; (3) the story of the search; and (4) what I learned or did not learn.

Models for I-Search Papers

When I wrote the book on I-Searching for high school students and college freshmen, I featured a dozen real I-Search papers from students that had been written in my classes and those of a few other teachers from throughout the country. For a book for middle school and elementary school students, I would need 12 similarly practical and passionate papers written realistically and for real purposes. After 26 years of teaching, during which I used approaches that elicited truthtelling from the majority of my students, I have had impressed on me the validity of the saying "We imitate the

behavior of our peers." The truth in that statement becomes apparent as we acquire our mother tongue and keep adding new languages and lingos to it, often without realizing what we are doing. Similarly, when high school and college students read truthful I-Searches anchored by real needs, those students produce more of that kind of writing. I thought that teachers in middle schools and elementary schools could simply look at the 12 high school and college papers in my book and ask their students for something analogous but not on the same level of complexity. Some of those models appear as follows:

- Carmen, a high school girl in New York state, wrote her search to find out how and why Jennifer, her newly adopted little sister, was given up by her blood parents and taken in by Carmen's mother. Carmen said that when Jennifer grew up, she would probably want to know where she came from. So Carmen interviewed the blood mother of the child, her own mother, and adoption officials in the community. She read three books about the physical ills Jennifer had been born with.
- A college freshman wrote her search to find the best camera that she could buy with money her parents had given her for Christmas.
- A Lebanese college student in California searched to find out whether or not she should have her nose remade by a plastic surgeon so that she could obtain an on-camera job from a television producer who thought she needed to look more American.
- A college freshman searched to find out whether he should try to realize a lifelong dream, keeping a wolf at his home. First, he put down why he wanted to do the search. Second, he told of what he knew and did not know about the topic. Then he told the story of his search. Here are excerpts from that story:

  > After a few more dead ends, I finally resorted to just asking anybody if they knew of any wolf breeders or anyone who owns a wolf. I must have asked over 50 people and gotten over 50 no's. I was telling my story to a girl down the hall and to my astonishment she said, "My

neighbor at home breeds wolves. . .". The wolf she owns she feeds scraps to only from her plate. In return her wolf will walk up to her when she is sitting somewhere and drop some of his food onto the lady's lap, as a gift to the lady for sharing her food with the wolf. "It is very important not to turn the food down because the wolf will be very hurt at this and might not come by you for days," she said.

He ended his paper by saying:

Right now I don't think I can give enough back to the wolf as far as room to run; but who knows, I have until Easter to figure out a way that won't tie me or a wolf down.

The student read four books and talked to two people who had owned wolves. He turned in a ludicrously incomplete bibliography. An item in it looked like this:

The Wolf (1970)   David L. Mesh

I printed his report unchanged in *The I-Search Paper* because I wanted to show that an incomplete bibliography could not ruin his excellent, useful search. His paper showed how a need—a drive to know—could powerfully affect the searcher's thoroughness, focus, and voice. This I-Searcher was not "interested in wolves," as disconnected students say when they are trying to impress a teacher with their intentions. He was almost consumed by a need to know what would allow him to make a right decision about keeping a wolf. Eventually, he decided against buying a wild animal to keep with him in urban surroundings. The driving question must be particular. Being "interested" in something will not do.

Dangers Inherent in the I-Search for Middle Schoolers

A middle school teacher sent me 20 of her students' I-Search papers. Apparently, she was teaching a course in career choice, but I did not know this when she wrote me about wanting to experiment with the I-Search idea. The papers were written in concise, unpretentious sentences. The writers described their searches in story form and meaningfully conveyed the essence of interviews with experts. But the content frightened me. At the end of these very short papers, many of the writers decided on a college or a career. For them college

was three to five years away and a career even further. Most of the writers had interviewed only one or two experts. One searcher who wanted to know about ROTC interviewed an ROTC colonel, read some ROTC literature, and decided to sign up. He did not interview students who had not liked ROTC and did not read any books dealing with the ROTC in a social and political context. For him the I-Search had been practice in making decisions on the basis of insufficient evidence, but I doubt that he ever realized this.

Two of the students searched to find out whether they would like to own shops that specialized in selling baseball cards. They wrote papers that were among the best from that class. They interviewed working owners of baseball card shops and asked them about the realities of their jobs. But even those two thoughtful and aware boys were trying to make decisions too far ahead of time. When they amassed the capital necessary for such an enterprise and completed what education they thought was right for them, they would be considerably different human beings than when they had written their papers. In some respects, their searches might have been good experience and preparation, but doing those searches kept them from the challenge of investigating a real, present-day need that would have had present-day consequences. A weakness of most schools is that they are forever preparing students for future acts. Students find this practice in artificiality very dull.

What I had expected middle school children to be searching for was which classes they might decide to take next year in middle school or high school, how to deal with the mice their mother complained about at home, or which basketball shoes they might buy that would fit their needs. They would be confronting real questions: Were they playing varsity basketball? How much money would they be able to get for the purchase? What sorts of basketball shoes had other boys in the school bought, and with what results? When did their parents become involved in such a decision, if at all? What if the opinions of basketball players or shoe clerks differed on the qualities of various shoes? How could the students judge the validity and authority of such differing opinions? In any genuine I-Search, such questions are similar to those that scientists or lawyers or priests ask when they are puzzled by major decisions. The issue may seem trivial to outsiders, but the methods of dealing with it may be complex, challenging, and useful in future situations.

A middle school student living with a person who has Alzheimer's disease, Parkinson's disease, or AIDS might decide to do an I-Search about the illness. If the student were to undertake a genuine I-Search, he or she would not read and summarize the vast amounts of printed or broadcast materials about the diseases. Instead, the student would consider his or her position in a particular situation and his or her relationship to the sick person, not just gather general knowledge about the disease. I-Searches of this nature carried on by students at any age and school level would require them to consider whether they should use the names of real persons in the search, including their own.

Misconceptions About the I-Search Paper

I received a telephone call from a person in Virginia who I thought was a graduate student. She said she was taking a course in which she had been asked to write an I-Search paper by a professor who seemed unable to explain clearly what it was, and the bookstore had not received copies of *The I-Search Paper* yet. She said that "the I-Search is apparently the 'in' thing right now," and I shuddered.

Another time I received a batch of papers written by children in the first grade. The teacher who sent them thought they were wonderful I-Search papers, but I saw them as I-Searches in name only.

> *To write in their own voices about things that count in their lives is surely the basic step for students learning to write.*
>
> **KEN MACRORIE**

The I-Search project was set up to counteract what some English teachers and I consider mistaken and wrongheaded about many school research paper assignments. I hope that the term *I-Search* is not applied to research assignments that produce papers that are uptight and superficial, or careless and unconvincing.

In a genuine I-Search project, most of the papers teach both the writers and their teachers. The I-Search paper should not be just another badly organized rehash of what unmotivated students have read. If the I-Search is carried out properly, the writers and teachers learn from the assignment, for writers as persons are a part of the equation. Past experiences of all writers affect their perceptions and the way they report them. The result in I-Search projects is that teachers read papers that have new and therefore live information in them, and the teachers are not bored.

Preparing the I-Search paper asks a lot from young people. Is too much required? I suspect that may be the case for elementary school students. When I once acted as a visiting teacher of writing in a fourth grade class, I quickly learned that the students were in the process of building their necessary egos. They were not good at helping other students improve their work, as I-Search projects require. But for middle school students, I think the chances for success with I-Search projects are better. Only some teachers brave and thoughtful enough to set up I-Searching realistically and prudently will be able to tell us. The only way that this telling can be accomplished is through eliciting thorough, responsible I-Search papers from students. When I finish some present projects, I may take on such a challenge myself. If other teachers do the same, I would like to hear from them.

EDITOR'S NOTE: For further information about Ken Macrorie's book, *The I-Search Paper*, one may contact Heinemann, Boynton Cook Publishers, Inc., 361 Hanover Street, Portsmouth, NH 03801-3959; telephone (603) 431-7894. Correspondence may be addressed to Ken Macrorie, Route 14, Box 257-A, Sante Fe, NM 87505.

Practical Ideas for Using the I-Search Paper

Adapting the I-Search Paper for the Elementary Classroom

By Anita Freedman

Former Teacher, Fairhaven Elementary School,
Orange Unified School District;
and Teacher/Consultant, UCI Writing Project

Remember the old saying, "Copy from one author and it's plagiarism; copy from several and it's a research paper"? Well, it is still true. We think we are teaching students how to do research when all we are actually showing them is how to assemble scattered pieces of information. It is time to redefine our goals and change our methods. We need to start at the beginning, in the elementary school, where we first tackle making a report.

What are our objectives when we assign reports? We are trying to help our students develop:

- The ability to recognize responsible sources of information and ideas
- The ability to distinguish between fact and opinion
- A knowledge of the accepted forms of writing research
- The habit of testing facts and drawing conclusions

A new approach suggested by Ken Macrorie, Allan Edwards, Iris Tiedt, and others is the I-Search paper. Here are some ideas for using the approach in the third grade and above.

Before you begin, be sure your students are ready. Can they write expository paragraphs? Expository paragraphs, in contrast to what we commonly call creative writing, must be tightly constructed. A topic sentence and two or more sentences to back up the topic sentence are required.

Dr. Tiedt suggests that teachers ask their students to write five "I think" statements. For example:

I think purple is a beautiful color.

I think my brother should get a haircut.

I think that——— is a good television program. (List your favorite program.)

I think we should have a school cafeteria.

I think dogs make better pets than cats.

After writing these statements, each student chooses one to develop into a paragraph. The first sentence becomes the topic sentence that is then followed by sentences supporting the statement made by the author.

Then, work with these formal paragraphs in different ways so that your students become familiar with them and write them easily. Have your students rewrite their paragraphs, placing the topic sentence at the end. Using the chalkboard, help the class develop paragraphs together. Duplicate and distribute to your class paragraphs taken from articles, and discuss the way the authors developed them. Find selections in your textbooks, and go over them with the class.

Now you are ready to start the I-Search paper. There are three steps to developing this paper:

1. Identifying a problem to be studied
2. Searching for information
3. Writing the report

As a prewriting exercise, each student can write several statements beginning with "I would like to know . . . ." These can be written about anything at all or specifically related to a topic the class is studying. After writing four or more statements, the students choose one topic that interests them. This warm-up activity stimulates thinking and assures students of having the key ingredient of the I-Search paper: finding a problem which they can get involved in.

Next, show students how to find information. Take them to the library so that they can investigate different reference books. Help them with the use of encyclopedias, atlases, almanacs, biographies, and the card or computerized catalog. Perhaps the library has a picture file or filmstrips available for them. Teach older boys and girls how to use the *Reader's Guide to Periodical Literature.* However, do not stop with the use of the library. Give the students practice in interviewing, in using the telephone book and then in telephoning resource people, and in writing letters to obtain information. Suggest sources for finding people who may be helpful to the students.

Here is a format for the actual report that elementary school students can follow:

1. Statement of the problem: What did I want to know?
2. Procedures followed: How did I find the information?
3. Summary of findings: What did I learn?
4. Conclusion: What will I do with this information?

Do not forget to have the students practice note-taking and to guide them in writing their final report.

All of this preparation will enable the students to tackle a report with confidence; the structure will guide them, and, most important of all, they will learn how to do actual research. Pages copied from the encyclopedia will not appear in the students' papers when this plan is followed.

An I-Search topic has to be of high interest to the child; yet in our crowded curriculum, we often feel we must cover certain topics. We can combine the two demands. For example, instead of assigning the topic American Indians, let the children tell about the tribe to which they would like to belong. Perhaps someone will report on why he or she would not like to be an Indian.

The children can write about whatever region you are studying in social studies and share with the class, "I would like to live in . . . ," and give their personal reasons for wishing to do so. In my class we talk about what qualities we want where we live, make a class list together, and duplicate it for each child. One class studying the Southeast had astounding results with this approach: Jill wrote to her grandmother for more information about Miami, and Glen wrote to all of his relatives in Atlanta for firsthand facts. The children did thorough research on amusement parks and

beaches, the number of school days in the year, and what kinds of jobs their parents could get. Blair chose Washington, D.C., because "my mom could take my brother to the hospital for his special treatments. They have excellent hospitals there [he listed some]. And my dad could be President."

When American history is taught, each child can research his or her own family. Parents and grandparents may appreciate the results. "Why My Family Came to the United States" or "Why All My Neighbors Moved to California" would interest many reluctant writers, as would "Why Orange County Is a Great Place to Live." Career education can be the source for much research when the children write about what they want to be. Science fits in with "My Trip to Outer Space" (or "Under the Sea . . ."). A health unit could get the class involved in checking school lunch habits or exercise programs among the adults they question. Students might also enjoy researching a favorite holiday or solving a local problem. Other suggestions are "My Favorite Sport," "How the Students in Our School Feel About Mathematics," "What We Watch on Television," or "The History of Our Street." The topics are endless, limited only by the interests of the children.

The information the students gather in the I-Search should be shared with the class and perhaps with other classes as well. I often publish the I-Search papers in a class or a school newspaper, or I send them to the local paper or magazine. I may display them on a bulletin board, bind several for the school library, or feature the reports during open house for parents. In one way or another, I make sure that the research serves a purpose other than being read and graded by the teacher. I want the students to become so involved that their search becomes an end in itself, and my evaluation is confirmation of work well done. The password in this form of a research paper is *I.*

> *Nothing is more scandalous in schools and colleges than what we call "writing a research paper."*
>
> **KEN MACRORIE**

My Search

By Laurie Opfell

Former English Teacher, Irvine High School;
and Teacher/Consultant, UCI Writing Project

Scott was a teacher's nightmare. He did not walk into a room; he pushed, shoved, and kicked his way in, leaving behind a wake of at least five outraged students, who reacted by howling and throwing their books at him or running to tell me. He was constantly stealing—pens, backpacks, teachers' editions of textbooks, or the coffee creamer. He was not selective. Since in all the time I knew him he never once did an assignment, he naturally had a great deal of spare time to throw spitwads, make nasty suggestions to the girls, and make loud, obnoxious comments about anything and everything that went on in my classroom.

However, because Scott directed his hostility primarily toward the other students, he was actually easier to deal with than the ones who considered school a boring war with the teacher— private enemy number one. The ones who were openly defiant, who called me names under their breath, who accused me of losing their work, who threw tantrums if confronted by their unacceptable behavior—these were the ones I lost sleep over. As this was my first year of teaching, I found that all my ideals and enthusiasm about "the learning experience" seemed to be getting lost under this issue of control. I found myself feeling confused, angry, somewhat powerless, and totally outraged over this onslaught of emotional behavior. I could not imagine how or why I was allowing this group of thirteen-year-olds to terrorize my life, but one thing I did know was that teaching could be an intense and often painful experience.

When I decided to do an I-Search paper along with my eighth grade English class, a topic readily occurred to me: frustration in teaching. After deciding to go on a quest of my own, I identified three questions that I knew I needed some answers to:

1. What made the students show so many negative behaviors?
2. What made me respond in stress-producing ways?
3. What could I do to handle their behavior more constructively?

As I went through the various stages of the search, I found myself enjoying the opportunity to find some solutions to problems that were bothering me. I interviewed the school counselor and the assistant principal on the topics of coping with student behavior, understanding games the students play, and maintaining discipline in class. I was quite pleased to get some humorous and practical advice that really worked. I studied various psychologists' views on adolescent behavior and gained some relevant information. After typing my research, I read it and tried to decide what to say in my conclusion.

I found that I had answered each of my questions but that, in the process, I had learned some fairly disturbing things about myself. One was the concept that we dislike most in others what is also hidden somewhere in ourselves. This meant that the emotional, irrational, attention-getting behavior of the students was also there, in some form, in myself. This was an uncomfortable idea that I had to admit was true. I also learned that adolescents who show especially outrageous behavior are often stuck at a painful stage in the growth process. In some ways being stuck was something I could look back and see in my own life.

Finally, I learned that all adolescents are expected to answer the questions "who am I?" and "where am I going?" to reach successful maturity. These are difficult questions that I realized I had not answered myself. I came away from the finished report feeling that there were some important unfinished issues still left to be dealt with. But I was now better able to deal with them.

> *The best teachers of teachers are other teachers who are believable as consultants, because their ideas and the specific teaching strategies they demonstrate have been developed with real students in real classrooms.*
>
> JAMES R. GRAY

I had gained a new self-awareness and a sense of compassion for the struggles of my students.

When I compare my first year of teaching in an intermediate school to this year, I realize that I still have a few Scotts and a few who direct their rebellion at me, but somehow they do not seem intimidating. I know that it is my search that has made the difference.

A Sample Prompt, Scoring Guide, and Model Paper for the I-Search

By Carol Booth Olson
Director, UCI Writing Project

I first learned about the I-Search paper at a California Writing Project Conference in Monterey. Allan Edwards, a Consultant from the Redwood Writing Project, had been experimenting with the concept that Ken Macrorie would introduce later that year in a book called *Searching Writing*.[1] He was so excited about the results he was getting that I decided to try the idea. (See "The Reawakening of Curiosity: Research Papers as Hunting Stories" by Ken Macrorie, which appears in this section.)

What I like best about the I-Search assignment is that it encourages research that the student conducts out of a genuine need to know. So often, the traditional research paper is a passive enterprise in which the student merely analyzes and restates the results of someone else's intellectual inquiry, an inquiry that he or she may have no personal involvement in. When I think of research, I think of more than a visit to the card catalog and weekends spent in the library stacks. I think of firsthand activities like—writing letters, making telephone calls, initiating face-to-face interviews, and going on field trips—supplemented by the valuable information that can be obtained from pertinent journals and books.

I agree with Ken Macrorie that the dictionary definition of research as a "patient study and investigation in some field of knowledge, undertaken to establish facts and principles" leaves out "the basic motivation for the whole effort" (*Searching Writing*, p. 162). My students are rarely patient about anything. I would rather have them get so involved in a topic that they launch their search for information in several different directions simultaneously than have them become bored before they begin, dragging their bodies down to the library, simply going through the motions of searching. Because the students have a stake in this paper, I find that after the initial excitement of getting started, they will sit down and take an objective look at what needs to be done and avail themselves of all the accessible secondary sources.

Using Allan Edward's handouts and Ken Macrorie's book, I developed a prompt describing the I-Search paper, which I distribute to students along with a scoring guide delineating criteria for evaluation and a model student paper. Samples of all three items follow:

A Sample Prompt

The I-Search Paper

DESCRIPTION

The I-Search paper is designed to teach the writer and the reader something valuable about a chosen topic and about the nature of searching and discovery. As opposed to the standard research paper in which the writer usually assumes a detached and objective stance, the I-Search paper allows you to take an active role in your search, to hunt for facts and truths firsthand, and to provide a step-by-step record of the discovery process.

TOPIC

The cardinal rule of the I-Search paper is to choose a topic that genuinely interests you and that you need to know more about. Topics written about by previous students have included "Not Exactly the Brady Bunch: Understanding and Resolving the Tension in Step Families"; "Reaching Out to Orange

---

EDITOR'S NOTE: For a more detailed account of how to implement the I-Search concept in the classroom, see this author's article, "Personalizing Research in the I-Search Paper," in the November, 1983, issue of the *Arizona English Bulletin*. Portions of this commentary have been reprinted from that article. An additional resource is Carol Booth Olson, "Out of a Genuine Need to Know: Personalizing the Research Paper," in *Thinking/Writing: Fostering Thinking Through Writing.* Edited by Carol Booth Olson. New York: HarperCollins College, 1992, pp. 378–95.

[1] *Searching Writing* in a later edition was titled *The I Search Paper.* See Ken Macrorie, *The I-Search Paper* (Revised edition). Portsmouth, N.H.: Boynton Cook Publishers, Inc., 1988.

County's Invisible Poor"; "Diabetes: What's the Prognosis?"; "Auuuggghh!: An Exploration of Stress and Burn-out"; and "Should I Invest in the Silver Market?" The important point is that you choose the topic you will investigate rather than having the instructor select a topic or even provide a number of options. (*Note*: Elementary teachers may need to bend this rule. See Anita Freedman's article, which appears in this section.)

FORMAT

The I-Search paper should be written in three sections: (1) what I know, assume, or imagine; (2) the search; and (3) what I discovered.

What I know, assume, or imagine. Before conducting any formal research, write a section in which you explain to the reader what you think you know, what you assume, or what you imagine about your topic. For example, if you decided to investigate the rain forest, you might want to offer some ideas about the reasons for the current deforestation, describe what you think might be the impact of deforestation on the physical environment of the rain forest, the wildlife, and the rain forest people, as well as speculate about what you think will happen to the world's ecology over time as a result of this destruction.

The search. Test your knowledge, assumptions, or conjectures by researching your topic thoroughly. Consult useful books, magazines, newspapers, films, tapes, and other sources for information. When possible, interview people who are authorities on or who are familiar with your topic. If you were pursuing a search on the rain forest, you might want to check several books on the subject (literary works and nonfiction); read several pertinent articles in a variety of current magazines; visit a store that specializes in nature conservation; watch a video or television special; subscribe to Lynne Cherry's environmental newsletter, *Nature's Course*; and so forth.[2] You might also ask an environmentalist who has been to one of the endangered rain forests for an account of his or her firsthand exposure to the problem.

Write your search in narrative form, recording the steps of the discovery process. Do not feel obligated to tell everything, but highlight the happenings and facts you uncovered that were crucial to your hunt and contributed to your understanding of the topic.

Document all your sources of information, using formal footnote form when it is appropriate.

What I discovered. After concluding your search, compare what you thought you knew, assumed, or imagined with what you actually discovered and offer some personal commentary and draw some conclusions. For instance, after completing your search on the rain forest, you might learn that the problem is far more severe than you formerly believed. You may have assumed that international attention to this issue has succeeded in diminishing the incidence of slash-and-burn deforestation, but you now find that the rain forest is still disappearing at an alarming rate. Consequently, you might want to propose that your class or school join The International Children's Rain Forest and raise funds to protect one or more acres of undisturbed tropical rain forest in Costa Rica. (For more information contact The International Children's Rain Forest, P.O. Box 936, Lewiston, ME 04240.)

BIBLIOGRAPHY

At the close of the report, attach a formal bibliography listing the sources you consulted to write your I-Search paper.

A Scoring Guide

This scoring guide was designed for high school and college-level students and should be modified according to the grade level that you teach. For more information on evaluation, see the last section of this book and Chapter 5 of *Improving Writing in California Schools: Problems and Solutions*, which the California Department of Education published in 1983.

9—8   This paper is clearly superior. It is well written, clearly organized, insightful, and technically correct. A 9—8 paper exhibits most or all of the following characteristics:

- Writing the paper was a genuine learning experience for the writer, and a person would benefit greatly from reading the paper.
- The paper displays evidence of critical thinking and offers special insight into the topic discussed.
- The topic lends itself to investigation and discovery.
- The paper is written in three sections. (The format may be explicit or implicit.):

---

[2]For information about *Nature's Course,* write to Lynne Cherry, Center for Children's Environmental Literature, Smithsonian Environmental Research Center, P.O. Box 28, Edgewater, MD 21037-0028. Lynne Cherry is the author of *The Great Kapok Tree: A Tale of the Amazon Rain Forest.* New York: Harcourt Brace Jovanovich, Inc., 1990.

A meaningful search grows from seeds in the writer's life, events which need to be revealed immediately to the reader.

KEN MACRORIE

- What I know, assume, or imagine (prior to the search)
- The search (testing knowledge, assumptions, or conjecture through documented research)
- What I discovered (comparing what you thought you knew with what you learned and offering commentary and conclusions)

• The author takes an active role rather than a passive role in the search.
• The writer uses research effectively as a supplement to, but not as a substitute for, his or her own ideas.
• The paper's tone and point of view convey a clear sense of the author's voice or style.
• The writer uses precise, apt, or descriptive language.
• The main points of the essay are well supported with examples.
• The writer uses ample transitions between ideas, paragraphs, and sections.
• The writer varies sentence structure and length.
• The search portion of the essay is properly documented with footnotes in correct form.
• The paper includes references to a minimum of two primary and two secondary research sources.
• The paper includes a formal bibliography.
• The writer generally uses effectively the conventions of written English.

7   This paper is a thinner version of the 9—8 paper. A paper rated 7 is still impressive and interesting, but it is less thoroughly researched, more loosely organized, less insightful, and not as informative as the 9—8 paper.

6—5 Scores of 5 or 6 apply to papers that are less well-handled than the 7, 8, or 9 paper. A 6—5 paper may be less interesting and informative, more superficially researched, and less insightful. It may contain problems in the conventions of written English. A 6—5 paper will exhibit some or all of the following characteristics:

• Writing the paper was a learning experience for the writer; but the paper is less informative than the 7, 8, or 9 paper, and thus, the lesson is less valuable for the reader.
• The paper does not display as much critical thinking or insight as the 7, 8, or 9 paper.
• The paper is written in three sections, but they are not equally complete or well handled.
• The author does not seem genuinely involved in his or her topic.
• The writer may rely too heavily on the research rather than use it to augment his or her own thoughts.
• The paper does not convey a clear sense of the author's voice or style.
• The language is not as descriptive, precise, or apt as that of a 7, 8, or 9 paper.
• The main points of the report are not as well supported with examples as they might have been.
• The three sections of the report are not tied together effectively with transitions.
• The sentence structure and length need more variation.
• The writer uses very few footnotes, indicating that little research has been conducted and the bibliography is sketchy.
• The paper does not refer directly to at least two primary and two secondary research sources.
• Some problems in the conventions of written English occur but none that seriously impairs the message.

4—3 These scores apply to papers that maintain the general idea of the writing assignment, but they are weak in content, thought, language facility, or the conventions of written English. A 4—3 paper will exhibit some or all of these characteristics:

• Writing the paper was not a genuine learning experience for the writer. A person would not benefit from reading the paper.
• The paper demonstrates little or no evidence of critical thinking.
• The paper is not written in three sections, or the sections do not follow the guidelines set up in the assignment's description.
• The writer either relies too heavily on research or conducts very little, if any, research.

- The writer's "voice" does not come across.
- The language is vague and imprecise.
- The discussion is overly general or superficial.
- The main points are not supported with examples.
- The research sources are not documented in the bibliography or footnotes.
- The reader may have a problem understanding the paper.
- The paper has serious problems in the conventions of written English that impair the writer's message.

2   This score applies to papers that do not follow the writing assignment and contain weakness of the paper rated 4—3.

1   This score applies to a paper that is completely off track and has no redeeming qualities.

An extremely well-written and well-prepared paper may receive a rating of 10. If a paper has serious problems in the conventions of written English that impair the writer's message, it can receive up to a two-point deduction.

Although the student paper reprinted below was written by a community college student, I believe the subject matter—the illness of a family pet—will be of interest to and have emotional appeal for elementary and middle school students. Notice how the author, Caren Rice, weaves her factual, informative account into a compelling narrative that involves the reader.

A Model Student Paper

Caren Rice, English 1 A (Olson),
Irvine Valley College

Canine Parovirus

Just recently, I experienced the pain and trauma of almost losing a loved pet. Mandy was only a four and one-half month old puppy when, on a Friday night in October, she was suddenly struck with a severe illness.

The sickness first began with the loss of her appetite, followed by severe, convulsive vomiting. This went on for 24 hours, when I decided to call the emergency pet clinic.

"What are the dog's symptoms?" asked the nurse.

"Constant vomiting, loss of appetite, and lethargy," I replied.

"Does she have diarrhea?"

"No, not at all."

"Oh, thank goodness! She isn't showing the symptoms of parvo. Just give her some Pepto Bismol, and she'll be fine in a few hours."

Well, Mandy was given the antacid, and she still wasn't "fine." I thought perhaps that my eyes were betraying me, but in the short time that she had been sick, Mandy looked as if she had lost half of her weight. Her eyes were bright red and to walk took all of her effort and strength. She refused to eat and drink.

This was only the beginning of what was to be a sleepless, heartsick week, and an eye-opener to the deadly dog-killing disease known as canine parvovirus.

What Is Parvo?

With a heavy heart and a guilty feeling, I took Mandy to the vet on Monday. I had heard of this disease and of the vaccine being given to ward it off. But I didn't take it seriously enough. I assumed that Mandy wouldn't get parvo since all of our neighbors' dogs had been vaccinated against the illness. Where else could she get it? Little did I know that Mandy could contract the disease just from walking on the grass outside our door. This was the beginning of my education on parvovirus.

Canine parvovirus was first identified at a Louisville, Kentucky, dog show in the spring of 1978 and spread to other dog shows throughout the country.[1] As a result of these dog shows, the disease soon spread overseas to Europe and Australia. Parvo was thought to have been a mutation of cat distemper, though it did not seem to affect cats in the same way. According to Dr. Martin Levin, scientists of veterinary medicine are still not sure what causes this almost always fatal disease.[2]

The question remains: How did canine parvovirus suddenly appear? The *Australian Veterinary Journal* has suggested openly that a contaminated batch of vaccine was responsible for the mutant virus.[3] Many doctors disagree with this theory because serial production lots of the vaccine are routinely monitored by the U.S. Department of Agriculture, which has yet to find a bad batch.

Now we are back to the same question: How did Parvo suddenly appear? From what I could gather at the clinic where Mandy was being treated, they still know very little about this disease.

---

[1] Jean Seligman, "A Viral Epidemic Without a Cure," *Newsweek*, (August 19, 1980), 57.
[2] Martin Levin, Doctor of Veterinary Medicine, El Toro Animal Hospital, El Toro, Calif., December 11, 1980.
[3] Mike Macbeth, "Dogs, That Virus Is Still Loose," *MacLeans* (March 3, 1980), 14.

Parvo and Its Cure

By Tuesday, it was confirmed that Mandy definitely had parvo, and her chance of survival was 15 percent. This really depressed me. I wanted to know why, what, and how. I pressed the doctor for more information.

"My knowledge is limited on this disease," he told me.

I asked him if he thought that Mandy would survive. Dr. Levin said that it was hard to determine. They knew that she had intestinal parvo, which if it could be called a plus, was one.

There are two known types of canine parvovirus. One is intestinal parvo. This virus grows in the intestinal tract of the dog, causing severe vomiting, loss of appetite, and diarrhea.[4] This can last for several weeks before the dog dies of malnutrition and exhaustion. If the disease is caught in its early stages, there is a chance of stopping it from spreading further, and a good chance of saving the animal. Mandy had suffered with the illness for 48 hours before I took her to the vet.

The other type of this disease is cardiovascular parvovirus. This virus starts in the arteries of the dog's heart and can kill the animal in as short a time as eight hours. The cardiac parvo is what usually strikes the very young puppies. The chance of survival of this form of parvo is almost zero.

Before veterinarians and pet owners became familiar with parvovirus, the mortality rate reached 40 percent among dogs with serious cases of the disease.[5] Puppies under ten weeks and older dogs are the most vulnerable.

Since parvo was first identified in the warmer months of spring and summer, it was hoped that perhaps cold weather would bring an end to the disease. But parvo proved to be a hardy virus, unaffected by temperatures.

When this disease began to break out in near epidemic proportions, many pet owners kept their dogs close to home, afraid that a trip to the vet might put a healthy animal in dangerous proximity to one carrying the virus.[6] Most pet owners, such as I, were naive to the fact that the shoes we wore could carry the virus into the house via contact with the feces of an infected animal.

Therapy is basically palliative—drugs to control vomiting and diarrhea, and fluids to prevent dehydration.[7] Without treatment, dogs often die of parvovirus within three days. It is one of the quickest killers of dogs known.

This was the therapy given to Mandy, as by Wednesday she still had not taken in any food or water, and her weight was dropping rapidly. I kept in close contact with Dr. Levin, and he, in turn, informed me of the effects of the disease on her. Her condition was stable, and despite loss of weight, there was a remote possibility that she would survive. After five days of being caught in a dark tunnel, I could see a spot of light in the distance.

The best protection against parvo is a new vaccine called parvocine. The lab that is producing it is working around the clock, turning out 1.5 million doses a month.[8] But there are 3 million doses on back order as clinics across the nation are operating at full capacity.

The vaccine does not cause immunity to parvo. Booster shots must be given every four to six months. It is not known just how effective the vaccine is, but there have been fewer cases of illness in immunized dogs than in ones that went untreated.

A Summary of Parvo

By Thursday, Mandy began to show signs of recovery. She became more responsive to the treatment and ate a small amount of food. I was told that if all went well, I could bring her home on Friday. I breathed a sigh of relief and thanked my lucky stars.

Mandy was one of the few dogs that survived this ravaging disease. The symptoms were still in their early stages when I brought her in and, therefore, the disease could be stopped from spreading further. When I picked her up on Friday, she was extremely thin, having lost half of her weight. But Mandy was alive and very glad to see me.

I can now reflect on the situation and realize how little we, as pet owners, know about our pets and their illnesses. We tend to take for granted that dogs are always healthy and need no help from us when they are sick. I realize now just how severely harsh diseases can affect our pets, especially when they cannot communicate their pain to us.

I am now well informed on canine parvovirus and through my own experience have learned a valuable lesson. The vaccine only

[4]Seligman, 57.
[5]Ibid.
[6]Ibid.
[7]Martin Levin, December 11, 1980.

[8]Seligman, 57.

costs about $7 to $14, but I chose not to buy it out of my own ignorance. Instead, I suffered a week of fear at the thought of losing my dog and a bill from the vet totaling over $140.

I cannot recommend highly enough that teachers of writing who are unfamiliar with the I-Search paper learn more about it and assign it on a trial basis in at least one of their classes. When students personalize research and bring everything they know about writing to their project, they produce some of their best work. In addition, they often discover something that is far more valuable to them than a letter grade or a numerical score.

The I-Search Paper: A Perfect Compromise

By Susanna Clemans
English Instructor, Cerritos College;
and Teacher/Consultant, UCI Writing Project

Feeling somewhat guilty about never having assigned a research paper to my students in English composition at California State University, Fullerton, because of a lack of time and my own dread of having to read the boring topics, I seized on Ken Macrorie's I-Search paper as the perfect compromise.

Luckily for me and my students, Carol Olson's handout (which is included in her commentary in this section) was extremely clear-cut and complete. While skimming the syllabus with my students on the first day of classes, I explained briefly that this paper (not due until the last week of the course) would be a modified research paper that would be explained in fuller detail with handouts and examples as the semester progressed. I could see the raised eyebrows and hear the barely audible groans. Something about a research paper seemed to induce these predictable displays. Was I wrong in tackling this paper along with all the other required compositions?

By the third or fourth week of the course, I spent time in class discussing the paper, read some examples of I-Search papers, and asked the students to begin seriously considering a topic, one which they knew comparatively little about, but one which they wanted to pursue. One by one, topics were given to me as possibilities, and in spite of themselves, the students began to get caught up with their searches. These questions and discussions continued throughout the semester: "You mean I can use *I* ?" "I don't have to give you a formal outline?" Relief permeated the class, and the most overheard question now became, "What are you doing your paper on?"

The "Saturation Report" (one of the required essays assigned the second month), interview sessions in and out of class, exercises in dialogue, and the various kinds of essays—narration, description, persuasion, classification, and so on—helped give students the confidence necessary for embarking on a new venture. By the time my students had completed the "Saturation Report" and discovered how they could apply different types of writing skills to the I-Search paper, they became very enthusiastic about the assignment.

Of course, my students, being human, were a mixture of those who worked hard and thoroughly as well as those who procrastinated. Yet all the students turned in an I-Search paper, and interestingly enough, no one wrote on the same subject. Many students personally told me how much they benefited from the assignment, even though they resented the extra work in the beginning. For many, this assignment was the first time they had really enjoyed looking for information because they did not have to worry about an overly structured format. Others felt the choice of subject matter finally allowed them to spend their valuable time earnestly searching out an interest, such as diabetes (in the case of the student who had just found out she had the disease) or mining (in the case of the student whose mother had just remarried to a miner).

For me the best part of this assignment was that I actually looked forward to reading the students' papers that were filled with their enthusiastic searches. And the students, who had enjoyed their superior position in almost always knowing more about their individual subjects after the search than I, had gained confidence in a mode of writing that will be useful to them in other classes. The compromise research paper worked.

Critical Thinking and Writing

Reforming Your Teaching for Thinking: The Studio Approach

By Dan Kirby

Professor, Teaching and Teacher Education,
University of Arizona, Tucson

Reforming your teaching to nurture thinking involves more than dreaming up new activities or offering students more decision-making freedom. At the heart of this reform is a new attitude toward knowledge and how it is acquired. This new view of knowledge does not mean you have nothing to teach students or that textbooks are no longer important or that old knowledge is no longer valuable. What it does mean is that teachers must plan for and structure their classes in ways that give students many opportunities to construct their own versions of old knowledge in new and more personal ways. But there is even more at stake here than preparing students to make meanings of what is already known. It is more than acquisition that we are after. We want our students to create new knowledge both now and in the future and be able to do something with that knowledge after they have it. Changing your class to make this happen may at first plunge you into an abyss of uncertainty, as Barbara Elmore, a biology teacher at Jones High School in the Houston Independent School District, relates:

> I thought I was pretty good at critical thinking skills. I knew Bloom's taxonomy; I had written curriculum for Houston Independent School District; and I taught science. I knew I was going to be really good at teaching this thinking stuff. But it wasn't that easy for me. At first I felt as if I was plunged into total darkness. I am a highly organized teacher, a real paper pusher, and this kind of teaching was asking me to let go, to let go of control. I'm the kind of teacher who knows where she wants every child to be at every moment. Finally, in frustration, I just turned to my kids. "What can we do to make biology more stimulating, more creative? What can we do to make it more fun?" It didn't take long for me to realize that students really do know a lot about how they can best be taught.

First of all, they liked being able to express themselves in class and do things their way. They wanted time to think. They didn't want me just shoving stuff down them—you know, quick, quick, quick, "You have 15 minutes." They want less test, less fill-in-the-blanks stuff, fewer handouts, more projects, more student-designed things, more role in decision making. They wanted more interesting problems. They wanted fewer problems. They wanted their problems. They were sick and tired of cookbook labs. So I took all of their ideas and thought about it awhile, and it wasn't all easy to take. But I was sick of most of that stuff too, so we embarked on real research in which they were given something to observe and inquire about. They designed their own labs; basically, designed them their own way, using the materials at hand. I just stopped dispensing information. It's more like an inquiry now. The students are the learners, and they are also the providers of their own learning. I'm the one who steers, but they have a big say-so in the route we take.

Identifying the Important Knowledge

Barbara Elmore has done more than cosmetic surgery in her classroom. She has changed more than assignments and tests. She has altered the balance of power and reshaped the definition of knowledge and knowing. To begin a comprehensive restructuring of your own class as Barbara has done will take some courage. I suggest that you begin by looking at your content and how you teach it. Ask your students what they think, as Barbara did. Is your attitude toward your content frustrating students? Are you teaching your content as stuff you know and they do not? Are you defining knowledge as facts in books or lectures or, worse yet, stuff on tests? That view of knowledge is the norm in many classrooms, and it's a kind of hangover from the nineteenth century when people believed that the essential mysteries of the universe had been encountered and solved by smart people. It's a view of knowledge as a containerized commodity locked in libraries and books that locks up the act of teaching, too. It leads teachers to do what Carl Rogers has called, "the exposition of conclusions."[1]

If you are presenting the central tenets of your content as issues already settled, as truth already known and uncontested, then your students aren't going to be inclined to interact with that content and raise questions of their own. They are going to feel locked away from content. "Knowledge must solve a problem or provoke inquiry for it to seem important," says Grant Wiggins.[2] Expository teaching has too often characterized major subject areas like science and social studies and English. Schooling has far too often been a kind of warehouse operation in which teachers load trivial knowledge into students—a teamster's kind of work. The term paper, the science report, the essay have often been mere copying exercises from other sources. If you are going to develop your students as thinkers, you must begin to look at knowledge and knowing in new ways.

How else can you view knowledge? What other ways can you teach domain-specific knowledge to students? What does it mean to *know* something? One important ingredient to stir into this stew of thinking about reform and change is that the knowledge that thinkers can use is socially constructed. Personal knowledge is made powerful and permanent as it interacts with that of other knowledge makers. Meanings are negotiated and sharpened by learners as they talk and write about them in social contexts. There is not an efficient way to shortcut or truncate the process of knowledge making. If students are to become authentic knowledge makers and acquire what Grant Wiggins has called "the habits of thoughtful inquiry,"[3] you will have to provide lots of time for them to talk—time to talk to you and to each other and to themselves. These inquiry-based conversations will place a continuing emphasis on the importance of the class-

[2] Grant Wiggins, "The Futility of Trying to Teach Everything of Importance," *Educational Leadership* (November, 1989).
[3] Wiggins, 1989.

This new view of knowledge does not mean you have nothing to teach students or that textbooks are no longer important or that old knowledge is no longer valuable.

DAN KIRBY

[1] Donald Schön. *Educating the Reflective Practitioner: Toward a New Design of Teaching and Learning in the Professions.* San Francisco: Jossey-Bass, 1987.

room as community, a community where more speculative talk is encouraged—an environment where thinking aloud talk and hypothetical talk and knowledge-building talk are ongoing. And more writing will be necessary—not more writing from encyclopedias and report writing but reflective, theory-building writing, student-owned writing like that done for logs and journals that feed thinking.

Building a Community of Learners

Grace Beam, a seventh grade life science teacher at Pershing Middle School in the Houston Independent School District, began her classes by bringing her students into a circle and placing a live hermit crab on the floor of the classroom and letting it crawl around. As her students oohed and aahed and sometimes screamed, she began to capitalize on their natural curiosity. She asked them what questions they had. And the talk began to focus on science. As they asked questions, she extended those questions and asked some of her own. Students jumped in to add personal knowledge and raise other questions. Within ten minutes or so, Grace and the crab had created an intense climate for inquiry and learning without telling the students anything. Finally, she said, "Class, this is how we're going to learn science this year. We're going to observe things and wonder about things and find answers and new questions. We're going to learn life science by thinking and acting like scientists."

Grace Beam began her year by signaling to her students that their questions were important, that they were responsible for their own learning, and that they were going to function as a community of thinking scientists. Classrooms as communities is the key to that kind of learning. Communities offer modeling and support for individual thinkers to extend the thinking of others while offering opportunities for mutual criticism and self-correction. Communities build dispositions to think.

Treating the Classroom as a Studio

Something that has helped me restructure my class, think in new ways about what I'm doing, and facilitate the creation of the same kind of community of learners that Grace Beam is striving for is to treat the classroom as a studio. What comes to mind when you hear the word *studio*? Freedom,

independent work, creativity, process, space, light, productivity? Those are all things I wanted in my classroom. I wanted to work toward building what Lauren Resnick and others are calling "cognitive apprenticeships."[4] I wanted to build a work environment where students learn thinking as a trade. A studio is a place where learners work in front of each other and where the studio master is both mentor and artist. I adopted the metaphor of classroom as studio to see how that might open my mind to new roles for me to play and to help me place more of the responsibility for learning on individual students.

My classroom does not look much like a real studio; it has desks in rows and far too many bodies to feel spacious. It's not interior decorating that I'm after, but the values and principles of a studio classroom. It's the psychological environment that is critical. In the studio, repeated practice and experimentation are the norm. Students do not expect to get it right the first time; getting it right may not be a primary value at all. Individual visions and versions are what is important. And thinkers come to those versions by experimenting, by trying out ideas. The teacher's role in the studio is to stay out of the student's way, but not too far out of the way. Studio teachers are highly selective with their instruction. They often respond to students' questions like, "What do you want?" with "I want to see your view of this" and to, "Does this look right?" with comments like "What do you think?"

Studio teachers often work in front of their students and share their own processes and quandaries. When studio teachers do give specific coaching suggestions, they try to give them while the students are at work. They abandon speeches to the whole class like the "Before you do this . . ." speech and the rules and guidelines speeches. They try to build a comprehensive frame for learning, giving students a sense of how they are going to proceed; then they set the whole thing in motion and go to work. I do some of my best teaching over the shoulder as I listen to individual students represent their questions and problems. I encourage students who need more help and support to

[4] Lauren Resnick, *ASCD Update* (February, 1990).

find it from within the classroom community by consulting with partners and group members. "See what your partner thinks about that" is my typical response to a student in need of direction.

Setting Up a Studio Classroom

Initiating an environment where students are encouraged to solve real problems and develop individual visions and versions, using their own strategies, substantially complicates the teacher's ability to know where each student is and what he or she is doing. In the studio classroom, you will need a plan for monitoring your students' progress and problems. Since you are going to give students lots of time to work independently in class and work in groups and work with partners, you want to be sure that they are using that time well. Giving students three or four weeks to complete a project and then finding out that half of them have not done very much is not acceptable. You need to monitor their work with regular reports. Three strategies that will help you know how well each student is doing, even if you have 95 students in three classes, are (1) a thinker's log; (2) a portfolio; and (3) a working plan.

A Thinker's Log. I have found it helpful to ask students to keep a log or journal as they work. Sometimes I assign specific log entries like, "Read this article and talk back to it in your log." Sometimes I just ask students to give me a free form response to something they did or talked about in class. I don't collect the logs very often, maybe sample pages each week, and I don't try to structure the recording very much. I want the logs to be the students' own collections of responses to readings and classroom experiences. But I learn how they are doing by sampling the logs, and I keep students on track by responding with encouraging comments.

A Portfolio. Students need a place to work and keep that work together, and I have found a portfolio to be an invaluable tool in the studio classroom. Portfolios, which are somewhat in vogue now as tools for evaluation, may contain samples of the students' best work, which are submitted for grading or assessment. The kind of portfolio I'm using is quite different, however,

from many of those being used. This portfolio is the place where students keep *all* of their work: trials, experiments, drafts, sketches, experimental notes, observations, and musings. I tell my students that their portfolios are the tracks of their work, the visible evidence of their minds at work. And when I grade their performance, I give the portfolio equal weight with their finished products, whatever those are. The portfolio is the record of process, and I view it as every bit as important as the completed products.

A Working Plan. At the very beginning of the class, try to have students develop a working plan on how they think they will proceed. This plan will vary, depending on what kind of work the students are going to do. The plan can be a map, a series of drawings, a list of steps, a time line, a list of concerns or obstacles, even a log entry on how they feel about the project before they launch into it. The plan is not a straitjacket, a rigid outline, or a pressure-packed set of deadlines. It's a way of getting them to think about where they are going, even before they know what they are doing. And it gives you a lot of information about what kind of problem solvers they are and how their minds are already working. As students proceed through the experiences that you have developed for them or with them or that they have developed for themselves, have them revise and alter their plans. As the plans unfold, discuss them with the whole class and with individuals.

Auditing the Work in Process

Devising some procedure for getting a progress report from each student each week is almost essential. I have been using something I call *audits*. My students prefer to give me these reports on Mondays. They know when they come to class that I'm going to ask them to document how the work is going. Since I teach writing, my audits have to do with how the students' writing is progressing; but your audits could focus on any specific task that students are to complete. Here are some sample questions from my weekly audits:

- What's in stock? How many pieces do you have in the portfolio, and in what shape are they?

- What's on back order? What is still in your head? What pieces are you thinking about and planning to write?
- Which pieces are working? Do you have any really solid pieces that may grow into longer ones? Do you have any pieces worth elaborating on?
- How are your work habits? How much time are you spending on your writing? Are you jotting notes and ideas? Working at the computer? Reading?
- What problems are you having? Is there anything I can do to help?

The following response is typical; it is from Ruthie Escalante, a student in my class when I was a visiting professor at the University of California, Santa Barbara:

> Dan,
>
> I now have five pieces in my writer's portfolio: the first being our first write starting with "My family is . . ." and it's in okay shape. It's rough, I did it in a hurry. It'll do, but I could fix it if you want me to. Then I have the summary of my "Life Parts," and that may as well be in Greek because only I could understand it. I thought we were just going to discuss it and not read it. My third piece is the first of a trilogy of memories; I am quite proud of it, in fact. I spent much time and thought on the piece and, although none of my group liked it, I still can't wait for your feedback. It's my best piece. The second part (4th piece) is written out and not bad, but I'd like to develop it more. The final work I have in my possession is that which I wrote last night; it is weak and I'm getting discouraged. To get something pulled together for next Thursday, I must really concentrate on my love of writing and the important, positive first impression I want to make. I will probably compile the three pieces for a large synopsis (I'll have to play around with them), I have to purchase some typewriter ribbon, and you can count on a finished project I will be proud of.
>
> Have a good weekend,
>
> Ruthie

Ruthie's audit, like most of my other students' audits, is honest and informative. I learn that she has five pieces in the portfolio, and she gives me a status report on each. I learn that she is still trying to please me, even though I've been emphasizing the importance of pleasing one's self: "I can fix it if

you want me to," and "I still can't wait for your feedback." But she closes with the line "a finished project I will be proud of," a hint that she really is beginning to see the work as her own. She also gives an updated plan for pulling the writings together by the deadline. As a teacher, I feel as if I know exactly where Ruthie is and how her work is going, and I have the feeling that Ruthie knows that, too.

Valuing Metacognitive Thinking

The most helpful and valuable metacognitive information I'm getting from students is coming from the reflections they write when the inquiry has drawn to a close and the final products and portfolios are ready for evaluation. This powerful information about how things went and how I can revise and change what I did is something most of us have been missing for all our teaching lives. Oh, I've asked students to evaluate a unit or even complete a self-evaluation, but those documents were almost always perfunctory and useless. Students either told me what I wanted to hear or didn't have much to say at all. It wasn't until I began the studio classroom approach that I realized my own mistake. If students do only the teacher's assignments to the teacher's specifications, there really isn't much they can say about their processes: "I did what you wanted; here it is." But if students have freedom to make individual decisions about how to proceed, they have important things to tell us about how it went. If students have to find their own ways through a problem, devise and think through alternatives, and consult with other class members, they can be quite articulate about the circuitous route that inquiry took.

I have been amazed at how seriously and thoughtfully students approach these reflection times. For the first time in my teaching, I know what students think they are doing, as well as what they have been doing, as shown in this example from Mark Mester, a student of mine at the University of Georgia:

> Dr. Dan,
>
> I am taking this time to respond about a few things I have had on my mind. The first item I would like to talk about is the nature piece. I have been wondering why I do not have the motivation I did for the

memoir piece. Part of the reason must be the winding down of the quarter. But I think there is more. I love being out in nature. I especially love going camping in the mountains with my friends, or going fishing (saltwater) in Florida. In both instances, I feel a sense of awe, and a sense of smallness?? It is a great feeling. I am not sure if I always feel a part of nature. Sometimes I feel like I belong, and at other times I feel I am an outsider. I do not know if I can find universal truths in nature; I guess I have tried such things in this class. But it is difficult to go out, observe nature, and rattle off truth. It is difficult to always compare nature to my life. Perhaps I didn't always have to do this, maybe I'm looking and writing the wrong way. In any case, the writing is unnatural. It is too forced, thus it lacks emotion, fire. I think it is dull. Still, explorations benefitted me.

First of all, even though my writing was scarce and poor, I believe my powers of observation improved. Often, I would be driving somewhere and I would just stop and think of how I would describe that field, or that sunset, and why. Why do I want to write about the sunset? I know that this is where my nature piece should start. An enforced observation is the beginning. (I suppose I do have a basic understanding of what I'm supposed to be doing, but still it isn't easy.) The second benefit is the crafting of the language. I enjoyed experimenting with the form, and I liked my Shakespeare piece because of this reason. It was fun to try new things. Sometime, I really want to write a great nature piece like Annie Dillard, but first I really need to get motivated; I need to feel that the piece is important, relevant, and natural. I'm hoping I'm developing this sense.

Mark's reflection comes after a class inquiry centered around observing and writing about nature. Obviously, Mark is not satisfied with his writings, but he has come to learn some things about himself as an observer, thinker, and writer. If I didn't collect this information, I might look at Mark's work and think he just wasn't interested or didn't work hard enough. I may think the observation of nature itself was the problem. I may blame myself or the readings or the explorations he chose. Worse, I may jump to all the wrong conclusions about Mark as a thinker if I grade only Mark's work. But in this reflection, I learned that Mark really had wrestled with important ideas about observing nature. Mark has a strong sense of what worked and didn't work for him in his writings

and in this inquiry. He gave me some specific clues as to what he might do next time: play with the outsider/insider dichotomy, continue to emphasize observation activities, encourage experimentation with form.

But Mark is only one student in the class. I need to know what triggers thinking for each student in my class. I need to know which explorations worked for which kinds of thinkers and whether my coaching and handouts were helpful. I need to know how well groups and collaborative time functioned. I need to know the effectiveness of my own attempts to mentor thinking. I must ask myself "What triggers my own thinking?" I need to compare my notes and observations and feelings with those of my students. When I collect and study the portfolios and audits and reflections from everyone in the class, I get a powerful composite picture of thinking and learning, information rich with potential to inform and improve my teaching.

The key to getting metacognitive information flowing in your classes is to emphasize and value that kind of thinking from the very beginning. Give students frequent opportunities and invitations to talk about how their minds work and how they went about solving problems or finding answers or creating artifacts before, during, and after the process. Value speculative, tentative talk; encourage risk-taking and hypothetical solutions. Engage in this kind of thinking yourself and in front of your students. And remember, students will make authentic observations of their minds at work only when they engage in real tasks and make independent decisions about how to pursue those tasks.

Restructuring Your Classroom: Getting Started

You want to begin the business of growing thinkers; you are going to find ways to bring these commitments alive in your classroom. You're not going to be pushed around by the curriculum or by habit. Great. You're resolved and enthusiastic, but how do you go about getting all this in place in your classes? Where do you go from here? How do you keep your edge, your mental sharpness, and your resolve to grow and change? And how do you go about enlisting colleagues and students in this process? Here is a suggestion. Don't try to change everything you've been doing overnight, but do more than just tinker with assignments. Start by reworking a unit that has never worked very well, or begin experimenting with concepts that have always been difficult for your students to grasp. Transforming my classroom into a studio was an experiment that worked for me and for my students. I encourage you to transform your class in ways that work for you. What's important is to work more toward the edges of your competence so that your students can work more toward the edges of theirs.

Teaching in a rich context that allows students maximum amounts of time to plan and work cooperatively and revise and redo their work and reflect on their processes will take a great deal of class time. You will not be able to assign as many stories to read or problems to work or reports to write as you have in the past. In fact, you may very well cover less ground than when you had a well-oiled, teacher-centered class. But look at what your students *are* doing. Look at the quality of their work, at the amount of pride and effort they have for their products, at the sense of community they

have developed. You may often feel uncertain about how you've organized the learning environment, but experience will make you progressively better at planning and managing this more complex, more dynamic and whole classroom. Above all, believe in what you are doing. As Robert Sternberg says, "What a good school provides is good role models. That is the main thing we can give to the next generation."[5] Reforming classrooms and restructuring schools begins with teachers renewing their own minds. I wish you well as you begin this renewal process in your own thinking about teaching and learning. In spite of occasional setbacks and frustrations and the fact that I still have an enormous tangle of student papers to respond to and keep track of, the time I have spent rethinking and revising my classroom has made my teaching more exciting and productive than it has ever been before.

Reprinted by permission of Dan Kirby and Carol Kuykendall: *Mind Matters* (Boynton/Cook Publishers, A subsidiary of Reed Elsevier, Inc. Portsmouth, N.H. 1991).

[5]Michel F. Schaughnessy, "An Interview with Robert J. Sternberg," *Human Intelligence* newsletter (spring/summer, 1986), n.p.

Practical Ideas for Teaching Critical Thinking and Writing

Adapting Dan Kirby's Portfolio to the Study of a Novel

By Esther Severy

Assistant Vice Principal, McFadden Intermediate School, Santa Ana Unified School District; and Teacher/Consultant, UCI Writing Project

All of a sudden, that Aha! of recognition hit me as I listened to Dan Kirby speak at the UCI Writing Project Conference in December, 1989. I had been hearing bits and pieces about portfolios—rumors, almost whispers. I had also been wondering how these portfolios might be different from

my in-class writing folders, collections of student writing, and culmination anthologies. Kirby, in his easygoing style, told us how he used portfolios as an approach to memoir writing with his college students. His approach seemed to be a refinement and an extension of my use of writing folders at the middle school. Ah, the Aha!

After hearing Dan Kirby's talk, I applied his portfolio approach to the study of the novel *Roll of Thunder, Hear My Cry* by Mildred D. Taylor. Set in the Deep South during the depression, this award-winning book is about social awareness, friendships, family, pride, and prejudice. The main character, Cassie Logan, a young black girl, and her family use their pride of family and pride of ownership to deal with prejudice and threats to their very existence. Because the book focuses on experiences as Cassie sees them, I thought it would serve as a perfect springboard for my students to use in recollecting their own experiences. By relating Cassie's experiences to similar ones in their past, they could make this novel their very own. My goal in using the portfolio approach was to encourage my students to generate several thoughtful pieces of writing which they could later reread and selectively weave into their own memoirs.

There are several components in Dan Kirby's portfolio approach to writing a memoir: journals (J), quickwrites (QW), audits (A), and drafts (D). Figure 1 demonstrates how he organizes the portfolio process.

I knew that if this approach were to succeed in a middle school class, each student would have to have his or her own folder, kept permanently in the classroom. Into this folder would go all writing connected with the novel: journal entries, Quickwrites, drafts, doodles, whatever we worked on that was in any way connected with the novel.

I had students write weekly progress reports about the work they had done so far, indicating which assignments were difficult, easy, beneficial, insightful, disturbing, and so forth. Students attached all work relating to the novel to this self-evaluation and turned it in as a progress check.

I adapted Dan Kirby's components in the following manner:

Journal. As the students read the novel, they made regular journal entries. These entries were based on reactions to the text: an emotion evoked, a feeling stirred, a memory recollected, a question raised. There was no limit to the number of journal entries students might make, but they had to make some. More important than the number of responses was their quality: They had to demonstrate reflection, application, and synthesis rather than merely summary. Although summary was allowed along with these other levels of thinking, the point of this exercise was to encourage the students to think at a deeper level about what they were reading.

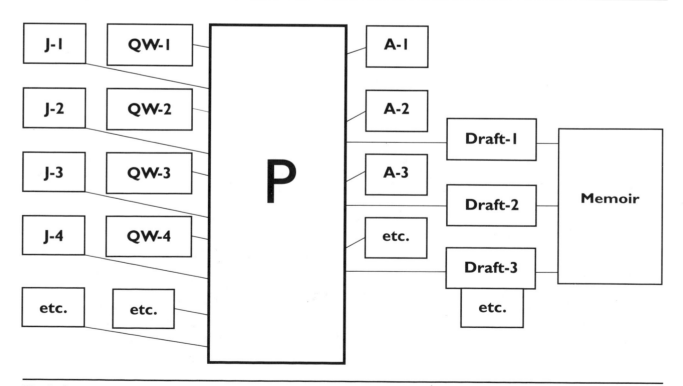

Fig. 1. Components in a Portfolio

Quickwrites. Throughout the teaching of this novel, I had the students do quickwrites that were based on some event in the novel but that reminded them of something similar that had happened to them. I might use selected study questions as subjects for quickwrites, but answering questions about the reading was not the purpose of the quickwrite. Instead, my purpose was to stimulate the students to think about a concept or a theme and apply it to their lives—to make them think about how this novel could affect them, not to test whether they had read the material.

Audit. Students wrote weekly audits, evaluating what they had accomplished. To do this, they culled their portfolios, looking for those things they wanted to share with me. They might write a summary of the week's activities. They might want to focus on one particular item and tell me about it, asking questions, reflecting on what they learned. This weekly audit gave students a chance to summarize what they had learned that week, to reflect on this learning, and to comment on it. It gave me a running account of each student's progress through the novel and an idea of what needed to be emphasized or explained, where the lesson might be bogging down, and who needed more help or wasn't doing the work.

Draft. The drafts were the students' working papers, reflections of their efforts to finalize the study of the novel. The drafts for this project came when I gave the final prompt at the end of the study of *Roll of Thunder, Hear My Cry.* All drafts were given credit but not graded. All drafts went into the portfolio.

To prepare my students to read *Roll of Thunder, Hear My Cry,* I first assigned as a prereading activity a newspaper article, written in 1968, titled "A Southern Idyll." It was the account of a town, inhabited primarily by African Americans, that had gained access to running water for the very first time. My students wrote a journal entry before discussing their responses in groups and then as a class. One of my students wrote the following:

January 10, 1990

"Southern Idyll," 1968

I know they used to call Black people Negroes, but that word . . . or label . . . just hit me the wrong way! I mean, if someone called me a Negro, I'd think they were talking down to me. You know, like if someone went calling me Whitey all the time. Why can't they just call them people, like we all are???? The whole article seemed to be doing that too. I mean, they just got water . . . running water??!!! I wonder how it must have felt to know that you had to haul up your water everyday from somewhere else? It must have been hard. And to think that all the little five year old girl could think of was a bath! I wish my little brother would think like that sometimes!

Addition: Some of the other kids thought it was great that the town just got running water. I still think they should have had it a long time ago. I found out that Jimtown, the name, might be a way people put down the Blacks then, too. Jim was a common name for anyone who was Black in those days. Wouldn't it be awful if someone saw that my skin was white and called me Mary, not caring what my real name was? Ugh!!!

This prereading activity, along with any notes garnered during the class discussion, went into the portfolio. As the students began to read Mildred Taylor's novel, they wrote more journal entries, which, as I mentioned previously, included emotional reactions and memories evoked by the novel and questions it raised. One student wrote the following in her journal:

January 10, 1990

Roll of Thunder, Hear My Cry

Chapter 1

Wow! On this very first page, page 1, I already know so much about Little Man. That's a crazy name for a kid. But, I know that he's always neat and clean. I like the way she shows it: "shiny black shoes" and "lifting each foot high before setting it gently down again." We've done some of this showing in class and now I see how it really works in books, too. I think I'll look for some more of that.

Another one . . . on page 3: "I dragged my feet in the dust, allowing it to sift back onto my socks and shoes like gritty red snow." I like the picture of red snow. It's weird but neat.

How awful again. They get used, and I mean USED books that have been thrown away by the white kids. Then, all the way down the front part of the book it has kids' names and White, but when the black school gets it, it says nigra. First of all, why does White have to be capitalized and nigra not? And second, why do they call them nigra? I think it's disgusting. I think that if I were Little Man, I'd have done the same thing. I mean, after all, all he wanted was a nicer book. I know what it's like to get an OLD book with writing all over it and stuff. It's gross. I'm glad we all have brand new books this year.

As the journal entries were being shared in the groups, students were encouraged to add to their own journals anything they heard that seemed of particular significance to them. These journal entries went into their portfolios.

In addition to the journal entries, I assigned quickwrites about each chapter, asking students to relate an event from the novel to their own lives. For example, I gave the students a choice of responding to one of the following prompts based on Chapter 1:

1. Little Man is upset about being given a discarded book that not only is old but is now assigned to the "nigra." Think about a time that you had to accept someone's discarded object. Maybe it was an old school book, maybe an old hand-me-down coat or jacket, or maybe an old used bicycle . . . anything that was given to you as a discarded item and not given out of love. Think about how you felt and what you thought at the time. Describe the situation, the object, and your feelings.

2. Miss Crocker seems to be a very strict, unbending teacher. Think back about all the teachers you have had so far. Has there ever been a teacher you didn't like because he or she seemed unfair, unbending, or uncaring? Tell about at least one incident you had with this teacher, a time when he or she seemed very unfair or uncaring to the whole class or just to you. Use dialogue and describe the situation that shows this teacher's nature. (Please use a fictitious name for the teacher to keep the teacher's identity confidential.)

My purpose in assigning these quickwrites was to stimulate the students to think about a concept or theme, to encourage them to apply it to their lives, and to make them think about how this novel could affect them. Students' responses, which they wrote before, during, or after each chapter of the novel, went into the portfolios and were part of their weekly evaluations.

Dan Kirby calls the self-evaluations *audits* because that is exactly what they are. They are progress reports, statements of accomplishment and understanding, questions, and summaries of the week's activities. Preparing this audit, or self-evaluation, gave each student a chance to focus on what he or she had accomplished or learned, to reflect on all of the activities, and to comment on them. At the same time, reading these status reports helped me determine what students thought and felt about the novel. A sample student audit follows:

January 17, 1990

Dear Mrs. S.,

This week I planned to do a lot with *Roll of Thunder* . . . I wanted to get the two quickwrites done, but only did one because I was sick on Tuesday. I really got a lot out of the group work, though, and think I at least know what you did when I was sick.

I'm not sure about T. J., though, and why he's friends with the Logans. If he were here at our school I think he'd be a gang banger like "you-know-who." Maybe on one of my quickwrites I could write about the gangs here? I mean, they're part of life in Santa Ana even if we don't want 'em to be. You know? Besides, I can remember just last 4th of July and all the guns going off and stuff. In a way, I understand T. J. and why he wants a gun and just to protect himself. You know? Anyway—if I can I'd like to. Okay?

This week could have been better. I don't like doing the journal right now cuz there's too much writing. But, I'll do it. I'll do better, too. Really.

Because my students wanted to be rewarded with grades for the quality of their efforts, I assigned the audits a letter grade. It was roughly equivalent to a spelling test grade in my book.

So far, I had used Dan Kirby's journals, quickwrites, and audits. Now, to the drafts. By the time we finished the novel, with richer discussions and more enthusiasm than any previous study of a novel had generated, the students had a wealth of information in their portfolios: their journal entries, plus added notes from class sharings of those journals; several autobiographical quickwrites that focused on their experiences with cultural awareness, prejudice, friendships, family, and pride; and several self-evaluations. I gave them the following prompt:

You have just finished the novel *Roll of Thunder, Hear My Cry* and have several journal and quickwrite entries in your portfolio. You have thought about symbols and how they portray meaning in one's life. You have been asked by an editor of a popular magazine to write a memoir for the magazine, to be published in June and distributed to your classmates. Write a memoir in which you link at least three events from your life together with a symbol. This memoir will reflect your values as it tells the magazine's readers, your classmates, more about you. Enhance your memoir with descriptive detail, use dialogue to show, not tell; and follow the conventions of written English.

As a precomposing activity, we discussed how symbols often hold separate events together in a memoir. I then asked the students to form groups of four or five and to brainstorm the kind of symbols Mildred Taylor uses in *Roll of Thunder, Hear My Cry* and what those symbols stand for. We combined each group's responses into clusters like those shown in Figure 2. Then, I asked the same groups to brainstorm some of the symbols we use today to reflect our values or emotions. The class came up with clusters like the ones shown in Figure 3.

After the group brainstorming and clustering, the students searched their portfolios, looking for three incidents that could be connected with a symbol. At this point, they had to keep their ideas of symbol fairly open. Some of them chose their three favorite pieces in the portfolio and then tried to fit a symbol to those pieces. Others chose a symbol and looked for those pieces that they might be able to fit under its heading. Some of the symbols were real, like a father's eyes that connected three memories in which the inner child in the father contributed to the child in his children. Another was a medal, an award that symbolized achievement in three different areas and at three different times for a student. Some of the students had to invent a symbol: an object that kept cropping up in their writing, but not all the time, or some imaginary object that seemed to float through

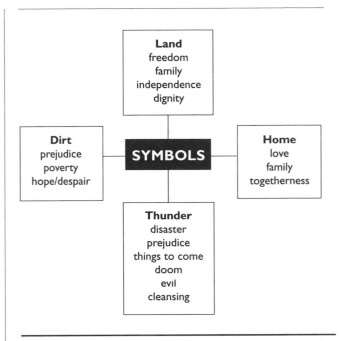

Fig. 2. Clustering of Symbols from *Roll of Thunder, Hear My Cry*

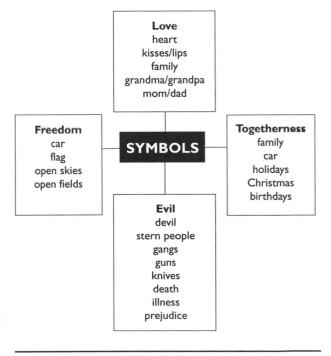

Fig. 3. Clustering of Symbols from Students

their pieces but that they never really had. For example, one student realized that sunshine seemed to play a big role in each of the three pieces he had chosen.

After identifying a symbol, each student drew a picture of it and wrote notes, radiating from that drawing, about each of the three parts of his or her memoir to show how each incident could be woven around the symbol.

Finally, before they drafted their memoirs, I gave students charts to help them organize their quickwrites, any journal entries that might be applicable, and their symbols. This chart, I hoped, not only would help them organize their multitude of writings and thoughts but also would guide them in the drafting of their memoirs. The chart appears below.

By the end of the study of *Roll of Thunder, Hear My Cry*, the students "owned" the novel: The hardships, triumphs, and pride of the Logan family had personal meaning for them. They also had a deeper understanding of themselves and how they relate to a world in which all races have the right to pride, a sense of family, friendships, and ownership. In addition, the students had had many opportunities to freely write their thoughts, reflections, ideas, and questions; had generated many kernels of ideas for future writings; and had earned many credits in the grade book.

I think that you will find the portfolio approach beneficial to your students in their study of a novel and that they will think more deeply, generate richer ideas, and produce better writing than they would have if the novel been taught in other ways. As you experiment with the portfolio approach, you will also benefit and be pleased as you watch your students' progress in their abilities to read, think, and write. This was certainly the case with my class.

Aha! and thank you, Dan Kirby!

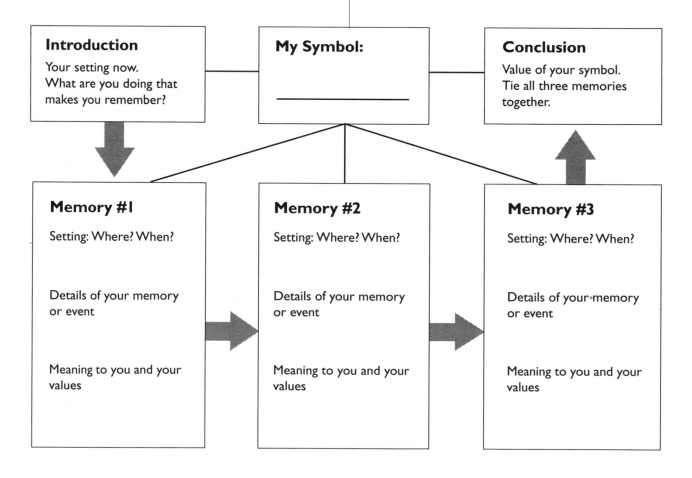

Introduction

Your setting now. What are you doing that makes you remember?

My Symbol:

_____

Conclusion

Value of your symbol. Tie all three memories together.

Memory #1

Setting: Where? When?

Details of your memory or event

Meaning to you and your values

Memory #2

Setting: Where? When?

Details of your memory or event

Meaning to you and your values

Memory #3

Setting: Where? When?

Details of your memory or event

Meaning to you and your values

Weaving an Autobiographical Web from Kirby's "Spider Pieces"

By Julie Simpson

English Teacher, Sunny Hills High School,
Fullerton Joint Union High School District;
and Teacher/Consultant, UCI Writing Project

Several years ago I attended one of Dan Kirby's workshops called "Images of Childhood." He showed us some of his techniques to help his students tap into their memories and make meaning by recreating their pasts. He used what he called "spider pieces"—bits of memories, sketches, snapshots, maps, "boundaries," and views of friends, neighbors, or parents—that in some magical way eventually wove together into a final memoir.

I was inspired. I loved what Dan was doing with autobiographical writing, and I wanted to do it, too. I wanted my students to read more autobiographical literature and more literature centered on childhood. Having students read about childhood and write about themselves would be a great way to introduce my year-long theme of the hero's quest. Students would see themselves as writers, a viewpoint that I want to foster. So I added and added and added—more writing, more autobiographical literature, more group work. And the unit I had planned to last two months took a whole semester, and we still did not complete all I had wanted to do. No more hours could be added to the 24. My inspiration did not lag, but it was frequently counterbalanced by my weariness and frustration at not being able to do everything.

I had not learned to give over control. I was creating an environment in which my students could make their own meanings, but I did not want them to develop those skills without my sharing in the process. Besides, if I let them go on their own too much, they would waste time; and the curriculum was much too full to allow for that.

As the years pass, I realize that what I need perhaps is not to give up *control over* the class but to exchange *control* for *guidance*. Every year I cut out more "stuff" to allow the class the time for thinking, sharing, and writing. Every year I am able to remain longer on the sidelines rather than in the center of learning. But this approach is not easy for me. And it is certainly not easy for my students. They come to me convinced that, as a teacher, I have the answers—that, as Dan Kirby says, knowledge is a "containerized commodity." School knowledge is not personal for them; it is what they regurgitate to earn a grade.

So we take our time in building a "community of learners," establishing credibility for each member of the class and learning to trust everyone's responses equally—other students', our own, and the teacher's. We start slowly, working in triads. (See "An Argument for Sharing in Triads," which appears elsewhere in this publication.) We all begin with the same "telling" statement written on the board:

- "I was so scared."
- "My broken arm hurt."
- "Mr. Johnson's house was spooky."
- "George was the nerd in my fifth grade class."

Each team rewrites the statement, and we share the different kinds of images we can present in one "showing" sentence. Then we take another telling sentence and practice again. All sentences are accepted equally. We talk about the differences between responding and evaluating, and we practice some nonjudging response language:

"This word makes me hear/smell/see, and so forth, the action."

"I wonder why you chose this word to describe such and such."

"What does this word mean?"

"I get chills from this house you portray."

Because our goal is to learn about writing by seeing ourselves as writers, we begin with the attitude that whatever any of our classmates write is exactly what they wanted to say. Our job as readers is to understand what they say, to interpret what we think they mean, and to respond to how their writing affects us personally. And that is the same approach we take when reading literature.

As soon as we have experimented with the group's showing sentences, we take a look at various kinds of literature and practice responding

As the years pass, I realize that what I need perhaps is not to give up control over the class but to exchange control for guidance.

JULIE SIMPSON

to the selections. We use a technique I call *active reading*, a combination of an inquiry approach to literature and Peter Elbow's responding to writing. (See "Some Guidelines for Writing-Response Groups" by Peter Elbow, which appears elsewhere in this publication.) The literary selections are short, so we read each one at least twice. We point out words and phrases that strike us each time we read the piece, underlining them as we go. We ask questions: factual questions about things we do not understand and interpretive questions to help make meaning of the author's intentions. We summarize, choosing from the piece one word or phrase that we feel best encapsulates it. And we give personal responses, stating how the piece makes us feel. For each piece, we take three minutes to elaborate on one of our responses. Because all of the selections of literature we read in relation to the Images of Childhood unit are short, xeroxed pieces, we write on the copies and respond on the back of the piece itself. With the first two pieces, we share our responses in class, listing and grouping all our questions, and coming to an understanding of each piece through the kinds of questions we ask.

Once we understand how to respond to literature from published writers, we begin our own writing and respond to it in the same fashion. When I have trained my students, I stand back and become more of a guide than a controller. As we work through the various "spider pieces" of our own memories, I introduce the approach, allow time for planning and at least for the beginnings of writing in class, and guide the feedback in class each day.

My plan for the unit, which follows, includes five "spider pieces" that, woven together, create an autobiographical web. Although the unit was originally designed for and used in the tenth grade, I have substituted some titles of literature and a few models more appropriate for the middle school.

1. Mapping Memories

   In class we brainstorm as many memories from our childhood as we can, discussing possible ways to categorize them. Each student creates a map, according to his or her own pattern, of as many childhood memories as possible, leaving room to add more later.

2. Snapshots (pictures we have etched in our memories)

   As an introduction to snapshots and as training for active reading, eighth graders might read any of several snapshot incidents from *The House on Mango Street* by Sandra Cisneros.[1] One example might be "Chanclas."

   From our maps we remember a scene that is very clear; Dan Kirby calls it a "mind picture that has edges." We jot notes about each scene, brainstorming it from lots of angles: Who is there? Where is each person? What is he or she doing? What does each person's face look like? What is each person wearing? What is said? What is the tone of the conversation? Where is the snapshot taking place? What does the place look like? What objects are in the picture? Where is each object? What time of day is it? What is the weather like? How do you feel as this snapshot is occurring? Then we sketch each scene, being sure

---

[1] Sandra Cisneros, *The House on Mango Street*. New York: Random House, Inc., 1991.

to place each object and person carefully in the picture. And, finally, we present the snapshot in writing, showing it as precisely as we can. We do this with three memories.

Here's an excerpt from eighth grader Matt Kivrizis' "Hockey":

I was so excited I was playing hockey for the first time. (It should have been my last!) We were playing this hoddendous game at McFadden Junior High School's tennis courts. I was playing with my older brother Brian and Brian's friends Danny and Anibal (Eyeball). The teams were Me and Danny versus Brian and Eyeball. We prepared for the start, but what we didn't know was as we began the game, a bundle of accidents were about to occur.

One, two, three, we're off. Brian won the face-off and was heading down the court. "WHAM!" Brian shot the ball with supreme force. "BAM!" right into the net. "SCORE." It was now 0-1. As they faced off again, Matt got the ball. Skating down the court, "KABOOM!" down I went. Eyeball knocked me on my @#&*. Brian stole the ball and hustled down the court. He passed it to Eyeball and they flew past Danny. It was now a two-man fast break. Eyeball smacked a thunderous ball to Brian who sent a speeding puck right into the goal. (0-2) I was starting to get mad. Eyeball had tormented me too much, just because I was a beginner; I didn't think Eyeball should treat me that way. Who cares if I was the youngest, I shouldn't get beat up like that.

We faced off again and Danny won the draw. Skating down the court, Danny batted the puck to me. I got tackled by Eyeball and went down. He hit me in the nose and it started bleeding. I came back punching. . . . The score was still 0-2, but Danny and I were determined to win. We faced off again, and Eyeball won. He was scurrying down the court when I pulled up next to him. I smashed my stick in his skates, and Eyeball smashed his face flat on the ground. Eyeball got up and chased me crazily around the court. He grasped me and chucked me into the fence. Danny hurried over, grabbed Eyeball, and launched him across the court. The score was still zip-2.

3. Places

As an introduction to places, eighth graders might read prose descriptions like "The Lake" from *The Legend of la Llorona* by

Rudolfo A. Anaya,[2] or excerpts describing Mary's room at Misselthwaite Manor or her secret garden from *The Secret Garden* by Frances Hodgson Burnett;[3] or they might read "Four Skinny Trees" from Sandra Cisneros' *The House on Mango Street*.

We discuss the physical limits of our worlds as children and draw a map for each general area, including where we could and could not go. We create maps for a neighborhood, house, and favorite place. On the back of each map, we list and categorize as many details as we can to recreate those places and then transfer the details to the maps when possible.

We talk about how a description of one of those places will compare with the snapshots we have been writing. Although some students may want to include a situation in their piece, the focus will perhaps be more on physical description and mood than on the incident. We write two pieces about places.

Here is an excerpt from sophomore Shin Hae Lee's "Haunted House":

I got real restless after dinner. I had to do something, anything. I went outside to the front porch and watched the dark streaks of tangerine cover the sun, cradled on top of the mountains. It was real peachy.

Soon, crickets in the bushes began to chirp in their perpetual way, telling one that it was getting late. I went down the stairs and strolled along the dirt street, stopping at the house next door. I stood there, waiting for my friends to come out. I had forgotten that they couldn't come out any more. It had been almost three weeks since they moved back to our homeland.

Wwwwhhh. Chills tingled up and down my back as the wind blew the moist air in my face. I put my hands in my pocket and I stared at the darkness inside the house. I felt like knocking at the door. Were they really gone? Taking two brave steps forward, I stopped abruptly as a funny feeling came over me. I lost my nerve. What if someone does open the door and it's not my friends? What if it's a witch, or even a ghost?

[2] Rudolfo A. Anaya, *The Legend of Llorona*. Berkeley: TQS Publications, Inc., 1984.
[3] Frances Hodgson Burnett, *The Secret Garden*. New York: NAL/Dutton, 1989.

4. Friends

To show how writers describe the people they know, eighth graders might read a story such as "Thank you, Ma'am" by Langston Hughes,[4] poems such as "For My Sister Molly" by Alice Walker,[5] or "The Secret Heart" by Robert Tristram Coffin.[6]

We choose one age of our childhood, say six or seven, and make clusters of all the friends we knew then. We include pets, family, relatives, neighbors and acquaintances, good and bad influences, and so forth. Then, we choose one of those people and create him or her in a firsthand biographical sketch. In the process, of course, we include some fond memories, too.

Here's an excerpt from Sang Han's letter to his friend, Josh:

Homerun hitting contests, Indian ball, football games. Those were some of the good times we had together. Throwing All-Star ballots through the fences at Wrigley Field. Remember the time when I hit a baseball and it hit your wrist, Josh? And how about the time you walloped the ball over the wall and onto the railroad tracks?

How many times did we sneak into Dyche Stadium to play football in the snow? Orrington vs. Lincolnwood. I would dump my bike in the bushes and squeeze in through the fence and onto the playing field.

As I reflect back to those times, I sometimes doubt if we'll ever see each other again. I know I said that I'll visit, but so far it hasn't happened and it's been two and a half years already since I moved from Chicago. I hate to think that we'll never see each other again, but that thought sometimes pops into my head.

As I sit here and ponder about my past, one thing jumps into my mind. Orrington Elementary School . . .

5. School Experiences

To introduce this spider piece, we read "Charles" by Shirley Jackson[7] and an excerpt

from Ernesto Galarza's *Barrio Boy*.[8] We talk about our earliest memories of school—the first day in kindergarten, the first day at a new school, the first time we were in a holiday program, and so forth. We choose one situation and sketch our memories of the event. Then we make clusters of the memories surrounding it. The focus here is on what we had expected before the event and how we felt during it. We write of one such time.

Here is eighth grader Thuy Nguyen's expectations of the first day of school:

One of the stories my family often mention was how much I adored school when I was little. They often tease me.

"Remember how you would cry every morning when we left for school," my sister would say.

I would chase after them yelling, "Wait for me!" "You forgot me!" They just ignored me. I would cry for hours.

When my sisters arrived home, I would carry their books and ask them about all the exciting things they did in school. They bragged about their numerous friends, their huge playground, and how nice their teachers were. I was always fascinated by their stories.

I imagined school as this beautiful place with all these toys and the slides and swings. I waited every day for my fifth birthday. Finally, I was able to attend kindergarten. I squealed with joy and was extremely excited. I was going to school!

After my first day, I was quite disappointed. Kindergarten hadn't been all that I hoped for. I felt lost. I didn't meet any new friends. My teacher seemed more mean than nice.

By the second week, I was used to everything. I was no longer happy when my alarm went off and I had to go to school. I would moan and groan. Now I'm pretty used to it. It's just ordinary.

6. Objects

To introduce this piece of personal reflection, we read stories and poems about remembered pets and objects from childhood: "Calling in the Cat" by Elizabeth Coatsworth,[9] "The Dog

[4]Langston Hughes, *Something in Common and Other Stories*. New York: Hill and Wang, Inc., 1963. *Best Short Stories by Negro Writers*. Edited by Langston Hughes. New York: Little, Brown and Company, 1969.
[5]*We Become New: Poems* by *Contemporary American Women*. Edited by Lucille Iverson and Kathryn Ruby. New York: Bantam Books, Inc., 1975.
[6]*Poems for Red Letter Days*. Edited by Elizabeth H. Sechrist. Philadelphia: Macrae Smith Company, 1951.
[7]Shirley Jackson, *Charles*. Mankato, Minn.: Creative Education, Inc., 1991.

[8]Ernesto Galarza, *Barrio Boy*. Notre Dame, Ind.: University of Notre Dame Press, 1971.
[9]*Book of Animal Poems*. Edited by William Cole. New York: Viking Press, 1973. *Poetry of Cats*. Illustrated by Samuel Carr. Stamford, Conn.: Longmeadow Press, 1991.

That Bit People" by James Thurber,[10] and "Four Skinny Trees" by Sandra Cisneros.[11]

Then we remember favorite childhood objects. For homework that night students are to search through closets and drawers and under beds to see what they still have that has endured through the years. If possible, they bring an old, favored object to share with the class the next day.

We use these objects to stimulate reflection, filling out a chart like this:

A. What the object is—what it looks like
B. What it meant to me new—how it looked, how I got it, what I did with it, and how I felt about it
C. What it means to me now—what it symbolizes

Here is an excerpt from Marney Cheek's reflection on her beanbag dog, "Polly":

Polly. As I admire your view of my room from atop my wall unit, your bulging brown eyes call to me and beckon my memory to journey back to the times we've shared.

I know; now your brown beanbag ears sag from years of restless nights when I would crush you under my body in pretzel twists. But you were patient with me, as my clammy palms squeezed your paws and fondled your ears.

Your orange fur, although thinning and faded in places, still radiates your warm disposi-tion and relentless spirit which has always kept you and me finely woven as one. You're thinner now, but since I no longer need you to squeeze in order to live through nightmares and homesickness, I suppose it doesn't matter . . .

It's strange that I would look to you, a bean-bag dog, for comfort. I guess I didn't see the line drawn between stuffed animals and people. I wanted to be needed. When I was little, I wanted the respon-sibility of mature friendship. I wanted to solve what I saw as life's problems.

Now I have real problems, and you aren't here to help solve them. Being a teenager isn't easy, you know. Sometimes I'm Sir Edmund Hillary,

conquering Mt. Everest, while other times I'm the Challenger, headed for disaster. I've grown away from you the moment I probably need you the most.

Now I understand why some thirty-five-year-olds still have their favorite stuffed rabbit or teddy bear. To help them through the seemingly impos-sible times. Now I understand why I still keep you atop my wall unit, watching over me. . . .

7. The Final Piece

Looking at everything we have written and drawn, we discuss how to sort through the material and then weave it together into a final autobiography. Possibilities include taking one piece and making it longer, taking two or three pieces and unifying them into a whole piece, or writing a new piece we did not have a chance to write earlier. We work with a partner first, sorting out what might work. Then we make a plan, share it with our writing groups for feedback, and create a draft to present to the writing group.

So that students can have a record of their progress, I ask them to print out each draft as they write it using the computer. Between one draft and the next, they write about what satisfies them so far about their piece and identify troublesome areas. They prepare a couple of questions to ask their response group. During the last meeting of this group, students share drafts rather than finished pieces; and before students write their final version of their drafts, I read their responses to the group.

Sophomore Ngoc Troung's final piece, "Loss of Identity," written in 1988, foretells what she might say two years hence:

Dear Mom and Dad,

Well, I'm finally eighteen. My four years of high school really zoomed by. It's hard to believe that I'll be graduating in just a few months. I want you to know that I owe all my success to you.

By now, you're probably wondering why I'm writing this letter. It's simple. I've been ashamed of something I believed a long time ago. Why bring it up now? Well, I'm an adult today. I finally feel ready to tell somebody. I know, I've been waiting too long. But I guess now is better than never.

---

[10]James Thurber, *My Life and Hard Times*. New York: HarperCollins, 1990. Thurber, James. *Thurber's Dogs*. New York: Simon and Schuster Trade, 1992.

[11]Sandra Cisneros, *The House on Mango Street*. New York: Random House, Inc., 1991.

Ever since I was in the first grade, I felt ashamed and embarrassed of not being an American. It was hard to adjust to a new environment when everyone else was completely different from me. Having straight black hair and yellow skin made me different from others. It felt awkward living in a land whose colors are red, white, and blue, and constantly being reminded of coming from a land of red and yellow.

Being Vietnamese made it even more difficult. I hated history classes: watching the war movies; reading the names of the deceased soldiers; listening to the lifeless lectures; knowing that most of my relatives perished in this battle that seemed endless. It was too much for me to handle. Red eyed and sniffled nose, I would try to hide my sorrow, but it was useless. My remorse was too obvious.

Having an unusual name was the worst part of all. I dreaded the first day of school, listening to my name being mispronounced class after class. Mom, you always told me I have such a beautiful name. Why, then, couldn't anyone pronounce it correctly? The teachers got the goofiest pronunciations out of my name. "Gok, Nyo, Gnok." But I was always prepared. They would say something like, "Please correct me if I pronounce this name wrong." Or they'd say, "This is a wild guess," before they attempted to read my name off the attendance sheet. That was my cue to hide my face as I silently slunk down into my wooden chair. If I was lucky, my face wouldn't turn red, but that didn't happen too often.

It didn't get any better after class. One kid after another would come up to me and tease me. It didn't matter whether I was playing in the sandbox, hanging upside down on the monkey bars, or just walking on the soggy field. Humiliation stuck to me like super glue. I didn't know how to shake it off. It seemed useless.

There was one boy in particular who always had a new name for me, "Knock on wood." Maybe a rhyme, "Knock, Knock. Who's there? Mickey Mouse's underwear." Or maybe just plain, "Knock! Knock!" I tried to ignore his crude remarks, but it wasn't easy. If I told him to shut up, he'd say, "Who's gonna make me?" Well, I couldn't make him. Sometimes I'd just cover my ears with my frail hands and walk away. Anywhere. He would follow me of course, but sooner or later, he'd get tired of his usual teasing and would leave me alone. For a boy as small as he was, he sure had a big mouth!

Excitement filled the atmosphere when you announced that we were filing for American citizenship. This was my chance! You had to pass the test for my sake. Becoming an American citizen was the only thing on my mind since that day. Everything would be perfect. No more teasing and no more Vietnamese . . . everything. I mean, no more Vietnamese language, and, hopefully, no more Vietnamese food. Don't get me wrong, Mom. Your meals were absolutely delicious, but I was craving for hot dogs and hamburgers. Perfect. I imagined red, white, and blue colors flashing in my mind as the authorities declared us American citizens; but I was thinking too far ahead. We sure hit the history books, didn't we? Sliding in and out of the Fullerton Public Library, testing while eating dinner. It was tough, but we had to think of the rewards.

Shockingly, I was more relieved than proud when you passed the citizenship test. Those red, white, and blue colors didn't flash the way they were supposed to. What went wrong? It wasn't supposed to be like this. I looked forward to the next day of school. I stalked crowded halls with an American flag sticker, the one that the naturalization authorities gave us, on my sweater. I had shoulder length hair at the time so I was sure everyone could see my sticker. At the end of the day, I was deeply disappointed. Sure, I received a lot of congratulations, but what I really wanted was to put an end to the teasing. That didn't happen. It was just an ordinary day for me. The mocking still plagued me as usual.

Being an American citizen didn't change my life at all. Well it did in a way. I felt secure knowing that I had so many rights that I never had before, but that was only an outer shell. Deep inside, I was still the same Vietnamese refugee. I ate the same food and spoke the few Vietnamese words I knew at home. The funny thing is that I didn't seem to mind. In fact, I didn't want anything to change.

Mom and Dad, you gave me many values that I can't erase. You taught me everything that makes me whole. It's like a jigsaw puzzle. If I lose one piece, I'm not complete. All of those Vietnamese customs you surrounded me with as a child grew up with me. I was still the same person then, and I'm the same person now.

Since I've matured with this thought in mind, I've learned to fight off the humiliation that once plagued me. Oh, I know I'll be facing this problem everywhere I go, but I have to go on. My values and customs are too important to waste. They are the substance that make me Vietnamese at heart.

I don't know how to express my emotions right now. Part of me is still ashamed, yet the other part of me is proud. Proud of being an American. Proud of being Vietnamese. Proud of having such wonderful parents who taught me my true values and customs. Truly proud.

Love always,

Ngoc

This whole unit as it now stands is planned to take seven-and-a-half weeks. That means I can finish it in the first quarter, allowing for extra time and time out for interruptions.

Basically, the first week-and-a-half are spent in creating groups and establishing the responsive environment. About five weeks are needed to go through the spider pieces. We start by discussing the literary models. These discussions are done in groups, using questions and responses as a starting point. I move from group to group, listening and perhaps asking a question or two, but not instructing. After ten or 15 minutes of discussion, each group reports to the whole class; and we continue discussion as needed. The literature is intended to stimulate and to spark ideas for writing. Then we begin our writing. Everything is written as drafts first and then shared in class. One day a week, one reworked piece is prepared to present in a formal writing group. In high school I can arrange for three groups to stay in the classroom for writing groups while the other three go to the computer laboratory to work on preparing their piece for their next group.

So a typical week would involve half a day for literature sharing; two and one-half days for talking, planning, and sharing our own drafts; one day in the computer laboratory; and one day in writing groups. The final piece takes a week of class time. I reserve the computer laboratory for four of those days, and the students decide where they can best spend their time.

If all goes well, when we put the whole thing together, we have seven spider pieces (three or four of which have been reworked for the writing group) and one final autobiography. Every now and then, a class becomes involved enough in this project to want to publish. When that happens, each student selects one piece he or she wants to publish (from any of the eight). An editorial board responds to, edits, and organizes each piece and compiles the book. There are always enough artists in a class to illustrate the material. Luckily, all of our work is done on computers now, so future publications will be much easier to complete.

As Dan Kirby suggests, I have set up a plan for monitoring the work as it progresses. For this unit each student is asked to have a loose-leaf notebook divided into four sections: Literature and Lit Log; Stuff About My Stuff; My Stuff; and Final Autobiographical Web. I have a collection of stamps that I use to note whether work is done on time. When the literature is assigned, stamps are given the next day for completed work. When pieces are due, stamps are given as the assignments are collected to be shared in samples. When I read the final portfolio and evaluate it, papers with stamps earn 10 points; those without, 7.

The section of the notebook that I read the most carefully and ask for throughout the unit is the Stuff About My Stuff (SAMS) log, the metacognitive work. Because the class members are working on their own, and I am trying not to control them, I need to know how things are going. So after each activity, I ask the students to write something in their SAMS logs:

- How do you feel about your last piece?
- How did your group respond?
- What do you think you will do for the next piece?
- How can you see your writing developing so far?
- What kind of piece have you most enjoyed?
- How was this piece different from the last one you wrote?
- Is there anything you want me to know about at the moment?

I read these logs once or twice a week and always include some kind of personal response to each student.

For the final portfolio, students select two of their spider pieces: their favorite and their most challenging. They write an introduction to each piece, explaining how and why it fits the given category. They also include all of the steps in creating their final web and, of course, the web itself. Each student decides how best to present his or her portfolio of childhood images.

I have found this autobiographical unit to be a favorite with my students. Whether we publish or not, they are proud of their work. They often want to take it home to share with their families. Parents enjoy sharing their memories when children ask about their family's past.

Tapping Multiple Intelligences Through the Literature Book Project

By Carol Booth Olson
Director, UCI Writing Project

Are you a jigsaw puzzle junkie, or do you quit in exasperation when you cannot find even two pieces that fit together?

Which is easier for you to remember—people's names or faces?

Can you walk into a meeting and "read" how people are feeling, or are you surprised when tempers flare halfway through the agenda?

Which sounds like a more formidable task— discovering the symbolic significance of a poem or balancing your checkbook?

Do people ask you to help them fix the sprinklers or the VCR, or are you the one who's asking for the assistance?

Would you rather make up the sayings for people to act out in charades, or would you prefer to be the mime?

Multiple Intelligences

Your answers to these questions may indicate which intelligences you favor as well as those that, given the choice, you might be apt to avoid. The concept that *intelligence* is plural may take some people aback. After all, *intelligence* appears as a singular noun in the dictionary. According to

Howard Gardner, however, studies of cognition and neurobiology suggest that we may have a number of different intellectual strengths, or domains of intelligence: each located in discrete parts of the brain; each responsible for a particular human ability; each relatively autonomous from other human faculties; and each progressing through Piagetian-like stages from novice, to apprentice, and, finally, to expert or master at rates influenced not only by heredity but also by cultural values. And although Gardner emphasizes that what he postulates is a theory only, that there will "never be a single irrefutable and universally accepted list of . . . three, seven, or three hundred intelligences,"[1] and that what he proposes are not "physically verifiable entities" but "useful scientific constructs,"[2] his work has given rise to more than a few Ahas! for both students and teachers alike.

Published in 1983, Gardner's book, *Frames of Mind: The Theory of Multiple Intelligences*, offers a provisional list and profiles of seven intelligences that have the "capacity to solve problems or to fashion products that are valued in one or more cultural settings."[3] Brief descriptions of these intelligences appear in the next section.

Linguistic Intelligence

As the most widely and democratically shared intellectual competence across all human beings, linguistic intelligence involves a sensitivity to the sounds, rhythms, and meanings of words, as well as to the functions of language. Four aspects of linguistic knowledge "have proved of striking importance in human society":[4]

Rhetorical Aspect—Ability to use language to convince and persuade others of a course of action or point of view
Mnemonic Aspect—Ability to use language as a tool for remembering

---

[1]Howard Gardner, *Frames of Mind: The Theory of Multiple Intelligences*. New York: HarperCollins Publishers Inc., Basic Books, Inc., Publishers, 1983, p. 60. Selected quotations are from Gardner, Howard. *Frames of Mind: The Theory of Multiple Intelligences*. New York: HarperCollins Publishers Inc., Basic Books Publishers, Inc., 1983. Reprinted with permission from HarperCollins Publishers Inc. Copyright © 1984 by Howard Gardner.
[2]Gardner, *Frames of Mind*, p. 70.
[3]Howard Gardner and Thomas Hatch, "Multiple Intelligences Go to School: Educational Implications of the Theory of Multiple Intelligences," *Educational Researcher*, Vol. 18, No. 8 (November, 1989), 5.
[4]Gardner, *Frames of Mind*, p. 78.

Explanation Aspect—Ability to use language to convey instructions and information, both orally and in writing
Metalinguistic Aspect—Ability to use language to reflect on language

Musical Intelligence

Often viewed as a gift rather than a form of thinking, musical intelligence calls for a keen auditory sense; a feel for patterns and rhythms, pitch and tonality; and an appreciation for the forms of musical expression. Whereas there is a considerable emphasis in the schools on linguistic attainment, music "occupies a relatively low niche in our culture."[5] However, in some cultures—China, Japan, and Hungary, for example—musical intelligence is highly prized.

Logical-Mathematical Intelligence

While linguistic and musical capacities originate in the auditory-oral sphere, logical-mathematical intelligence "can be traced to a confrontation with the world of objects."[6] It requires sensitivity to and the ability to discern logical or numerical patterns, memory for and the capacity to handle long chains of reasoning, an appreciation of the links between propositions, and a love of abstraction and problem solving. Whereas linguistic intelligence is the most democratically shared of all the intelligences, logical-mathematical intelligence is spread unequally across the population. Further, some of the most lasting contributions in humanistic scholarship have been made by individuals in their sixties, seventies, and even eighties; however, the peak period for contributions in the logical-mathematical domain is during the third and fourth decades of life. Logical-mathematical intelligence has been placed at a premium in the schools, largely because of Piaget's influence. He perceived logical thought as "the glue that holds together all cognition,"[7] and his theories have been a driving force behind intelligence testing.

Spatial Intelligence

Spatially intelligent people have a heightened capacity to perceive the visual-spatial world and to mentally recreate aspects of visual experience—

even in the absence of physical stimuli. Three components of spatial ability are the ability to (1) recognize the identity of an object seen from different angles; (2) imagine movement or internal displacement among the parts of a configuration; and (3) think about spatial relations. Psychologist Rudolph Arnheim has argued that the most important operations of thinking come directly from our perceptions of the world because unless we can conjure up a visual image of a concept, we will be unable to think about it clearly. Albert Einstein, who derived many of his insights from spatial models, is a case in point. As Einstein once said:

> The words or the language, as they are written or spoken, do not seem to play any role in my mechanism of thought. The psychical entities which seem to serve as elements in thought are certain signs and more or less clear images which can be voluntarily reproduced or combined. . . . The above mentioned elements are, in my case, of visual and some of muscular type.[8]

Bodily-Kinesthetic Intelligence

In recent years psychologists have seen a close link between the use of the body and other cognitive powers. Bodily-kinesthetic intelligence involves a well-honed sense of timing, an ability to anticipate what an opponent will do next, a control of one's bodily movements, an overall smoothness of performance, and an automaticity of certain reflexes or activities. Interestingly, Gardner identifies the use of tools by primates as the first developmental sign of bodily-kinesthetic intelligence.

The Personal Intelligences

Two forms of intelligence that are almost virtually ignored by students of cognition are **intrapersonal** and **interpersonal** intelligence. It is easy to understand how those that see a clear division between thought and emotion would relegate both intrapersonal intelligence (access to one's own feeling life) and interpersonal intelligence (ability to read the intentions and desires of others) solely to the affective domain. However, Gardner sees the personal intelligences as "infor-

---

[5]Gardner, *Frames of Mind*, p. 109.
[6]Gardner, *Frames of Mind*, p. 129.
[7]Gardner, *Frames of Mind*, p. 134.

[8]Albert Einstein quoted by Jacques Hadamard in *An Essay on the Psychology of Invention in the Mathematical Field*. Princeton, N.J.: Princeton University Press, 1945, pp. 142–143. Reprinted by permission of the publisher.

mation-processing capacities—one directed inward, the other directed outward."[9] The integration of these two intelligences, which leads to a firmly developed sense of self, "appears as the highest achievement of human beings."[10]

Just as it takes the integration of the personal intelligences to foster a well-developed sense of self, so too it is the interaction and integration of "complexes of intelligences functioning together smoothly, even seamlessly [that enable us to engage in and] execute intricate human activities."[11]

Because the theory of multiple intelligences has profound implications for educators and education itself, I include this concept as an essential curricular component in my Elementary Language Arts Methods class for teaching credential candidates at the University of California, Irvine. My students need to know, for example, that as teachers we are apt to lead with our strong suit, a tendency that, to use an analogy, may leave certain "players" in the classroom out of the game. Further, we may be unconsciously drawn to those students who share our intellectual preferences. Given that we are obligated to provide all schoolchildren with opportunities to learn and to feel successful, we must identify and capitalize on their strengths and use them as tools to foster their less-developed or practiced intelligences.

The Literature Book Project

To help my students translate this conceptual framework into something practical, I ask them to illustrate their understanding of Howard Gardner's theories by creating a tangible teaching material with a work of children's literature as a springboard. The directions I give the students for their literature book projects are as follows:

> You will be given an opportunity to choose a work of literature that you would like to use in the classroom and to design a literature book project. After you have

read a work of children's literature of your choice and thought about how you might teach it, your goal is to think of a tangible teaching material that you can use to introduce students to your book or to use as a teaching tool during the course of reading or writing about the work of literature. You are encouraged to use your imagination and make this project fun as well as something you can use in your teaching career. Book projects in a previous class included game boards, collages, dioramas, mobiles, models, felt boards, objects containing other objects, greeting cards, and so forth. As you design your project, keep Howard Gardner's theory of multiple intelligences in mind. Your project should tap two or more intelligences and give students with diverse learning styles an opportunity to shine. Literature book projects should be accompanied by a one-page statement of their purpose, including an explanation of how your project relates to the theory of multiple intelligences. Your literature book project will be shared in class and evaluated on a 1 to 6 scale determined by you and your classmates.

I never cease to be amazed by the thoughtful, creative, entertaining, and educational projects devised by my teaching credential candidates. Five of these projects are described on the pages that follow.

My hope is that, influenced by the theory of multiple intelligences, a host of new and experienced teachers at all grade levels will enrich their teaching repertoire with a variety of strategies that tap not just one or two but the full spectrum of the intelligences so that all students have an opportunity to shine. One step toward discovering students' strengths, after modeling a teacher-designed literature book/multiple intelligences project, might be to encourage your students to give their imaginations free reign and design their own projects based on a work of literature of their choice.

---

[9]Gardner, *Frames of Mind*, p. 243.
[10]Gardner, *Frames of Mind*, pp. 242–43.
[11]Gardner, *Frames of Mind*, p. 279.

EDITOR'S NOTE: We are grateful to ECS Learning Systems for their permission to reprint "Tapping Multiple Intelligences Through the Literature Book Project," from *THINK*, Vol. 2, No. 2 (December, 1991). *THINK* magazine is published by ECS Learning Systems, Inc., P.O. Box 791437, San Antonio, TX 78279-1437.

JUMP, FROG, JUMP

Designed for kindergarten through grade one students, Kathryn Smirl's project uses the book *Jump, Frog, Jump* by Robert Kalan (New York: Greenwillow Books, 1981) as a springboard to give beginning readers an opportunity to practice oral and written language. She constructed a spin board, with the main character of the book, the frog, as the spinner and with his tongue as the pointer. *Jump, Frog, Jump* is a pattern book that recounts the adventures of a frog, as in the following excerpt:

This is the snake that dropped from a branch
and swallowed the fish
that swam after the frog
that was under the fly that climbed out of the water.
How did the frog get away?
Jump, frog, jump.[12]

Fig. 1. *Jump, Frog, Jump*

After the teacher reads the story to the class, the children can play the game in groups of three to six. To stimulate linguistic intelligence, the child spins the frog, whose tongue will point to a word that refers to one of the people or things the frog in the story must jump away from. The child then tries to sound out the word and say it out loud. Beneath each word is a lily pad stuck to the board with velcro. Beneath the pad is a picture of the person or thing the word refers to. A child who was stumped by the written word can lift up the lily pad and use his or her spatial intelligence to match the picture with the word and then try to sound out the word. A child who made a guess at the word can confirm his or her answer by looking at the picture. The child must then place the lily pad back over the picture, matching the two shapes. Finally, the child must kinesthetically trace the raised letters of the word with his or her fingers and write the word on a piece of paper. Then, it is the next child's turn to spin the frog. As Kathryn says, "The spin board was designed so that children may have a visually appealing medium and a relaxing environment in which to stimulate learning how to read and write."

---

[12]Reprinted by permission of Greenwillow Books, a division of William Morrow & Co., Inc., and by permission of Walker Books Limited, London. Copyright © 1981 by Robert Kalan.

THE VERY HUNGRY CATERPILLAR

Ronda Triegsted's literature book project dramatizes *The Very Hungry Caterpillar* by Eric Carle (New York: Philomel Books, 1969). The caterpillar is represented by a green sock that fits over the reader's hand. As the caterpillar eats its way through the book (which literally has holes in it), the reader places a laminated representation of the piece of food over the arm with the sock on it. Finally, when the caterpillar has finished eating, it crawls into the cocoon made by two laminated pieces of brown construction paper with an opening at the top. Inside, the reader maneuvers the sock off and takes out a butterfly made from egg cartons and tissue paper. After reading the book and studying the life cycle of the butterfly, the children will use their spatial and interpersonal intelligences by working in groups to make their own sock puppet, laminated fruit, and butterfly for a group performance of the story. The children will also be required to use their linguistic intelligence by writing a few sentences about what happens to the caterpillar once it becomes a butterfly and their logical-mathematical intelligence by adding the number of various pieces of fruit draped on their arms. Once the groups complete their readings, each child gets a turn to take the props home for a performance for the family. "The primary goal of this project," says Ronda, "is to make reading fun and to encourage students to want to read."

Fig. 2. *The Very Hungry Caterpillar*

THE MAGIC SCHOOL BUS: INSIDE THE HUMAN BODY

Kathleen Whiting made the life-size (child-size, of course) game board shown in Figure 3 so that third grade students can journey through the human body in much the same way that the students do with their teacher, Miss Fizzle, in *The Magic School Bus: Inside the Human Body* by Joanna Cole (New York: Scholastic, 1990). Kathleen designed the board to be played at the end of a unit on health and the body. According to her the game board pieces, consisting of small fruit erasers and some real fruit props, were chosen to appeal to the spatial and kinesthetic learner. The game itself demands both oral language and reading skills. A group of about four students works together on the floor. Each person selects a piece of fruit as his or her marker in addition to one bill of paper money. Students roll the die and, using the number shown, move forward to that number of arrows. After moving ahead, the student selects a yellow card and hands it to the person on his or her right who will read the question printed on it. Information to be recalled appears on some of the cards; for example, "True or False: The more active you are, the faster your heart beats." But other questions, such as, "Tell us what your favorite organ is and why," have no right or wrong answers. If the student answers a recall-level question correctly or attempts any response to a higher-level question, he or she receives a paper money bill. At the end of the game, when students reach the brain, they use the bills to buy a healthy snack provided in class. All students will progress at about the same rate around the board because they will not be penalized (made to go back a space) for being unable to answer a question or

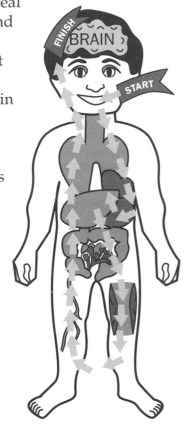

Fig. 3. *The Magic School Bus: Inside the Human Body*

for answering incorrectly. Kathleen notes, "I want to stress that this is not a digestion game, since it doesn't follow the right path. It is simply a 'get to know myself' game that incorporates a 'healthy me' attitude."

THE SECRET GARDEN

Fig. 4. *The Secret Garden*

ased on *The Secret Garden* by Frances Hodgson Burnett (New York: Bantam Books, 1987), Jody Ann Sinclair Jones's project integrates science, art, reading, and writing. The project itself has two visual aids: a diorama of a garden (complete with trellis, strawflowers, walkway, white picket fence, and painted backdrop), which is designed to stimulate the children's imaginations about flowers and plants and what gardens look like; and a flower chart, painted in watercolors, which is the centerpiece of a botany lesson. Both are intended to be prominently displayed while the story is being read orally to the class (for students in fourth through sixth grades) during a two- to three-week period. The role of the diorama, displayed early in the reading of the book, is to stimulate curiosity about the secret garden. Later, this display becomes a model for dioramas that the students make of their own secret gardens. The flower chart is intended as a visual referent and as an inspiration to the students when they begin studying flowers at the point in the story when Mary finds the key and gains access to the secret garden. In addition to using spatial intelligence to design their dioramas and draw their own flowers, students use kinesthetic intelligence to dissect flowers and also to choose several types of flowers to plant and grow in class.

Once students complete their art project, they will use linguistic intelligence to write a creative story about their own secret garden—what it would look like, whom they would invite there, and what magical qualities it would have. Sinclair notes, "Originally when I planned this project, I was excited about the creative writing aspect. But, when I started drawing the flowers, I remembered how interesting that activity was and how exciting planting seeds and watching them grow in a class setting was." Therefore, the culmination of the project is the planting of a class garden, if a small plot of earth is available at the school site. Sinclair writes, "I think that studying flowers and creating a class garden could be especially meaningful to children who grow up in apartments and who have never had that 'little corner of earth' that Mary eventually acquires from her guardian."

THE PHANTOM TOLLBOOTH

When you walk into the sixth grade classroom that Sabrina La Rocca has planned for the not-too-distant future, you will be entering the Kingdom of Wisdom. But first you must pass through the Gateway to Knowledge, a life-size replica of the tollbooth from *The Phantom Tollbooth* by Norton Juster (New York: Random House, 1961). "Just as Milo had to pass by the tollbooth on his journey to the Kingdom of Wisdom, so too my students will have to pass by on their journey to their seats," writes Sabrina. The students go into the tollbooth each day to discover the day's assignment, which might be oriented intrapersonally or interpersonally. Each of the lands Milo visits is the springboard for an activity center. For example, the Coin-a-Phrase box on the side of the tollbooth, which relates to Milo's adventures in Dictionopolis, asks students to use their linguistic intelligence to coin a new phrase and slip it into the box for extra credit.

In the Forest of Sights, students will listen to selections of music and write their reactions in learning logs. In Digitopolis students are urged to write at least six mathematical equations or story problems that will challenge their classmates and so forth. With each new land come new educational adventures. "After two chapters of reading, I predict that the kids will be hooked," says Sabrina. Using basic instructions to assemble a tollbooth, the students will also individually design a new tollbooth, select one as a class, and use spatial and kinesthetic intelligence to construct it. "Before Milo entered the tollbooth, he was a bored kid with no interest in learning, studying, or observing," writes Sabrina. "After his experiences in the Kingdom of Wisdom, he was transformed; he wanted to embrace knowledge and all that life had to offer him. Perhaps his biggest realization, by the end of his adventures, was that he could take responsibility for his own knowledge. My hope is that my students, like Milo, will enter the Kingdom of Wisdom with a strong desire to embrace knowledge."

Fig. 5. *The Phantom Toll Booth*

Sharing/
Responding

WRITER/READER

RESPONSE PARTNERS

Some Guidelines for Writing-Response Groups

By Peter Elbow
Director of Composition,
State University of New York, Stony Brook

To improve your writing, you do not need advice on what changes to make, and you do not need theories of what is good and bad writing. You need *movies* of people's minds while they read your words. But you need the movies for a sustained period of time—at least two or three months. And you need to get the reactions of not just a couple of people but of at least six or seven. And you need to keep getting them from the *same* people so that they get better at transmitting descriptions of their experiences and you get better at hearing them. And you must write something every week. Even if you are very busy, even if you have nothing to write about, and even if you experience writer's block, you must write something and try to experience it through those other people's eyes. Of course the writing may not be good; you may not be satisfied with it. But if you learn only how people perceive and experience words you are satisfied with, you are missing a crucial area of learning. You often learn the most from reactions to words that you hate.

In the paragraphs that follow, I will try to help you set up and use a writing-response group. If you get confused, remember that everything is designed to serve only one utterly simple goal: The writers should learn how their words were *actually* experienced by their particular readers.

Setting Up the Class

Learning to make use of a class that depends heavily on students' responses to each other's writing is a struggle. To develop this kind of class,

EDITOR'S NOTE: We are grateful to Oxford University Press for permission to reprint excerpts from *Writing Without Teachers* by Peter Elbow. Copyright ©1973 by Oxford University Press, Inc. For further information on the use of writing-response groups, see *Writing Without Teachers* (1975) and *Writing with Power: Techniques for Mastering the Writing Process* (1981), both published by Oxford University Press, Inc., 198 Madison Avenue, New York, NY 10016.

you need a committed group of students. You need the same people writing and taking part every week so that they have the time to get better at giving reactions and hearing them. You need to maintain the initial commitment of the class so that everyone continues to participate.

The main thing to remember in setting up the class is that *what* you and your students write does not matter as long as you write something. Treat the rigid requirement as a blessing. Since the class must produce something every week, expect some of the writing to be terrible. You and your students cannot improve your writing unless you put out words differently from the way you put them out now and find out how your readers experience these new kinds of writing. You cannot try out new ways of generating words unless many of them feel embarrassing, terrible, or frightening. But you and your students will be surprised in two ways. Some passages that you currently hate you will discover to be good later. And some of the reactions that most improve your writing are brought on by terrible writing—writing you would not have shown to someone if you had had more time to rewrite the material.

Use whatever procedure you think is best for deciding what to write. Write the same kind of thing over and over again—even the same piece over and over again if you wish. Or try out wildly different things. There is no best or right way. If you have the desire to write, you probably dream of doing some particular kind of writing. Do it. Or if there is something different that you believe you should work on first, follow your own advice.

Should you hand out copies of what the class has written or read the writing out loud? Both ways have their advantages. Giving out copies to the class saves class time because silent reading is quicker; you can stop and think, go back, read more carefully, and if the piece of writing is long, you can let students take it home and read it there. This procedure may be more possible than you think. Many photocopying processes are cheap; or making three to five copies from carbon paper is easy, and writing or typing onto duplicating masters is easy. Class members may leave a single copy of their writing where everyone else can read it carefully before class.

But reading out loud is good, too. When you and your class read your writing out loud, you often hear things in it that you do not experience any other way. Hearing your own words spoken gives you the vicarious experience of being someone else. Reading your words out loud stresses what is most important. Writing is really a voice spread out over time, not marks spread out in space. The audience cannot experience words all at once as they can a picture. They can only hear one instant at a time, as with music.

When you read something out loud in class, always read it twice and allow at least a minute of silence after each reading for impressions to become clearer for your listeners.

Giving Movies of Your Mind

As a reader giving reactions, keep in mind that you are not answering a timeless, theoretical question about the objective qualities of those words on that page. You are answering a time-bound, subjective but *factual* question: What happened in *you* when you read the words *this time?*

Pointing to the words. Start giving your reactions by simply pointing to the words and phrases which most successfully penetrated your skull: Perhaps they seemed loud or full of voice, or they seemed to have a lot of energy, or they somehow rang true, or they carried special conviction. Any kind of *getting through* is possible. If I have the piece of writing in my hand, I tend to put a line under such words and phrases (or longer passages) as I read. Later when telling my reactions, I can try to say which kind of *getting through* it was if I happen to remember. If I am listening to the piece read out loud, I simply wait until the end and see which words or phrases stick in my mind. I may jot

> *I always try to write on the principle of the iceberg. There is seven-eighths of it under water for every part that shows. Anything you know, you can eliminate, and it only strengthens your iceberg.*
>
> ERNEST HEMINGWAY

them down as they come to me in the moments of silence after the readings.

Point also to any words or phrases which strike you as particularly weak or empty. Somehow they ring false, hollow, or plastic. They bounce ineffectually off your skull. (I use a wavy line for these when I read with a pencil.)

Summarizing the writing. Another way to give your reactions to a piece of writing is to summarize it. This can be done by following these procedures:

1. First, tell very quickly what you found to be the main points, main feelings, or centers of gravity. Just sort of say what comes to mind for 15 seconds; for example, " Let's see, very sad; the death seemed to be the main event; um . . . but the joke she told was very prominent; lots of clothes."
2. Next, summarize the writing in a single sentence.
3. Then choose one word from the writing which best summarizes it.
4. And, finally, choose a word that is not in the writing to summarize it.

Do this procedure informally. Do not plan or think too much about it. The point is to show the writer what things he or she made stand out the most, what shape the thing takes in your consciousness. This is not a test to see whether you got the words right. It is a test to see whether the words got *you* right. Be sure to use different language from the language of the writing. This ensures that the writing is filtered through your perception and experience, not just parroted. Also, try this test a week later: Tell someone what you remember of his or her last week's piece.

Pointing and summarizing are not only the simplest ways to communicate your perception but also the most foolproof and the most useful. Always start with pointing and summarizing. If you want to play it safe and make sure your class is successful, if you are terribly short of class time, or if your class is coming apart, try skipping all the following ways of giving feedback.

Telling the writer what happened. Simply tell the writer everything that happened to you as you tried to read his or her words carefully. It is usually easiest to tell what happened in the form of a story.

First this happened, then this happened, then this happened, and so on. Here is an example of *telling* from the tape recording of an actual class:

> I felt confused about the man in the gray suit and the men gathered around you. I suppose they're the cops and the escorts. I had first thought [that] the [person in the] gray suit was a cop, but then I thought he was a dignified person who got arrested. I was uncertain about it. And then you talked about the men gathered around at one point—fairly early. I felt like they were cops, and I wanted you to contrast them to the fantasies.
>
> There was one point where you talked about—I think you were going down the stairs—and I felt like that whole part with the father of the bride and the gown was like the flash a person has supposedly, when he's going to drown and his whole life flows before him. I thought it was like an initiation of a girl—or a woman, particularly—out of her whole parental, social, ball-gown past into this new thing. And I was, I just, I was surprised. I didn't expect you to describe things that way. I was really happy. Then for some reason I felt like when you talked about the men who were gathered around—I felt like they were cops—and if I heard it again I might feel like I didn't need to have you say it, but at the time, as you said it, I wanted them to be blue-suited or something contrasting. Perhaps that wouldn't be necessary for some other reader.
>
> I had a very sort of happy feeling when you went to drinking songs. But it felt like the whole history of someone's life from being a young bride to becoming an old fishwife. I felt like it was a social comment in a way. One gets brought up and goes from the ideal fantasies to being fat and a drinking companion in pubs. And I was just very happy at that change in age. It seemed like the whole thing was—if it were a movie it would be going around like this—but the history of a whole person in a way retold in capsule form.

The important thing in telling is not to get too far away from talking about the actual writing. People sometimes waste time talking only about themselves. But on the other hand, do not drift too far away from talking about yourself either, or else you are acting as though you are a perfectly objective, selfless critic.

To help you in *telling,* pretend that there is a whole set of instruments you have hooked up to yourself that record everything that occurs in you, not just pulse, blood pressure, and so on, but also ones that tell every image, feeling, thought, and word that happens in you. Pretend that you have hooked them all up and that now you are just reading the printout from the machines.

Showing the writer your reaction. When you read something, you have some perceptions and reactions which you are not fully aware of and thus cannot "tell." Perhaps they are very faint, perhaps you do not have satisfactory language for them, or perhaps for some other reason you remain unconscious of them. But though you cannot *tell* these perceptions and reactions, you can *show* them if you are willing to use some of the metaphorical exercises listed below. These may seem strange and difficult at first; but if you use them consistently, you will learn to tap knowledge which you have but which is usually unavailable to you:

- Talk about the writing as though you were describing voices; for example, shouting, whining, whispering, lecturing sternly, droning, speaking abstractedly. Try to apply such words not only to the whole thing but also to different parts.
- Talk about the writing as though you were talking about weather; for example, foggy, sunny, gusty, drizzling, cold, clear, crisp, muggy. Use this approach not just with the whole thing but with different parts.
- Talk about the writing as though you were talking about motion or locomotion; for example, as marching, climbing, crawling, rolling along, tiptoeing, strolling, sprinting.
- Other ways to use this approach to talk about writing are as follows:

    Clothing: for example, jacket and tie, dungarees, dusty and sweaty shirt, miniskirt, hair all slicked down.

> . . . to write well, there are required three Necessaries. To reade the best Authors, observe the best Speakers: and much exercise [one's] owne style.
>
> BEN JONSON

Terrain: for example, hilly, desert, soft and grassy, forested, jungle, clearing in a forest.
Color: for example, what color is the whole? the parts? *Shape:* for example, square, round, oblong, triangular, cylindrical.
Animals: for example, cat, lion, mouse, frog, moose, bear, elephant, gazelle.
Vegetables: for example, carrot, broccoli, cauliflower, lettuce.
Musical instruments: for example, trumpet, flute, drum, clarinet, tuba, trombone, violin, oboe.
A body: for example, what kind of body? which parts are feet, hands, heart, head, hair?

- Think of the piece of writing as having magically evolved out of a different piece of writing, and it will eventually evolve into some other piece of writing that again is different. Tell where it came from, where it is going.
- Describe what you think the writer's intention was with this piece of writing. Then think of some crazy intention you think he or she might have had.
- Assume that the writer wrote the piece that is being discussed *instead* of something very different from what was really on his or her mind. Guess or fantasize what you think was really on the writer's mind.
- Assume that soon before the author wrote this piece, he or she did something very important or something very important happened to him or her—something that is not obvious from the writing. Say what you think it was.
- Pretend that this piece was written by someone you have never seen. Guess or fantasize what he or she is like.
- The writing is a lump of workable clay. Tell what you would do with that clay.
- Pretend to be someone else—someone who would have a very different response to the writing from what you had. Give this other person's perception and experience of the writing.
- Draw quickly the picture or doodle that the writing inspires in you. Pretend that the

writing was received only by your arm with its pencil; now let them move.

- Make the sound the writing inspires or imitate the sound of the writing. Make different sounds for different parts.
- Jabber the writing; that is, make the sound you would hear if someone were giving a somewhat exaggerated reading of it in the next room—in a language you had never heard (also compress the writing into 30 seconds or so).
- Let your whole body make the movements inspired by the writing or different parts of it. Perhaps combine sounds and movements.
- Do a ten-minute writing exercise on the writing, and give it to the writer.
- Meditate on the writing and try to tell the author about what happened. Do not think about his or her writing. Try, even, to make your mind empty, but at the same time fully open to the writing. It is as though you do not chew and do not taste—just swallow it whole and noiselessly.

These *showing* procedures are not very useful until you get over being afraid of them and unless you give two or three at a time. Therefore, I make it a rule that for your first four classes, you make at least a couple of these oblique, metaphorical statements on each piece of writing. This procedure may seem strange and uncomfortable at first. Indeed, the reason I make this an explicit demand is that I have discovered that people in some trial writing-response groups were too timid to use them. In other classes where people did use them, almost everyone came to enjoy them and find them useful.

Do not struggle with these procedures. Try to let the words just come. Say the thing that comes to mind, even if it does not make any sense. And for the first few weeks, do not expect satisfactory results.

There is an easy way to think of the relation between telling and showing. Telling is like looking inside yourself to see what you can report. Showing is like installing a window in the top of your head and then taking a bow so the writers can

see for themselves. There is no need to try to remember what was happening as you read. Just bow. Showing conveys more information but in a more mixed and ambiguous form than telling.

Further Advice to Readers

The following additional advice is given to help readers become more effective in the writing-response group:

- Make sure you have had a good chance to read the writing.
- Never quarrel with someone else's reaction.
- Give specific reactions to specific parts.
- No kind of reaction is wrong.
- Though no reactions are wrong, you still have to try to read well.
- Sometimes you may not want to give your reactions; respect this feeling.
- You are always right and always wrong. (You are always right in that no one is ever in a position to tell you what you perceive and experience. But you are always wrong in that you never see accurately enough, experience fully enough.)

Advice to Writers on Listening

The following advice is given to help writers benefit from their readers' comments in a writing-response group:

- Be quiet and listen.
- Do not try to understand what people tell you; just listen and take it all in.
- But do try to understand *how* they make their comments.
- Do not reject what readers tell you.
- Do not stop them from giving you reactions.
- But do not be tyrannized by what they say.
- Ask for the specific feedback you want, but do not play teacher with them.
- You are always right and always wrong. (You are always right in that your decision about the writing is always final. But you are always wrong in that you can never quarrel with their experience—never quarrel even with their report of their experience.)

Practical Ideas for Sharing/Responding

Implementing Sharing Groups in the First-Grade Classroom

By Michael Carr

Teacher, Valley Junior High School,
Carlsbad Unified School District;
and Teacher/Consultant, UCI Writing Project

Writers of all ages need feedback in order to develop a concept of audience. Students of all ages can be trained to be an audience and to give specific, meaningful responses to each other's writing. This is true as early as the first grade.

I have been implementing peer sharing groups in my classroom since my exposure to Peter Elbow's response group techniques during the 1981 UCI Writing Project. One major modification I made when I taught first grade was to the model for children by having one large rather than several small groups. After the children have completed their writing, they assemble on the rug and sit in a large circle. Our rules were simple. The author read his or her piece of writing, and the group listened. There could be no talking during the reading, as that took away from the piece of writing. The reader needs to have the center stage. Because of this rule, the children developed a sense of mutual respect and trust—both of which are essential elements in a sharing group.

After completing the reading, the author chose three people to respond to the writing. All comments, to begin with, had to be positive. Later I hoped to show the children how to tell whether or not the piece of writing was on the topic and whether the writing worked for them as listeners. The group responded to certain parts of the writing or corresponding illustration and could not make general, evaluative statements, such as, "I like your writing." The children had to be very specific about which words or sentences they liked by using Peter Elbow's pointing techniques. This approach gave the writer specific feedback and increased the ability of the group to recognize vivid language,

effective use of details, and so forth. After three people shared their reactions, the writer had the option of responding to the sharing group or letting the next writer share his or her work.

This process of sharing gave the first graders in my room a sense of purpose for their writing, an audience for sharing, and a forum for positive feedback. The enthusiastic attitude toward writing in my classroom could be traced back to the successful sharing group.

An Argument for Sharing in Triads

By Charles L. Reichardt

English Teacher, McAuliffe Middle School,
Los Alamitos Unified School District;
and Teacher/Consultant, UCI Writing Project

Of the stages of the writing process inherent in the model advocated by the California Writing Project, I believe that the concept of sharing is the most important. As I sit down to write this commentary, I am thinking of my audience, mentally anticipating the needs of those individuals with whom I will share my thoughts, and remembering that my experience with peer groups was the most positive aspect of my participation in the UCI Writing Project.

I first heard of Peter Elbow's writing-response groups at a weekend conference. When I first attempted writing groups with my sixth grade class, I followed Mr. Elbow's model closely and found that the logistics of the process did not suit my classroom situation. The meeting time was too lengthy, my students had trouble remaining on task, and it was hard to form groups of five or six members without moving a great deal of furniture. Having the students prepare five or six copies of their work was difficult. Photocopies were costly for the students to make, and carbon copies were messy. Eliminating these problems took over a year, yet finding the correct formula for my classroom's needs has been both creative and rewarding.

My groups now meet in threes, forming a triangle with the reader at the apex and the response partners at the base, as shown in Figure 1.

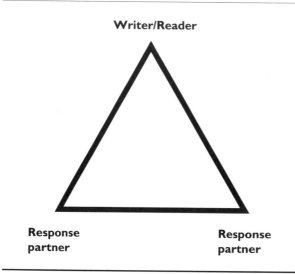

Fig. 1. Sharing in Triads

When sharing, the writer reads his or her piece aloud to the two peer responders and then passes it to them to read silently. This reading process eliminates the need for either photocopies or carbon copies and means that my class has only to move chairs to form the groups. Time is very easy to control because the process of reading, rereading, and sharing rarely takes more than seven minutes. The three members of the group can share in about 20 minutes. Rewriting often begins during the remaining minutes of a 45-minute period. My students love that!

There are other benefits of meeting in groups of three. With about ten groups in a class, you can disperse your best writers, making them leaders in the group. At the same time, your weakest writers are not congregated together, and they have the leadership and talent of a peer to rely on when there are problems. I was also able to control problems of concentration arising from close friends discussing topics other than writing by separating friends and making sure that each group had at least one girl and one boy. Careful grouping can help students, especially middle school students, stay on task and promote meaningful interaction among the writer and his or her peer partners. While these triads meet, I can hold conferences with individual students, circulate from group to group, or simply make myself available as a response partner when a group requires a third opinion.

Sharing in triads remains a key component of my writing class. I have found that limiting the size of peer groups to three students makes sharing more efficient for my classroom situation and student population without lessening the quality of the feedback. I recommend that other teachers who have found larger peer groups too unwieldy or the paperwork too cumbersome try sharing in triads rather than abandoning this valuable group interaction.

Reader Responses

Dialogue with a Text

By Robert E. Probst

Professor of English Education,
Georgia State University

A Story:

The entire class, but especially one girl sitting directly in front of me, was intrigued by the story. It was C. D. B. Bryan's "So Much Unfairness of Things," and the unfairness of which it spoke seemed to trouble and awaken the students.[1] They stirred, noticeably uncomfortable and disturbed, when the time came to discuss the reading.

The story is that of a student at a tough preparatory school in Virginia who finds himself in difficulty with his Latin course and succumbs to the temptation to cheat on an examination. He regrets the lapse immediately and painfully, but too late. He is reported and is summarily removed from the school. The story ends as his father takes him away from the campus.

Many of the students must have been painfully aware of the complexity of the situation Bryan had created. P. S., as the student is called, had no intention of cheating. It wasn't planned or premeditated. He hadn't even considered the possibility. Not until well into the examination does he realize that the translation of the test passage is in his desk—he hadn't brought it to the exam planning to use it—and even then he fights the temptation. But he *is* in desperate straits, having failed the exam the year before. He needs to pass it to graduate, and he doesn't want to stay at the school another year or go to summer school. Things are not going well on the exam, he is obviously in bad shape, and the

EDITOR'S NOTE: We are grateful to the *English Journal* for permission to reprint excerpts from "Dialogue with a Text" by Robert Probst (January, 1988). For further information on the reader response approach to literature, see Robert E. Probst, *Response and Analysis: Teaching Literature in Junior and Senior High School* (1987), published by Boynton Cook Publishers, Heinemann Educational Books, Inc., 70 Court Street, Portsmouth, NH 03801.

[1] C. D. B. Bryan, "So Much Unfairness of Things," in *Literature and Life*. Edited by Helen McDonnell and others. Glenview, Ill.: Scott, Foresman Co., 1979, pp. 342–367. Originally published in *The New Yorker*, 1962.

> *Readers must analyze and think, producing their own understandings, not simply remember information provided by teacher or textbook.*
>
> **ROBERT E. PROBST**

notes are there in his desk. The temptation is just too great. He slides the sheet out, copies the translation, and goes off to his room in terror.

If somewhat too casual about his work, too easily distracted from his studies, P. S. is nonetheless a pleasant, good-natured, likable fellow, not habitually dishonest and corrupt and not the sort of character whose punishment the readers could watch with equanimity. It must have been easy for the students to imagine themselves in a similar situation. On the other hand they could not permit themselves the satisfaction of railing against the teacher and the headmaster who expel P. S. Both the Latin teacher, Dr. Fairfax, and the headmaster, Mr. Seaton, appear to be kind men, nearly as upset and unhappy with the situation as P. S. is. Bound by the school's strict honor code, they have little choice but to abide by its demands. Even the student who reported P. S. is a good fellow whose motivations are respectable. There is no villain to blame and thus relieve the reader of his problem.

Before the teacher could begin the discussion, the girl sitting in front of me raised her hand, and, without waiting for the teacher to call on her, began to talk.

"I know exactly how he felt," she said, obviously troubled. "My parents expect me to become a doctor, and if I were going to fail I'd *have* to cheat."

Her remark provoked a flurry of comment, some students confirming the point, almost sadly and shamefully, as if revealing an unhappy truth about their lives; some casually amoral—"Everyone cheats," one student said, "that's the way it works"; and some almost belligerently, as if expecting the teacher to reprimand them for asserting that they would, if they thought it necessary, cheat to succeed in school. But the teacher didn't reprimand them. She tolerated the outpouring for a few brief moments and then waved the class into relative quiet and asked,

"What techniques does the author use to reveal character in this story?"

The girl in front of me waved her hand this time, waited until the teacher acknowledged her, and said, "My father has warned me what medical school is going to be like, and I'm not sure I can get through it—I'm not even sure I want to be a doctor. . . ."

Which was understandable, since she was at the moment in the eighth grade. The teacher acknowledged that, replying, "Yes, Jane, well you have plenty of time to make up your mind. Now, there are three ways an author reveals character—can you tell me what they are?"

Jane slumped a bit in her seat, in a gesture that often reveals ignorance, but that in this case seemed an expression of indifference, and another student joined in: "The kid who turned him in for cheating is a character, all right—he ought to be shot. Nobody turns you in for cheating."

Another flurry of argument followed that remark, with several students agreeing but with several others objecting that there were good reasons not to tolerate cheating, even if it did mean turning in a friend. One argued that there were reasons for having rules against this kind of behavior, and others responded that no circumstances justified turning in a friend. A few of them tried to defend the concept of a code of ethics, while others spoke for unconditional loyalty among friends. They were searching for their arguments when the teacher again interrupted. Bending slightly to the path the discussion insisted, against her will, on taking, she asked, "All right, how does the author reveal the character of the student who turns P. S. in?"

The students stared blankly, apparently unable to turn their thoughts away from the moral complexities of the story toward the teacher's questions, and the room was, for the first time, silent.

One child, introspectively, as if speaking to himself, muttered quietly, "I *did* cheat once, on a test, and I was scared to death, but no one turned me in."

"What techniques," the teacher repeated, sternly now, "does the author use to reveal character in this story? We've had them before, you studied them last year, you know what they are, there are only three—now *what are they?*"

The class was subdued.

"Well, the author can just tell you about somebody's character," one student responded.

"He can show how the character acts," said another.

And the little girl in front of me, still preoccupied with other thoughts, offered distractedly, "He can show other characters reacting to him or talking about him."

"Good," said the teacher, breathing a sigh of relief, "now let's go on. . . ."

But I forget what she went on to. She had to move on, she explained later. There were other stories to cover, other skills and techniques to learn, and a test to be taken on Friday. They had to be ready for that test. It had to do with techniques of characterization, and it was important. Those kids, that little girl, would be under a great deal of pressure to pass it, one way or another. They might even be tempted to cheat.

The Argument:

I'm sure that all of the pressures the teacher felt were real, almost as real as those her students felt and wanted to talk about, and the discussion might have served her as it might have served them; but her vision of literature and its function led her to other matters. She saw her job as the teaching of skills and terms and techniques. The students, on the other hand, wanted to address the moral dilemmas presented in the story. Their instincts and inclinations led them to talk about the intense pressure to succeed that comes to bear upon some of them, about the temptation to cheat that confronts them all, about the weight of parents' expectations, about the conflicting values of friendship and honesty, about the burdens of a demanding honor code that is supposed to be valued even above friendship. But their teacher wanted to conduct a recitation on the three techniques of characterization.

Louise Rosenblatt would argue that the students in that class had the clearer, more vital conception of literature:

> Surely, of all the arts, literature is most immediately implicated with life itself. The very medium through which the author shapes the text—language—is grounded in the shared lives of human beings. Language is the bloodstream of a common culture, a common history. What might otherwise be mere vibrations in the air or black marks on a page can point to all that has been thought or imagined—in Henry James' phrases, to "all life, all feeling, all observation, all vision."[2]

Had the teacher viewed literature that way, she might have considered the students' questions and interests more significant—they came, after all, from the life, the feeling, the observation, the vision of the students. They were focused clearly and intently on the connecting links between the text and their own lives. The story was, for them, implicated with life itself, and they wanted to consider those implications. To have done so would have been to invite the students into the literature in the most powerful and effective way, allowing it to be, not an exercise or a drill, but a shaping experience, one out of which students could make meaning. They could have, if the teacher had allowed it, participated in the making of meaning about their own lives as well as about the text, engaging in real thought rather than in simple recall of terms and definitions.

Rosenblatt has suggested some principles for that sort of teaching:[3]

First, the students must be free to deal with their own reactions.

These students clearly were not free to deal with their own reactions, which were strong and clear. They were instead constrained to ignore them in favor of the teacher's exercise.

Second, there must be an opportunity for "an initial crystallization of a personal sense of the work."

[2] Louise M. Rosenblatt, "Language, Literature, and Values," in *Language, Schooling, and Society*. Edited by Stephen N. Tchudi. Upper Montclair, N.J.: Boynton Cook Publishers, 1985, p. 65. Reprinted by permission of Louise M. Rosenblatt.

[3] Louise M. Rosenblatt, *Literature as Exploration* (Fourth edition). New York: Modern Language Association, 1983, pp. 66, 69, 71, 74.

The personal sense of the work *was* crystallizing quickly for these students. They had begun to articulate the personal implications of the story even before the teacher was able to start her lesson, and it took some effort for her to interrupt them so that she could proceed with her work on characterization.

Third, the teacher should attempt to find the points of contact among the opinions of students.

These students were finding the connections easily. Some said "cheating cannot be tolerated"; others, "you can't betray your friends." They had begun to notice and discuss their different perspectives on cheating, on the honor code, on the issue of loyalty. There was great potential in that discussion, because there *was* conflict, in their lives and in the story, between two codes of behavior. An opportunity to talk about those matters would have been valuable for them.

Fourth, the teacher's influence should be "an elaboration of the vital influence inherent in literature itself."

In this incident, the teacher was working—struggling—*against* the influence inherent in the literature, rather than allowing the students to pursue it.

None of Rosenblatt's principles eliminate careful, reasoned analysis in the study of literature, but they suggest that the basis for intelligent and productive reading is the unique, individual, idiosyncratic connection between the reader and the text. Rosenblatt has demonstrated that the meaning made of a literary text depends on the reader as well as on the text itself, that meaning is the transaction between an active mind and the words on the page—it does not reside in the ink, to be ferreted out, unearthed, uncovered. Rather it is created, formed, shaped by the reader in the act of reading, and thus it is *the reader's* meaning.

That doesn't, however, condemn us to intellectual isolation. Language has both idiosyncratic and social dimensions, and meanings can, to an extent, be shared. Even widely accepted conceptions are the result of such sharing and negotiating among individuals. What we understand by such terms as *love, justice, good*, and others, is the result of our

immersion in a culture that has dealt with these issues in its art and literature and law, continually refining and modifying its understandings in the light of new experiences. All of these crucial concepts have their roots in concrete human experience and emerge from continual reinvestigation of that experience—it is literature's role to present and explore those roots.

Instruction in literature should enable the readers to find the connections between their experience and the literary work. If it does so, it may enable them to use the literature, to employ it in making sense of their lives.

The Dialogue:

If we were to devise instruction consistent with Rosenblatt's principles, what shape might that instruction take? It must provide students a comfortable setting, freeing them, at least for the moment, of some of the customary burdens of classroom discourse—the obligation to prove all assertions, the shackling concern with accuracy and correctness, and the competitiveness that often rules the talk. Further, they must be invited to attend to matters that are often considered extraneous and irrelevant in classrooms—their feelings, perceptions, memories. They must be given time to articulate all of those thoughts and help in finding the links between their various reactions that will reward talk. They may need assistance in identifying the elements in the text that have contributed most powerfully to shaping their responses and help in figuring out how they have worked. And they are likely to need a great deal of assistance in learning the difficult process of talking with others. Finally, they need an opportunity to shape the discussion, directing it toward their own goals. They need to sense the influence inherent in the literary work and attempt, in the discussion and writing, to articulate it, define it, explore it.

The following activity is intended to lead students to the sort of literary experience implicit in Rosenblatt's principles and to demonstrate for them some of the potential satisfactions in beginning a consideration of a literary work with their own responses. It asks students to read a short literary work, probably a poem, although a short story—Bryan's, for instance—might work as well, and then to discuss it by responding to a series of questions designed and arranged to encourage reflection on several aspects of the act of reading.

The teacher can guide the talk gently, without interfering too much, by providing a selection from these questions—perhaps five to ten, depending on the time available and the maturity of the group—reworded suitably for the group, of course, and prepared without the side-note (the column labeled "Focus"). Placing each question to be used on a separate small page (4" x 5") stapled into a small book provides a place to jot down notes and encourages the readers to address each question more thoroughly before going on to the others. The first page of the booklet might give such instructions as those following, reworded appropriately for the group:

> Please read the text and take a moment or two to reflect on it. Then turn to the next page and begin. Take a few minutes—as much time as you need or want— with each question. Please reflect on each question for a moment or two, perhaps jotting down brief notes, before discussing it. Some may be more productive than others for you, and you may wish to give those more time. There is no rush, no need to finish them all. Please don't glance ahead in the booklet.

The discussion might be conducted in pairs, or in small groups of perhaps four or five students. Each arrangement has its virtues and its problems. In pairs, if the students are compatible, the talk may be more intimate, more personal, and more likely to lead to discoveries about the self. The small groups, however, are sometimes better able to sustain the discussion because they have more minds at work on each question. Decide how you wish to arrange the talk, give the students a copy of the text and the booklet, and explain the activity. If you've chosen a poem, you might read it aloud, and then let them begin.

The questions guiding the discussion of the text reflect a concern for the variability of readings and for the possibility of moving from response into analysis without denying the validity of students' unique personal reactions and associations. They are generic questions, tied not to a particular text but rather to a conception of the reading process. They invite students to attend to themselves, to

their own experiences with the work; to identify aspects of the text that seem significant; to consider their readings in the light of other readings by other students; and, finally, to reflect on what they have observed about themselves and their classmates in the process. (See the next page for sample questions.)

After the pairs, or the groups, have finished with the booklet and reconvened, consider reactions to the activity. In particular, you might raise questions such as these:

> Do you have any first reactions to the discussion, any thoughts or observations about its results for you or for the group?
>
> Did differences in readings of the text emerge as you talked? Did those differences reveal the possibility of other legitimate experiences with the text? Did the talk lead to any insights into the text, or yourself, or others at the table?
>
> Did the discussion occasionally drive you back to the text to find examples, evidence, sources of ideas? Did you find yourselves engaging in analysis, either of the text or of your interpretations and associations?
>
> How did your understanding of the text or your feelings about it change as you talked? Do you view the text differently now that you have discussed it extensively with others?

Conclusions:

If discussion of students' experiences with a text seems productive, it should suggest that the teaching of a literary work might begin with the reader's response, whether that response is emotional, visceral, aesthetic, or intellectual. The teacher might then encourage students to examine that response, looking at themselves, the text, other readers, and other texts. That discussion might lead to several possible outcomes. Students might find that their initial impressions or interpretations are reinforced and confirmed, that they are refuted, or, most likely, that they are modified in the course of discussion and writing. This is not, however, necessarily a matter of right and wrong, of dispelling error, but rather a process of refining and clarifying. The confirmation, modification, or refutation resulting from the discussion indicates not simply that mistakes have been corrected, though of course that may have happened, but rather that there has

Questions to Help Students Focus on Significant Aspects of Their Reading

Focus	Questions
Introductions	Introduce yourself to your partner(s)—where you are from, what your interests are, and so on. You may ask your partner(s) any questions you wish.
First reaction	What was your first reaction or response to the text? Describe or explain it briefly.
Feelings	What feelings did the text awaken in you? What emotions did you feel as you read the text?
Perceptions	What did you see happening in the text? Paraphrase it; retell the major events briefly.
Visual images	What image was called to mind by the text? Describe it briefly.
Associations	What memory does the text call to mind—of people, places, events, sights, smells, or even of something more ambiguous, perhaps feelings or attitudes?
Thoughts, ideas	What idea or thought was suggested by the text? Explain it briefly.
Selection of textual elements	On what, in the text, did you focus most intently as you read—what word, phrase, important idea?
Judgments of what is important	What is the most important word in the text? What is the most important phrase in the text? What is the most important aspect of the text?
Identification of problems	What is the most difficult word in the text? What is there in the text or in your reading that you had the most trouble understanding?
Author	What sort of person do you imagine the author of this text to be?
Patterns of response	How did you respond to the text—emotionally or intellectually? Did you feel involved with the text or distant from it?
Other readings	How did your reading of the text differ from that of your discussion partner (or the others in your group)? In what ways were they similar?
Evolution of your reading	How did your understanding of the text or your feelings about it change as you talked?
Evaluations	Do you think the text is a good one? Why or why not?
Literary associations	Did this text call to mind any other literary work (poem, play, film, story—any genre)? If it did, what is the work and what is the connection you see between the two?
Writing	If you were asked to write about your reading of the text, on what would you focus? Would you write about some association or memory, some aspect of the text itself, something about the author, or some other matter?
Other readers	What did you observe about your discussion partner (or the others in your group) as the talk progressed?

been some growth in understanding, some change in perspective. To see the changes simply as rejection of error is to suggest once again that there is a single correct interpretation.

Discussion beginning with response might then extend to biography, history, criticism, culture, intellectual history. Beginning with the personal and unique does not necessitate a purely egocentric study that denies the validity of other lines of inquiry; it simply asserts that the fundamental literary experience is intimate, personal, and dependent on the nature of the individual. It is, in fact, quite likely that these discussions of personal readings will lead the students naturally into close analysis of the texts, and that other questions—biographical, historical, and others—will emerge as students attempt to understand and reconcile their different readings.

Not used to an approach that emphasizes working with responses to texts, students may not like it, and they may fight it. If they have learned well to play according to other rules—predicting the interests and interpretations of the teacher, for instance, or memorizing details, or whatever other pattern may prevail—they may not be happy with a sudden change in the game. Although it may seem to them, as it does to many teachers, permissive and indulgent, this sort of reading—and teaching—can be rigorous and demanding. It requires the reader to consider not just the text, but also one's self and the readings of others. Readers must analyze and think, producing their own understandings, not simply remember information

provided by teacher or textbook. This exploration of responses can be fascinating or exhausting or both. It may reveal much about the individual who engages in it. It is easy to resist, however, since the teacher cannot spell out expectations precisely. There are no absolutes in such a classroom—each reader must make his or her own sense of things. The exploration of responses can be hard work, and the uncertainty may be nerve-racking; but the process has its rewards. It keeps the class alive, allowing it to be a vital exchange of ideas rather than the working out of a script.

If we accept the idea that literature ought to be significant, that the reader has to assimilate it and work with it, that transforming it into knowledge is more significant than memorizing the definitions of technical terms, then we need to find ways of bringing the reader and the text together and of forcing on the reader the responsibility for making meaning of the text. First efforts are very likely doomed to fail, for obvious reasons—the students aren't used to it and don't trust it; we aren't used to it and haven't figured out all of its complications; it places tremendous responsibility on everyone involved, not the teacher alone; it requires that we deal with 30 evolving poems at a time, rather than just one stable text; it requires that students accept a new and frightening notion of what knowledge is; and it demands a tolerance for ambiguity and digression. But if meaning is a human act rather than a footlocker full of dusty facts, then we need to focus attention on the act of making meaning rather than simply on the accumulation of data.

Practical Ideas for Reader Responses

Responding to a Reader Response: An Adaptation for Kindergarten Through Grade Six—Based on *Knots on a Counting Rope*

By Sandi Wright

Principal, Leo Carrillo Elementary School,
Garden Grove Unified School District;
and Teacher/Consultant, UCI Writing Project

Looking back, I think that the statement "there is no one perfect answer" first grabbed my attention. Bob Probst's presentation to the 1989 UCI Writing Project's Summer Institute on "Literature Response and Analysis" had a strong, immediate impact. His approach was exciting because of its important implications for our students as we looked forward to implementing a literature-based language arts program for students in kindergarten through grade six. The potential seemed strong for reaching and working with students of varied backgrounds who make up our classrooms. Probst developed this approach for college students, yet it seemed to offer much for the culturally diverse population in our elementary schools. It included many elements identified in the research on effective schools, such as cooperative learning, writing to learn and to clarify thinking, peer learning and heterogeneous grouping, whole-group instruction—and all based on instruction in literature! No wonder this approach piqued my interest so intensely; it involved listening, speaking, reading, and writing. It was an integrated language arts approach at its best. I was hooked!

Presentation of a Response-Based Approach

During Bob Probst's presentation, my thoughts flew back to my junior year in high school and Miss Williams' English literature class. How I dreaded the study of poetry—the interpretation part in particular. How did I know what the author meant in each line? It was always a game of chance to me—one with unfavorable odds. Probst's interpretation of Louise Rosenblatt's theories made so much more sense to me: no single "perfect" or "right" interpretation of a piece of literature.

As I quickly refocused on the presentation, I listened intently to the poetry selection as it was read to us. We were given a moment to collect our thoughts and feelings about the piece. Then we were given several predetermined questions and were asked to write about our first reactions, whatever they might be. There were to be no right or wrong answers. How good that sounded! After a quick freewrite response to the questions, each group of four was asked to have its members share their written thoughts, one at a time and without comment. How different our reactions were and how fascinating. We all listened intently to each other's words, amazed at the range of responses or understandings from the same poem! In some cases our responses revealed similarities. Of greater interest to me, however, were the differences. Where did these divergent interpretations come from? Hadn't we all heard the same piece of literature? As our group discussed our responses further, we were fascinated to learn about the bits and pieces of our personal lives from which our responses were formed. As I listened, I realized that I had misinterpreted an important event in the poem. Soon, the discussion moved from our foursome to the entire group. More similar responses and even more differences were expressed. This was fascinating!

Bob Probst skillfully guided and directed the discussion to help us make connections or links between responses as a group and then between our responses and the poem. My understanding of the poem changed, not because I had erred in my original response but because my understanding had been clarified—first through my written response, then through small-group discussion, next through the whole group's sharing of responses, and finally, through returning to the original text. I remember thinking how much richer my response to the poem was because of the reader-response process as I wrote down and underlined this quote from Probst in my notes:

> Reading without anyone else to talk to, a student too easily puts a work of literature aside without articulating his [or her] thoughts and, thus, without fully digesting it. Without the talking or writing that might follow reading, the student's reaction to the work remains undefined, unspecified.

There it was again, that emphasis on integrated language arts. I found this approach so natural, so empowering, that I began to wonder whether it could make reading literature more accessible to elementary students and responding to it not only more meaningful but also more fun.

At this point I began to develop the literature-response lesson to *Knots on a Counting Rope,* provided below, which was my attempt to adapt what I had learned from Bob Probst to a specific piece of literature at the elementary school level.

A Response-Based Approach to *Knots on a Counting Rope*

This section shows how the activities described previously can be adapted for the elementary school classroom.

Lesson Abstract

The purpose of this lesson is to have students use writing as a tool for thinking and as a basis for the discussion of a literary selection. As students consider the text and their own personal responses, as well as the responses of others, they will create their own understanding of and meaning from the text. Therefore, emphasis is placed on the thinking process, not on the final piece of writing.

The Process

The material that follows describes how the stages in the writing process can be used with the response-based approach. The stages discussed are prewriting/precomposing, writing, sharing, revising, editing, and evaluating.

PREWRITING/PRECOMPOSING

The steps for prewriting/precomposing follow:

1. Have the class, as a whole group, cluster ways in which they *see.* (See Figure 1.)

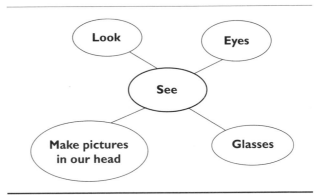

Fig. 1. Clustering of *See*

To stimulate a variety of responses, invite students to close their eyes while you lead them through a short guided imagery:

"Picture yourself at the beach on a warm, lazy summer afternoon—with your eyes closed. Think about the sand as you walk toward the surf, the waves breaking nearby, and all the activity going on around you. Think about how you know you are at the beach. Remember, your eyes are closed the entire time you are there." Now have your students open their eyes and ask the class, "How did you know you were at the beach?" Continue to brainstorm additional ways to *see* and add to the cluster. (See Figure 2.)

Ask your students whether their personal definitions of seeing have changed or broadened as a result of clustering.

2. Read aloud *Knots on a Counting Rope* by Bill Martin, Jr., and John Archambault. (It is most

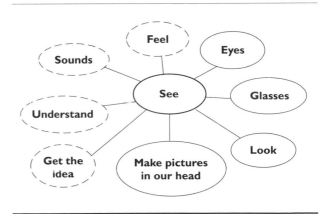

Fig. 2. Clustering of Additional Ways to See

effective if you have two different people read the parts of the grandfather and the boy.)

3. Invite students, after you have read the book, to close their eyes and think about the story for a moment. Then ask students to freewrite on any of the following questions, which you have written on the chalkboard:

   - What is your first reaction to the text?
   - What feelings did you have as you read or listened to the story?
   - Does it remind you of anyone you know? Of anyone you have ever seen? Of any experience you have had?

4. Have the students freewrite for five to ten minutes on their personal responses to the story. (Students in primary grades, limited-English-proficient students, and ESL students may illustrate their responses.) Immediate writing gives students the opportunity to think and write about their reactions to what they have heard or read before hearing the responses of others. According to Probst, "The brief writing period is intended to force students into solitary, unassisted thoughts about the work read and to obtain those thoughts from them so they can be discussed by the group."

5. Organize the class for small-group discussion. In groups of four, students take turns reading their responses without comment. After all have shared, students take turns commenting on the responses. The following questions may be used as a discussion guideline:

   - How did your individual responses to the story differ?
   - In what ways were they similar?

6. Organize the class for whole-group discussion. This is the opportunity for the groups to come together to hear the ideas developed in the smaller groups. The discussion should concentrate on the students' responses and provide the opportunity to find the links or the common strands between the various responses. The following questions may be used as a whole-group discussion guideline:

   - Do you have any first reactions to the discussion, any thoughts or observations

As students shared their responses, each child's reaction, feeling, and personal recollection became one more knot in the class's own symbolic counting rope, linking us all together.

SANDI WRIGHT

about its results for you or for the group?
   - Did differences in responses to the text emerge as you talked? Did the talk give you any insights into the story, or yourself, or others in the group?
   - Did the discussion occasionally drive you back to the text to find examples, evidence, or sources of ideas?
   - How did your understanding of the story or your feelings about it change as you talked? Do you view the story differently now that you have discussed it with others?

WRITING

After the students have had several opportunities working with this response technique, you may want to have them develop a piece of writing based on their responses to the text or on the text itself. Some suggestions for follow-up writing are as follows:

1. Return to the freewrite. Are there ideas that could be developed further?
2. Write about an association or memory that the text may suggest.
3. Write a letter to the author describing your personal response to the text. You may want to include the following information:

   - What you especially liked about the story (Be specific.)
   - Any part of the story you did not understand
   - Something you would like to know more about in this story

SHARING

Share papers in groups of four. Each student is to read his or her paper without comment. Each listener, in turn, comments on the following:

- I especially like . . .
- I didn't understand . . .
- I would like to know more about . . .

REVISING

Students revise their writing based on the feedback from the sharing.

EDITING

List the editing criteria on the chalkboard or on a chart and discuss them with the class. The criteria are to be determined by the teacher, according to the current expertise and needs of the class. Students can exchange their papers with partners to have them checked for editing criteria. Students then edit their own papers based on the suggestions from their editing partners and their own careful proofreading.

EVALUATING

The method of evaluation will depend on the nature of the writing prompt. (Suggestions for evaluation are available elsewhere in *Practical Ideas*.)

When I tried this approach with elementary students, I was struck by how different it was from the instructional methods in my high school English literature class. The children were not intimidated by the story. They eagerly shared their responses—assured that no one had the "right" or "wrong" answer. And, as students shared their responses, each child's reaction, feeling, and personal recollection became one more knot in the class's own symbolic counting rope, linking us all together.

Reader Response Logs

By Jenee Gossard

Language Arts Consultant; Former English Department Chair, Culver City High School; and Former Codirector, UCLA Writing Project

Of the many tools designed to improve reading comprehension, the readers' log is one of the most effective and economical. It enhances comprehension by supporting the student's continued growth as a reader. And it is truly economical because it requires little teacher time outside of class for preparation or follow-up.

Readers' logs deepen students' ability to construct meaning from texts by encouraging students to notice their responses and to examine them for patterns and insights. Readers' logs are simple to use: Whenever readers come to a stopping place, they record a response *of any sort* in their log books. These entries can serve many purposes: as stimuli for discussions, as springboards for writing and further reading, and as seeds of literary analysis. Students who keep logs of their reading demonstrate improved comprehension.[1]

How readers' logs improve comprehension is no mystery. Research studies of the reading process have shown that what we call *reading comprehension* does not depend solely on decoding words.[2] In fact, the decoding of words accounts for less than 70 percent of comprehension. More than 70 percent of comprehension occurs from the interplay between the text and all the other matters in readers' minds: feelings, attitudes, knowledge, experience, opinions, relationships, state of health, and so forth. To help students become good readers, increasingly capable of making meaning from texts, we need to teach them strategies for using all the relevant aspects of their personal experience as they read. Readers' logs increase comprehension by deepening the relationship between the text and the readers' life.

The idea of readers' logs had interested me for some time. I was intrigued by students' responses that teachers had shared in workshops and impressed by the range of students, from kindergarten through college, who had used the log format effectively.[3] Most of all, I was captured by the natural insights and perceptions of even very young children when they were encouraged to bring their own experiences to the process of

[1]See Nancie Atwell, *In the Middle: Writing, Reading, and Learning with Adolescents*. Portsmouth, N.H.: Boynton Cook Publishers, Inc., 1987, and Sondra Perl and Nancy Wilson, *Through Teachers' Eyes: Portraits of Writing Teachers at Work*. Portsmouth, N.H.: Heinemann Educational Books, Inc., 1986.
[2]See Yetta M. Goodman and Carolyn L. Burke, *Reading Strategies: Focus on Comprehension*. Katonah, N.Y.: Richard C. Owens Publishers, Inc., 1980.
[3]See *The Journal Book*. Edited by Toby Fulwiler. Portsmouth, N.H.: Boynton Cook Publishers, Inc., 1987.

making meaning from a text. On the basis of all I had read and heard, I decided to try the technique with my own classes.

Getting Started with Readers' Logs

When I began using readers' logs in my high school classroom, I was still under the delusion that *telling is teaching*, so I *told* my students exactly what to do. I *told* them to bring a small spiral notebook to class each day with their reading textbooks. I *told* them to write a response after each reading session in *any way they liked*; that is, spelling, sentence structure, and grammar did not count. I *told* them that their responses might include feelings, images, ideas, questions, and so forth. Finally, I *told* them to write in their logs every day in class and at least three times a week at home. Any questions? Yes, two: "How long should it be?" "What are we supposed to write?" Patiently, I *told* them again that there was no set format, no "right answers," and no way to do it wrong except not to do it at all.

After I had *told* them everything they needed to know, they began using their logs in class. At the end of the week, I took home a few logs from each class to enjoy the candid, perceptive, and insightful responses I believed would appear on every page.

The responses were disappointing. Students in my honors class, for example, offered cautious, inhibited responses: "The protagonist is interesting, the foreshadowing is good, and I liked the symbolism too." From another sort of class, I got different but equally disappointing responses: "Boring." "Stupid."

This experience finally forced me to accept the idea that telling *isn't* teaching. It became clear that if I wanted spontaneous, perceptive, and candid responses, I would have to *demonstrate* the use of readers' logs.

Using Metacognition and Response

At first I thought I needed to teach my students *how to respond* to their reading. But I quickly realized that a lack of response was not the problem. The human mind responds automatically, incessantly; unless it goes dead while reading, the human mind *cannot be prevented from responding*. What my students needed to learn was that their

personal responses were valid, appropriate, and useful. To track these responses, I ask the students to practice a metacognitive exercise: noticing and recording the responses they had while reading.

To demonstrate metacognition, I begin by talking with students about the kinds of responses readers often notice, giving examples from books or movies that they are familiar with.

Common responses follow:

- *Feelings* (boring, sad, exciting, weird)
- *Reactions* to characters or events (That Templeton is such a rat!—Ha, ha!)
- *Questions* (I wonder why the author put in the boring parts?)
- *Images* (pictures in the mind, with full sensory response)
- *Favorite (or detested) words or parts*
- *Echoes* (of other books, movies, television shows, headlines, songs, or poems)
- *Memories* (people, events, or places you have known)
- *Connections* (to other ideas, people, feelings, or books)
- *Lots more possibilities*

Then I ask the students to practice metacognition by noticing their own responses as I read a short passage aloud. When I stop reading, I give them about 45 seconds to write down their responses. Then I read a bit more from the work, asking the students again to notice their mind's activities and write their responses when I finish reading.

Sharing in Pairs

After the two readings I ask the students to share their responses, first with a partner and then with the whole class. The pair-sharing period is short: only a minute and a half. The procedure is simple: the first person reads his or her responses aloud to a partner, *without elaboration or discussion*, as the listening partner metacognitively considers how these responses are like his or her own and how they differ. As soon as the first partner has finished sharing, the second partner shares his or her responses, *also unelaborated*, while the first partner considers how the responses are similar to or different from his or her own. After both partners have shared their responses, they use the remaining time to discuss whatever they noticed: similarities, differences, new responses, and so forth.

Sharing with the Whole Class

To begin the whole-class discussion, I ask how many pairs had *similar* responses. As they describe the shared responses, I list them on a large chart on the board in a column headed "Similarities." I start with similarities because students often volunteer an idea more confidently if their partner had also thought of it. When a student contributes an idea, I repeat it, sometimes asking a question to make sure I've understood the idea, and note the idea on the chart in an abbreviated form. Since one of my goals is to build confidence, I take a deliberately positive attitude to the students' ideas—no response is wrong or weird and all are equally interesting *as responses*. Factual mistakes are treated matter-of-factly and corrected on the spot: "Wasn't it the *mother* who sent the letter, not the aunt?"

I continue encouraging the students to offer responses until they begin to share some risky ones. If I have done a good job of reducing anxiety, eventually someone will admit thinking that the reading was "a little boring." Or someone will ask, plaintively, "Is this one of those books where the dog dies?" or "Do we have to read another 'girl' book?" On the chart I write "boring," "dog dies?" and "girl book?" in the same accepting manner as I wrote the safer, more conventional responses.

After collecting as many similarities as I can extract, I make a column headed "Differences" and collect responses that partners did not share in common. Here again, I press the class for responses until some of the students become willing to take risks: "I didn't like the long descriptions." "I just zoned out and started thinking about the prom." "My partner hated the part about the frog." All responses, no matter how divergent, are recorded on the chart.

During the whole-class sharing, I listen especially for five kinds of responses: images, questions, words, feelings, and echoes. I find those responses particularly useful because they are among the most common ones and also because they are most likely to lead to more in-depth discussions later on. I do not specifically request those types of responses;

but after collecting a number of different ones on the chart, I comment on them. For example, if several questions or images have come up, I may ask whether anyone else had a question or an image that we could add. I might do the same for feelings, echoes, and words and phrases from the text as several of those responses begin to emerge.

Whole-class sharing and pair sharing accomplish three important purposes. Primarily, they validate and celebrate the students' responses, letting students know that I am unconditionally interested in their ideas and reactions. The sharing reinforces the point that *there is no way to do a readers' log wrong except not to do it at all*. As a teacher what I find most delightful is that from the wildly divergent responses on the board, a network of relationships among images, ideas, and feelings begins to emerge quite naturally. Key ideas and themes that lead students to deeper levels of understanding appear as if by magic. But the most freeing aspect of the group's sharing is the validation of personal response.

A second purpose for sharing in pairs and with the whole group is that these discussions fill in gaps in the reading. Even the best readers miss bits as they read, and some students miss from three to five words out of every ten. The shared discussions help to remind the class of what the reading was about and to fill gaps in students' memories or processing.

A third (minor) purpose for showing students' responses visibly and publicly on the chart is that I can model a note-making process. Log responses need not be full sentences with correct spelling and punctuation. My chart notes are fragmentary and abbreviated, full of arrows, circles, and other shorthand symbols representing the student's idea. Students observe the advantages of capturing the essence of ideas in ways that enable them to extract the longer, more complex version later.

Seeing Possibilities with Readers' Logs

The first time I demonstrated readers' logs in class, I was encouraged by the students' high level of engagement in the sharing sessions. The pair sharings were animated and noisy—a good sign, I have found—and the class did not want to stop when the short sharing time was up. During the whole-class sharing, students were eager to contribute their ideas and reactions; and, again, they did not want to stop. At this point I thought that I had done a pretty good job of teaching them what "response" could mean—and now they should be able to use this tool *on their own*. I had no intention of spending any more class time looking at readers' logs.

However, the next day, one of my "teach-me-if-you-dare" students looked in before class and asked whether we were going to do "that book thing" again today. When I shook my head, he looked disappointed, an unexpected response from a student who normally hated *anything* we did in class. But as I thought about it further, I caught a clue: *I* had enjoyed the readers' log demonstration, and apparently *they* had enjoyed it, too. And we had all learned a lot about the book I had used in the demonstration. Why not do it again? What I had written off as a one-time demonstration turned out to be a highly successful teaching strategy that I began to use once or twice a week in every class.

Organizing Discussion Groups

Readers' logs also gave me a new strategy for organizing discussion groups. At the end of each week, I ask the students to review their log responses for the week and then write a "reflection" entry for eight to ten minutes in which they might:

- Expand a response.
- Relate an idea or image to their own lives.
- Recall a memory.
- Explore a new idea.
- Play around with an idea or structure.

After writing, the students form groups of four or five, with a "designated starter" in each group. The designated starter opens by reading his or her reflection aloud to the group, after which each group member reads his or her reflection aloud in turn. The group does not discuss or react to any reflection until all the reflections have been read aloud. While listening to each reflection, group members ask themselves:

- How is it like mine?
- How is it different?
- What do I like about it?

After hearing all the reflections, group members discuss whatever they noticed about the set. A group recorder keeps track of ideas and issues as they arise. At the end of the time for discussion (five to ten minutes), I ask a spokesperson from each group to tell the whole class about what their group discussed. He or she might tell us about common themes that emerged from the group's reflections, the most interesting ideas that came up, or an issue that the members disagreed about. A group might share a reflection that the members think the whole class would enjoy hearing. This activity produces a rich mixture of ideas and reactions and again leads to increased comprehension and insight.

I learned to follow Nancie Atwell's practice of sitting in on each group for a few minutes—not to check up on the members but to hear what they have to say. Like her, I found that a primary-size chair—one that puts me just a little below the group's eye level—works best. At that level the students know I am *listening* to them. Of course, sometimes when I sit in on a group, the person to my left finishes reading; and it becomes *my turn* to share. But that is all right, because while they were writing their eight- to ten-minute reflections, I wrote one, too. And when I share mine, they accept my ideas as they do each other's, not as the "right answer" but as simply another point of view.

Eliciting Sample Responses from Fifth and Sixth Grade Students

After using reading logs successfully in my high school classroom, I arranged to implement this strategy with fifth and sixth grade students.

To introduce readers' logs, I read Chapter 1 of *The Indian in the Cupboard* aloud in three parts and asked the students to write responses after each part. After sharing in pairs and with the whole class, the students wrote five-minute reflections. Since this was their first experience with readers' logs, their initial responses were somewhat tentative and mechanical, qualities that disappear with lots of experience in responding and sharing.

James began by labeling his responses as "feelings," "reactions," and "images"; but by the third reading, he was responding spontaneously:

First response: Feelings—boring, cool. Reactions: The boy turned the key and it was quiet then he yelled mom! What is going to happen next? Images—I saw the skateboard that the boy got [for a gift]. How big was the cupboard.

Second response: Cool. Reactions: I like when the Indian cut the boy with his knife. What is the boy going to do to the Indian?

Third response: I like when he said, "I'm not small—you're big." I picture the Indian yelling at me.

Before I read the selection, the class discussed how it feels to receive unappealing or inappropriate gifts (in *The Indian in the Cupboard*, the plastic toy Indian seemed at first a thoughtless birthday gift). That discussion prompted many responses about gifts; for example, the following one from Russell:

I remember something I got for christmas. It was a Teddy bear and I was 10 when I got it. When I got it my mom saw the disapporntment on my face.

During the whole-class sharing of responses, many children brought up *Child's Play*, a television movie about a doll that comes to murderous life. They found the scene of the Indian stabbing Omri with his tiny knife similar to events in the movie. In his reflection James summarized the plot of *Child's Play*:

I like Childs Play because it is a good movie and it tells about a man the does voodoo and his soul go into a doll. The doll's name is Chucky. A little boy gets Chucky and Chucky come to life. He kills a black man and a baby sitter. The boy's mother looks into the doll box and see's the badoces [?] in the box. At the end Chucky tries to kill the little boy but a cop stops him they set him on fire and it kills Chucky.

The range of responses and reflections from the fifth and sixth grade classes on their first experiences with readers' logs was impressive. As we discussed responses, new ideas emerged that deepened our understanding of the chapter. Many children asked questions or reflected on ideas that could stimulate future discussions of issues, values, or literary devices. Sophy wanted to locate the magic—is it the fancy key or the cupboard itself that brings the Indian to life?

I wont to know why he chose that key. Is ther something special about that key that made the Inden come to life. Or is it the couberd that made the Indina come to life?

Jennifer felt a great deal of empathy for the three-inch Indian who does not want to be handled by a teenager.

I feel that the Indians wright because just because he little dosnet mean he wants to be picked up sure you can pick up a dog or a cat because there furry and fun to play with but this is another human being thats smallar and he has feeling just like other human beings.

Some children used their reflections to invent stories of their own, often borrowing details and plot elements from *The Indian in the Cupboard* as well as from other books and television shows they were familiar with. Michael reworked events, sound effects, and dialog from *The Indian in the Cupboard* in writing his own story:

One day on christmas I got a trip to the bahamas and as soon as I got on the plain I heard a noise. It sounded like the streatching of rubbr. it would go on for a wile then stop. Then I felt a breas come throw my hair and all of asuden I looked up and saw a humenges dragen and it said may I pick you up, and so I said Yes, and so it did and said your so small how did you get so small.

They even asked questions I had not thought of:

hocome he dident put one of his other plastic men in theair?

now it is giteing weaired. how come the indian wouldent let him pick him up, and how come he lost his magnifying glass.

Questions like these can lead naturally to a discussion of the writer's craft: How would it change the story if Omri had put a plastic soldier in with the plastic Indian? Would both have come to life? Then what? And what does Omri's misplaced magnifying glass have to do with the story? Is it a clue, a symbol, a revelation of character?

Grading and Recording

One reservation that teachers have about using readers' logs is the fear that at grading time they will be crushed under the paper load: "I don't even have time to *read* all that writing, let alone correct and grade it!" Take heart. One of the nicest aspects of readers' logs is that the teacher does not need to read, correct, or grade each one. For grading purposes log entries are either done or not done.

Since I allot time in class each day for reader response, I can easily spot those who typically write in their logs and those who do not. For grading purposes *what they write* is less important than *that they write*. I actually do read individual log entries on a fairly regular basis, but I do so for my own delight or to find a particularly perceptive idea to share with the class, *not to grade them*.

There is also no need to correct logs. Since log entries simply record the students' reactions while reading, there is no "correct" or "incorrect" response. Misunderstandings or highly idiosyncratic interpretations are often cleared up or shifted during the sharing sessions as students articulate, modify, and deepen their responses. During the whole-group sharing, I can easily help to clarify the major issues or confusions produced by the reading. Sitting in on discussion groups also helps me know which issues are important or meaningful to the students—and which ones I may want to address in later lessons.

At first students demanded points for their logs. I chose the simplest approach: At grade time I had them count the total number of responses and reflections they had written. I made a curve roughly based on the number of days we had read in class (usually every day) plus the times I had asked them to read at home (about three per week). If my total was 60 entries, then I might say that 50 to 60 entries = A on Readers' Logs, 35 to 50 = B, and so on. However, after a while grades ceased to be an issue. Most students enjoyed responding, found their logs useful for many purposes, and no longer worried about getting points for writing entries.

Discovering Benefits for the Teacher

As a teacher I find readers' logs an effective and particularly satisfying way of engaging students with literature. Students' sharing of divergent, idiosyncratic responses inevitably reveals patterns, relationships, and new understandings. Almost every element of literary analysis I might ever want to teach emerges quite naturally in the discussion of responses. And the students discover that the exploration of literature can be a shared

enterprise, one in which the teacher is not only learning along with them but often from them.

Selections for Introducing Readers' Logs

Passages from the opening pages or later sections of these books make excellent selections to introduce the idea of readers' logs. The grade levels in parentheses indicate the lowest levels at which I or other teachers have used the work for readers' response.

Babbitt, Natalie. *Tuck Everlasting*. New York: Farrar, Straus and Giroux, Inc., 1975. (Third grade and above)

Banks, Lynne Reid. *The Indian in the Cupboard*. New York: Avon Books, 1982. (Fourth grade and above)

Cooney, Barbara. *Miss Rumphius*. New York: Puffin Books, 1985. (Preschool and above)

Gertstein, Mordicai. *The Mountains of Tibet*. New York: HarperCollins Children's Books, 1989. (Second grade and above)

Giff, Patricia Reilly. *Today Was a Terrible Day*. New York: Viking Children's Books, 1984. (Preschool and above)

MacLachlan, Patricia. *Sarah, Plain and Tall*. New York: HarperCollins Children's Books, 1985. (Third grade and above)

McLerran, Alice. *The Mountain That Loved a Bird*. Illustrated by Eric Carle. Saxonville, Mass.: Picture Book Studio, Ltd., 1991. (Preschool and above)

Maruki, Toshi. *Hiroshima No Pika*. New York: Lothrop, Lee and Shepard Books, 1982. (Fourth grade and above)

Munsch, Robert. *Love You Forever*. Buffalo, N.Y.: Firefly Books, Ltd., 1986. (Preschool through kindergarten and above)

Paterson, Katherine. *The Great Gilly Hopkins*. New York: HarperCollins Children's Books, 1978. (Fifth grade and above)

Peck, Robert Newton. *A Day No Pigs Would Die*. New York: Dell Publishing Company, Inc., 1979. (Fifth grade and above)

Sperry, Armstrong. *Call It Courage*. New York: Macmillan Publishing Co., Inc., 1940. Reprint. New York: Collier Books for Young Adults, 1973. (Fourth grade and above)

EDITOR'S NOTE: Several of the publications in this list are available from more than one publisher.

Strategies for Interacting with a Text

By Carol Booth Olson
Director, UCI Writing Project

When I first began teaching literature, as a graduate student at UCLA, I thought that my job was to guide students toward an "accepted" interpretation of each text. So, with yellow highlighter in hand, I went back through each line or page of the poem, story, play, or novel, carefully framing questions that would enable us all to arrive at a place and a reading predetermined by my previous experience with the text, the readings of my professors culled from old class notes, and the insights of literary critics. I will even admit to occasionally taking a look at that old standby, *Cliffs Notes*, for an annotation of some obscure textual reference or to see how this source interpreted something I myself felt rather uncertain about. I did a lot of fishing in those days—fishing for the right answers to what were sometimes ill-framed questions. When the class didn't bite, I would often just answer the question myself so that we could move on. As it was to the teacher in Bob Probst's story at the beginning of this section, moving on was important to me at the time, although I cannot recall precisely why. It was often, although not always, a laborious journey. But, as I think back, the journey may have been more laborious for me than for my students. After all, I was the one who was painstakingly trudging through each text, giving the guided tour, as it were.

Since I have been exposed to all of the wonderful strategies shared within the Writing Project, I am much more willing and better able to let students embark on their own journeys through texts and arrive at diverse destinations. I say much more willing because people like Bob Probst, Sheridan Blau, Dan Kirby, and Ann Berthoff have helped me to redefine learning and literacy and to respect and acknowledge the power of students' responses. I feel better able because the innovative

ideas of Gabriele Rico, Jenee Gossard, Rebekah Caplan, my UCI Writing Project colleagues, and others have expanded my repertoire of strategies beyond the traditional question-answer approach so that I can help facilitate my students' interactions with texts.

Provided in the sections that follow are just a few strategies for interacting with a text. Although some of these strategies were originally popularized as tools to facilitate the writing process, teachers have naturally and easily adapted them to enhance the reading process as well. For the purposes of illustration, all are discussed in relation to *The Velveteen Rabbit* by Margery Williams.[1]

Clustering—A Prewriting Strategy

As Gabriele Rico says, "Clustering is a nonlinear brainstorming activity that generates ideas, images, and feelings around a stimulus word until a pattern becomes discernible." As students cluster around a stimulus word, the encircled words rapidly radiate outward until a sudden shift takes place, a sort of Aha! that signals a sudden awareness of that tentative whole that allows students to begin writing.

Clustering, which was once an exciting Aha! in and of itself, is now an essential and frequently used prewriting strategy for teachers and students alike. But it also is a stimulating idea-generating strategy for thinking, talking, and writing about literature before, during, and after the reading process. Clustering and freewriting about a book title, as shown in Figure 3, can cause important themes, issues, questions, and feelings about the text to surface. Clustering of characters, setting, events, and symbols can offer students a chance to take a closer and deeper look at a text and to experience some of their own Ahas!

Dialectical Journal—Responses to Literature

As described by Ann Berthoff in *The Making of Meaning*, the dialectical journal is a collection of double-entry notetaking and notemaking responses

AUTHOR'S NOTE: All examples are from fifth-year teaching credential students in my class, Education 110D: Teaching Language Arts in the Elementary School.

[1]Margery Williams, *The Velveteen Rabbit: Or How Toys Become Real.* Illustrated by Michael Hague. New York: Henry Holt and Company, 1983. A second version of *The Velveteen Rabbit* (New York: Alfred A. Knopf Publishers, 1985) is adapted for both a video and an audio version narrated by Meryl Streep. The audiotape with Streep's narration and George Winston's music is especially effective for the guided imagery exercise.

First, I am the boy's favorite Christmas gift—loved, new, and very important.
Then, I am on the shelf in the nursery; the skin horse is my friend.
And then, I am in the sick boy's bed, once again cared for and caring.
And then, I am in the trash. I cry my first tear. It hurts to be real.
And now, in the nursery, the Magic Fairy has made me real. I have hind legs. I can hop.

Fig. 3. Clustering and Freewriting About *The Velveteen Rabbit*

that the student can keep while reading literature. The journal's two columns, which are in dialogue with one another, not only encourage the students' cognitive responses, such as analysis, interpretation, and reflective questioning, but also elicit affective feelings and reactions as well. "The reason for the double-entry format," says Berthoff, "is that it provides a way for the student to conduct the continual 'audit of meaning' that is at the heart of learning to read and write critically."[2]

Guidelines for readers' logs appear in "Reader Response Logs" by Jenee Gossard in this publication. Figure 4 illustrates a notetaking and notemaking response to a preselected passage of *The Velveteen Rabbit*.

Guided Imagery—Drawing Mental Images

Guided imagery enables students to tap their creative imagination and visual thinking skills.

[2]See Ann Berthoff, *The Making of Meaning: Metaphors, Models, and Maxims for Writing Teachers*. Upper Montclair, N.J.: Boynton Cook Publishers, Inc., 1981.

While the teacher slowly describes a setting or narrates a story, using vivid sensory detail to elicit impressions or images, the students watch the "movie screens" in their minds—using visualization to develop their own mental pictures of the words they are hearing. Most guided imagery exercises are written by teachers or other professionals and are expressly designed to evoke certain impressions; yet literature itself is a rich and often untapped source for visualization. One might say that all literature is a form of guided imagery. However, as Dan Fader, a professor of English at the University of Michigan, pointed out during a talk at the University of California, Irvine, many of today's students, conditioned by the pictures already manufactured for them by the television industry, often have difficulty creating their own mental pictures to accompany the text they are reading. Ongoing practice in visualizing vivid passages from works of literature, such as the one that follows, can help to free the imagination and make literature come alive.

Note Taking	Note Making
"What is real?" asked the rabbit one day. . . . "Real isn't how you are made. . . . It's a thing that happens to you. When a child loves you for a long, long time, not just to play with, but REALLY loves you, then you become Real!"[3]	Real doesn't come from within; "it isn't how you are made." Real comes from without. It is a gift someone gives to you. They affect the very essence of who you are because of the love they have for you. Real isn't automatic. It happens to you as a result of a process of being loved by another.

Fig. 4. Notes on a Passage from *The Velveteen Rabbit*

And while the Boy was asleep, dreaming of the seaside, the little Rabbit lay among the old picture-books in the corner behind the fowl-house, and he felt very lonely. . . . He thought of those long sunlit hours in the garden—how happy they were—and a great sadness came over him. He seemed to see them all pass before him, each more beautiful than the other, the fairy huts in the flower bed, the quiet evenings in the wood when he lay in the bracken and the little ants ran over his paws; the wonderful day when he first knew that he was Real. He thought of the Skin Horse, so wise and gentle, and all that he had told him. Of what use was it to be loved and lose one's beauty and become Real if it all ended like this? And a tear, a real tear, trickled down his little shabby velvet nose and fell to the ground.

And then a strange thing happened. For where the tear had fallen a flower grew out of the ground, a mysterious flower, not at all like any that grew in the garden. It had slender green leaves the colour of emeralds, and in the centre of the leaves a blossom like a golden cup. It was so beautiful that the little Rabbit forgot to cry, and just lay there watching it. And presently the blossom opened, and out of it there stepped a fairy.

She was quite the loveliest fairy in the whole world. Her dress was of pearl and dewdrops, and there were flowers round her neck and in her hair, and her face was like the most perfect flower of all. And she came close to the little Rabbit and gathered him up in her arms and kissed him on his velveteen nose that was all damp from crying.[4]

Moreover, asking students to respond to a guided imagery experience by having them draw

what they saw, as shown in Figure 5, will often bring to the surface important images which can be discussed.

Fig. 5. A Student's Image of the Velveteen Rabbit

Reader's Theatre—Dramatizing a Text

Reader's Theatre is a way of dramatically rendering a text as if it were a play, thus bringing it to life in the classroom. The text can be scripted for the students, as shown in the accompanying example on the next page, or students can choose the roles and write out the lines themselves. The same passage can be read or "performed" by more than one group of students, allowing the class to see how the lines have been interpreted and, therefore, read with more or less feeling, delivered in different tones of voice, accompanied by different body language, and so forth by different groups.

Showing, Not Telling—Painting Pictures

Like clustering, the concept of showing, not telling, is well known to most teachers. As Rebekah

[3]Williams, Margery. *The Velveteen Rabbit: Or How Toys Become Real.* Illustrated by Michael Hague. New York: Henry Holt and Company, 1983, p. 4. Reprinted by permission of the publisher.
[4]Williams, *The Velveteen Rabbit*, pp. 22–26.

233

The Velveteen Rabbit in Reader's Theatre

ON: Omniscient Narrator
VR: Velveteen Rabbit
VRN: Velveteen Rabbit's Narrator
FR: First Rabbit
FRN: First Rabbit's Narrator
SR: Second Rabbit
SRN: Second Rabbit's Narrator

ON: One evening, while the Rabbit was lying there alone, watching the ants that ran to and fro between his velvet paws in the grass, he saw two strange beings creep out of the tall bracken near him. They were rabbits like himself, but quite furry and brand-new. They must have been very well made, for their seams didn't show at all, and they changed shape in a queer way when they moved; one minute they were long and thin and the next minute fat and bunchy, instead of always staying the same like he did. . . . They stared at him, and the little Rabbit stared back. And all the time their noses twitched.

FR: "Why don't you get up and play with us?"

FRN: one of them asked.

VR: "I don't feel like it,"

VRN: said the Rabbit, for he didn't want to explain that he had no clockwork.

SR: "HO!"

SRN: said the furry rabbit.

SR: "It's as easy as anything."

ON: And he gave a big hop sideways and stood on his hind legs.

SR: "I don't believe you can!"

SRN: he said.

VR: "I can!"

VRN: said the little Rabbit.

VR: "I can jump higher than anything!"

VRN: He meant when the Boy threw him, but of course he didn't want to say so.[5]

(Continue the dialogue.)

[5]Williams, *The Velveteen Rabbit*, pp. 11–14.

Caplan explains elsewhere in *Practical Ideas*, the assumption behind the showing, not telling, technique is that most students have not been trained to show what they mean. Showing, not telling, encourages students to dramatize their writing by *showing* with specific details that paint pictures in the reader's mind. This technique involves giving students a *telling sentence* such as "The room was vacant" or "The lunch period was too short" and asking them to expand the thought in that sentence into an entire paragraph. Students are challenged not to use the original statement in the paragraph at all. Rather, they must show that *the room was vacant* without making that claim directly. Giving students telling sentences about plot, setting, characters, and symbols in works of literature is a great way to prompt them to reflect on and interact with the text, as shown in Figure 6. Asking cooperative learning groups to generate their own telling sentences about a work of literature for another group to *show* is also an excellent way to facilitate discussion about and the discovery of literature.

TELLING SENTENCE

"Being loved by the boy made the Velveteen Rabbit very happy."

SHOWING PARAGRAPH

Night after night, the boy snuggled up close to his Velveteen Rabbit and slept with his hands clasped close around it, refusing to ever lie down to rest without the feel of its heart-warming softness beneath his chin. During these tender moments, the Rabbit's plastic eyes seemed to twinkle, his thread whiskers twitched, and the sides of his yarn-lined mouth appeared to rise and remain that way throughout the night.

Fig. 6. Showing, Not Telling, Through Writing

Time Line—Creating a Graphic Sequence of Events

A time line is a graphic representation of a sequence of events or activities. In the study of literature, developing time lines often helps students to reconstruct and reflect on what happens in the text. I got the idea from Joni Chancer, a Teacher/Consultant from the South Coast Writing Project (at the University of California, Santa Barbara) and the author of "Minilessons and Lit Letters," which appears in this section of *Practical Ideas*. She suggests that students list above their time lines events that they interpret to be positive (+) and list below their time lines events that they feel are negative or problematic (–), as shown in the portion of a time line represented in Figure 7. This task elicits a great deal of animated discussion and sends students back to the text as they discuss their varied interpretations of events. Students may also wish to illustrate their time lines with pictures and symbols.

Venn Diagrams—Comparing Relationships

Venn diagrams are overlapping circles often used in mathematics to show relationships between sets. In language arts instruction Venn diagrams are useful for examining similarities and differences. In responding to literature, students find that Venn diagrams can be especially helpful for comparing and contrasting characters, themes, settings, and so forth, as shown in Figure 8.

Letting Go of Leading the Guided Tour Through Literature

As Dan Kirby has noted elsewhere in *Practical Ideas*, "Reforming your teaching to nurture thinking involves more than dreaming up new activities or offering students more decision-making freedom. . . . This new view of knowledge does not mean you have nothing to teach students or that textbooks are no longer important or that old knowledge is no longer valuable." He continues

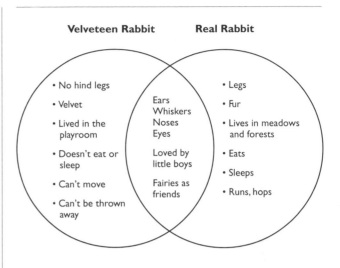

Fig. 8. Venn Diagram of Velveteen and Real Rabbits

with the statement that what it does mean is that we have to plan for and structure our classes in such a way that students construct their own versions of knowledge in more personal ways. And allowing students to construct their own versions of knowledge in more personal ways means that you, as a teacher, have to allow students to embark on their own journeys through texts and possibly arrive at destinations that may be unfamiliar to you. As students interact with the literature and with each other, I find their own fresh questions and concerns replacing my prepackaged ones. I no longer lead the guided tour through the literature. The students' own responses lead the way.

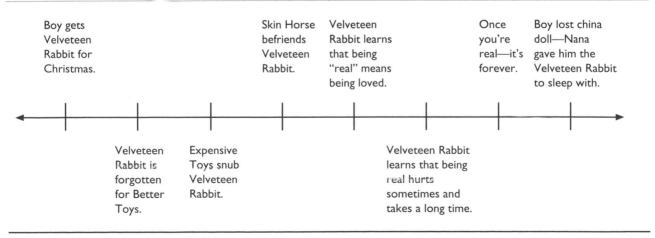

Fig. 7. A Time Line of *The Velveteen Rabbit*

Sharing What Belongs to You: Minilessons and Lit Letters

By Joni Chancer

Teacher, Red Oak Elementary School,
Oak Park School District;
and Teacher/Consultant, South Coast Writing Project

"Before I can share something, it has to belong to me." Two years ago, Amy, a student in my sixth grade class, wrote this statement in a letter about a book she had just finished reading. It was followed with a question: "Do you know what I mean?"

I do know what Amy meant, and I believe that giving students a sense of ownership is the purpose of the reading and writing workshops that Nancie Atwell describes in her book, *In the Middle: Writing, Reading, and Learning with Adolescents.*[1] In the reading workshop, interpretation, response, and meaning belong first to the student and are then shared with the community of readers that includes the teacher and peers. Atwell identified what I hoped to create in my classroom, a "dining-room table" where readers could share the excitement, stimulation, and pleasure of talking about good books in the company of friends. The conversations, or book talks, are extended and enriched through two effective strategies: minilessons and lit letters.

Minilessons

The research of Donald Graves[2] and Lucy Calkins[3] reveals how short, focused lessons based on response to student writing can provide opportunities for helping students to "read like writers" and write with conscious awareness of audience, purpose, style, and technique. Nancie Atwell describes how similar introductory lessons can help set the tone and focus of self-selected independent reading.

During the past three years, I have found several minilessons that are basic to the success of the reading workshop. The common factor is the emphasis on metacognitive thinking—a reflective understanding of the personal process of reading.

The way to begin any reading workshop is to read. The students and teacher have regularly scheduled opportunities for self-selected reading at least three times a week. When first starting the workshop, I begin each session with quick discussions on four basic questions:

How do you feel about reading?
What kinds of books do you like best?
What kinds of books have you read?
How often do you read?

Written and oral responses to these questions reveal significant information about the readers in my class. Typically, some students write that they do not enjoy reading because they "don't read well out loud" or they "don't read fast enough." Others report that they have read only the books they have been given in school. Many students read a certain type of book or a particular series of books over and over. Some students respond with enthusiasm about their love of reading.

This initial discussion has to take place. Collectively, we need to discard notions that students are labeled as good or bad readers. We discuss how some books need to be read slowly, while others can be read and understood quickly. Students are not expected to read aloud on command. We acknowledge that students have difficulty getting into a book if their only reading opportunities are ten minutes long. Students are often relieved to hear others admit their difficulties in sticking with some books. We discuss how the first chapter frequently sets the scene for the more exciting parts and builds relationships with the characters. We discuss how long a student should stay with a book before abandoning it and the fact that not finishing a book is a choice in the reading workshop.

Starting with the first day, students realize that there is no one right answer in a discussion during a minilesson. Rather, students are encouraged to express their interpretations and opinions. As the conversations become increasingly focused, students are encouraged and challenged to support their opinions with evidence from the text. The transformation from passive reading to responsive, critical reading has begun.

---

[1]Nancie Atwell, *In the Middle: Writing, Reading, and Learning with Adolescents.* Portsmouth, N.H.: Boynton Cook Publishers, Inc., 1987.
[2]Donald Graves, *Writing: Teachers and Children at Work.* Portsmouth, N.H.: Heinemann Educational Books, Inc., 1989.
[3]Lucy Calkins, *The Art of Teaching Writing.* Portsmouth, N.H.: Heinemann Educational Books, Inc., 1989.

Inevitably, students begin to mention favorite books ranging from childhood classics to contemporary selections. As this activity continues, I have the sense of chairs being pulled up around the dining room table. Someone will suggest a book to someone else, and I pass around books that former students have chosen as particular favorites. Finally, I read a few passages from some of the classroom library books I have especially enjoyed. The teacher's role diminishes as students converse about characters and books, and soon everyone is settled with something he or she has chosen to read.

Subsequent minilessons during the initial days of the reading workshop focus on books the students are enjoying. A few minutes are set aside for quick whole-group and individual conversations about favorite parts, particular characters, and exciting events. I encourage the students to "text-render," or quote favorite lines from their books at the end of the session. How different this activity is from forced oral reading! When the students have selected personally meaningful passages or individual sentences by themselves, they read with confidence and pleasure. What results is a taste for and a celebration of the best of what they are reading. Students savor the sound of words, particular descriptions, humor, drama, style, and voice in writing. Often, they record these lines on notecards and post them on a bulletin board in the classroom. The excitement grows, and the workshop belongs to the students collectively and individually.

By the end of the second week, I focus the minilessons on particular elements of reading. The questions deal with the author's development of a character in a work as shown in the following examples:

Who are the characters in your book?
What makes a character a **main** character?
How would you describe certain characters in your book?
Can you find passages that support your opinion?
What techniques has the author used to bring a character to life?
Have you ever written a similar character description?

Initially, the responses are superficial. Students label characters as good or bad or nice. Events involving characters are easily described, but students commonly do not have the vocabulary to state their opinions fully. The minilessons significantly improve the students' abilities to make interpretive descriptions.

In this case the reading workshop is complemented by the shared text experience. Although most of our reading time is spent with self-selected materials, we read together from a common core book during another time of the day. Often, I read this text aloud to the students, or we read together, using "jump in reading" or instant Reader's Theatre strategies. The common text provides a referent point, the "mental velcro," that ideas, descriptions, and opinions can stick to and be used for comparison.

During a minilesson we might discuss how Leslie Burke and Jesse Aarons, characters in the novel *Bridge to Terabithia*, differ. Descriptions of the characters' behavior in certain situations are matched to words that help the students express their opinions; for example, *sensitive, outgoing, shy, self-confident,* and *unique*. The discussion comes back to the self-selected books. Soon students are relating characters' actions to interpretations of personalities and motivations and eventually to opinions that are well supported with examples from the books. Not surprisingly, students' personal writing about fiction becomes richer with more developed character descriptions that reflect "reading like a writer."

As the weeks progress, new questions emerge for the minilessons:

What type of book are you reading?
What are the characteristics of this type of book?
Have you read others like it?
Have you written stories similar to the one in this book?

The connections to personal writing are invaluable. Discussions in the reading workshop about characteristics of genre frequently provide a prewriting structure for students who might not otherwise have attempted risking an experiment in a different style of writing.

Within a few months distinguishing between the reading and writing workshops becomes difficult.

In many ways achieving this integration is my goal. Teachers who take a process approach to reading and writing know that the two cannot be separated. Soon minilessons in the writing workshop provide the focus for discussions or log entries in reading. After we have written "show, not tell," descriptions, we look for examples of this technique in our self-selected books. As we share different lead sentences in our books, we discuss our various options as writers in beginning our own pieces. When we look for passages that exemplify effective descriptions of setting, the settings described in student-authored books soon become increasingly rich and mood-evoking.

As a teacher I particularly delight in leading minilessons that combine the writing of my students and passages from the works of published authors. When the students "text-render" favorite lines from a piece written by a peer in the same way as they do with the work of published authors, I know the community encompasses all members of what Frank Smith refers to as the club of literacy. (Frank Smith is an author of several books about language and writing, a researcher of language, and the Chair in Language Education at the University of Victoria, British Columbia.)

The minilessons allow me to be creative in providing a focus to discussions in the reading and writing workshop. They provide a structure that is not preset or strictly defined. Instead, the minilessons are shaped in response to what the students find meaningful in their reading. The same question is answered differently by each student and will be answered differently with each new book that students read.

Inherent conversations about books in minilessons lead to a different type of dialogue, the talking on paper that Nancie Atwell describes as "lit letters."

Lit Letters

In the reading workshop, log entries are written for personal reflection and processing and help students express their connections with the text. When Nancie Atwell describes the writing of "lit letters," she introduces a new dimension to the workshop. Writing a letter to another student reflects an awareness of that person's identity as a reader and invites sharing of responses and information. For example, if Kyle knows that Jonathon enjoys mysteries and fantasies, Kyle might write a letter encouraging Jonathon to read the book *The House with a Clock in Its Walls*.

Although the sharing of lit letters between students is a powerful motivator in reading workshop, the effectiveness of this activity touches students in many ways. When students write the letters to their peers or to me, they are sometimes surprised at their discoveries about themselves. Dennis writes in his lit letter:

Dear Mrs. Chancer,

I've been reading *Ghost Host* for about two days now but I'm only on page 45 because I read a few pages and then I stop and think about what I read and what the setting is, the mood . . . I just try and get into the book a lot. It works for me. The book was sort of boring at the start, but when you get into it, it's pretty good. The ghosts in this book aren't weird and like Halloween goblins, but are believable. I'll stick with this book.

Recognizing his patterns as a reader, Dennis feels positive about the process of reading and rereading. He felt differently on the first day of school. He had considered himself to be a poor reader because he did not always read quickly.

In Amy's letter about the book she is reading, *The Dark Is Rising*, she responds to someone else's comment about the book. A student reported finding the novel hard to get into and saw little reason for its popularity. Amy loved the books in this series and was moved to defend the writing of Susan Cooper, the author. In her letter she states:

I feel that the books of *The Dark Is Rising* are the kind of books you have to take your time on. They aren't books you can just skim through and get information. You have to be the kind of reader that enjoys reading slowly and figuring things out. I can't picture anybody getting bored with this book! It is my favorite set of books so far in my journey. There are little clues and hints that all fit together like a puzzle at the end of the chapters or the book. I suggest these books to anyone if they just stick with it! I admit that parts are hard to follow along with, especially in *The Grey King*. It is written in Welsh which is not easy to read. I showed my dad and he couldn't even read it. We read it together at night. It is neat because I get a chance to share this gift with him. I can't believe I used to hate!!! reading! Now I like it very much, and I am a good reader. I can't believe how many books I've read this year!

Amy sees that reading is not something that you do for a teacher or because it is good for you. She has become a reader by choice. Sheridan Blau, director of the South Coast Writing Project at the University of California, Santa Barbara, describes several characteristics of personal literacy, each of which Amy demonstrates. She is willing to take risks, to read and reread, to sustain and focus her attention, and to be patient with ambiguities of the text.

The reading of shared texts or core literature books is a welcome addition to the reading workshop. The critical element of self-selection is in the response to the text, not exclusively the individual choice of text itself. Students must have regularly scheduled opportunities for self-selected reading; however, the shared enjoyment of a common book augments the community established in the reading workshop. Frequently, lit letters about self-selected books include comparisons to core books. Renea writes as follows:

> *A Taste of Blackberries* reminds me a lot of *Bridge to Terabithia*. In *A Taste of Blackberries*, Jamie and the author are good friends, and the author doesn't want to believe Jamie died. Remember in *Terabithia* how Jesse didn't want to believe that Leslie was dead?

Whether the lit letters are written about self-selected or shared books, I am always struck by how students respond at many levels of comprehension. The focused discussions of the minilessons provide the underlying structures for natural critical thinking. The synthesis of thinking and comprehending skills is evident in the lit letters—as in the reflective piece Kristin wrote to me:

> I've just finished reading *Prairie Songs*. It wasn't an "exciting" book that quickly took you here and there, here and there. It was a feeling book that led you through an ordinary life day by day. Pam Conrad had wonderful pacing in her story. She would bring back things she said in the beginning of the book. It had a shocking ending, though, and I could picture Mrs. Berryman's face, touched with terror.
>
> She described Lester so well! She didn't just say, "Lester was shy." She told me in other ways too. For example, he hid in the house when they were taking pictures, and he didn't talk at all to strangers.
>
> It seemed like all the women in this book didn't like living alone. Remember when Mrs. Downing compared herself with the cattle on the plains? For a project on the book, I'd like to paint the prairie.

Giving Reading Back to the Reader

The reading workshop supports process teaching in effective ways; but, more important, the workshop gives reading back to the reader. In the *Primary Language Record: Handbook for Teachers*, Myra Barrs includes a continuum that describes students' levels of reading, ranging from inexperienced to exceptionally experienced.[4] The reader at the top of the scale has the following characteristics:

- Is enthusiastic and reflective, with strong established tastes in fiction or nonfiction
- Enjoys pursuing own reading interests independently
- Can handle a wide range of texts, including some adult materials
- Recognizes that different kinds of texts require different styles of reading
- Is developing critical awareness as a reader

Through the conversations of minilessons and the written dialogues of lit letters, all students can become exceptionally experienced readers. The reading workshop becomes the place to share what belongs to you.

---

[4]Myra Barrs and others, *Primary Language Record: Handbook for Teachers*. Portsmouth, N.H.: Heinemann Educational Books, Inc., 1989, p. 46.

RAGS
for Sharing/ Responding

good details consistent interesting begin...

Using Read-Around Groups to Establish Criteria for Good Writing

By Jenee Gossard

Language Arts Consultant; Former English Department Chair, Culver City High School; and Former Codirector, UCLA Writing Project

A few years ago, I realized that the only way my students were ever going to learn to write better was for them to write more often, revise more willingly, and edit more effectively than they had been doing. In addition, they needed a wider and more "real" audience to write to as well as a clearer sense of the purpose for each piece of writing. In short, their entire writing experience needed to be much more extensive and much more realistic than it had been.

On the other hand, I definitely did not want to read and mark any more papers of the kind my students typically handed in—dashed off the night before, bloated with generalizations and cliches, riddled with irritating errors of expression and conventions. As I began to experiment with solutions to this dilemma, I found myself relying more and more on a modified small-group technique that seemed ideally suited to the special needs of a writing class.

The Read-Around Group Approach

Basically, the read-around group (RAG) approach gives students the opportunity to read and respond to each other's writing at various stages in the process of any assignment. For example, they read each other's first drafts to discover how others solved the problem of finding a subject and getting started. They read second and third drafts to note progress in shaping the paper according to criteria established in discussions of earlier drafts. Later, they help each other edit nearly finished papers for specific requirements of form, language use, and the conventions of writing. At the end of the process, they read and evaluate final drafts, celebrating improvements and editing for surface errors.

With each reading, students develop a more precise idea of what they want to say, to whom, and how. They experience writing as a process, and they discover that good writing rarely springs full-blown from the author's brow but must be carefully shaped over a period of time. They begin to recognize the importance of their audience as they become accustomed to writing for real readers—their classmates—instead of just for the teacher, a most unreal creature, in their eyes. From the student's point of view, perhaps the most helpful aspect of using the RAG method is that, for the first time, each student has a clear notion of what other students do to solve writing problems. Papers written by their peers provide much more useful models than do the professionally written examples in textbooks.

For the teacher, one of the most important advantages of using RAGs is that the students read, discuss, and revise their papers three or four times before ever handing them in, which means not only that the submitted papers are at a fairly advanced stage of development but also that they are relatively free from gross errors in language and mechanics. As a result, the teacher can comment more directly on issues of composition—organization, development, tone, point of view, and effective use of language—rather than devoting so much time to matters of spelling, grammar, punctuation, and other conventions.

The Steps in the RAG Process

As I began to use RAGs regularly, I devised several procedures to streamline the process and make it more effective. I learned that small groups work best when they have a very specific task to perform and not quite as much time to complete it as they would like. Several of the procedures are so useful to me that I will describe them for you in some detail.

The first day. On the first day, after a brief prewriting activity (clustering or brainstorming—anything open-ended), students write for ten minutes on a topic, using code numbers instead of their names to identify their papers. Then they form groups of four. At my signal, each group leader passes his or her group's papers to the next group, where they are distributed and read quickly—30 seconds for each paper. At the end of each 30-second interval, I give the signal to pass the papers to the next reader in the group. When the set of four papers has been read, each group chooses the paper it liked the best in that set. The group's recorder notes the code number of the chosen paper, while the leader holds up the set of papers to indicate that the group has finished making its choice. When all groups have made a choice (generally, this takes less than a minute), I give the signal for the leaders to pass the papers on to the next group. We repeat this process until all groups have read every set except their own.

When all the sets of papers have been read, I print the code numbers chosen by each group on the chalkboard. Students enjoy seeing whether any group chose their papers as best in the set of four papers theirs traveled with. Inevitably, some code numbers appear more than once. I call for any papers chosen several times and read them aloud, asking the students to identify the qualities of the best papers they read. As they enumerate the specific "best" qualities they noticed in reading around, I write them on the chalkboard. Their list usually includes such items as good details and description, interesting beginning, consistent tone, good beginning, and so forth. The list on the chalkboard becomes a simple rubric which the students are to follow in revising their ten-minute paper for the next day. In their new drafts, I ask them to include from the rubric two or three specific items related to organization and development. The new versions, stapled on top of the originals, must be at least one full page, but no longer than one and one-half pages.

The second day. On the second day I use the same RAG procedure, but this time I ask my students to use the criteria from the rubric in choosing the best paper in each set. Among the second day's "best" papers will be several that had not been chosen in the first day's RAG. Thus, students who worked hard to improve their original versions are rewarded for their efforts, while some of the first day's "stars," who rested on their laurels by simply recopying their popular originals, find themselves back in the middle of the pack.

After this second RAG I generally spend a few class sessions discussing sample copies of some of

From the student's point of view, perhaps the most helpful aspect of using the RAG method is that, for the first time, each student has a clear notion of what other students do to solve writing problems.

JENEE GOSSARD

the papers the class chose most often in order to refine the rubric on which their third versions will be based.

The third day. On the day the third version is due, I use a modified RAG procedure in which I ask the students to focus on very specific elements of the rubric. In this first editing phase, students pass their papers within their own group only, checking and marking each other's papers for only one element at each reading. For example, in the first turn, readers may be asked to make a note in the margin next to the opening and closing lines if these lines contain the required content or form. In the second and third turns, I may ask readers to underline concrete details, specific examples, or lines of dialogue—whatever the rubric specifically requires in terms of organization and development.

The second phase of this editing RAG requires the students to pass the papers around their groups again to identify problems in language use. This time, on the first turn, readers are to circle all forms of *to be*. On the second turn they circle all *dead words* (e.g., *thing, very, so, really, a lot,* and other empty or overused words), while on the third turn readers bracket all repeated sentence openers (e.g., "There is," "And then," "The boy . . ."). Later in the semester, I may ask them to star all repeated words and bracket short, choppy sentences for sentence-combining work. After this RAG session, their final draft is due. It should incorporate appropriate changes suggested by the marks of the student editors.

The fourth day. When the students submit the fourth version of their papers, I repeat the RAG procedure from the first day, allowing a little more time for the reading of each paper (up to one minute), as these final versions tend to be more

concentrated than earlier ones. After posting the chosen numbers, I have the students proofread each other's papers for spelling and sentence errors before handing them in. Then I read aloud the best of the best, compliment the writers on a job well done, and take the whole set home to read for the first time. And a pleasant reading it is, too, compared to what it might have been had I taken home their first or second drafts. Because all earlier versions are handed in along with the newest ones, I can easily see the changes that have been made from the original writing. Thus, I can praise a student's efforts to revise, even if the overall quality of the latest version is only average in comparison with others in the class.

For longer papers (more than two pages), or more complex assignments, I use variations of the RAG method in which students read their papers aloud to their group, followed by a discussion of each paper's strengths and weaknesses. For essays of argument, I use RAGs to teach thesis paragraphs, counterarguments, supporting arguments, and concluding paragraphs, spending one RAG session on each element separately. In remedial classes I use the editing-style RAG procedure, requiring readers to find and note paragraph indentions, capitals and end punctuation, dead words, contractions, fragments, run-ons, and other specific items related to the skills we have been working on. The read-around group technique can be easily modified to suit almost any situation arising in a composition class.

Suggestions for RAG Sessions

Here are some general considerations for setting up a successful RAG session:

1. Students should use code numbers instead of names on their papers to reduce anxiety by preserving anonymity.
2. Groups should be as nearly equal in size as possible. If your class number is not divisible by four or five, make sure that the odd-sized group(s) is (are) smaller than the others rather than larger. Groups of four or five students are best for most tasks; fewer than four provide too little interaction; more than five may have difficulty sticking to the task.
3. Appoint a leader and a recorder in each group; define their duties clearly.
4. Give the groups a specific task to perform in a strictly limited amount of time. For example, you might ask them to read quickly and select the best paper in the set or circle all forms of *to be*. As an alternative to choosing the "best" paper in each round, a different criterion could be used for each new set. For example, one round might be used to choose the paper with the best opening; the next, to choose the paper with the most information, an unusual or unexpected element, the most vivid visual images, the strongest arguments, the best ending.
5. Keep close track of time. I use a stopwatch so that students learn to pace themselves against a fixed time period. Do not let students pass papers on until you give the signal; otherwise the reading process will quickly become chaotic.
6. Set up a simple system for reading and passing papers. My students follow this system:
   a. Group leaders collect papers from their own group members and, at my signal, pass the set to the next group in a counter-clockwise direction around the room.
   b. Students read each paper in the prescribed time, passing it to the person on their *right* in their group. Students pass papers only when I give the signal to pass—not before and not after.
   c. When the set has been read (I keep a tally as I time the reading so that I know when each set is finished), I tell the groups to choose the best paper, reminding them of the specific criteria for that day.
   d. Recorders write the number of the chosen paper on a self-sticking note. Leaders then collect the papers and hold them up to signal that their group is finished.
   e. When all the leaders indicate readiness to continue, I say, "Change groups," and the leaders pass the set on to the next group.
7. Do not ask students to choose the best paper from among the papers in their own group. This approach is too threatening, at least at first.
8. Keep the papers short for whole-group read-around sessions. Papers longer than two pages can be handled better by being read aloud in a small group and followed by discussion.

Advantages of Using Read-Around Groups

There are many advantages to using read-around groups. For the student, the following advantages are most important:

1. Writing for, and getting response from, a "real" audience
2. Gaining useful ideas, approaches, and perspectives from reading and hearing other students' writing
3. Revising their papers several times before having them graded
4. Knowing where they stand in relation to other students
5. Gaining a clearer understanding of writing as a process
6. Sharpening editing skills

For the teacher, these advantages stand out:

1. Students write more often, but the teacher does not read more papers.
2. Gross errors decline significantly with each revision following a RAG session and discussion.
3. Papers are better written and more interesting to read.
4. Students learn to evaluate their own and others' work.
5. Students have fewer complaints about grades.
6. Students' handwriting improves. This last phenomenon occurs when students with good ideas but poor handwriting realize that their papers are being passed over in the choosing process because they are too hard to read.

Of all the techniques I have used over the years, the RAG has been the most useful and the most versatile. Though it requires careful planning and strict monitoring, the extra effort pays off in better writing and improved attitudes. Students enjoy it, too, for it gives them a chance to share. Most important, it focuses attention on the act of composing itself, demystifying the process and thereby giving students more confidence in their abilities to write better at every new step.

Practical Ideas for Read-Around Groups

Using RAGs to Teach Revising and Editing at the Elementary Level

By Diane Dawson

Coordinator of Programs and Curriculum,
Beverly Hills Unified School District;
and Teacher/Consultant, UCLA Writing Project

It has been my impression that the revising and editing stages of the writing process are rarely emphasized at the elementary school level. As a fifth-grade teacher in a self-contained classroom, I have found the read-around group (RAG) to be a powerful tool for teaching these skills. In fact, of all the techniques I have used to encourage my students to revise and edit, none has been as successful as this procedure. It provides students with a "real audience" of their peers, and it creates for them the personal motivation to rethink and rework a piece of writing. For the first time, I feel that my elementary students see writing as a valuable process.

I use the first few exposures to RAGs as a way to get students thinking about what constitutes effective writing. After selecting the "best" papers, we talk about what specific elements make certain papers stand out from the rest. The list we generate from this discussion and print on the chalkboard becomes a rubric we use for revising our papers. Students can then be trained to look for and mark particular items in papers as they read around in groups. For example, I teach them to mark a plus (+) in the margin to indicate an excellent topic sentence, to draw two lines under a strong, vivid verb, and to put parentheses around effective sensory descriptions. Other notations can be used to call attention to a particular aspect of the writing assignment while the papers are being read, such as the use of transition words in a narrative or the clarity of instructions in a how-to paper.

During later stages of the writing process, as revising moves into editing, I have found RAGs particularly effective when I have been focusing on specific skills, such as using quotation marks and correct end punctuation, eliminating forms of *to be* in favor of strong, vivid verbs, identifying basic sentence patterns (declarative, interrogative, and so forth), and checking spelling after sentence dictation.

RAGs serve as outstanding support for teaching writing. Students working in groups not only learn the stages of the process but also analyze what they have written and come up with ways to make it better. The total success of this approach can be measured by the fact that my students do not believe that the writing task is complete unless they have had at least one read-around experience to help them revise their papers.

Using Read-Around Groups for Holistic Scoring

By Trudy J. Burrus

Former English Teacher, El Toro High School,
Coordinator Healthy Kids,
Saddleback Valley Unified School District;
and Teacher/Consultant, UCI Writing Project

Having first learned about read-around groups (RAGs) in their second or third generation, I did not know the finer details of RAGs; so I took the essence of the approach, as I knew it, and improvised. What I ended up with was a RAG that incorporated holistic scoring, too. Thus, in one final-stage RAG, I get the top papers in the class and scores for all papers.

I have been training my students to score compositions holistically for several years, and I recognize the critical need for a clear, strong rubric. At the same time that it must reflect the individual assignment, I prefer a rubric that is standard in form and mechanics. As a result, I use a basic six-point rubric as the foundation for the individualized versions. (For more information on holistic scoring, see the evaluation section later in this book.) The students become quite skilled at focusing on the specifics of an assignment, so we can agree on a final rubric quite rapidly. Once it is in final form, the rubric gets three to four minutes of silent attention from everyone. If the students request additional time to internalize the rubric, they are given it without question.

Ideally, students are placed in groups of four or five. I often sit in to round out the number, and my participation in the process lends a measure of formality that seems to encourage an even more conscientious attitude from my students. A group leader and clerk distribute papers and materials and record scores.

The leaders gather the papers from the members of their groups. (Students do not score their own papers.) Attached to the back of each set of papers are seven or eight score sheets, one for each group in the room. Each student writer has entered an identification number at the top of each score sheet and has written the letters *A* through *E* on the sheet (if there are five in the group) for the readers' scores. Each leader passes the group's papers clockwise to the next group, and they are redistributed there. Each member of each group has an assigned letter (again, usually *A* through *E*, depending on the number in the group), and the clerk records the letters on an index card for future reference. The group leader is always *A*; the person on the leader's left is always *B*. Then the holistic read-around begins.

I allow one minute for the reading of each paper. This provides ample time for the students to read the papers and to determine holistic scores. Each student turns the paper over, records in pen a holistic score on the top score sheet beside his or her letter, and holds the paper until given the signal to pass the paper to the person on the left. After all papers have been read by the group, the leader records the best paper of the stack and collects the papers. Then the clerk collects the completed score sheets and clips them together. (Because the scores given by any one group are not seen by the next group, it is easy for me to tell if one group is grading consistently high or low and to remedy the situation rapidly. Using the clerk's record of readers' letters assigned before the RAG began, I can also tell if any one student is grading inconsistently.) The scored stack of papers is passed to the next group, and the process is repeated until the stack is returned to the originating group.

The final step is for the clerks to hand the clipped score sheets to the leader of the appropriate group, who then distributes them to the writers. Each student can immediately figure his or her average score. The students staple their score sheets to the back of their papers before they turn them in. I also call for the best paper from each stack, and we discuss those papers, focusing on their outstanding aspects.

With a well-trained class and an efficient handling of the papers, a class of 35 can complete the entire RAG process in a 50-minute period. While my students are scoring, they are internalizing criteria for evaluating the papers of others; they can apply the criteria to their own first and final drafts of subsequent papers. At the same time, I am lightening my own paper load without reducing the number of writing assignments. I can then respond to selected papers or particular assignments in more depth and can provide the kind of content-based feedback that will genuinely help students improve their writing.

Rewriting/ Editing

Competence for Performance in Revision

By Sheridan Blau
Vice-Chair, Department of English;
and Director, South Coast Writing Project,
University of California, Santa Barbara

Once we begin to think seriously about revision, we are likely to feel some confusion about what acts of mind or writing behavior ought to be called by that name. All composition theorists warn us against making the easy mistake of thinking of revision as merely the last stage in a linear three-stage composing process. That is because, in composing, revision can and does take place at any time. Studies of the thinking processes of writers show that nearly every writer is constantly reviewing, evaluating, and changing words and ideas at every moment in the composing process—as much perhaps while the writer is planning what he or she might want to say as when the person has already begun to write sentences on paper.

Our conception of revision will be only momentarily clarified if we forget about when it takes place in the linear organization of the composing process and define it more operationally as the thinking and behavior that writers engage in whenever they rework any piece of a text that they have already drafted or partially drafted. As every writing teacher knows, however, not all redrafting entails revision. For many students, rewriting means copying a draft over neatly in ink. And if nothing counts as revision except what gets written and rewritten on paper, what will we call the mental activities of writers who in their minds perform the same operations of selecting, altering, and deleting that less experienced writers might have to carry out in more obvious stages on paper?[1]

---

[1] Donald H. Graves and his colleagues at the University of New Hampshire noticed precisely such a progression as a mark of development in the young writers they studied. That is to say, they observed children at one stage making language choices and alterations on paper which, at a later stage in their development, they would make mentally.

Toward a Unified Theory of Revision

In spite of all these complications in our understanding of revision—or perhaps because of them—there has begun to emerge a fairly clear picture of what revision—in any and all of its manifestations—entails as a thinking process or set of intellectual skills. These are skills that can be taught and learned or at least encouraged and nourished in the context of an instructional program in composition.

We can take an important step toward a unified theory of revision by recognizing that all of the various activities we might want to call revision can probably be said to belong to one of the two classes of revision that Donald Murray has designated "internal" and "external."[2] Internal revision refers to the process through which writers, in the production, evaluation, and amendment of their own emerging texts, gradually discover for themselves what it is that they mean to say. External revision, in contrast, entails the amending of an already written *text for the sake of a reader,* so that the reader will be able to understand it as unambiguously and efficiently as possible.

Virtually every theory of the composing process implicitly or explicitly postulates internal and external revision. Sondra Perl speaks of them under the headings of "retrospective" and "projective" structuring.[3] She defines the first as the process through which writers, in composing, use their language not to communicate something they already know but to come to know for themselves something they do not yet know except as a vague feeling or "felt sense." She points out, furthermore, that when we discover and give articulate shape to our inchoate felt sense of a meaning, we necessarily restructure our sense of what the meaning is that we are trying to articulate. Retrospective structuring, then, refers to the way in which during composition we oscillate between expression and revision—attempting to express what we do not yet know and, through that attempt, revising our sense of what it is we are trying to come to know.

Projective structuring, on the other hand, is directed not to the discovery and construction of our emerging meaning for ourselves but to the communication of a meaning we already know to our readers. It refers to the effort writers make to accommodate the expression of their ideas to the needs of their auditors or to the requirements of a situation. It would include revising in order to use more acceptable diction, to achieve mechanical correctness, or to meet the requirements of a specialized form (a laboratory report, research paper, and so forth).

All competent writers engage in some projective structuring. All want to meet the needs of their readers. However, studies of the differences between the composing processes of competent and incompetent writers consistently reveal that competent writers, in most of their composing, are principally engaged in retrospective structuring, turning more to projective structuring only after they have discovered the substance of their ideas in a fairly complete form. Incompetent writers, on the other hand, seem to give most of their attention to form rather than content from the moment they begin writing. Typically, poor writers pause so frequently to amend their language or correct real or imagined mechanical errors that they are unable to develop or follow any continuous line of thought long enough to see what it is. Their thinking, therefore, appears to be discontinuous and impoverished.

The Dimensions of Competence in Revision

If we reflect on the kind of thinking that is entailed in revising, in any of its modes or stages—that is, in the early stage of revising to discover one's ideas, in the later stage of amending a text to suit the needs of one's readers, or even in the stage of copy editing and proofreading—we will see that two apparently opposite acts of mind are required. These are *commitment* and *detachment.*

In identifying the writer's commitment as a dimension of his or her competence to engage in revision, I am acknowledging the fact that writing—insofar as it calls for revision—is characteristically a difficult, frustrating, and time-consuming process. Inexperienced writers frequently experience the difficulties of the task as evidence of their

[2]Donald M. Murray, "Internal Revision: A Process of Discovery," in *Learning by Teaching: Selected Articles on Writing and Teaching.* Upper Montclair, N.J.: Boynton Cook Publishers, Inc., 1982.
[3]Sondra Perl, "Understanding Composing," *College Composition and Communication,* Vol. 31 (December, 1980), 363–369.

No inducement to revision is likely to carry us as far through the difficulties of the process as the prospect of having our work published.

SHERIDAN BLAU

own incompetence as writers. Experienced writers know that frustration and feelings of incompetence are among the most difficult challenges any writing task is likely to pose for any writer.

Only if we attribute enough value to what we have to say are we likely to make the effort required to get our ideas straight, even for ourselves. The less commonplace our ideas and the more they derive from our own independent thinking, the more difficult it is likely to be for us to discover them for ourselves or to articulate them precisely for our readers. When the task of articulation feels impossible or too arduous to endure (as it often will in composing any piece worth writing), then we must depend in spite of such feelings on our faith that the job we have taken on for ourselves can be completed and that we are capable of completing it. Thus, of the two qualities of mind that account for a writer's competence in revision, the first of them, commitment, requires two underlying acts of the will—one finding value in the completion of the writing task and the other, consisting of faith (despite feelings to the contrary) in one's capacity to meet the challenge of the task.

The second enabling or prerequisite skill for competence in revision is the intellectual skill of *detachment*. This entails distancing ourselves from our own writing in order to take the perspective of a reader. Such a perspective is especially necessary as writers move from retrospective structuring to projective—from getting their ideas straight for themselves to getting them straight for a reader, or in moving from writer-based to reader-based revising. To the degree that writers appear able to make such a shift in perspective, we may say that they are exhibiting *empathy*. As a competence underlying detachment, *empathy* refers to a writer's

or speaker's ability to see things from someone else's point of view. The more writers want to have an impact on their readers, the more they need to understand how readers are likely to respond to their discourse.

Empathy does not quite describe the underlying skill that enables writers to achieve the kind of distance or detachment that is necessary for internal revision—the revision through which writers gradually discover and take possession of their own emerging ideas. Here it is not necessary to project oneself imaginatively into the mind of some other reader but to assume the detached perspective of oneself as reader rather than writer of the text being produced. Competent writing and revising requires writers, at intervals, to step back from the production of their texts with sufficient distance to judge whether or not the words appearing on the page match their sense of the intended meaning. When writers as readers find a mismatch, they also find opportunities to work further to discover their intended meaning or, just as likely, to revise their intention.

Competence in revision, as I have defined it, may therefore be said to have two principal dimensions: an affective dimension, which I have called *commitment;* and a cognitive dimension, which I have called *detachment*. The first is a function of writers' attitudes toward themselves and their tasks; the second, of their cognitive abilities to perform the tasks. For any task of composing, writers will be committed to the degree that they value the assignment they are engaged in and retain faith or confidence in their capacity to complete it. Their capacity for the competent completion of the task will, in turn, be a function of their having learned to detach themselves sufficiently from their text to engage in the evaluative and empathic procedures that revising entails as they attempt to discover their ideas for themselves and adjust their discourse to the needs of their readers. Graphically, we may represent the dimensions of competence in revision as shown in Figure 1.

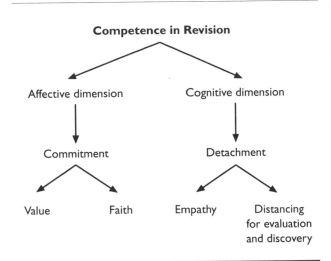

Fig. 1. Dimensions of Competence in Revision

Strategies to Develop Competence in Revision

A variety of instructional strategies are available for the teacher who is intent on helping students acquire the disciplines of commitment and detachment that underlie competence in revision. Many of them are described elsewhere in this book. They include the use of writing-response groups of the sort proposed by Peter Elbow; the use of "read-around groups," as described by Jenee Gossard; and considerable effort at following Mary K. Healy's advice about finding genuine situations that call for real communicative writing for students instead of "dummy runs." Taken together, activities like these help students discover the value of writing as a genuine communicative act directed toward a real audience whose differing perspectives must be taken into account.

Building Communities of Writers. Students in writing-response groups, in particular, learn to become more empathic readers, not simply from getting the responses of others to their own work, but from reading the work of peers and thereby

seeing through their own experience what readers need and can expect from writers like themselves. Writing-response groups can also be important for what they contribute to turning the writing class into a community of writers. In such a community much of the conversation and instruction are focused on the difficulties and challenges that the student writers encounter while they are engaged in the composing process. Through such discussions students usually find themselves better able to work out the self-management strategies they need to sustain the effort that revision often requires.

Ideally, teachers will become active members of their classroom communities of writers by writing along with their students and sharing their experiences of anxiety, frustration, and satisfaction in the composing process. Students need to see their teachers write in order to see that the most accomplished writers are not those who write most easily. They need to see how much it is the case that the competence of most writers consists less of facility than of staying power—a power that derives from their recognition of the value of the enterprise they are engaged in and from their faith in their capacity to continue making progress in it, even after they begin to feel defeated by it.

Inviting Drafting and Redrafting. If we want our students truly to revise, we need to give them opportunities to get a number of writing projects started so that they may choose to revise only those that hold the most interest or promise for them. Most of us produce many starts—a few notes, some pages of an early draft—on projects that are simply not worth revising or else need to be put aside for the months or years it might take before we ripen to the challenge they pose. Teachers who want to make their classes into authentic environments for writing and revising will, therefore, deliberately cultivate the production of a great many starts on pieces in progress—quick rough drafts that may or may not be taken any further. Only when students have had the opportunity to produce three or four such pieces in rough first-draft form (and perhaps received some responses on them from peer readers) should they be required to commit themselves to the further revision of their most promising pieces in progress. Real *reseeing* (revision), rather than obedient tinkering with the surface features of the text, will occur when writers have a sense of the value of their thoughts and have a need to enhance, clarify, recast, or elaborate on their original messages.

A related way to nurture revision as an integral part of the composing process for our students is to provide them with lots of experiences in experimental and exploratory writing in journals or notebooks. These can serve as repositories for ideas, lists, clusters, and starts on drafts that writers may return to selectively to find material worth developing into completed pieces of writing. Students will benefit particularly from being encouraged to do a good deal of free-writing (nonstop recording of a writer's continuous thoughts on a subject) in such notebooks. The virtue of free-writing in teaching revision is that it helps writers discover the value of their "naked" thoughts—thoughts that can sometimes be discovered most fully when the writers attend only to them, putting aside momentarily the distractions of a concern for correctness or form or the needs of a reader. Even for very young writers, one of the first steps toward learning to revise seems to come with the recognition that in the initial stages of one's writing, it is an acceptable and proper procedure to produce messy, incorrect, and hastily composed work that is intended as material for revision.

Authorship as a Motive for Revision

Among the most effective strategies teachers can use to help students discover the value of their own ideas (and hence the value of clarifying and communicating them) is that of taking those ideas seriously—examining them not with the eye of a corrector but with the respect of one who would learn from them. A teacher who can give the time and concentrated effort required to respond to student writing as a partner in an intellectual dialogue will find that several benefits flow from it. First, the teacher's actions testify to the value of a student's ideas. Second, the teacher will be modeling a mode of response that students would do well to imitate in responding to each other's work as well as to literature and other assigned readings.

Finally, the dialogue between student-writer and teacher-respondent (which can be continued with an answering response from the student and another from the teacher) offers both participants an opportunity for additional learning through their continuing exchange and clarification of ideas—an exchange that continues to take place in writing.

School writing assignments often subvert the normal relationship that emerges between the writer and reader by asking students to write on subjects about which they are less well-informed than their teachers are. In such a transaction the writer is relieved of most of the responsibility that a real author bears for accommodating what he or she has to say to the understanding of his or her readers. Teachers who would have their students develop a capacity for detachment will therefore encourage them to write on topics about which they (the students) have more authoritative knowledge than their readers.

Metaprocessing as a Strategy for Revision

Aside from having their students write about what they know with some authority (i.e., as "authors"), teachers can help students develop their ability for detachment or perspective-taking by employing a number of instructional methods that may be loosely characterized as *metaprocessing* activities. These are activities that call on students to treat their own texts and writing processes as objects of inquiry. Metaprocessing describes most of the talk that takes place in writing-response groups and in teacher-student conferences. Such talk can sometimes become more focused and productive if students are asked to keep writing-process logs in which they record and reflect on their composing processes, including their responses to each of their own completed drafts for each writing task they undertake.

Most of the revising and editing tricks that experienced teachers are fond of showing to their students also entail metaprocessing. One such trick is to have students outline drafts of their essays after they finish them. From such an outline students can gain new perspectives on the structure of their essays—on the relative emphasis they have given to main and subordinate points and on the progression of their arguments.

In another metaprocessing activity students write brief summary statements of each of their completed drafts (or of each paragraph) in the form of what Linda Flower calls a *WIRMI* statement: "What I Really Mean Is . . ."[4] Having written WIRMIs, students may be able to stand far enough back from their essays to ask productively if they actually said in the essays what they meant to say. An exceptionally promising activity of this sort is to ask students to write revised drafts of their essays without looking back at their first drafts and then to have students write a comparison of the two versions. Since the two versions will tend to be very different (especially for the poorest writers), the task of comparing them forces the writers to pay close attention to the written content of their two essays, separate from whatever intentions may have informed either or both of them.[5] This distancing exercise provides practice in assuming the detached perspective that one needs to revise effectively.

A much simpler distancing assignment, yet one that almost always yields surprising benefits for unskilled writers, is to have students read drafts of their essays aloud before they revise or submit them. This can be done in the presence of another person, in the context of a writing group, or even in private. When writers read their texts out loud—to themselves or to other persons—they become more apt to hear the text themselves. Unskilled student writers rarely reread their texts out loud as they compose. Skilled writers almost always do.

Publishing as a Strategy to Encourage Revision

Publishing is the last instructional strategy I want to mention here for its role in encouraging revision. However much we may want through our writing to gain possession of our thoughts or to communicate with our readers, no inducement to revision is likely to carry us as far through the

---

[4]Linda Flower, *Problem-Solving Strategies for Writing.* New York: Harcourt Brace Jovanovich, Inc., 1981.
[5]Will Garrett-Petts of the University of British Columbia has experimented with the technique of withholding first drafts while students create a second version.

> *Pruning writing is the same as pruning apple trees: The point is not so much to get rid of the dead branches (which are easy enough to spot) as it is to shape the tree to produce the best possible fruit.*
>
> **BRUCE O. BOSTON**

difficulties of the process as the prospect of having our work published. Many forms of publishing are possible within the context of a classroom, particularly if we think of publication in its root sense of "making public." These forms can range from having students read their work out loud to the entire class, to posting work on bulletin boards or in school display cases, to producing dittoed, mimeographed, or photocopied anthologies of student work from a single class. Many teachers have found that in working on long-term projects, students will be encouraged to revise carefully when they know that they will individually make a hard-cover binding for their completed work so that it might be kept in the classroom or library for reference by future students. The promise of publication is a promise of fame, however limited. If that makes it appealing to a student's vanity, it is surely a tolerable vanity and one that can do a writer much good.

The strategies I have identified here are all aimed at fostering in students the commitment necessary to communicate something of value and the detachment required to discover, articulate, and reformulate an intended meaning for an intended audience. Taken together, they imply respect on the part of the teacher for the process of composing and an appreciation of the importance of a humanly rich communicative context, both for the acquisition of competence in composition and for its realization in performance.

Practical Ideas for Revising

Yes, There Is a Better Way: Revising on the Word Processor

By Russell Frank

Principal, Altimira Middle School,
Sonoma Valley Unified School District;
and Teacher/Consultant, UCI Writing Project

I remember the drudgery of learning how to write as a child—of painfully scratching out letter after letter with sore, tender red fingers. Meanwhile, my mind raced ahead of my hand, and, as a result, only I could interpret the scrawl left on the page. There had to be a better way.

My typing ability quickened my composing process, but revising and editing remained just as tedious. I remember the times just before a paper was due—when it was no longer worth the pain of erasing and retyping a page to clarify a vague point or argument buried in the text. There had to be a better way.

In the summer of 1982, I experienced how word processing could improve my composing and revising skills. My writing kept closer pace with my thoughts, and I no longer needed to type draft after draft, shaping my ideas on a typewriter. This technology can also improve many students' writing by making composing and revising physically less demanding.

A word processor is any type of system for typing text material into a computer and editing, changing, or correcting the text easily and efficiently. Essentially, a word processor is a computer loaded with a word processing program, written on a storage device—usually a floppy disk. With a word processor, the author discovers or creates content and shapes and edits this content while the computer holds the text in memory. The author can revise and edit his or her piece by pushing the appropriate keys. When the piece is finished, the author presses other keys to obtain a paper copy that is clean from cross-outs, inserts, carets, smudges, and deletion marks. The process is simple, legible, and immediate and leads to easier and faster writing and revision.

Word processing is a potentially powerful tool in the quest to improve student writing. In order to explain how word processing can be used to help students, I would like first to review the characteristics of competent and incompetent student writers. Research shows that competent writers generally write longer essays, spend more time on writing tasks, and pause more often to reflect on their writing. Competent writers also revise their texts while rereading them and are far more concerned with planning, more aware of audience, and more considerate of purpose and stylistic concerns of an assignment than incompetent writers are. Competent writers also view revision as restructuring of content and ideas. These characteristics reflect the high degree of commitment competent writers feel for their writing.

Incompetent writers generally are concerned too soon during their writing with form and mechanics and, therefore, spend less time developing the content of their piece. They try to "follow the rules" of writing in an attempt to make their first draft their final draft. Incompetent writers view revision as a patchwork—of getting what was written worded correctly and of correcting mechanics and spelling. These writers, according to Sheridan Blau, are deficient in two dimensions of writing and revising: an affective dimension that includes commitment and a cognitive dimension that includes detachment. Incompetent writers generally have a low sense of commitment to their writing because (1) they do not value the piece's importance; or (2) they do not believe in their ability to complete the writing task. They also usually lack detachment from their writing—an ability to step back from their piece and view the content from a reader's point of view.

The word processor can help students to improve their writing in both the affective and cognitive dimensions of writing and revision by making the writing act easier, faster, and more efficient. Word processing enhances the affective dimension by increasing the student's faith in his or her ability to complete the writing task. Additions, deletions, substitutions, and the reordering of words, phrases, sentences, and paragraphs can be executed immediately without cluttering the page or necessitating the recopying of an entire text. This power for immediate revision is the word processor's greatest power, because students are freed from early concerns regarding correctness and form. Students learn that they can make editing corrections as well as reshape entire paragraphs late in the process with the same ease that they made earlier modifications. With the teacher's nurturing and coaching, writing becomes a mode of discovery of thought and meaning—of creating and developing content—what Sondra Perl labels retrospective structuring.[1] By understanding the characteristics of competent writers, teachers can encourage and foster those characteristics in incompetent writers, using word processing as a budge toward competence. I have seen a child move from total rejection of writing to intense interest and involvement within a few weeks of being introduced to the word processor. Clearly, that child's ability, desire, and commitment to complete a writing task increased with the mechanical advantages of the computer.

To develop the cognitive dimension of writing and revising, the word processor can also be used in conjunction with peer response groups, which encourage detachment from a piece of writing in order to see an audience's point of view. During small-group interaction students read their work to each other to obtain feedback on its effectiveness. My own observation of writing response groups without accessibility to a word processor indicated that, even after successful group interaction, many students failed to incorporate their classmates' suggestions in their second drafts, probably because it was too much bother to write the extra text needed to clarify a point. With electronic editing such revisions become simple and quick. Instead of taking home an essay to revise overnight, students can obtain some feedback from their groups, incorporate the suggestions in the essay, and often obtain a paper copy within the same class period. By allowing students to incorporate peer feedback immediately, the word processor assists the writer in seeing his or her work from the perspective of a reader. As this concept of audience broadens, the student may gain enough critical distance (or detachment) to begin to anticipate how the reader will respond or, better yet, to plan his or her writing to manipulate the reader's response.

The teacher plays a major role in helping students achieve enough detachment to revise what they have written. By writing comments in the electronic text that require clarification or explanation, teachers can encourage students to see their writing as a reader might interpret it.

For word processing to have a significant impact on the quality of student writing, teachers as well as students must internalize what is meant by revision—that it is not just copying over or correcting mechanical errors but reseeing and reshaping an intended message for an audience. A teacher's own sense of what revision is will probably have the greatest influence on students' attitudes and how students use word processing. For most

AUTHOR'S NOTE: In my own personal experience, I am aware of how much more I utilize retrospective structuring when I write with my computer. In this article, for example, each paragraph and many sentences have been restructured during my initial composing during my search for the "right" meaning. In contrast, I am less willing to experiment with ideas and text when I am composing with pen and paper.

[1]Sondra Perl, "Understanding Composing," *College Composition and Communication*, Vol. 31 (December, 1980), 369.

> *For word processing to have a significant impact on the quality of student writing, teachers as well as students must internalize what is meant by revision—that it is not just copying over or correcting mechanical errors but reseeing and reshaping an intended message for an audience.*
>
> **RUSSELL FRANK**

students a human being is still a more effective motivator than a machine is. But the word processor can contribute greatly to the writing process if it is used wisely.

Yes, there is a better way!

EDITOR'S NOTE: For additional information on the use of computers in writing, see pages *8, 9,* and *59–62* in *Handbook for Planning an Effective Writing Program,* which was published by the California Department of Education in 1983.

Revising with Sentence Combining

By Jerry Judd

English Teacher, Irvine High School,
Irvine Unified School District;
and Teacher/Consultant, UCI Writing Project

Writing is one of the few communication processes that allows the communicator the luxury of revision. This can involve revision of thought, of structure, of style, of writing to an audience, and generally of writing to produce a certain effect on the reader. When one is transforming initial thoughts to print, ideas do not generally flow in an orderly, linear, well-planned manner. In fact, many writers need to generate ideas on paper in the form of fragments, jottings, and disconnected sentences before they can make composing decisions that are compatible with their purpose and their audience.

Sentence combining can be an invaluable tool in the evolution of a piece of writing from prewriting to rough draft to finished product. Teaching sentence combining is not, in itself, teaching writing; rather, it is a means of increasing a writer's options in terms of fluency, form, and correctness, enabling the writer to create his or her own style.

I have found the practice of sentence combining in my classroom to be beneficial for a variety of reasons. If sentence combining is introduced early in a writing class and practiced regularly, it can have a positive influence on the attitudes of writers, especially beginning writers. Generally, there is a built-in tension and pressure in the act of composing a piece of written text. This anxiety is often self-imposed by the writer who is struggling to "get it right" the first time around. Mina Shaughnessy points out in *Errors and Expectations* that:

> The practice of consciously transforming sentences from simple to complex structures . . . helps the student cope with complexity in much the same way as finger exercises in piano or bar exercises in ballet enable performers to work out specific kinds of coordination that must be virtually habitual before the performer is free to interpret or even execute a total composition.[1]

This practice, or prewriting, not only raises the ability of student writers to manipulate language, but it also raises the level of confidence that student writers have in their ability to manipulate language. This releases them to generate more fluent first drafts that can be reworked and polished in the later stages of composing.

Sentence combining can enhance form and correctness as well as fluency. Sentence patterns, pronoun usage, and punctuation can all be introduced and mastered through practice and problem solving. I usually begin with the first part of Charles Cooper's "An Outline for Writing Sentence-Combining Problems."[2] I write sample sentences, such as the ones below, and challenge students to combine them in as many ways as they can.

> The people on the boat asked us to come aboard.
> The boat was *alongside.*
> We sailed in the boat.
> The boat was the one *with the blue sail.*

To encourage students to experiment with language use and sentence structure, I give full credit for each variation of the initial sentences.

Once students are adept at sentence combining, I use it as a means to teach not just sentence variation and length but also style. Using the literature we study as a resource, I either select or let students choose passages that they must break down from complex into kernel or base sentences. Then they must recombine them by adding their

---

[1]Mina P. Shaughnessy. *Errors and Expectations: A Guide for the Teacher of Basic Writing.* New York: Oxford University Press, Inc., 1977, p. 77. Used by permission of the publisher.
[2]Charles Cooper, "An Outline for Writing Sentence-Combining Problems," in *The Writing Teacher's Sourcebook.* Edited by Gary Tate and Edward P. Corbett. New York: Oxford University Press, Inc., 1981, p. 372.

own modifiers and clauses. As they "reconstitute" the styles of professional writers, they begin to internalize elements of successful writing through imitation.

After students are practiced in the sentence-combining technique, I turn their attention to its use in the revision of their own prose. To begin the process, I take a section from one of my own stories, which I originally wrote with short, choppy sentences and then later revised using sentence-combining techniques:

> His hair was dark, matted, and graying. It was pushed back and was shiny with hair oil. It was wavy and neatly trimmed around his ears and neck.

> His dark, matted, wavy hair was shiny from hair oil and neatly trimmed around his ears and neck.

> A newspaper was on the stool next to Spence. He picked it up after the first shot of whiskey. He read the names of writers given by-lines on the first page.

> After Spence downed his first shot of whiskey, he picked up a newspaper on the stool next to him and read the names of writers given by-lines on the front page.

We discuss the differences between the two versions, and we point out the changes in style created by longer, more complex sentences.

To integrate sentence combining into the revision of their own writing, I have students select an earlier journal entry or free-writing exercise that they are interested in revising. They find paragraphs, sentences, or sections from their writing which are short and choppy and need work. They pull these excerpts from their papers and experiment with revising them in a variety of ways through sentence combining. Peer groups can provide valuable feedback for the author when he or she must decide which of the new variations

> *Rewriting is when playwriting really gets to be fun . . . In baseball you only get three swings and you're out. In rewriting, you get almost as many swings as you want and you know, sooner or later, you'll hit the ball.*
>
> **NEIL SIMON**

represents the greatest improvement over the original. These selections are then inserted in the revised version of the student's writing.

Having students make up their own sentence-combining exercises from spelling lists, vocabulary lists, or other units of study can also be done. Here is an example of part of a student-produced sentence-combining activity from an eighth grade spelling list:

Spelling List	Student-Produced Sentence-Combining Activity
1. sophomore	He was a wrestler
2. wrestler	He fought on Wednesday.
3. colonel	He was full of haughtiness.
4. Wednesday	She was a sophomore.
5. laboratory	She works in a laboratory.
6. haughtiness	He was an old colonel.
7. yacht	He liked sailing his yacht.
8. autumn	He sails in autumn.

After having the students do the activities described previously for several weeks, I have found that an instructional unit on the different sentence patterns can be invaluable. When I am about halfway through my sentence-combining unit, I teach students the simple, compound, complex, and compound-complex sentences over a several-week period. Once students are writing longer sentences, they want to know that their longer sentences are correct and not run-ons.

In the end perhaps the single most important criterion in teaching writing is the amount of time students spend thinking about writing. The more students write, the more they begin to think like writers. Sentence combining is an excellent teaching tool to help students gain control and confidence over their own writing. When students write often and have confidence in themselves as writers, they begin to do more offstage thinking about writing, composing, and revising in their heads before committing pen to paper. They also have more options in how to go about communicating an intended message and can consciously plan not only what they want to say but also how they can best express it. Revising, then, becomes an integral component of each stage of the writing process.

Two Activities That Encourage Real Revision

By Trudy J. Burrus

Former English Teacher, El Toro High School,
Coordinator, Healthy Kids,
Saddleback Valley Unified School District;
and Teacher/Consultant, UCI Writing Project

I spend considerable time and energy each year fighting the same battles, and one that I never seem to win is the battle over rewrites. I say, "Rewrite," and somehow it is translated as "recopy." However, I have come up with a solution. It is not infallible, but it has been successful. Simply stated, I collect and keep the draft, and then I ask for a rewrite.

The reactions are what one might expect them to be. Looks of horror and disgust abound, and someone almost always cries "Foul." It is then that we discuss one more time, for the record, the variety of approaches one can make to a topic. We review voice, point of view, and methods of organization and development. I follow this discussion with an extensive precomposing phase during which I introduce a variety of topics that the students orally practice writing.

I may suggest a potentially suspenseful event to begin the discussion. One student will invariably arrange the parts of that event in chronological order while another might offer a news story account with the most important information first. Given a controversial issue, one will attempt to persuade, and one might choose to remain objective. One approach may be to begin with the least significant items; another will lead with the most important. One may support with facts; another could offer examples. The students spot avenues open to them that they would not have considered before.

Often the goal is for the writers to revise their work in essentially the same form. In this instance, the earlier draft has been a rehearsal for the purpose of blocking and pacing. When the student writers are forced to act without their original scripts, they become more familiar with their purposes and their unique messages; their rhythm becomes more even and their style more apparent. The writers move more ably within their topics, and their writing develops tones of confidence and authority.

An adjunct activity is to have one student rewrite another's paper. This exercise is especially useful for response partners. Each has a clearer understanding of the weaknesses in the other's draft and of the difficulties in handling the topic. The writer then has the benefit of a peer model when he or she begins his or her own revision. The partner's version may offer fresh ideas; it may also expose unworkable alternatives. Either way, it is helpful.

> *I tell my students that to bury an idea, a sentence, or even a topic may be to give it an honorable death.*
>
> **TRUDY J. BURRUS**

These revision activities seem to bring about the most consistent change when repeated several times early in my course and then resurrected at random intervals thereafter. Probably the greatest long-range effect is an increased opportunity for the students to gain some distance from their work. With this distance, students take command of the subject. Without it, they do not control their writing; their writing controls them.

I tell my students that to bury an idea, a sentence, or even a topic may be to give it an honorable death, and that to keep a poor draft in its flawed form is to condemn it to a life of pain and distortion. I like to draw an analogy between the revision process and an incident in which a ceramics instructor admonished me to destroy the first hundred pots I threw on the potter's wheel. He said, in effect, "To keep each pot is to treat it as your child. It is not, and you are not obligated to love it or to give it a home. Work until you create something that deserves your admiration."

Revising for Correctness

Some Basics That Really Do Lead to Correctness

By Irene Thomas
Educational Consultant, IOTA, Inc.

When many English teachers hear the word *basics*, they think of drills on grammar—drills that lead to the identification of nouns, adverbs, subjects, and so forth. When parents and the society at large call for *the basics*, however, what they usually mean is that students should be able to correct such usages as "we was" and "he done," write in complete sentences with proper punctuation and spelling, and so on. We have been led to believe by the writers of textbooks and traditional English curricula that a connection exists between these two definitions of the basics; indeed, it is assumed that a teacher's drills on grammar will satisfy society's demands for correct performance. I question that assumption. In fact, I would attribute much of the so-called writing crisis in our schools to that very assumption. When drills on grammar are used as *the* means toward better writing, precious time is wasted—time that could be better spent on actual writing tasks. First, let me suggest some reasons why drills on grammar are a waste of time.

Grammar—the analysis, or parsing, of sentences—is an abstract skill. It bears little or no relationship to the production of a correct sentence. Anyone who has taught knows that children or adolescents who can locate an adverb in a sentence do not necessarily use effective or correctly formed adverbs in their writing. And the reverse is also true: Many students who write well do not necessarily perform well on standardized grammar tests. The fact is that the two skills are indeed just that—two different skills. Consider these findings from research studies:

1. Controlled studies attempting to link the teaching of grammar with improvement in writing ability have so far been unsuccessful.*

**EDITOR'S NOTE. For specific citations on the research regarding grammar and the teaching of writing, see pages 3 and 4 of *Handbook for Planning an Effective Writing Program,* which the California Department of Education published in 1983.*

> *The teaching of formal grammar, if divorced from the process of writing, has little or no effect on the writing ability of students.*
>
> HANDBOOK FOR PLANNING AN EFFECTIVE
> WRITING PROGRAM

2. The work of Piaget, the prominent cognitive psychologist, strongly suggests that preadolescents are not developmentally ready for the levels of abstraction demanded in the process of parsing. (That may be why so many ninth graders come to you still not knowing what a verb is, much less a predicate.)

3. The most recent studies of right and left brain domains suggest that the tasks involved with composing are right brain tasks and those of analyzing are left brain tasks. We can at least hypothesize, at this early stage of the research, that the two kinds of skills, when taught simultaneously, may create a neurological conflict during the acquisition of writing skills.

4. Finally, from what researchers know about the acquisition of oral language, we can safely say that oral language is acquired biologically and with data provided by the normal linguistic environment. In other words, children are biologically equipped to learn a language quickly. The language spoken around them serves as data to be internalized. They know, for example, that *er* comparative endings are added to only one class of words. And they will add the *er* to those words predictably, even though they may not understand the term *adjective* until they are fifteen years of age.

Now you might say that oral language and written language differ considerably, even though the latter is roughly based on the former. Moreover, the special requirements of the written forms and conventions (spelling, punctuation, sentence structure) require practice—even drill. Yes, I fully agree; but it is the *kind of practice needed* that we should consider carefully.

All too often in the language arts, we spend our time allotted for *revising* skills on practice material that is essentially impractical. We use textbook drills on verbs or "grammar games" and then, we are led to believe, our students will write correct sentences. What tends to be missing in the process are those intermediate steps of copying, imitating, and manipulating good models. Such models, in fact, can provide the linguistic input to writing skills that is analogous to the "natural language data" necessary to oral language development. Many teachers have found that working with models tends to encourage carryover of the information conveyed in models—information about punctuation, spelling, sentence structure, verb forms—into the students' independent composing. And do not miss an opportunity to use the students' own writing as a learning tool. The idea of being "correct" takes on a new importance when a student is genuinely concerned about communicating his or her message to an audience or in class publications.

Listed below are some examples of practical sentence exercises that you can use almost daily in either your prewriting activities or your warm-up to the revising stage of the writing process. They can be adjusted for any grade level. The overall objective of these exercises is to develop students' *eyes and ears* for identifying the correct written form of sentences. If you have students keep these exercises in a permanent notebook, you can refer to a specific exercise or specific sentence when they need to "correct" something in their independent work. In almost every case, your demonstrating an example first is enough instruction to allow students to work on their own or with a partner. Whenever possible, create examples that relate to actual people, places, and activities to capture the interest of your class. Use the sentence exercises to reinforce the curriculum you are teaching. Most teachers have found that when they integrate the basics with other content areas and present them as they occur naturally in written expression, the need for grammatical terminology is substantially reduced—even eliminated. Here are 12 practical sentence-exercises that I hope you find helpful:

1. Copying a sentence or two from the chalkboard or from a specific passage in a text.

What could be more basic? (These can later serve as models to imitate, as in exercise 2.)

2. Replacing a word or phrase in a sentence with some other word or phrase—also a very practical way to recycle a spelling list.

    Third grade example: Jill sat on my **hat**.

    Ninth grade example: We won the competition because of our **tremendous** speed.

3. Unscrambling a scrambled sentence to produce a real sentence.

    Third grade example: like We boats. to sail (Punctuation and capitalization clues can be dropped later.)

    Ninth grade example: are faster than he and I Harry (three possibilities)

    A series of these scrambled sentences with pronouns helps to establish the relationship between form and position.

4. Replacing nonsense words with real words.

    The **tizz** is **mimming** in the **fass**.
    The **tizzes** are **mimming** in the **fass**.
    The **tizz mims timly**.
    The **tizzes mimmed** yesterday.

    This kind of exercise focuses attention on structural clues and subject-verb agreement.

5. Changing declarative sentences into negations, questions, or imperatives. (Again, you can recycle spelling words.)

6. Using the sentence machine. Make a sentence by choosing one word from each column, as in the examples below. Then repeat the process and make as many other sentences as you can.

Example for Grade Three

They	made	the	same	game
We	ate	a	eight	cages
Ray		an	late	lunches

Example for Grade Nine

Because	I	were	late	we	were	punished.
Since	we	was	sick,	I	took	medicine.
Although	they		obedient,	they	was	

7. Mixing and matching (subjects and predicates) to produce as many sentences as possible.

Example for Grade Three

Those girls		was naughty.
Henry	+	is silly.
My cat		are my friends
		were away today.

8. Punctuating sentences in discourse.

    Third grade example: I want some bubble gum may I go to the store

    Ninth grade example: Reproducing any series of sentences, or a paragraph, from a text everyone has (eliminate capitalization and punctuation). Read the sentences aloud so that students can associate punctuation with intonation clues. Then ask them to proof and correct the copy. Finally, let the students compare their corrected versions with the original text.

9. Writing sentences, later whole paragraphs, from dictation. At any grade level, read a passage from a common text and then compare with the original to allow for self-correction.

10. Playing the Why game (invented by Frank O'Hare). This game both teaches and reviews mechanics. Have students look at a paragraph in the text they have. Begin by asking a question about a specific use of punctuation or capitalization; e.g., Why is there a period after the word *time*? The student who answers correctly may then ask a similar question of the class and so on. You can provide the answer when students cannot.

11. Expanding the world's shortest sentence. This technique works well in grades four and above to help students develop a sense for the two-part structure of the English sentence. The terms *subject* and *predicate* can be added, if you wish, once the students can easily perform the tasks involved.

    Example for grade four: Children/play. Have students add one word at a time to each part of the sentence, always keeping it a real

The starting point in the teaching of writing must be the teacher's belief that children possess the requisite linguistic knowledge.

OWEN THOMAS

sentence. You can write their suggestions on the chalkboard, always retaining the line between subject and predicate. You can invite prepositional phrases (treating them as single-word adverbials) by asking the questions beginning with *where, when,* and *how.* Here is an example that students might produce: Some of the <u>children</u> in our class <u>play</u> tetherball every day at recess.

If you are concerned about the recognition of predicates on standardized examinations, you can point out that the second part of a sentence almost always begins with a verb (a word that can take past tense). To draw attention to helping verbs, you can follow up the original exercise by demonstrating the variations of *play*—played, have played, are playing, will play, and so forth—all of which have a time dimension. The reverse of this whole process, perhaps most appropriate to upper grades, is the paring down of an expanded simple sentence to its barest essentials. This is a most practical way to aid the conceptualization of subject/predicate.

12. Taking dictation. Just as we know how important dictation is for whole language/ language experience instruction, we can also trust our instincts about dictation for older children and adolescents. The teacher or a student can dictate to the others a paragraph or so from a text that everyone has in common. Then students can check their writing against the original and self-correct. This process is bound to alert students and their teachers to which writing conventions need attention. Students, moreover, are encouraged through this activity to engage in revision and proofreading as a natural and practical part of learning to write. With published models in front of them, students also take in a great deal of sentence informa-

tion on their way toward internalizing that information.

13. Sentence combining. This is probably the best method yet developed for teaching all the important skills of sentence building. See the illustration on the next page for a suggested sequence of sentence-combining exercises that are appropriate for students in grades three through six. Additional material on sentence combining may be found in *Sentence Combining: Improving Student Writing Without Formal Grammar Instruction* by Frank O'Hare;[1] in *Sentence Combining: A Composing Book* by William Strong;[2] and in the commentaries by William Lomax and Jerry Judd that appear in other sections of this book. Sentence-combining exercises have also been adapted for computer instruction[3] and for word-processing activity files.[4]

By way of a conclusion, I offer two suggestions to those teachers who agree that the approaches I have described are both basic and sound alternatives to traditional grammar:

1. If your school district uses standardized examinations, ask for a periodic review and evaluation of these examinations. If their measure of writing ability is limited to the skill of identifying subject and verb, press for

---

[1]Frank O'Hare, *Sentence Combining: Improving Student Writing Without Formal Grammar Instruction.* Urbana, Ill.: National Council of Teachers of English, 1973.
[2]William Strong, *Sentence Combining: A Composing Book.* New York: Random House, Inc., 1983. (Also see William Strong, *Creative Approaches to Sentence Combining.* Urbana, Ill.: National Council of Teachers of English, 1986.)
[3]Irene Thomas and Owen Thomas, *Sentence Combining I and II.* St. Louis, Mo.: Milliken Publishing Co., 1984. (P.O. Box 21579, St. Louis, MO 63132) (Consists of six diskettes, teacher's guide, reproducible masters, and a binder).
[4]*You Are the Editor,* series for Humanities Software, P.O. Box 950, Hood River, OR 97031.

A Possible Sequence of Sentence-Combining Exercises for Grades Three Through Six

Note: The grammatical terminology used here is directed to the teacher, not the pupil.

GRADE THREE

1. **Inserting adjectives and adverbs**

   Examples:

   I ate the hamburger.
   The hamburger was *soggy.*   } *I ate the soggy hamburger.*

   Harry is a roller skater.
   He is *good* at it.   }

   Harry roller skates.
   He is good at it.   [good → well]   }

   Children are playing.
   They are playing *in the school yard.*   }

2. **Producing compound subjects and objects**

   Examples:

   Maria wanted some bubble gum.   [and]   } *Maria and Jose wanted some bubble gum.*
   Jose wanted some bubble gum.

   Maria wanted bubble gum.   [and]   }
   Maria wanted *popcorn.*

3. **Producing compound subjects and objects with pronouns**

   Examples:

   He likes bubble gum.   [and]   } *He and I like bubble gum.*
   I like bubble gum.

   Peter gave her a puppet.   [and]   }
   Peter gave *me* a puppet.

GRADE FOUR

Review of the above, plus:

1. **Producing compound sentences with *and* and *but***

   Example:

   John went to the movies.   [, but] }   } *John went to the movies, but I didn't want to go.*
   I didn't want to go.

2. **Producing parallel sequences**

   Example:

   Maria wanted a bike.
   Maria wanted *a doll.*   [,___,___and__]   } *Maria wanted a bike, a doll, and a baseball bat.*
   Maria wanted *a baseball bat.*

3. **Producing possessive nouns**

   Example:

   I like the sailboat.
   It is *Henry's*.   } *I like Henry's sailboat.*

4. **Producing sentences with adverbial clauses, using connecting words, such as *because*, *after*, *until*, and *when***

   Examples:

   We went to the store.
   We wanted some bubble gum.   [because] } *We went to the store because we wanted some bubble gum.*

   I finished the book.
   I went back to the library.   [when____,____] }

GRADES FIVE AND SIX

Review of the above, plus:

1. **Producing sentences with relative clauses**

   Example:

   The girl will win a prize.
   The girl *is the best player*.   [who] } *The girl who is the best player will win a prize.*

2. **Inserting participial phrases**

   Examples:

   My favorite book is **Charlotte's Web**.
   It was *written by E. B. White*.   } *My favorite book is **Charlotte's Web**, written by E. B. White.*

   My father is busy.
   He is *playing football*.   }

3. **Inserting appositives**

   Example:

   Grandma is coming to visit.
   Grandma is *a famous cook*.   [,____,] } *Grandma, a famous cook, is coming to visit.*

4. **Multiple combinations (with more than one possible answer)**

   Examples:

   I ate the hamburgers.
   Henry also ate the hamburgers.
   They were *soggy*.
   They were *stale*.
   We ate them *quickly*.   } *Henry and I ate the soggy, stale hamburgers quickly.*

   A *Wrinkle in Time* is a book.
   It is written by Madeleine L'Engle.
   I would recommend it.
   People my age would like it.   }

the elimination of such examinations. A district-made test that uses the kinds of tasks described above, combined with a writing sample, will provide much sounder indices of a student's writing ability.

2. If your district and community insist that grammar be taught somewhere in the curriculum, press for the creation of an elective course in grammar (perhaps two semesters) at the high school level. Such a course, highly recommended to students studying foreign languages or preparing for college, can be designed for pure grammar instruction as an intellectual exercise. We all know that a course like this taught by someone who is enthusiastic about parsing and diagramming can be great fun as well as a rewarding challenge.

In these ways we will be "putting grammar in its place," doing no one a disservice, and realizing our mutual priorities at a time when our profession is being called on to do so.

Practical Ideas on Revising for Correctness

Making Correctness Creative: The "Snurdles" Project

By Sandra Barnes

Vista High School, Vista Unified School District; and Teacher/Consultant, UCI Writing Project

As English teachers, we are usually required to teach grammar because, supposedly, it will help students write better. However, research indicates that a knowledge of grammar has very little effect on how well students write. Despite these data, most public schools still give instruction in grammar. With that in mind, I tried in my "Snurdles" project to bring the teaching of grammar and writing together. I postulated that if students were challenged to apply what they knew about grammar in their own compositions, then correctness could be a creative enterprise that would foster long-term editing abilities.

I was inspired to make correctness creative by a set of posters called "Snurdles," published by the Perfection Form Company.[1] The set tells a short funny story, with each poster emphasizing one part of speech. I thought it would be educational and entertaining to have students create their own posters illustrating the parts of speech.

I use the original "Snurdles" posters as models for the students. They read the posters and use them as points of departure to create their own characters and stories. After providing a working definition of the parts of speech, I ask the students to work in groups of six to collaborate on a "Snurdles" project.

Each group decides on a character and a series of events or adventures for their story. Each student in the group writes one paragraph that emphasizes one part of speech. The whole group then reviews what has been written and polishes the writing to provide transitions and continuity between the parts. When the story is finished, each paragraph and its part of speech are written and illustrated on posters. The entire group is responsible for the correctness of the finished product.

When working on this unit, I have the students do most of the writing in class with their groups. I move among the groups giving help and advice and monitoring their progress. Usually, the project takes about five class periods. I give each student two letter grades—one for his or her contributions to the group and one for the individual poster.

I have found that students enjoy this project and have much greater success in identifying parts of speech in their own work than in isolated examples written by someone else. Because the students are applying grammatical knowledge to their own writing, they become more aware of when and where parts of speech are used in sentences. The

---

[1] *NOTE:* The address for the Perfection Form Company is 100 North Second Ave., Logan, IA 51546; telephone 800-831-4190.

need for transition to build in continuity is also important in the project and helps students in future writing assignments. Overall, the project can positively affect the students' attitudes toward grammar as well as their aptitudes for using parts of speech appropriately in their own writing.

The following is a sample of an eighth grade group's "Snurdles" project, as written by the students and with the parts of speech underlined by the students:

Close Encounters of the Itchy Kind

NOUNS

This is a <u>story</u> about a poor <u>canine</u> named <u>Butch</u>, who had a terrible personal <u>problem</u>. Well, you see, he had a <u>flea</u> <u>family</u> of who knows how many living in his <u>fur</u>. They began "living in" <u>Butch</u>, well, his <u>fur</u> that is, last <u>summer</u> while he was at an annual <u>flea</u> <u>market</u>. Now there are millions of them infested in <u>Butch</u>. <u>Butch</u> had gone so crazy because of these <u>fleas</u>

that he had even tried to get an <u>exterminator</u> to exterminate him. He figures that if he jumps in a <u>pool</u>, he will drown all of these <u>fleas</u> and that will be the <u>end</u> of this "itchy" <u>ordeal</u>!

ADJECTIVES

All of a sudden the <u>little</u> fleas saw a <u>mean</u> looking dog named Butch, running toward a <u>deep</u> pool. The <u>tiny</u> fleas decided to try to build a <u>giant</u> ark very quickly. They spent all of the long day chopping down <u>big</u> <u>thick</u> trees (his <u>thick</u> hair) and trying to put their <u>huge</u> ark together. The <u>big</u> ark had <u>five</u> <u>little</u> rooms—one for Mr. and Mrs. Fleaster, one for <u>little</u> Fleapé, one for baby Flease, and one for their pet tick, Toc. They all got in the <u>large</u> ark, when suddenly a <u>huge</u> <u>tidal</u> wave came. They all started screaming loudly and they started floating faster and faster to who knows where.

INTERJECTIONS

As the fleas jumped on the ark, there was noise and excitement. Everyone was yelling things back

The storm and the whirlpool quickly put the fleas to sleep! Unknowingly, the fleas slept through forty-three days of their terrifying adventure. Suddenly, they awoke. Almost immidiately, Mr. Fleaster got up and carefully started searching the worn boat. He went outside. He felt a tingling sensation throughout his body. Sometime in the night they had peacefully sailed to the top step of the pool. The Fleaster family quickly hopped onto the cement which enclosed the pool. They eagerly went looking for a new home and found it on a nearby rose. Now, the Fleaster family and their pet tic, Toc, were saved and joyfully lived happily ever after!

Adverb

and forth. As baby Flease walked aboard the ark, she yelled, "Yippee! This is fun." Then a huge wave came upon the ark, and Fleapé exclaimed, "Hey! I am getting seasick." Later, Mrs. Fleaster sat down and yelled, "Yea! This is great." But as soon as Mr. Fleaster looked on the deck of the ark, he screamed, "Ugh! There is a leak." Five minutes later Grandma Fleaster slowly started walking toward the ark and said, "Nuts! I'm still hungry," in a very screechy, high voice. Following her, baby Flease yelled, "Hey! Wait for me." A few minutes later everyone was on board, and all were happy till Mr. Fleaster saw a big water-fall close by. (The waterfall was really some water going down into the jacuzzi from the pool.)

VERBS

As the fleas sailed down the waterfall, sudden panic fell over all the Fleaster family. Flease, one of the fleas in the Fleaster family, lost her hat. The hat glided into the big ocean lying before her. One of the fleas was chatting to another about new hairstyles. They probably did not realize what danger they soon would be facing. I think they started to get the hint when they were submerged in water from their little tiny toes to their teeny little arms. I imagine the fleas at least felt safe when they reached the bottom of the waterfall.

PREPOSITIONS (PHRASES)

Then, all of the sudden, there was another big tidal wave. The flea ark was floating in the violent sea for what seemed like hours. The four little fleas and their pet "tick," Toc, were becoming very seasick. Mr. Fleaster saw a drop in the water. They were coming to another waterfall. Down the falls went the flea ark into a giant whirlpool. They started in a big spin.

CONJUNCTIONS

The fleas were jumping and falling all over the place. They were stunned by the whirlpool, for it was spinning and turning around and around. The fleas were going down and down. Finally, the spinning stopped (because the jacuzzi, which they were in, was turned off), but the fleas didn't stop spinning.

PRONOUNS

The flea family's ark was drenched from going through the whirlpool. Flease got dizzy. She was sick to her little flea stomach. They saw only misty and slightly foggy weather. Suddenly a light shone. They realized it was the sun shining. Then they emerged from the wet wonderland. Slowly rising out of the water they all rejoiced. After rejoicing, father flea was very tired and ordered them all to bed.

ADVERBS

The storm and the whirlpool quickly put the fleas to sleep. Unknowingly, the fleas slept through 43 days of their terrifying adventure. Suddenly, they awoke. Almost immediately, Mr. Fleaster got up and carefully started searching the worn boat. He went outside. He felt a tingling sensation throughout his body. Sometime in the night they had peacefully sailed to the top step of the pool. The Fleaster family quickly hopped onto the cement which enclosed the pool. They eagerly went looking for a new home and found it on a nearby rose. Now, the Fleaster family and their pet tick, Toc, were saved and joyfully lived happily ever after!

Teaching Correctness with Competition Day

By Russell Frank

Principal, Altimira Middle School,
Sonoma Valley Unified School District;
and Teacher/Consultant, UCI Writing Project

I know my students need to master the conventions of written English, but I have always dreaded the task of teaching them. In every lesson it seemed as if I were dragging a group of tug-of-war opponents through the mire.

"Well, class, today we are going to study the use of the comma in setting off an introductory dependent clause." When you make a statement like that to a group of courteous students, you are probably greeted with a combination of yawns and blank stares. In my eighth grade classes, the moans of pain remind me of milking time at the dairies in nearby Chino. However, because of Competition Day, the thought of teaching correctness now excites me. It is fun watching "terminally cool" eighth graders leap from their seats in their enthusiasm to answer questions.

Competition Day is designed around a game format that encourages class participation in learning through the following :

1. High interest through competition (especially effective at the middle and high school levels)
2. Immediate knowledge of results
3. Success according to level of difficulty (game

> *The idea of being "correct" takes on a new importance when a student is genuinely concerned about communicating his or her message to an audience.*
>
> **IRENE THOMAS**

can be individualized to ensure success for each student)

In addition, Competition Day encourages discussion in small groups. In essence you will be using the students in your classroom as teachers.

At some time we have all made the mistake of asking a class a question and immediately picking one person to answer it, without allowing time for thinking. Meanwhile, the other students in class have stopped thinking about the question because a classmate has already been singled out. Thus, this practice minimizes effective learning. In Competition Day, on the other hand, everyone is responsible for answering a question and earning points for his or her respective team.

To start the competition, you must have first introduced a correctness skill: the use of commas, appositives, difficult spelling words, capitalization rules, and so forth. The necessary materials include an overhead projector, chalkboard space, chalk, scorekeeper, and a set of small numbered cards. You divide the class into groups of between four and eight members, depending on the size of your class and the number of teams you wish to have. Assign a number to each person on each team. If you have four teams competing, you will have four people from opposing teams with the same number. Each player must have a sheet of paper and pencil and must answer each question. This paper is turned in at the end of the game, and you can review the paper to check a student's mastery of a particular skill.

Basically, students compete against students who have the same number on the other teams. This allows you to group students according to ability levels if you wish to do so. Highly skilled or highly competitive students can all be given the same number and, thus, will compete against each other. In like manner less skilled or shy students can be given the same number.

After assigning numbers, I may ask the teams to punctuate or capitalize a sentence properly. I dictate the sentence or use an overhead projector to display it. As the students are writing their answers, I draw a numbered card (1–4 or 1–6, depending on the number of players on each team), and anticipation mounts. Nobody knows what number I will call. Finally, I read the number.

At this point, I can ask all those people who have the number to give their answers orally or write them on the chalkboard. Another option is to have them hold up their papers, which I can check at their desks. Correct answers earn a point for that person's group; incorrect answers receive no score.

In a variation of the game, I ask a question and have each group come to consensus regarding its answer. This option is especially useful when I ask the students to do higher-level thinking, such as composing sentences that contain certain grammatical structures. Group discussion also provides students with opportunities for evaluation. In doing sentence combining, for instance, I ask my students to select the most effective sentence combination written by group members. These can be displayed on the chalkboard and compared with sentences chosen by other teams. When the competition comes to a close, I tally up the scores of each group and pronounce a winner.

Although Competition Day can be used in any content area, I have had success in using the approach to reinforce skills in punctuation, capitalization, spelling, grammar, vocabulary, and sentence combining. Using this game to help my students gain mastery over correctness skills has kept student motivation high when it usually ebbs. I no longer feel as if I am having to drag my students through a mire of tedium. By making a game of the learning of the conventions of written English and holding students responsible for each other's success, I have enjoyed cooperation and enthusiasm instead of a tug-of-war.

Building Vocabularies

Word-Sprouting: A Vocabulary-Building Strategy for Remedial Writers

By Barbara Morton

Former English Teacher, Villa Park High School,
Orange Unified School District;
and Teacher/Consultant, UCI Writing Project

Gabriele Rico coined the term *clustering* to describe a writing warm-up exercise that she developed as a result of her research at Stanford University in right brain functioning. Briefly, clustering is a formalized kind of brainstorming. The writer encircles a nucleus word, such as *blue* in Figure 1, and arranges the words he or she associates with the nucleus word in a free-form diagram around the nucleus. (For more information on the clustering technique, see Dr. Rico's essay in the "Prewriting" section that appears near the beginning of this book.)

Dr. Rico's research indicates that through the process of clustering, writers, particularly those at the remedial level, can generate a network of related thoughts from the nucleus word; i.e., clustering assists them in writing coherent paragraphs. Visualizing the relationships between the nucleus word and its satellites helps these students organize their thinking, eliminate nonessential elements, and write in an orderly, systematic manner. It is particularly useful as an alternative to outlining for students who have difficulty developing their thoughts sequentially. Similarly, a distant cousin of the clustering technique enables remedial writers to bypass the often counterproductive grammar lesson and deal directly with usage and word manipulation, as you will see as we examine the procedure of word-sprouting.

In Figure 2, which closely resembles Dr. Rico's clustering diagram, you will find an assortment of words related to the nucleus word *fool*. However, instead of random associations, the cluster is limited to inflections of the nucleus word.

Because the method of identifying inflections departs substantially from the clustering technique,

267

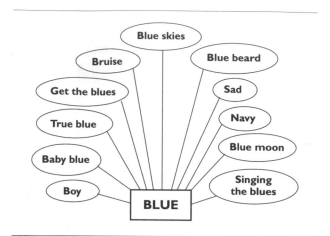

Fig. 1. The Clustering of *Blue*

Fig. 2. Clustering with Inflections of the Nucleus Word

I have substituted the term *sprouting* for Dr. Rico's *clustering*. Language teachers, already familiar with the linguistic terms *root* and *stem*, will readily comprehend the metaphor of *sprouts*, or grammatical variations, growing from *wordseeds*.

As each sprout is labeled and classified according to its grammatical identity, the fickleness of grammar becomes apparent, as shown in the following chart:

Verbs/ Verb variations	Nouns/ Noun variations	Modifiers (adjectives and adverbs)
fool	fool	foolish
fools	fools	foolishly
fooling	(to) fool	fooling
fooled	fooling	fooled
	foolishness	
	fools	

The confusion that results from attempts at arbitrary classification might discourage the most

able of students. *Fool* appears as both a noun and a verb, as does *fools*. And *fooling* is included in all three categories, because the participial form qualifies as a modifier as well.

Until the word is considered in the context of the sentence, its grammatical classification is, of course, impossible. Even then, frustrated remedial learners flounder in a morass of linguistic terminology with no improvement in their usage skills.

The word-sprouting approach abandons the traditional grammarian's approach to language and capitalizes on the student's inherent ability to distinguish the appropriate inflection of a familiar word according to its position in a spoken phrase. It is a vocabulary expansion and usage drill that deals with nouns, verbs, and modifiers without labeling them. Spared the burden of learning new definitions and assigning grammatical categories, as is often the procedure in standard vocabulary lessons, the student concentrates on the usage that "sounds right" for a given problem structure.

To introduce this exercise, the teacher generates a diagram of sprouts from a familiar word on the chalkboard or transparency as the class spontaneously provides them, adding new forms of the seedword. Before assigning the written segments of the exercise, the teacher must determine that the diagram includes an exhaustive list of sprouts. With speakers of substandard English, it may also be necessary to repeat the words with appropriate examples: "We don't say, 'I fooling you,' we say, 'I _____?' "

Even though the word may be familiar, it is also important for the class to decide on a working definition. Remedial students often have a great deal of difficulty arriving at simple definitions, particularly if they are not allowed to use a form of the word to phrase the definition.

Next, using the completed diagram of sprouts, students work with a partner to select the most appropriate sprout for use in carefully structured sample sentences. Allowing them to complete the exercise aloud with a partner reinforces aural perception and provides an opportunity for peer involvement.

In the final phase of the exercise, students are expected to write original sentences, developed from a list of words and phrases that incorporate

The word-sprouting approach capitalizes on the student's inherent ability to distinguish the appropriate inflection of a familiar word according to its position in a spoken phrase.

BARBARA MORTON

the sprouts in a variety of syntactic problems. They are allowed to use the sample sentences as models, and they may refer to a set of sentence-grading criteria that will later be used to determine their letter grades. Although they are expected to work independently, a peer-evaluation session in which students read their sentences aloud to one another allows them to correct errors before submitting their papers for final grading.

The teacher's use of the grading criteria allows for a rapid, "no surprises" return of papers. Students who score less than 89 should choose two sentences to rewrite as a follow-up.

Phase One: Word-Sprouting

The group session in which the class provides sprouts of the seedwords combines auditory, visual, and kinesthetic modes of learning. Because remedial learners need constant reinforcement in all modes, the teacher's presentation should be painstakingly thorough. In the first phase of the exercise, the teacher must help the students create the most complete word-sprout.

For example, the sprouts the group might create for the seedword *decide* are shown in Figure 3.

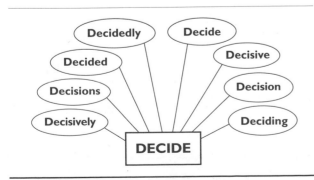

Fig. 3. Word-Sprouts of a Seedword

Even though the definition of a familiar word like *decide* may seem obvious, a brief session to arrive at a consensus is necessary before students continue with the written segments of the exercise.

Phase Two: Completing Sample Sentences

In phase two of the word-sprouting exercise, the students are asked to use the words they sprouted from the seedword *decide*, and they are given the following instructions:

- Write the most appropriate form of *decide* in the blanks provided in the accompanying sample sentences. Use each word from our word-sprout at least once.
- Say each sentence aloud to help you decide on the correct form.
- You may work with a partner. Refer to the word-sprouting diagram if necessary.

Sample Sentences

1. Louise always has difficulty making her own _____.

2. Yesterday, Louise _____ to give up the tennis team to take a job at a fast-food restaurant.

3. She had to _____ whether the money she would make was important enough to take the place of her first love, tennis.

4. "I just can't _____," she told me unhappily.

5. Louise always talks things over with me when she has trouble _____.

6. I usually _____ carefully to avoid making a mistake.

7. That is why _____ is usually easy for me.

8. Leaving the tennis team was a tough _____ for Louise.

9. Louise has never been a very _____ person; now she wants to change her mind and go back on the tennis team.

10. Coach Burns will not let favoritism be a _____ factor.

11. Having already _____ to remove her name, he's not likely to change his mind.

12. He is _____ today whether to let Louise come back on the team.

13. I hope he _____ in favor of Louise.

14. Louise just called to tell me it has all been _____.

15. Coach Burns said he _____ that he would give Louise one more chance.

16. It is _____ in the team's best interest to have Louise as a starter.

Phase Three: Writing a Sentence

In phase three of the word-sprouting exercise, the students are given a list of words and asked to create their own sentences. They are given these instructions:

- Using the words or word groups suggested below, write a sentence at least eight words long:

   1. decide
   2. to decide
   3. they decide
   4. decides
   5. Mary decided
   6. had decided
   7. having decided
   8. decision
   9. decisions
   10. deciding is
   11. is deciding
   12. Mary, deciding
   13. was decided
   14. decisive
   15. decisively
   16. decidedly

- Do not change the form of the word and do not separate or rearrange the word groups.
- You may refer to the "Sample Sentences" and the "Grading Standards for Sentences" as guidelines.

Grading Standards for Sentences

Possible score

90–100 (Superior)

To earn maximum points, you must show the following in each sentence:

- An understanding of the meaning of the vocabulary word.
- Correct use of the form of the vocabulary word.
- No spelling mistakes.
- No punctuation mistakes.
- Construction according to the rules of standard English.
- Originality and inventive use of language.

80–89 (Good)

This paper does not receive maximum points because of one or more of the following:

- Minor confusion about the meaning of the vocabulary word.
- Mistaken use of the form of the vocabulary word.
- Minor errors in grammar, punctuation, or spelling.
- Little apparent effort and originality in sentence construction.

70–79 (Fair)

This score is reserved for sentences that:

- Show uncertainty about exact meaning or use of the word in three or more instances.
- Have occasional awkward grammatical constructions.
- Show difficulty with internal punctuation.
- Have frequent spelling errors.

60–69 (Weak)

This score is reserved for sentences that:

- Show that the writer has little understanding of the vocabulary word.
- Have abundant errors in spelling, including the word being studied.
- Show elementary punctuation errors, indicating failure to proofread.
- Are elementary in structure; have run-on sentences or fragments.

Sample Seedwords—High School Remedial Level

Verbs/ Verb variations	Nouns/ Noun variations	Modifiers (adjectives and adverbs)	Verbs/ Verb variations	Nouns/ Noun variations	Modifiers (adjectives and adverbs)
separate separates separating separated	separation separations (to) separate separating separator	separate separately separating separated separable	pursue pursues pursuing pursued	pursuit pursuits (to) pursue pursuing	pursuant pursuing pursued
obey obeys obeying obeyed	obedience (to) obey obeying	obedient obediently obeying obeyed	change changes changing changed	change changes (to) change changing	changeable changeably changing changed
anger angers angering angered	anger (to) anger angering	angry angrily angering angered	picture pictures picturing pictured	picture pictures (to) picture picturing	picturesque picturesquely picturing pictured
create creates creating created	creation creations (to) create creating	creative creatively creating created	analyze analyzes analyzing analyzed	analysis analyses (to) analyze analyzing	analytical analytically analyzing analyzed
deceive deceives deceiving deceived	deceit deception (to) deceive deceiving	deceitful deceitfully deceptive deceptively deceiving deceived	experiment experiments	experiment experiments (to) experiment experimenting	experimental experimentally experimenting experimented

Practical Ideas for Building Vocabularies

Deceptive Definitions: Making the Dictionary a Treasure Chest

By Mindy Moffatt

English and History Teacher,
White Hill Middle School, Ross Valley School District;
and Teacher/Consultant, UCI Writing Project

The dictionary is a treasure chest, but too often students see it only as Pandora's box. The mere mention of a dictionary often suggests punishment, or it is associated with boring, endless, mindless ditto sheets which ineffectively "teach" vocabulary skills. Unfortunately, the dictionary may also be viewed the same way by some teachers. (Contrast the availability of dictionaries in teachers' workrooms and in a school's detention halls.)

When I was confronted with the dilemma of turning Pandora's box into a treasure chest, one of my eighth grade students gave me the key—a game called Deceptive Definitions. I have been told that a version of this game, called "Fictionary," which has slightly more elaborate scoring rules, is popular with many teachers.

Although the explanation for Deceptive Definitions was complicated, one of my students and I

271

had played the game a few times, and we became aware that the treasure was *ours*. The more often the game is played, the more self-motivated students become in order to improve their own skills of dictionary use (especially with pronunciation key and guide), vocabulary building, imitative writing, listening and reading comprehension, memorization, and spelling. The directions for playing the game are presented in the accompanying chart.

Deceptive Definitions		
	Directions	*Example*
Introduction to the Game	The teacher arranges to play two rounds.	
Round 1	1. The teacher chooses a word from the dictionary and writes it on chalkboard with pronunciation guide (if needed for review of skill).	1. merl (mərl)
	2. The teacher writes four deceptive definitions and the true definition on the chalkboard.	2. a. to rotate in a counterclock-wise direction b. blackbird c. corner spring in a mattress d. fiber used in elastic e. Neanderthal weapons
	3. Students write down the letter identifying the definition that they believe is the correct one.	
	4. The teacher identifies the correct answer.	4. merl b. blackbird
	5. Each student who chose blackbird earns 1 point.	
Round 2	1. The teacher writes a new word on the chalkboard and selects four students to write deceptive definitions for the word.	1. anlace (an ləs)
	2. The teacher collects the definitions.	
	3. The teacher writes all the definitions on the chalkboard.	3. a. tropical flower b. type of sour cherry having blue-green fruit c. therapeutic psychologist d. leather strip used for tying e. a tapering medieval dagger
	4. The students again choose the definition that they believe is the true definition and write the identifying letter on their papers.	
	5. The teacher announces the correct definition and the names of students whose deceptive definitions were chosen.	5. anlace e. a tapering medieval dagger
Scoring	Each student who chose the true definition earns 1 point. Any student whose deceptive definition was chosen by others earns 1 point for every student who was fooled.	

After playing two rounds of the game with the teacher, the students can play the game without additional guidance. Each student can have a turn at selecting a word from the dictionary, for which deceptive definitions can be written and then presenting the definitions to a peer group of four to five students. (*Note*: To promote listening comprehension skills, the definitions can be read aloud and then written on the chalkboard or notepaper.) Or, working in small groups, students can select an intriguing vocabulary word; each student can then contribute a definition for the word and let other groups in the class come to consensus on which is the true definition. The rules remain the same: one point for each group that chooses the correct definition and one point for the small group each time one of its deceptive definitions is chosen by another group.

The point of Deceptive Definitions in the first few rounds of the game is simply to get students interested in the dictionary and excited about learning new words. While they may not use the specific words gained in the Deceptive Definitions game in their own writing, they may reach for a new word to convey what they do want to say. In subsequent games, the teacher can supply a list of words that relate more directly to the content of the course. At the same time that they are building vocabulary skills, students are also practicing imitative writing. The deceptive definitions they write must sound as if they came from the dictionary in order for their definitions to stump their classmates. This aspect of the game can be a rehearsal for the stylistic writing they will do later in the semester.

Deceptive Definitions is, indeed, a treasure chest. It can be adapted to any grade level and tailored to any student population. It promotes active rather than passive learning and it is fun.

> *The most valuable of all talents is that of never using two words when one will do.*
>
> THOMAS JEFFERSON

Verbal Density: Expanding Students' Use of Verbs

By Evelyn Ching

Former English and Fine Arts Teacher,
Villa Park High School, Orange Unified School District;
and Teacher/Consultant, UCI Writing Project

Although I stress several aspects of vocabulary to show high school students how diction contributes to a mature writing style, one of the most useful concepts I have found is that of verbal density, or the ratio of verbs and verbals to the total number of words in a piece of writing. It is an easy concept to demonstrate in the writing of various authors and becomes simple for the students to use in evaluating their own or others' writing styles.

For the lesson I first explain the rationale: that *moving pictures* created by interesting active verbs are far more fascinating to read than almost any still *portrait* that depends largely on the verb *to be* and its various forms. Even John Steinbeck's descriptions in which very little *happens* are full of evocative verbs that move the reader's mental eyes around the picture much as an artist, such as Cezanne, skillfully manipulates the eye of the viewer in one of his still lifes.

After the rationale is explained, students need to be reminded of what a verb and a verbal are; e.g., any verb, its conjugational parts and constructs, gerunds, participial and infinitive phrases, and participles used as modifiers. Also counted are those words in which the noun form and verb form are the same: *strike, slide, ride, smile,* and so forth. Do not be surprised by how many of these words come from sports. Encourage students to make this connection, because sports broadcasting, particularly on radio, has a high verbal ratio.

Next, it is useful to show how the process works by providing several samples. I distribute a selection in which I have previously counted the total number of words (between 200—300 is best). Then I *walk* my students through the selection by reading it aloud, emphasizing the verbs and verbals, which they underline on their copies. I purposely *forget* several to encourage them to look actively, not just

273

listen to me. Here is one of the selections I have used:

1904—The Forgotten Games

ST. LOUIS—It was late one spring afternoon. A watery sun tried fitfully to pierce the clouds that hung over the city. In Forest Park, the trees were bare, their branches tracing stark patterns against the dull gray sky.

In a far corner of the Washington University campus, great mudstreaked Caterpillar tractors and bulldozers eased their way between the ranks of parked cars, their exhausts sending puffs of dirty smoke into the afternoon air.

Workmen, warmly bundled against the cold, sloshed through the rain-filled potholes, already thinking about the end of another shift. Huge trucks, piled high with debris, carried away the results of the day's demolition.

Francis Field, its turf churned to mud by the treads of the giant earth movers, had a sad look about it. The black wrought-iron fence surrounding the field lay flat in places, as if having given up trying to keep the future from tearing away at the past. Already, the once-proud cement grandstand, the first of its kind in the United States, had been reduced to little more than a mound of broken concrete, twisted wire, and splintered wood.

Not so, however, for the giant stone pillars and ornate gates at the east end of the field. There they stood, as they had done for four-score years and more, and there they will remain.[1]

(220 words; verbal density = 1:7.3)

Before counting the total number of words in the selection, I ask a volunteer to read aloud just the verbs and verbals. The students will be able to follow the action with almost no help at all from nouns, adverbs, or their "great, fabulous, fantastic" adjectives.

The verbal density is figured by dividing the total number of words by the number of verbs and verbals.[2] The resulting number will be the denominator of the verbal-density fraction. Studies have shown that professional writers consistently achieve a verbal density of about 1:6; college students, 1:10; and many high school students, 1:12—15 .

Usually, I follow the demonstration by distributing two selections, such as the following, for which I have already calculated the verbal density:

Excerpt from "The Most Dangerous Game"

An apprehensive night crawled slowly by like a wounded snake, and sleep did not visit Rainsford, although the silence of a dead world was on the jungle. Toward morning when a dingy gray was varnishing the sky, the cry of some startled bird focused Rainsford's attention in that direction. Something was coming through the bush, coming slowly, carefully, coming by the same winding way Rainsford had come. He flattened himself down on the limb, and through a screen of leaves almost as thick as tapestry, he watched. . . . That which was approaching was a man.

It was General Zaroff. He made his way along with his eyes fixed in utmost concentration on the ground before him. He paused, almost beneath the tree, dropped to his knees and studied the ground. Rainsford's impulse was to hurl himself down like a panther, but he saw that the general's right hand held something metallic—a small automatic pistol.

The hunter shook his head several times, as if he were puzzled. Then he straightened up and took from his case one of his black cigarettes; its pungent incense-like smoke floated up to Rainsford's nostrils.

Rainsford held his breath. The general's eyes had left the ground and were traveling inch by inch up the tree.[3]

(212 words; verbal density = 1:5.05)

Excerpt from An Introduction to Shakespeare

An actor also had to be a trained swordsman, for the London audiences knew a great deal about the art of fencing and the Theatre was often hired for exhibition matches by professionals. A good fencer needed years of training and a great deal of physical endurance, for the heavy Elizabethan rapier was a brutal weapon and the fencer was trained to make for his opponent's eyes or strike below the ribs. Actors had an even more difficult problem, since they had to face a critical

[1]Grahame L. Jones, "1904—The Forgotten Games," *Los Angeles Times*, Part VIII, p. 4, July 24, 1984. Copyright, 1984, *Los Angeles Times*; used by permission of the publisher.

[2]In counting the number of verbs and verbals, a verb and its helping verb are counted as one; infinitives, as one; hyphenated words, as one; gerunds, as one; participles, as one; and nouns that are identical with the verb form, as one.

[3]Richard E. Connell, "The Most Dangerous Game." Copyright, 1924, by Richard Connell; copyright renewed 1952, by Louise Fox Connell. Reprinted by permission of Brandt & Brandt Literary Agents, Inc.

audience on an open stage in the glare of the after-noon sun and stage a duel which was realistic enough so it would look as though a man had actually been killed.[4]

(118 words; verbal density = 1:5.9)

After we have read the selection, we discuss it as a class. This follow-up makes students especially aware of the impact of verbals in a given selection.

When students begin to have confidence in their own writing and, in particular, to feel secure about their ability to fix errors and to improve their effectiveness as writers, I have them run a verbal density test on a piece of their own writing or the work of an author they admire or enjoy.

At this point, I ask students to apply what they have learned by using an idea I picked up from Barbara Morton's word-sprouting technique—having students apply the missing words in a paragraph. But instead of having them use only forms of a root word, like *decide*, I encourage them to use as many original verbs and verbals as they can think of, as I did in the following exercises:

Supply the Verbs for the Blanks:

An ancient popcorn machine _____ the door, and a long glass counter _____ down the narrow aisle. Mounds and pounds of candies—most of them homemade—are in baskets gaily _____ with ribbons and red plastic roses.

A little boy _____ in his jeans for a dime—the price of an ice cream cone. Another youngster _____ down a dime for a bag of popcorn and _____ out. A man enters and _____ the walkways, _____ something, that special, certain something to _____ a sweet tooth.

Slowly he _____ toward the end of the counter.

[4]Marchette Chute, *An Introduction to Shakespeare*. New York: E. P. Dutton and Co., Inc., © 1951, p. 26. Used by permission of the publisher.

At last the man's jaw _____ firm; he stands erect, no longer _____ over the stronghold of sweets, his decision _____.

List the Verbs and Verbals You Supplied:

_____

_____

_____

_____

More Original Verbs and Verbals:

_____

_____

_____

_____

We share the different student versions of the exercise as a class and, in the process, develop a word bank of effective verbs and verbals that students can draw on in upcoming writing assignments. Having students perform this same task on the work of prominent authors (with the verbs and verbals removed) helps the students enlarge their vocabularies, increase their use of dictionaries and thesauruses, and gain a better understanding of the elements of style.

The final step in the lesson is to ask students to perform a verbal density analysis on something they have written. This concrete experience with their own work is the best motivator for using a more action-oriented vocabulary in the future. Invariably the ratio of verbs and verbals in my students' writing increases as a result of this lesson and, as a by-product, their vocabulary is enhanced and their style becomes more vital.

MADDOG: Choosing Nouns to Create a Dominant Impression

By Scott Edwards

English Teacher, La Habra High School,
Fullerton Joint Union High School District;
and Teacher/Consultant, UCI Writing Project

Many types of writing—such as autobiography, observation, and even evaluation—call on students to portray people, places, objects, or events and make them seem real to the reader. I find that when students attempt to revise such pieces, to bring them to life, many only toss in a few adjectives. Some students include more action verbs. Few, however, realize the importance of nouns, the words they choose to name specific objects and details. MADDOG prompts students to build a base of names for the details in their writing and then choose from this base to dramatically convey a dominant impression. This lesson helps students tap their own vocabularies to find alternatives to lifeless nouns.

Prior to this lesson, the class reads several descriptive or narrative pieces to practice identifying the dominant impression, the central feeling or mood of a piece. These dominant impressions are frequently what Rebekah Caplan would call the "telling sentences."

To begin our look at nouns, I read students a rough draft of a paragraph recalling an adventure I had with a dog when I was a paperboy:

> Even though I knew where the dogs were, I could occasionally get caught off guard. At one house, the dogs would usually be in the front yard, waiting for me. Having learned the hard way that the dogs would chase me if I rode past them on my bike, I parked my bike and walked the newspaper to the door. One day I only saw two of the dogs in the yard. I walked cautiously past them, watching their lips curl and hearing the growls which came from deep in their throats. Then, just as I was about to set the paper down, I saw the third dog. He walked toward me and everything about him filled me with terror. We both stopped and stared, waiting for each other to make the next move. He waited for me to turn and flee; I waited for him to pounce.

The class then acts as my writing group to help me focus on the dominant impression. We recognize that I'm trying to re-create the feeling of terror, but that I don't really show a clear picture of the dog, the cause of my fear.

I model, with the class's help, how I go about finding more details with which to create my portrait of terror. I begin by drawing the outline of a large dog on the chalkboard. Seeing my drawing (which students think is a sloth, horse, or pig before I tell them it's a dog) makes the less artistic students comfortable later when I have them draw.

Students suggest possible names for dogs, such as *Fido, Brutus, Butch, Fifi, Killer*—all of which indicate qualities of the dogs' personalities. I list these on the chalkboard above the dog. Students then provide different words meaning *dog*, such as *cur, mutt, hound, pooch,* and *mongrel*. If students are unfamiliar with these names, their classmates can usually define them. I then proceed around the dog, from part to part, asking for synonyms for these parts. I write these words next to the respective part on the board. The dog's mouth area, for example, might also be named its *jaw, muzzle, chompers, kisser, licker,* or *destroyer. Claws, dukes, pads, feet, shredders* could replace the more common word *paw*. Students may suggest words that are part of their personal vocabularies, even if these words can't be found in a dictionary. I also encourage the students to make comparisons, so the dog's tail might, for example, become a whip or spike. (See Figure 4.)

After the dog has been surrounded by nouns, we discuss their connotations, what these different words imply. What kind of dog, for example, would be named Fifi? What kind of dog would have *shredders* instead of *paws*? We look at the words we have listed and circle those words that could be used to describe the dog in my paragraph, the cur that frightened me as I attempted to deliver the daily news. We choose words like *Brutus, Killer, fangs, chompers,* and *shredders*. In identifying the dog as my enemy, we might come up with alternatives like *villain, opponent, nemesis, terror,* and *fiend*.

Just a few sentences show how much power more precise nouns generate:

> Killer narrowed the slits of his eyes and lifted his gums to reveal chiseled, saliva-covered fangs. His

dog, cur, mutt, mongrel, wolf, pooch, cuddly wuddly, terror
Biff, Spike, Brutus, Fifi, Fido, Spot, Killer, Phoebe, Mookie

tail, wagger,
pointer, whip,
spike, sword

eyes, lamps, beads,
fire, slits, sights

jaw, muzzle, kisser,
licker, destroyer,
ripper, shredder,
grin, chompers,
razors, fangs,
daggers

rear, rump, butt,
hindquarter,
haunches

belly, stomach, gut,
chest, ribs, paunch

legs, limbs,
appendages, paws,
pouncers, feet,
springs

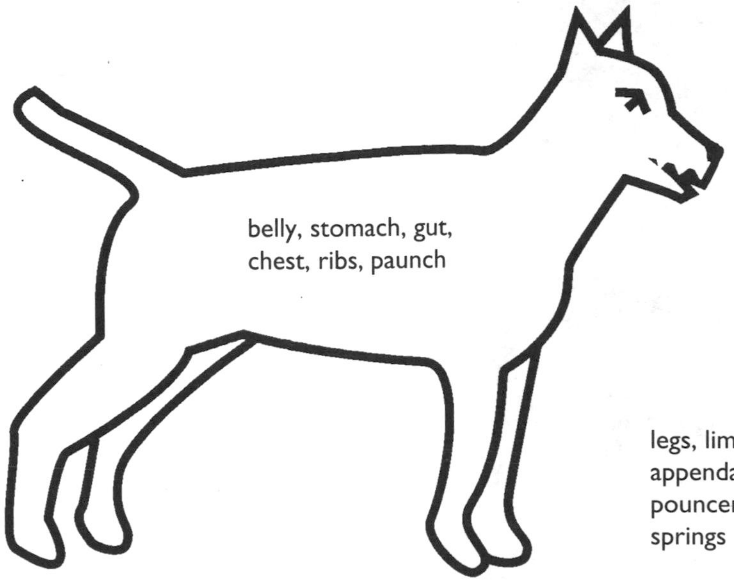

Fig. 4. Nouns Generated from MADDOG

ears went back as his hairs stood up along his spine like soldiers answering a bugle call. His tail went stiff, a sword waiting for the attack. As I watched his muscles clenched around his haunches, I knew who would emerge victorious from this contest.

At this point, students are usually ready to repeat the process to describe a situation they have experienced. I have them select from their writing folders a descriptive piece with which they would like to work. The students do a quick sketch of their subjects. If they are revising a longer narrative, then they choose a key moment, scene, or object. The sketch needn't demonstrate artistic ability; its only purpose is to help the students reexamine their subjects. As I did with the dog, the students label their drawings, using as many possible names for each feature as possible. Students enjoy helping each other, since their lists are different. They can also use a thesaurus to expand their choices.

Students then return to their written pieces and select nouns which support the dominant impres-

sion they wish to convey. When the students revise, they usually do more than simply replace the nouns, since reaching for more precise names makes them think of new details and actions to add as well.

Extensions to this activity provide further practice in vocabulary building. If the students have a less powerful vocabulary, many of the possible nouns might be new words. Having students order the noun list for *dog* (or one of the body parts) from most fierce to most gentle would help reinforce the new vocabulary. Students might also rewrite an effective descriptive passage from a literary work, changing the nouns and, thus, the dominant impression. Additionally, they can use literary works as the basis for a discussion of word choice, speculating on why authors choose the words they do.

Careful word choice—of all parts of speech, not just nouns—is characteristic of all effective writing. MADDOG helps students consider the impressions conveyed by precise language.

Evaluation

Holistic Scoring in the Classroom

By Glenn Patchell
English Teacher, Irvine High School,
Irvine Unified School District;
and Teacher/Consultant, UCI Writing Project

Holistic scoring is a technique of evaluation that solves many of the problems of a writing teacher. The conscientious English teacher concerned with teaching writing effectively is often burdened with the obligation of reading several class sets of papers a week. Even the best-intentioned and most dedicated teacher burns out after several weeks. I found that after 12 weeks I could hardly stand to look at a student paper. The results of the burnout were that students did not get immediate feedback; they did not write as often; and I felt guilty for offending the principles of good teaching. I welcomed the use of holistic scoring because it gave me needed relief from the paper load, involved my students in a more effective learning experience, and provided parents and administrators with concrete evidence of the students' progress and the program's effectiveness.

Simply put, holistic scoring is evaluating the paper as a whole. It assumes that each writing skill is related to the others and that no one skill is more important or should receive greater emphasis than another. The evaluation is achieved through the use of a rubric (scoring guide) which lists the criteria for each score. The rubrics that readers use may be based on various scales, usually ranging from nine points to four points. I personally find the four-point scale less desirable because it relates too closely to the common grading scale of A through F. Each rubric should be tailored to the specific writing task described in the prompt (assignment). Holistic scoring is used by school districts to evaluate proficiency tests, staff development projects, class progress, and individual improvement. Holistic scoring also serves the English teacher or any teacher of writing in the classroom to facilitate evaluation of the students' work. I soon found that one of the most practical

Holistic scoring is evaluating the paper as a whole. It assumes that each writing skill is related to the others and that no one skill is more important or should receive greater emphasis than another.

GLENN PATCHELL

uses of holistic scoring was in the classroom with students as the readers.

As a tool for the teacher, holistic scoring provides more time to instruct because less time is spent evaluating the students' papers. For example, before I used holistic scoring, I spent most of my evaluation time marking errors and writing suggestions or basic comments on the papers. Unfortunately, the students rarely read or understood my comments. Through the use of the prompt and rubric, the teacher establishes a clear purpose for each assignment, the student is exposed to the criteria for evaluation of each writing assignment, and the writer is directed to the strengths and weaknesses of each writing sample. For instance, the UCI Writing Project used the following descriptive prompt in an evaluation of the writing skills of tenth, eleventh, and twelfth grade students in the classes of teachers trained in the Writing Project and in the classes of comparable teachers who had not been exposed to the Writing Project's techniques:

> Write a paper in which you describe a restaurant that you remember vividly. It could be the best, worst, or most unusual. Include in your description the senses (sight, smell, touch, hearing, and taste).

Note that the prompt was designed to stimulate writing and was broad-based enough so that every student could draw on his or her experience. Moreover, the student received specific directions as to what to include in the essay. Based on the prompt, a rubric was established that clearly delineates the criteria for scoring each writing sample (see the next page).

Although the prompt and rubric described above were used for a large-scale evaluation, the same principles apply to holistic scoring in the classroom.

Some students have a hard time understanding why they received a particular grade on a paper, but I have never had a student who had difficulty comprehending why he or she received a certain score when a rubric was available and clearly explained in advance. The careful use of a rubric will provide the student instruction in specific areas of usage, spelling, sentence structure, word choice, and so forth. For example, one area that always concerns me is the variety of sentence patterns. Most high school student writers have little understanding of the value of subordination. Requiring several complex sentences or the use of clauses beginning with *because, if, since, although,* and so forth and listing the use of subordination as a criterion on the rubric make the student aware of complex sentences. When writers find that their papers received scores that indicate a lack of sentence variety, they know that they must learn the concept of subordination.

One of the greatest boons of holistic scoring in the classroom is that it actually involves students in the evaluation process. As the students learn to use the rubric, I have discovered that they can be trained to score writing assignments effectively. The rubric is now viewed in a new light as they try to apply it to the papers of other students. Then, not only do they better understand the rubric, but they also become responsible for helping other writers improve by directing them to the appropriate criteria by the score they select for each paper. The experience of Carolyn is a case in point. Carolyn was one of those students who always excelled. She worked hard to complete each assignment and to produce quality work. Soon, her reputation earned her such respect that the presence of

Rubric: Description

9—8 This paper is clearly superior. The writer developed the topic with excellent organization, content, and insight, and he or she displayed facile use of language and mastery of mechanics. A person who has written a *9—8* paper has done most or all of the following well:

- Developed a good introduction.
- Maintained an appropriate point of view throughout the paper.
- Employed precise, apt, or evocative descriptive vocabulary.
- Did not shift in tense or person.
- Organized ideas effectively and provided an introduction, some closure, and an orderly progression from one idea to another.
- Varied sentence structure and length.
- Used effectively the conventions of written English—spelling, usage, sentence structure, capitalization, punctuation.
- Used at least three examples with specific supporting details.
- Used at least three of five senses.
- Wrote legibly.

7 This is a thinner version of the *9—8* paper— still impressive, cogent, convincing, but less well handled in terms of organization, insight, or language.

6—5 A score of 5 or 6 applies to papers in the upper- half category that are less well written than a *7* paper. This paper may exhibit less maturity of thought than was exhibited in the papers with higher scores, and the writer has not handled organization, syntax, or mechanics as well. The *5* paper is a thinner version of the *6*. A *6—5* paper will exhibit these characteristics:

- Has a clear introduction.
- Has an appropriate point of view.
- Communicates clearly.
- Shows some sense of organization but is not fully organized.
- Uses less variety of sentence structure and length.
- Contains some errors in mechanics, usage, and sentence structure.

- Usually has three examples with support- ing details.
- Uses at least two of the five senses.
- Handwriting can be easily read.

4—3 These scores apply to a paper that maintains the general idea of the writing assignment, shows some sense of organization, but is weak in content, thought, language facility, and mechanics. A *3* paper is a thinner version of the *4* paper. A *4—3* paper has these character- istics:

- Introduction lacks clarity.
- Has shifts in tense and person.
- Displays a minimal overall organization.
- Has little variety of sentence structure and many sentence errors.
- Has some misunderstanding of the prompt.
- Contains serious errors in mechanics, usage, and sentence structure.
- Examples and supporting details are not clearly stated or defined.
- Uses at least one of the five senses.
- Handwriting can usually be easily read.

2 This score applies to a paper that makes no attempt to deal with the topic and compounds the weaknesses found in a *4—3* paper. A *2* paper exhibits several of the following:

- Has no sense of organization.
- Shifts constantly in tense and person.
- Shows little or no development of ideas; lacks any focus on specific and related details.
- Distorts, misreads, or ignores the topic.
- Contains disjointed sentences, lacks sense of sentence progression and variety, and contains many sentence errors.
- Shows serious faults in handling the conventions of written English to the extent of impeding a reader's understanding.
- Has no discussion of the five senses.
- Handwriting cannot be read easily.

1 This score is used for any response that is not on the topic and has almost no redeeming qualities.

her name on an assignment often earned her an *A*. However, during a class holistic scoring session, Carolyn received a *3* from her peers. Because the scorers were all boys, she appealed to me for a second opinion. I inserted her paper in a group of papers to be scored by another class. A second scoring again produced a *3* evaluation. Carolyn was then convinced to go back to the rubric and determine what the weaknesses in her essay were.

Training students to score holistically takes time and patience. Students will not become proficient overnight. But with the same training given to teachers, I have seen students score with the same consistency as adults. In the process of scoring, students also become aware of the criteria for good writing and learn to identify areas which need improvement not only in the papers of others but also in their own compositions. Significantly, in seeing their peers' writing and receiving group feedback on their own papers, student writers suddenly become conscious that they have an audience other than the teacher. This situation clearly lessens the burden on the teacher as the sole evaluator of student work.

Although holistic scoring is a valuable tool, I would never recommend it as the only method of evaluation. When I take the time to evaluate and completely edit a student's paper, I want to be able to have a conference with the writer about his or her paper. I now have the time for individual conferences because holistic scoring does help moderate the paper load, as well as provide specific criteria for evaluation, improve assignments, allow more writing, and motivate students to understand what constitutes good writing. The student writes with purpose, recognizes good writing, and learns to take responsibility for learning about the writing process through reading, scoring, and responding to the efforts of his or her peers through the use of holistic scoring.

I find that I use holistic scoring more and more. My students respond to holistic scoring and learn from it. Much of the anxiety is removed from the act of writing, for the student writer is freed from the red pen of correction, and the teacher is freed from the stress of editing and grading excessive amounts of student work.

As an added benefit, holistic scoring provides the teacher with a more objective means of evaluation, which can be demonstrated to interested parents and administrators. I have found the use of folders containing a sequential record of each student's prompts, rubrics, first drafts, and final scored papers to be an effective means of documenting students' progress as well as making my short-term and long-term composition goals clear.

Practical Ideas for Using Holistic Scoring

Prompts and Rubrics for Second Grade Teachers

By Barbara Farrell Brand

Former Teacher, Sycamore Elementary School, Orange Unified School District; and Teacher/Consultant, UCI Writing Project

I have been using a modified version of holistic scoring in my classroom since 1978. By modified, I mean that I use the concept of holistic scoring but simplify the process to make it comprehensible to my students. I have found that I get much better writing from my students when I present them with a clear prompt that specifies exactly what I want them to include in the writing assignment. But rather than evaluating them on any kind of involved point system, I have three basic categories: A Very Good Composition, A Good Composition, and a "Needs Improvement" Composition. Drawing from the directions in the prompt, I list the key elements a paper must contain in order to be very good and what elements the paper will lack if it falls short of the "very good" range. The important factor is to keep the prompt and rubric clear and simple.

Three sample prompts and rubrics that I have used with success in my class follow. My purpose in each lesson is twofold: to give students practice in using the conventions of written English (capitalization, end punctuation, possessives, and so forth) and to use imaginative and problem-solving skills in composing.

"Keep Out" Lesson

Prewriting

Review skills of sentence writing with capitalization and end punctuation.

Make available two pictures, such as girl and dog looking at an abandoned house or boy and dog looking at a Keep Out sign.

Prompt

Think of something that could happen if a child went into a place even when the sign said, "Keep Out." It could be dangerous or funny. Choose one picture to write about. Write a complete story. When you finish, mount your picture and your story on colored paper.

Writing Assignment

The teacher establishes heading, margin, and spelling standards.

Write a story of at least five sentences and:

- Tell what the child saw.
- Tell why the child went in or why the child stayed out.
- Tell what happened.

Rubric

- *A Very Good Composition*

  Has fewer than three errors in capitalization and end punctuation of sentences.

  Tells what child saw, why child went in or stayed out, and what happened.

- *A Good Composition*

  Has fewer than five errors in capitalization and end punctuation of sentences.

  Includes two of the three assigned items.

- *A "Needs Improvement" Composition*

  Has frequent sentence errors.

  Includes fewer than two of the items of information.

Postwriting

Share and display the stories.

Add-On Story

Prewriting

Enjoy the game of telling an Add-On Story (unrehearsed, with each person building on the previous sentences).

Example: The teacher or first person gives a starter:

I saw a strange animal yesterday.

Second person: The animal was eating my lunch.

Third speaker: He ate all the lunches in the school.

Fourth child: He got a terrible stomachache! (Four or five sentences usually complete a story.)

Other starters: Once upon a time there were three spiders that lived in a big web . . .

My friend and I had two dollars to spend . . .

A shiny round spaceship landed on the lawn . . .

Identify *imagination*. Encourage its use. Review skills of capitalizing and centering a title. Share rubric before children write.

Prompt

Use your imagination to write a story. Here are some starters:

My dad and I . . .
Once there was . . .
I heard a strange noise last . . .
In the spring . . .

Writing Assignment

- Make a title for your story.
- Write an imaginary story using the starter you chose.
- Tell who is in the story.
- Tell what interesting things happened.

Rubric

- *A Very Good Composition*

  Has a centered, capitalized title.
  Has fewer than three errors in capitalization and end punctuation of sentences.
  Uses one of the starter phrases, tells who is in story, and uses imagination in telling what happened.

- *A Good Composition*

  Has a title.
  Has fewer than five errors in capitalization and end punctuation of sentences.
  Includes two of the three requirements.

- *A "Needs Improvement" Composition*

  May have omitted a title.
  Has frequent sentence errors.
  Includes fewer than two of the items.

Postwriting

Partners read and hear each other's stories. Partner tells author a part he or she liked and what grade (Very Good, Good, or Needs Improvement, based on the rubric) he or she thinks it should receive. Share stories orally with class or "publish" copies.

Storefront Lesson

Prewriting

Review skills of adding 's for plurals and adding 's for possessive proper nouns. Conduct class discussion and cluster the *businesses* or *services* or both that a town needs, as shown in Figure 1.

Students choose a kind of enterprise each might like to have; draw furnishings or counter and wares inside the store (on Sheet 1); and cover with a storefront (using Sheet 2) with door, plastic window, and space for signs, as shown in Figure 2.

Prompt

Think of a store or business you might like to have. Name your business, using your name

Fig. 1. Clustering of *Businesses* for Storefront Lesson

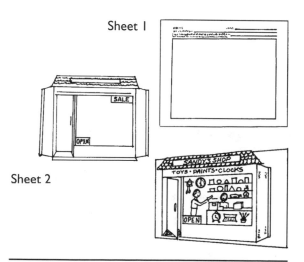

Sheet 1

Sheet 2

Fig. 2. The Storefront Lesson

and 's, and tell what you sell or do. It could be Jimmy's Supplies, and Jimmy sells pool supplies. It might be Garcia's Shop, and Miss Garcia sells records. Decide where you buy supplies and how many people work for you. Think of everything you will need to know in order to run a business.

Writing Assignment

- Make a title for your composition.
- Tell what your store or business is called.
- Tell what you sell or do.
- Tell more about your business.

Rubric

- *A Very Good Composition*
  Has a well-written title and sentences.
  Has fewer than three -s or -'s errors.
  Includes name of business, what is sold or done, and thoughtfully written details.

- *A Good Composition*
  Has acceptable title and sentences.
  Has fewer than five -s or -'s errors.
  Includes name of business, what is sold or done, and a few other details.

- *A "Needs Improvement" Composition*
  May have no title. Has frequent sentence errors.
  Has frequent -s or -'s errors.
  Includes fewer than four of the required items of information.

Postwriting

Have the partners share "stores" and stories and suggest improvements. Display storefronts and interiors in class. Discuss how the businesses might be related and interdependent.

Many elementary teachers discount holistic scoring because it seems too complicated for their students. But, if adapted, it can be just as effective at the second grade as it is at the high school or college level.

Sheet I

Name _____

Store or business _____

What do you sell, or what service do you provide? _____

Draw the inside.

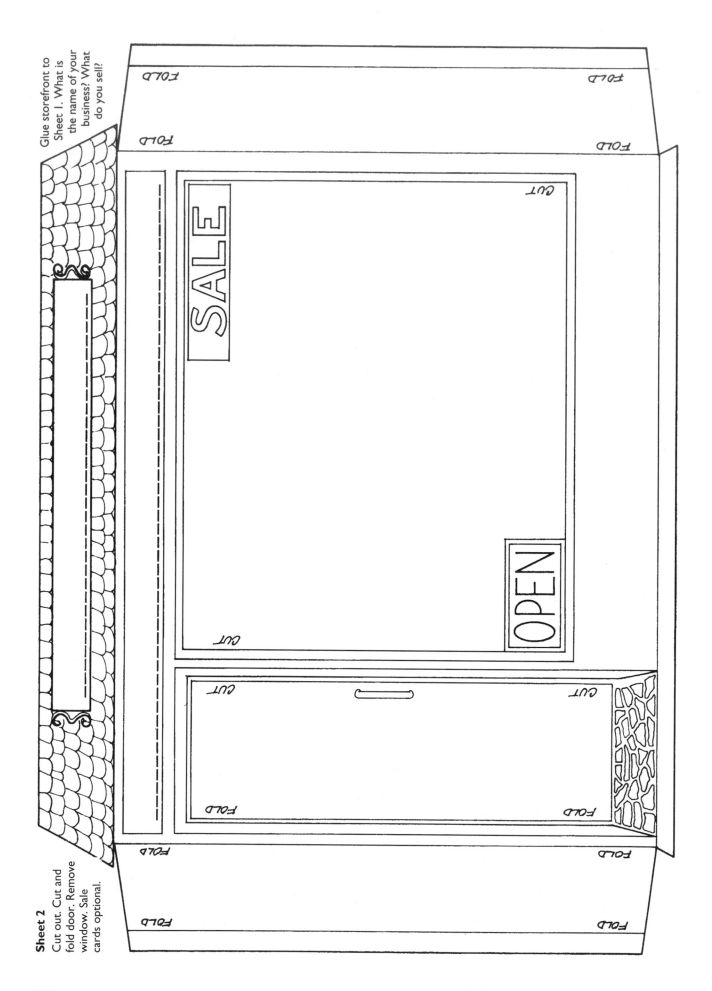

Sheet 2
Cut out. Cut and fold door. Remove window. Sale cards optional.

Glue storefront to Sheet 1. What is the name of your business? What do you sell?

SALE

OPEN

286

Using Visual Prompts for Holistic Scoring

By Pam Burris

Teacher, Masuda Middle School,
Fountain Valley Elementary School District;
and Teacher/Consultant, UCI Writing Project

A picture is worth a thousand words. That is why I often use a visual motivator when I ask children to write.

Holistic scoring has been an integral part of my writing program for the last several years. It seems to me that we create a situation for children to fail when we require them to write and then neglect to provide them with a focus, a specific situation, and a list of criteria on which they will be evaluated. Holistic scoring lends itself to making these aspects of an assignment clear.

While working on a prompt, I usually share a picture as a springboard for writing to lower the anxiety of the children and spark their imagination. The picture is a rich resource for children who lack experiences, imaginative ideas, or confidence. Total group mindmapping of words related to the picture is a great technique to use in vocabulary development of ESL students. It also provides the children with the follow-up activity of decorating or coloring the visual prompt or perhaps of creating a new picture of their own to illustrate what they have written. The written and visual

prompt appear as follows for an assignment I give called "Roller Boogie":

WRITTEN PROMPT

Imagine that you are able to skate anywhere you want to, even to a faraway country. Write a paper in which you:

- Describe your skates or roller blades. Use details and adjectives.
- Tell where you want to go and why.
- Describe your journey.

VISUAL PROMPT

Color your skates or roller blades and turn in the picture with your papers. In the background you may choose to draw a picture of the place you skate to.

After the papers have been written, the teacher has an instant "Roller Boogie" bulletin board. In fact, the pictures of the skates or roller blades can be placed all over the room.

Many sources are available to get good pictures to use as a stimulus for writing. Magazines, student-oriented publications, and newspapers contain excellent materials. Political cartoons work well for those writing about current events. Diagrams and pictures from science and social studies textbooks can easily be adapted for interdisciplinary development of children's writing skills.

Holistic Scoring and Peer Rating Groups in the Elementary Classroom

By Lois Anderson

English Teacher, Fred L. Newhart Middle School,
Capistrano Unified School District;
and Teacher/Consultant, UCI Writing Project

Although holistic scoring may seem complex and best suited for intermediate and high school students, it can also be successful at the upper elementary level. The use of holistic scoring and student rating groups has worked well for my fifth grade students. I find these activities to be worthwhile for a number of reasons. Students have an opportunity to analyze and evaluate writing similar to theirs. In doing so, they gain a clearer

In the process of rating the papers as a group, the students sharpen their awareness of the elements of good writing and develop critical thinking skills.

LOIS ANDERSON

picture of what works and what does not in their writing assignments. In addition, the process provides an audience of their peers to evaluate their writing. Often, they will take the comments received from their peers more seriously than any I make. Bonuses of the peer rating groups are the group interaction and the experiences students have of defending an opinion, reaching a compromise, and arriving at a group consensus.

The processes of introducing and using rubrics and rating groups may take several weeks. The first step is to teach the elements of the particular type of writing that the students are to learn. I usually begin with descriptive writing, so we study and practice using precise sensory descriptive words and figurative language. We then listen to several descriptive examples from literature, as well as to pieces I have written myself, and have a brainstorming session during which we list the ways the authors were able to create vivid descriptions.

At the next session I present a rubric constructed from the most important elements of our brainstorming session. I explain the purpose of a rubric, and we clarify the meaning of the statements on the scale. We use a six-point rubric, but a four-point rubric would also work well.[1] I hand out a copy of a descriptive paper from a previous year, which we read orally and then rate as a group exercise. Reaching a consensus at this point is very informal. My goal is to introduce the rubric and show how it relates to a piece of writing.

After my students have written, revised, and edited their next descriptive papers, I use the rubric as a guide, and I score each piece. I also

point to one or two elements of the paper that helped me determine the rating. Students then respond to my evaluation by writing, "I agree with my _____ rating because . . ." or "I disagree. I should have a _____ rating because . . . ." I sometimes give a letter grade to these rating responses, even though I have not graded the actual piece of writing. This approach takes some of my time, but it pays off in getting students to think carefully about evaluating their own writing.

In the next session we take a look at another student paper. This time we break into groups of four, and I introduce the use of a rating sheet. I have taken spelling and penmanship out of the rating because if I include them, students tend to concentrate on those aspects of the paper rather than on the writing itself. Later in the year, we add a 1, 2, or 3 rating for the conventions of writing, in addition to the scoring of the piece of writing itself. Students use the rating sheet and rubric to rate the piece. Then each group of four spends several minutes comparing ratings and reaching consensus. Last, we compare the ratings from all the groups and reach a group consensus.

After I prepare my students to work in independent rating groups, I teach them the procedure to use in the groups. As soon as they complete their writing assignments, I divide the students into groups of four. Each group gets four papers to rate (none from their own group). Each student reads and fills out a rating slip for a paper; then he or she passes that paper to the next person in the group until all of the students in the group have rated the four papers. Nothing is written on the paper itself; comments and ratings are marked on the rating slip, which each scorer keeps until consensus time. During this session, I insist on silence in the

---

[1] For sample rubrics, see the other articles in this section or Carol Booth Olson's article in the section titled "Writing the I-Search Paper."

classroom. Students or groups that finish early read silently or do other work silently.

When all groups have rated all four papers, I call for consensus time. At this point the members of each group compare ratings and study each piece of writing to arrive at consensus. Students present arguments in defense of the score they marked. After a few minutes, a compromise is usually made and consensus is reached.

The group score is printed at the top of the piece, and the four rating slips are attached to the paper. I collect and redistribute them to the appropriate writers. The needs of the students determine whether papers are identified by secret number or by name. My students have always wanted their names on their papers.

When students receive their papers, they respond to the ratings; then they turn in their papers, rating sheets, and responses. At this point, the teacher has a number of options:

1. Read and rate each paper.
2. Read the students' responses and make comments.
3. Do 1 and 2 above.
4. Read the papers but do not rate or grade them.
5. Skim the papers and record that the work was done, but make no comments or ratings.
6. Record the students' ratings; read only those papers in which the responses disagree with the ratings.
7. Do any combination of the above or whatever suits the program.

My students respond seriously and enthusiastically to the holistic scoring/group rating sessions. They read and consider each paper carefully because they want others to do the same for their writing. And in the process of rating the papers as a group, the students sharpen their awareness of the elements of good writing and develop critical thinking skills.

> *Holistic scoring provides more time to instruct because less time is spent evaluating the students' papers.*
>
> **GLENN PATCHELL**

Primary Trait Scoring

By Virginia Bergquist

Teacher, Meadowpark Elementary School,
Irvine School District;
and Teacher/Consultant, UCI Writing Project

Primary trait scoring (PTS) is a versatile evaluation system in which the strengths and weaknesses of student writing are described. The system, developed by the National Assessment of Educational Progress, can be adapted for use in elementary, intermediate, and high school classrooms across the curriculum and can be used to:

- Measure the presence of particular characteristics or elements of style.
- Value content, yet consider correctness in assessment.
- Create a sense of purpose and audience during prewriting.
- Provide a focus for peer interaction during sharing and revising.

The PTS system is akin to holistic scoring because it is based on a rubric or set of criteria on which a paper will be evaluated, but the scoring system differs. With PTS the person evaluates a single characteristic, or primary trait, rather than a piece of writing as a whole. PTS scoring guides focus on the most important characteristic, or critical attribute, of a successful response to a given writing prompt. Other traits may also be identified as characteristics of a successful response and evaluated as secondary traits.

The following are two examples of teacher-generated prompts and primary trait scoring guides at the elementary and high school levels:

News About Hands at School
(Kindergarten through grade three)

PROMPT

Today you are a newspaper reporter. Choose one person who works at our school that you would like to write a news story about. Choose one activity that the person does and write a news story that describes and tells how the person's hands help him or her do the activity. Since your news story will be placed in the classroom's "News About Hands at School" book, it should be interesting and informative so your classmates and other people will want to read it.

EVALUATION

Primary Trait Scoring Guide

 This news story is interesting to read. It accurately describes how a person who works at our school uses his or her hands to do his or her job.

 This news story is not as interesting as it could be. It tells about some of the person's duties but does not accurately describe how he or she uses his or her hands to do a job.

 This news story does not give enough information about how the person uses his or her hands to do the job. This lack of information made the story less interesting to read.

Secondary Trait Scoring Guide

 This paper is neat and easy to read. Fewer than three total errors were made in capitalization, punctuation, and/or spelling.

 This paper is not as neat or easy to read. Three to five total errors were made in capitalization, punctuation, and/or spelling.

 This paper is not neat or easy to read. More than five total errors were made in capitalization, punctuation, and/or spelling.

Pac Man or Kick the Can?
(Grades seven and eight)

PROMPT

Interview your grandparents or other older adults who grew up during the Depression. Ask them to describe the toys and games they remember from their childhood. Then write a three-paragraph analytical/expository essay in which you:

- *Describe* one or more toys and/or games of the Depression era, and
- *Describe* one or more toys and/or games you enjoy.

After describing the two types of toys and games, show the *similarities* and *differences* between them. From your study of toys and games, *compare* what it was like to grow up during the Depression to what it is like to grow up now.

EVALUATION

The teacher will evaluate according to the following rubric. The paper is worth a total of 10 points:

    5 points—Drawing Conclusions/Content
    3 points—Structure
    2 points—Mechanics/Format

Primary Trait—Drawing Conclusions/Content

- A *5* paper draws conclusions—compares childhood during the Depression with childhood today by giving examples of one or more toys/games from each era and by analyzing the similarities and differences of each.
- A *4* paper draws only one conclusion but otherwise fulfills the same criteria as a 5 paper.
- A *3* paper discusses only the toys/games and distinguishes between the two eras without drawing conclusions.
- A *2* paper does not discuss the similarities and differences of the toys/games in each era.
- A *1* paper does not provide sufficient detail about the toys/games or does not give one example from each era.

Secondary Traits—Structure and Mechanics/Format

STRUCTURE

- A *3* paper follows a three-paragraph structure using topic sentences, details, and transitions.
- A *2* paper omits one of the elements of a 3 paper.
- A *1* paper omits two of the elements of a 3 paper.

MECHANICS/FORMAT

- A *2* paper has neat margins, handwriting, and indentions; it uses proper spelling and capitalization and has a title.
- A *1* paper is not neat or does not follow the format given in class.
- A *0* paper addresses neither neatness nor format.

In lessons of the type just cited, the teacher can design a scoring system that weighs more heavily on the primary trait he or she wishes to highlight. For example, in the lesson on "News About Hands at School," the teacher made *an interesting story line and accuracy of description* the key elements; neatness and error-free writing were reinforced but considered as secondary to content. In the "Pac Man or Kick the Can?" scoring guide, the teacher stressed thinking skills, followed by organizational writing skills, appropriate paragraph form, and correct mechanics and grammar.

When creating the scoring guide, one must identify the purpose for writing, the audience to whom the writing will be addressed, and the domain or mode of the writing requested. Once these objectives are established, it is easy to determine the primary and secondary traits of the lesson. For instance, if the prompt asks the writer to explain how to make a peanut butter sandwich, it is of primary importance that the directions be clear and in the proper sequence in order for the reader to understand and follow them. If the writer fails to tell the reader to open the jelly jar, it will not matter how vividly he or she describes its contents.

The major goal of the PTS system is not to provide a grading or ranking device for writing. The goal is to describe the strengths and weaknesses of individual compositions so that students will understand clearly what the characteristics of a successful response are and be able to write and revise with those characteristics in mind. Having identified the primary and secondary traits, the teacher can plan prewriting activities which will help students achieve a successful response.

At the same time that the system clearly delineates for students the writing tasks they are being asked to perform, it enables the teacher to formulate his or her priorities in regard to writing instruction and to tailor assignments to foster the development of specific skills. Teachers who wish to stress fluency first and then form and correctness will find this system useful, as will teachers in

> *Primary trait scoring is a versatile evaluation system in which the strengths and weaknesses of student writing are described.*
>
> **VIRGINIA BERGQUIST**

curriculum areas other than English who wish to emphasize content. PTS can also be used to help transfer grammatical concepts, syntactical structures, and mechanical rules to students' writing, because mastery of a specific conventional skill (such as use of proper dialogue format in a narrative or the use of the colon in a descriptive essay) can be built into the scoring guide as a primary trait.

After some exposure to PTS, the students themselves will be able to contribute to the creation of primary and secondary trait scoring guides for future writing assignments. As their understanding of this process deepens, they will begin to develop an inherent set of criteria for what good writing is—not just on specific assignments, but good writing in general—and be better able to evaluate and revise their own papers before turning them in.

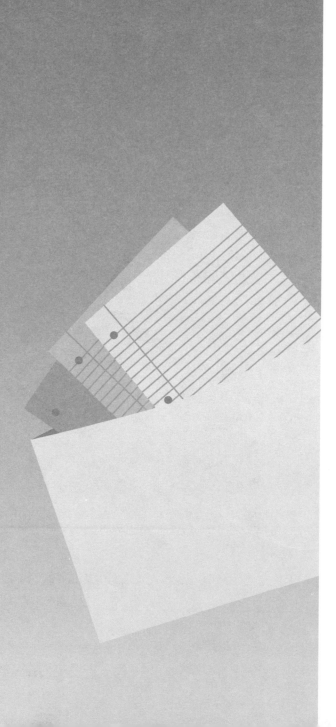

Evaluation Techniques

Some Techniques for Oral Evaluation

By Michael O'Brien

English Instructor,
Allan Hancock College, Santa Maria;
and Teacher/Consultant, UCI Writing Project

Oral evaluation of student papers is like the bicycle in my garage: neglected but patiently waiting in the corner. Well, I decided to pull oral evaluation out of the cob-webbed corner, clean up the moving parts, and try it. With the help of a lecture I heard by Dorothy Bray of Sacramento City College, I found that oral evaluation is a very effective vehicle.

My motivations for trying oral evaluation were not entirely selfless: I got very tired of grading papers after school or at home. Also, I got frustrated about how my carefully written comments were either neglected or misunderstood. So I began to evaluate papers orally in class. I found through my own experience and from listening to Dr. Bray at a meeting of the University of California at Irvine's Writing Project that the following techniques are effective:

1. I assign papers of about 400 words so that I can evaluate six or seven of them in a 50-minute period and, thus, can plan on completing a class set in about five days.
2. While I work individually with a student at my desk, the others are working on writing assignments or on work sheets to help them in areas of weakness.
3. I structure the conference to the needs of each student by asking at the outset whether he or she had any problem or questions with the writing of the paper.
4. I try to give favorable comments early if I sense that the student has given a good effort. (The oral evaluation is a much more positive experience because written evalua-

EDITOR'S NOTE: We are grateful to the National Council of Teachers of English for granting us permission to reprint this article, which appeared in the January, 1982, issue of the *English Journal.*

I have each student bring his or her journal to the conference to record my comments, both favorable and critical. Thus, the student has a log where he or she keeps all of my comments.

MICHAEL O'BRIEN

tions tend to be overwhelmingly negative, no matter how I try.)

5. In my criticisms I try to cover one or two major problems, realizing that this is about as much as most of the students can work on at one time.

6. I give the student a chance to respond and ask questions. Often, a short explanation can clear up major concerns.

7. I have each student bring his or her journal to the conference to record my comments, both favorable and critical. Thus, the student has a log where he or she keeps all of my comments. This approach is very effective for isolating chronic problems and areas of improvement.

8. I do not grade the assignment. After doing two or more of the same type of paper, the student will choose the one that has the most promise and rewrite it. Then I evaluate the final copy and grade it in the traditional way.

After using this method in my three composition classes for one quarter of a school year not long ago, I asked the students to write their anonymous responses to the following questions:

1. Should we continue oral evaluations?
2. If so, why? If not, why not?
3. How would you suggest they be improved?

Of 98 students all but one felt we should continue. This was a typical comment about why we should continue:

Yes, I would like to see oral evaluations continue. I get a much better understanding of whether or not my paper is well written. You can explain things in detail whereas you couldn't simply by writing down comments. I also like being able to tell you what I think is wrong with my paper and learning if it is or it isn't.

To the question regarding suggested improvements, most students had none to suggest. Some, however, were frustrated that it took me five days to get to the last students. Others felt that I should have taken more time with each paper. Both of these were valid concerns, but I could solve these problems only by having smaller classes, a solution that was not in my power, unfortunately.

I do not purport that my informal survey is conclusive evidence that oral evaluation works. And, certainly, little in the professional literature either confirms or denies the effectiveness of oral evaluation. For example, the Educational Resources Information Center (ERIC) lists only one study, done from 1967 to 1980, and it was deemed inconclusive. But in my experience oral evaluation has increased appreciably the effectiveness of my teaching while decreasing the time I spend after school grading papers. No, I do not spend my extra time bike riding. (My bike is still in the garage, the old tires rotting.) I spend it doing lesson plans.

The teacher is a facilitator of the writing/learning process by creating an environment that is conducive to learning; assigning writing is not the same thing as teaching writing.

JAMES R. GRAY

Practical Ideas for Evaluation

The Writing Folder: A System for Responding to Students' Writing

By Jim Hahn

English Teacher, Fairfield High School,
Fairfield-Suisun Unified School District;
and Teacher/Consultant, Bay Area Writing Project

I have been marking papers and wrestling with the problem of responding to student writing for ten years. I have found that traditional systems of feedback trap us in the frustrating cycle of myriad comments and corrections aimed at students who continue to make the same errors. The frustration stems from these areas: there are too many papers to mark, the students do not read our comments, and the same students make the same errors again and again, regardless of how often we point them out. An analysis of the process of responding to students' writing will help illuminate some of the causes of these problems.

Part of the problem with providing feedback on papers is that we try to do too many things at once. If we take all the marks teachers put on students' papers, we could place them in three categories: (1) comments related to content and organization; (2) notations related to grammar, mechanics, and spelling; and (3) remarks related to evaluation. Each of these categories sends a different message to students. A comment on content implies that the students will rewrite the composition to correct the problem. A mark about grammar or mechanics implies that the students need to make minor corrections to solve the problems. Marks of evaluation, such as grades or even statements like "Good work," imply that the composition is finished. When we consider all of these areas simultaneously, we are telling our students (1) rewrite and rethink the paper; (2) correct the paper, but do not necessarily rethink it; and (3) the paper is finished. Given the three choices, it is no wonder that our students seldom do more than look at the grade. I shudder every time I think of the number of hours I spent commenting on student papers only to find them in the wastebasket soon after I passed them back.

The frustration teachers often feel after responding to and returning papers is easily explained when one realizes that students and teachers are both trying to save time while dealing with the difficult task of writing. On the one hand, teachers, pressed for time, develop shorthand methods for communicating with the student.

awk. frag. rts. ¶ #

On the other hand, students, who are also in a hurry, usually accept the grade, ignore the cryptic marks, relegate writing to the realm of things they will never master, and throw their papers in a nearby trash can.

If marking the papers for content and grammar and evaluating them should not be done simultaneously, then the next step is to find out when to do what. (See Figure 1 for a diagram showing what you may want to emphasize during each stage of the writing process.)

Comments about content and organization are pertinent at several stages in the process. They can help clarify thinking anywhere from the prewriting to the revising stages. The conventions of writing belong to the editing stage. If you make notations to your student writers regarding conventions (spelling, grammar, and so forth) too early in the process, they will correct the word or sentence; but then they often will find it very difficult to revise the content of the paper later because they are committed to the correct form, regardless of the sense (or nonsense) of the passage. Since evaluations, especially letter grades, imply that the work is finished, they should be used only at the end of the process.

Acceptance of the preceding analysis leads us overworked teachers to the unwelcome conclusion that instead of marking papers once, we should mark them three separate times, with the student making changes after each step. If I had to teach

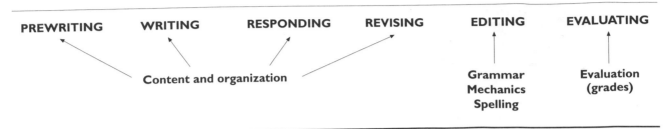

PREWRITING   WRITING   RESPONDING   REVISING   EDITING   EVALUATING

Content and organization

Grammar
Mechanics
Spelling

Evaluation
(grades)

Fig. 1. Items to Emphasize in Each Stage of the Writing Process

only one person to write, I might do that; however, with 150 to teach each semester, I look for options. I have designed a system for responding to writing at different stages in the composing process; and the system, which I will describe in the paragraphs that follow, provides students with feedback they can use and alleviates some of the burden of the paper load.

Students are constantly collapsing the writing process by taking shortcuts. Our job as teachers is to expand the process—to get students to think and rethink their work as much as possible. The writing process (and, consequently, the learning process) is kept open when evaluation is postponed as long as possible. Instituting writing folders for all written work helps accomplish this. Students often wish to throw out old papers. (If the papers have been graded, why should they be kept?) However, if the papers are evaluated en masse at the end of the grading period, the writing folders can be evaluated by the teacher or by the teacher and student in conference, or they can be self-evaluated by the student. The use of these folders has the added benefit of teaching students to be responsible for their work while demonstrating how much they have learned.

All of my students keep writing folders, which they must turn in to me at the end of a grading period (anywhere from two weeks to a semester in length) to get credit for their work. I collect these folders intermittently to provide feedback on the students' work, but I withhold grades until the end of the grading period. Before the students turn in work in progress for my review, I ask them to fill out a cover sheet that includes a self-evaluation of their paper, a classmate's comments on the piece, and a space for my response (see Figure 2).

You will note that the cover sheet (Figure 2) also requires the signature of three proofreaders. When

we teachers correct our students' errors, we train them to be lazy proofreaders. I transfer this responsibility to the students by making them the editors of each other's work. In the same way that students gain an intuitive sense of the criteria for good writing by participating as peer respondents to the work of others, they can improve their grasp of grammatical concepts and mechanical rules when they must be attentive to the conventions of written English in their classmates' papers. When a question arises, I can always serve as a resource.

In order for the students to track their progress, I also have them use a paper log sheet that is kept in each student's folder (see Figure 3). Students transfer the comments from the cover sheets of individual papers (theirs, a peer partner's, and mine) to this cumulative log. Now, they can begin to see that writing is a craft that one can improve with practice. In addition to gaining ideas for revising specific pieces of writing, they can recognize how the assignments fit together as a sequence and determine what skills they need to strengthen in future papers.

All of my students' writing goes into their folders, but I do not necessarily read or evaluate everything. Much writing is only for practice, and some rough drafts are not meant to be final copies. I can spot-check the folders at intervals throughout the semester, establish a set grading period, and evaluate an entire body of work as a whole. I require that certain assignments be revised for evaluation, or I allow my students to select from their folders items for review that they believe represent their best work.

Once students become used to the writing folder and accept the idea that developing writing ability involves practice and that not every draft must be evaluated, teachers will no longer become "bottlenecks in the writing process," and students can write as much as they need to.

295

Cover Sheet

Name _____

Title _____

Date _____

Proofreaders

1. _____

2. _____

3. _____

Author's Comments

The thing I like most about this paper is _____

_____

_____

_____

The thing I like least about this paper is _____

_____

_____

_____

The things I tried to improve in this paper are _____

_____

_____

_____

_____

Student's comments _____

_____

_____

_____

_____

_____

_____

Teacher's comments _____

_____

_____

_____

_____

Things to work on in your next paper are _____

_____

_____

_____

_____

_____

Fig. 2. Evaluation Sheet for Student's Writing

Name _____

Topic	Title	What I tried to improve	What I need to work on in my next paper

Fig. 3. Log of Student's Writing

Adding an Analytical Commentary to Holistic Scoring

By Carol Booth Olson
Director, UCI Writing Project

I have found holistic scoring to be a fair, fast, and efficient method of providing comprehensible evaluative feedback on student papers. But, in its pure form, it does not allow for the descriptive feedback that most students need in order to determine what specific skills they should work on to improve future papers. Not only do students need this input, but I feel *guilty* if I do not provide them with it. It just does not seem equitable for a teacher to require students to write and then not respond with some form of written commentary of his or her own. On the other hand, I do not want to fall back into my old habit of spending hours writing essays in response to students' essays.

I think I have come up with a workable solution to this dilemma. I read each student's paper, give it a holistic score, and then fill out a form which breaks down the paper into its key elements: quality of thought, structure, diction, syntax, and so forth. Each assignment requires a slightly different form.

The categories for my analytical response sheet come straight from the rubric on which the paper is evaluated. For example, here is the scoring guide I developed for a 9—8 paper (on a 1—9 scale) for "A Sample Prompt, Scoring Guide, and Model Paper for the I-Search," which appears earlier in this book:

9—8   This paper is clearly superior. It is well written, clearly organized, insightful, and technically correct. A 9—8 paper exhibits most or all of the following characteristics:

- Writing the paper was a genuine learning experience for the writer, and a person would benefit greatly from reading the paper.
- The paper displays evidence of critical thinking and offers special insight into the topic discussed.
- The topic lends itself to investigation and discovery.

- The paper is written in three sections. (The format may be explicit or implicit.):
  - What I know, assume, or imagine (prior to the search)
  - The search (testing knowledge, assumptions, or conjecture through documented research)
  - What I discovered (comparing what you thought you knew with what you learned and offering commentary and conclusions)
- The author takes an active role rather than a passive role in the search.
- The writer uses research effectively as a supplement to, but not as a substitute for, his or her own ideas.
- The paper's tone and point of view convey a clear sense of the author's voice or style.
- The writer uses precise, apt, or descriptive language.
- The main points of the essay are well supported with examples.
- The writer uses ample transitions between ideas, paragraphs, and sections.
- The writer varies sentence structure and length.
- The search portion of the essay is properly documented with footnotes in correct form.
- The paper contains references to a minimum of two primary and two secondary research sources.
- The paper includes a formal bibliography.
- The writer generally uses effectively the conventions of written English.

I use an abbreviated list of the criteria from the scoring guide to establish the headings for my feedback:

**Overall Comments and Suggestions
    for Improvement
Paper as Learning Experience
Analysis of the Three Sections
Research (Quality and Quantity)
Support with Examples
Transition
Author's Role
Footnotes and Bibliography
Diction
Syntax
Conventions of Written English**

Paper's score _____

Although I feel compelled to provide students with a written reaction to their work, I am also one of those people who eagerly embraces almost any opportunity to procrastinate. I find that having a response sheet makes the task of evaluating students' papers seem less formidable. I get to the job earlier and keep on task because the headings and the limited space provided (I try to keep the form to one page) necessitate that I keep focused and to the point. When filling out the form, I write a brief paragraph of four to five sentences in length in which I share my general reactions to the piece—in terms of both its strengths and its weaknesses. Beyond that initial remark, I do not feel obligated to write in complete sentences. If an "OK," "Nice work," or "More specific examples needed" will do, I leave it at that. If more explanation is required, then I provide it.

Adding an analytical commentary to holistic scoring has eased my conscience in regard to my responsibility to give students feedback on their written work. The method is certainly not as fast as using holistic scoring alone. But it is still more efficient than coming to each student's essay with a blank piece of paper and an undefined set of expectations, on the one hand, or an elaborate system of points for each component of the writing assignment, on the other. In my opinion, this combination is the best of both worlds.

Portfolio Assessment

By Catherine D'Aoust

Coordinator, Instructional Services,
Saddleback Valley Unified School District;
and Codirector, UCI Writing Project

One of the greatest challenges faced by writing teachers is assessment. Despite the fact that the National Writing Project and the writing reform movement in general have encouraged teachers to adopt a process approach to teaching composition, most teachers still rely solely on finished products to determine grades for students' writing. So, while the classroom pedagogy fosters the discovery and development of writing as a process—namely, the discovery by each student of his or her unique writing process—the assessment component continues to value only the final stage of that process. The challenge for today's teachers is how to grade students' writing in a way that reflects both the process and the product. One method that addresses these dual concerns is portfolio assessment.

Portfolios are more than just "storage bins" for students' papers. Borrowed from the tradition of portfolios in the arts, a writing portfolio is an ongoing representation of a student's ability to generate and craft thought. Through the portfolio, which contains numerous pieces of writing, the teacher has access to a student's processes as well as to her or his products. By piecing together numerous pieces of writing, the teacher begins to complete the puzzle of process and development in writing. The teacher has evidence of a student's writing as a process in generating ideas, taking risks, making errors, revising, and so forth. Rather than looking at a student's writing as an isolated *product*, the teacher can view in the portfolio the panorama of each student's struggle to capture and convey thought through writing.

Classroom writing portfolios seem to be taking one of two forms. *Process portfolios*, sometimes called *working* or *evolving* portfolios, are collections of all that a student writes over a period of time, which may be a quarter, a semester, a year, or several years. These portfolios include finished and unfinished pieces as well as ideas for future writing. They may include writing from a single subject area, or they may represent cross-curricular or thematic writing.

Another type of portfolio is the *exemplary portfolio*, sometimes called a *résumé* or *representative* portfolio. The writing in this portfolio represents the best writing by a student. It may include various pieces of writing in a particular genre or a representative piece from a variety of genres. The decision about what is "best" can be made by the student, the teacher, or a collaboration of both.

Often a teacher may use both types of portfolios. Students collect all their writing in the process portfolios; from that collection, they can create an exemplary portfolio. For example, the process portfolio may be a large manila folder that holds a brightly colored exemplary folder within it.

Within either type of portfolio, students often include *metacognitive responses* to their writing. These responses direct the student's attention to their writing and create awareness of their own processes. Through these responses, students listen to and learn from their inner voices as they become better writers. A metacognitive entry might describe the process a student used in generating a piece of writing, how the student overcame writer's block, how the student feels about himself or herself as a writer, what strategies the student will use in future writing, and so forth. The following are three examples of metacognitive responses from students at different grade levels:

> Joel wanted to see more "showing, not telling details" in my story. Sometimes, though, it is much better to tell. Often, in casual writing, we tell. When a book or story is told in first person like mine is, its point is to think like that person. Usually one doesn't talk or think in a show, not tell method. So, here it is better to tell as the first person sees things.
>
> *Karli—Eighth grade*

> The dialectal journal provided me with a relatively easy method by which I could get my initial thought formalized. Generally, this is a difficult step that requires much trial-and-error. But I now find that I can allow my thoughts to lead wherever they might—and still be able to find a "theme" within.
>
> *Arthur—12th grade*

> How do I transform my thoughts into writing? Hmm . . . I grasp onto one thing, a symbol, a moment, a color, a feeling. I feel and think with the camera eye. Then I mull and stew, compare it, contrast it, synthesize, humanize my symbol, hopefully twist it into a new shape or feeling, different from the trite. From there, I knock it out without thinking; then I go over and over and over it, rewrite. Mostly, if it is good, the guts are out on the page. My first write is 80% good or basic stuff; then a lot of throwing out goes on. Finally, I edit, but it is a two-week process. I live inside of it. Sometimes, I go into great pain—and I know it because it is part of the process. But when I really write something good, the child in me feels a certain awe and wonder (I'm still a knobby-kneed little kid about it), and I am pleased. I feel as if I have shared or done something, so I trudge on willingly.
>
> *Chris—University*

> *The challenge for today's teachers is how to grade students' writing in a way that reflects both the process and the product.*
>
> **CATHERINE D'AOUST**

In some cases, the teacher determines what types and how many pieces of writing are included in the portfolio. Other teachers believe that the power of the portfolio resides in each student's making that choice. In this situation, a teacher asks students to choose for their exemplary portfolios those pieces that are representative of their progress as writers. The degree of direction provided by the teacher depends on the needs of the students and, of course, on the reason for using portfolios in the first place. In both instances, a major strength of the portfolio is that students can "travel" through their portfolios, review their writing over a period of time, and gain an understanding of themselves as writers.

Teachers grade portfolios in a number of ways. Some teachers give points for everything that is included in the process portfolio: prewriting activities, first drafts, revisions, final products, unfinished products, metacognitive entries, and so forth. Other teachers grade all finished products but have students choose those which will be included in their exemplary portfolios. Their final grade becomes the average of the graded products in their portfolios. In some instances, the teacher encourages students to evaluate their own writing, and the final grade is a collaboration between the teacher and the student. If the assessment is to be authentic and legitimate, it should be the natural outcome of a process in which students generate both finished and unfinished texts, experiment and take risks, discover more about themselves as writers, and gain confidence as writers.

Portfolios are not just "containers" for a year's samples of writing. Besides providing a means of addressing the assessment issues of process and product, they are also symbols of students' struggles with the written word and of their eventual victories. Finally, portfolios provide students tangible proof that they are, indeed, writers.

Selected References

This list of selected references was compiled from the publications cited in this document. The references are organized according to whether they are works of literature, other sources, or publications about writing.

Literature

Some works of literature cited in this section may be available from more than one publisher. For such citations only the title and the author's name are listed. Publishers' names are listed if a work is available from only one publisher or if an author of an article identified or quoted from a work from a certain publisher. Works of literature are listed below the articles in *Practical Ideas* in which they appear.

Prewriting in the Elementary School

A Potpourri of Prewriting Ideas for the Elementary Teacher—Virginia Bergquist

    Allinson, Beverly. *Mitzi's Magic Garden*. Westport, Conn.: Garrard Publishing Co., 1971.

    Brown, Margaret W. *The Important Book*. New York: Harper & Row Pubs., Inc., 1949.

    Jensen, Virginia A. *Sara and the Door*. Reading, Mass.: Addison-Wesley Publishing Co., Inc., 1977.

    Katz, Bobbi. *Nothing but a Dog*. Old Westbury, N.Y.: Feminist Press, 1972.

    Martin, Bill, Jr. *David Was Mad*, one of the Kin-der Owl Books. New York: Holt, Rinehart & Winston, Inc., 1971.

    Mizumura, Kazue. *If I Were a Cricket*. New York: Harper & Row Pubs., Inc., 1973.

    Simon, Norma. *I Know What I Like*. Niles, Ill.: Albert Whitman & Company, 1971.

    Zolotow, Charlotte. *Janey*. New York: Harper & Row, Pubs., Inc., 1973.

The Rock Experience—Erline S. Krebs

    Baylor, Byrd. *Everybody Needs a Rock*. New York: Charles Scribner's Sons, 1974.

Developing Fluency Through Poetic Dialogue—Michael Carr and Erline S. Krebs

    Lurie, Toby. *Conversations and Constructions*. 1429 Page St., Apt. E, San Francisco, CA 94117, 1978.

    Sandburg, Carl. "Summer Grass," in *Good Morning, America*. New York: Harcourt Brace Jovanovich, Inc., 1928, 1956.

Pattern Writing with Novels for Elementary School Students—Elizabeth Williams Reeves

    Twain, Mark. *The Adventures of Tom Sawyer*.

Showing, Not Telling

A Training Program for Student Writers—Rebekah Caplan

    Doctorow, E. L. *The Book of Daniel*. New York: Random House, Inc., 1971.

Using Cooperative Learning to Facilitate Writing

Using Structures to Promote Cooperative Learning in Writing—Jeanne M. Stone and Spencer S. Kagan

    The Three Billy Goats Gruff

Cooperative Writing for Little Ones (Kindergarten Through Second Grade)—Lorna Curran

    Lionni, Leo. *The Alphabet Tree*. New York: Alfred A. Knopf Books for Young Readers, 1990.

Fable Writing: A Lesson from Aesop . . . and Spencer Kagan—Linda Bautista-Pappert

    Aesop's Fables. Edited by Michael Hague. New York: Henry Holt and Company, Inc., 1985.

Teaching Writing in the Culturally and Linguistically Diverse Classroom

The Missing Piece: Enhancing Self-Esteem Through Exposure to Culturally Diverse Literature—Pamela Jones

    An extensive list of selected works of literature appropriate for culturally and linguistically diverse students in kindergarten through grade eight appears at the end of this article.

A Literature Unit of Study About Vietnamese Children—Lea Kiapos

    Surat, Michele Maria. *Angel Child, Dragon Child*.

My Name, My Self—Brenda Borron

Cisneros, Sandra. *The House on Mango Street*. New York: Random House, 1991.

Haley, Alex. *Roots*.

Heller, Joseph. "Major, Major," in *Catch Twenty-Two*. *Lives of the Saints*

Martin, Bill, Jr., and John Archambault. *Knots on a Counting Rope*. New York: Henry Holt and Company, Inc., 1987.

Megged, Aharon. "The Name." Translated by Minna Givton. In *Israeli Stories*. Edited by Joel Blocker. New York: Schocken Books, Inc., 1962.

Wolff, Tobias. *This Boy's Life: A Memoir*. New York: Harper Collins Publishers, Inc., 1990.

Getting Off Track: Core Literature for All Students— Mifanwy Patricia Kaiser and Michelle Lindfors

Conrad, Joseph. *The Heart of Darkness*.

Eliot, T. S. "The Hollow Men."

Hawthorne, Nathaniel. *The Scarlet Letter*.

Miller, Arthur. *Death of a Salesman*.

Sophocles. *Oedipus Rex*.

Domains of Writing

Expanding the Different Domains of Writing — Julie Simpson

Little Red Riding Hood

Teaching Practical/Informative Writing Through Novels—Elizabeth Williams Reeves

Tolkein, J. R. R. *The Hobbit*. Boston: Houghton Mifflin Company, 1966.

Point of View in Writing

A Lesson on Point of View . . . That Works— Carol Booth Olson

Steinbeck, John. *Of Mice and Men*.

A Seventh Grade Approach to Point of View— Marie Filardo

Simon, Marcia L. *A Special Gift*. New York: Harcourt Brace Jovanovich, Inc., 1978.

A Parent's Point of View—Dale Sprowl

Jackson, Shirley. *Charles*.

The New Kid—Mark Reardon

Heyert, Murray. "The New Kid" in *Stories*. Edited by Frank G. Jennings and Charles J. Calitri. New York: Harcourt Brace Jovanovich, Inc., 1957.

When Clay Sings: A Point of View Lesson Integrating Art, Writing, History, and Literature—Erline S. Krebs and Mindy Moffatt

Baylor, Byrd. *When Clay Sings*. New York: Charles Scribner's Sons, 1972.

Writing the I-Search Paper

A Sample Prompt, Scoring Guide, and Model Paper for the I-Search—Carol Booth Olson

Cherry, Lynne. *The Great Kapok Tree: A Tale of the Amazon Rain Forest*. New York: Harcourt Brace Jovanovich, Inc., 1990.

Critical Thinking and Writing

Adapting Dan Kirby's Portfolio to the Study of a Novel—Esther Severy

Taylor, Mildred D. *Roll of Thunder, Hear My Cry*.

Weaving an Autobiographical Web from Kirby's "Spider Pieces"—Julie Simpson

Anaya, Rudolfo A. *The Legend of Llorona*. Berkeley: TQS Publications, Inc., 1984.

Best Short Stories by Negro Writers. Edited by Langston Hughes. New York: Little, Brown and Company, 1969.

Book of Animal Poems. Edited by William Cole. New York: Viking Press, 1973.

Burnett, Frances Hodgson. *The Secret Garden*. New York: NAL/Dutton, 1989.

Cisneros, Sandra. *The House on Mango Street*. New York: Random House, Inc., 1991.

Galarza, Ernesto. *Barrio Boy*. Notre Dame, Ind.: University of Notre Dame Press, 1971.

Hughes, Langston. *Something in Common and Other Stories*. New York: Hill and Wang, Inc., 1963.

Jackson, Shirley. *Charles*. Mankato, Minn.: Creative Education, Inc., 1991.

Poems for Red Letter Days. Edited by Elizabeth H. Sechrist. Philadelphia: Macrae Smith Company, 1951.

Poetry of Cats. Illustrated by Samuel Carr. Stamford, Conn.: Longmeadow Press, 1991.

Thurber, James. *My Life and Hard Times*. New York: HarperCollins, 1990.

Thurber, James. *Thurber's Dogs*. New York: Simon and Schuster Trade, 1992.

We Become New: Poems by Contemporary American Women. Edited by Lucille Iverson and Kathryn Ruby. New York: Bantam Books, Inc., 1975.

Tapping Multiple Intelligences Through the Literature Book Project—Carol Booth Olson

Carle, Eric. *The Very Hungry Caterpillar*. New York: Philomel Books, 1969.

Cole, Joanna. *The Magic School Bus: Inside the Human Body*. New York: Scholastic, Inc., 1990.

Hodgson, Frances Burnett. *The Secret Garden*. New York: Bantam Books, 1987.

Juster, Norton. *The Phantom Tollbooth*. New York: Random House, Inc., 1961.

Kalan, Robert. *Jump, Frog, Jump*. New York: Greenwillow Books, 1981.

Reader Responses

Dialogue with a Text—Robert E. Probst

Bryan, C. D. B. "So Much Unfairness of Things," in *Literature and Life*. Edited by Helen McDonnell and others. Glenview, Ill.: Scott, Foresman and Company, 1979.

Responding to a Reader Response: An Adaptation for Kindergarten Through Grade Six—Based on *Knots on a Counting Rope* —Sandi Wright

Martin, Bill, Jr., and John Archambault. *Knots on a Counting Rope*. New York: Henry Holt and Co., Inc., 1987.

Reader Response Logs—Jenee Gossard

The last page of this article contains a list of 12 selections for introducing readers' logs.

Strategies for Interacting with a Text—Carol Booth Olson

Williams, Margery. *The Velveteen Rabbit: Or How Toys Become Real*.

Sharing What Belongs to You: Minilessons and Lit Letters—Joni Chancer

Bellairs, John. *The House with a Clock in Its Walls*.

Conrad, Pam. *Prairie Songs*. New York: HarperCollins Children's Books, 1987.

Cooper, Susan. *The Dark Is Rising*.

Paterson, Katherine. *Bridge to Terabithia*.

Smith, Dorris B. *A Taste of Blackberries*.

Singer, Marilyn. *Ghost Host*. New York: Scholastic, Inc., 1988.

Building Vocabularies

Verbal Density: Expanding Students' Use of Verbs—Evelyn Ching

Connell, Richard E. "The Most Dangerous Game" in *Stories*. Edited by Frank G. Jennings and Charles J. Calitri. New York: Harcourt Brace Jovanovich, Inc., 1957.

Other Sources

"Building Bilingual Instruction: Putting the Pieces Together," *BEOUTREACH*, Vol. 3, No. 1 (February, 1992), 6–8.

Chute, Marchette. *An Introduction to Shakespeare*. New York: E.P. Dutton and Co., Inc. 1951.

Gardner, Howard. *Frames of Mind: The Theory of Multiple Intelligences*. New York: Basic Books, Inc., 1983.

Gardner, Howard, and Thomas Hatch. "Multiple Intelligences Go to School: Educational Implications of the Theory of Multiple Intelligences," *Educational Reseacher*, Vol. 18, No. 8 (November, 1989), 4–9.

Goodman, Yetta M., and Carolyn L. Burke. *Reading Strategies: Focus on Comprehension*. Katonah, N.Y.: Richard C. Owen Publishers, Inc., 1980.

Hadamard, Jacques. *An Essay on the Psychology of Invention in the Mathematical Field*. Princeton, N.J.: Princeton University Press, 1945.

Johnson, Roger, and David Johnson. *Learning Together and Learning Alone*. Englewood Cliffs, N.J.: Prentice Hall, Inc., 1987.

Kagan, Spencer S., and Laurie Robertson. *Cooperative Learning: Coop Across the Curriculum*. San Juan Capistrano, Calif.: Kagan Cooperative Learning, 1993. (Binder containing charts and handouts)

Krashen, Stephen. *The Input Hypothesis: Issues and Implications*. New York: Longman, 1985.

Krashen, Stephen. *Insights and Inquiries*. Hayward, Calif.: Alemany Press, 1985.

Krashen, Stephen, and Tracy Terrell. *The Natural Approach*. New York: Pergamon Press, 1983.

Kunjufu, Jawanza. *Developing Positive Self-Images and Discipline in Black Children*. Chicago: African American Images, 1984.

Model Curriculum Standards, Grades Nine Through Twelve. Sacramento: California Department of Education, 1985.

Nature's Course. Perspectives in Environmental Education: Tropical Rain Forests. Vol. 2, No. 2 (November/December, 1993).

Resnik, Lauren. *ASCD Update* (February, 1990).

Scarcella, Robin. *Teaching Language Minority Students in the Multicultural Classroom*. Englewood Cliffs, N.J.: Prentice Hall, Inc., 1990.

Scarcella, Robin, and Rebecca Oxford. *The Tapestry of Language Learning: The Individual in the Communicative Classroom*. Boston: Heinle and Heinle, 1991.

Schön, Donald. *Educating the Reflective Practitioner: Toward a New Design of Teaching and Learning in the Professions*. San Francisco: Jossey-Bass, 1987.

Schaughnessy, Michael. "An Interview with Robert J. Sternberg," *Human Intelligence* (spring/summer, 1986).

Taxonomy of Educational Objectives: The Classification of Educational Goals. Handbook I: Cognitive Domain. Edited by Benjamin S. Bloom. New York: David McKay Company, Inc., 1956.

Whitehead, Alfred North. *The Aims of Education*. New York: Free Press, a Division of Macmillan Publishing Co., Inc., 1967.

Wiggins, Grant, "The Futility of Trying to Teach Everything of Importance," *Educational Leadership*, Vol. 47, No. 3 (November, 1989), 44–48; 57–59.

Publications About Writing

Atwell, Nancie. *In the Middle: Writing, Reading, and Learning with Adolescents.* Portsmouth, N.H.: Boynton Cook Publishers, Inc., 1987.

Barrs, Myra, and others. *Primary Language Record: Handbook for Teachers.* Portsmouth, N.H.: Heinemann Educational Books, Inc., 1989.

Berthoff, Ann. *The Making of Meaning: Metaphors, Models, and Maxims for Writing Teachers.* Upper Montclair, N.J.: Boynton Cook Publishers, Inc., 1981.

Britton, James, and others. *The Development of Writing Abilities (11–18).* (Schools Council Research Studies) Houndmills Basingstoke, Hampshire: Macmillan Education Ltd., 1975.

Calkins, Lucy. *The Art of Teaching Writing.* Portsmouth, N.H.: Heinemann Educational Books, Inc., 1989.

Caplan, Rebekah. *Writers in Training: A Guide to Developing a Composition Program.* Palo Alto: Dale Seymour Publications, 1984.

Caplan, Rebekah, and Catherine Keech. *Showing Writing: A Training Program to Help Students Be Specific.* Berkeley: Bay Area Writing Project, University of California, 1980.

Cooper, Charles. "An Outline for Writing Sentence-Combining Problems," in *The Writing Teacher's Sourcebook.* Edited by Gary Tate and Edward P. Corbett. New York: Oxford University Press, Inc., 1981.

Curran, Lorna. *Cooperative Learning Lessons for Little Ones: Language Arts Edition.* San Juan Capistrano, Calif.: Resources for Teachers, 1990.

Elbow, Peter. *Writing with Power: Techniques for Mastering the Writing Process.* New York: Oxford University Press, Inc., 1981.

Elbow, Peter. *Writing Without Teachers.* New York: Oxford University Press, Inc., 1975.

Enright, D. Scott, and Mary Lou McCloskey. *Integrating English: Developing English Language and Literacy in the Multilingual Classroom.* Reading, Mass.: Addison-Wesley Publishing Co., Inc., 1988.

Flower, Linda. *Problem-Solving Strategies for Writing.* New York: Harcourt Brace Jovanovich, Inc., 1981.

Graves, Donald H. *Balance the Basics: Let Them Write.* New York: Ford Foundation, 1978.

Graves, Donald H. "We Won't Let Them Write: Research Update," *Language Arts*, Vol. 55 (May, 1978), 635–40.

Graves, Donald. *Writing: Teachers and Children at Work.* Portsmouth, N.H.: Heinemann Educational Books, Inc., 1989.

Handbook for Planning an Effective Writing Program, Kindergarten Through Grade Twelve (Revised edition). Sacramento: California Department of Education, 1986.

Healy, Mary K. *Using Student Writing Response Groups in the Classroom.* Berkeley: Bay Area Writing Project, University of California, 1980.

The Journal Book. Edited by Toby Fulwiler. Portsmouth, N.H.: Boynton Cook Publishers, Inc., 1987.

Kagan, Spencer S. *Cooperative Learning.* San Juan Capistrano, Calif.: Kagan Cooperative Learning, 1992.

Kirby, Dan, and Carol Kuykendall. *Mind Matters: Teaching for Thinking.* Portsmouth, N.H.: Boynton Cook Publishers, Heinemann Educational Books, Inc., 1991.

Levine, Harold. *Vocabulary for the High School Student.* New York: AMSCO School Publications, Inc., 1983.

Lomax, William. "Sentence Combining Across the Curriculum," *California English*, Vol. 16 (November-December, 1980), 18–21.

Macrorie, Ken. *The I-Search Paper* (Revised edition). Portsmouth, N.H.: Boynton Cook Publishers, Inc., 1988.

Macrorie, Ken. *Searching Writing.* Rochelle Park, N.J.: Hayden Book Company, Inc., 1980.

Macrorie, Ken. *Twenty Teachers.* New York: Oxford University Press, Inc., 1985.

Moffett, James. *Active Voice: A Writing Program Across the Curriculum* (Second edition). Portsmouth, N.H.: Boynton Cook Publishers, Inc., 1992.

Murray, Donald M. "Internal Revision: A Process of Discovery," in *Learning by Teaching: Selected Articles on Writing and Teaching.* Upper Montclair, N.J.: Boynton Cook Publishers, Inc., 1982.

O'Hare, Frank. *Sentence-Combining: Improving Student Writing Without Formal Grammar Instruction.* Urbana, Ill.: National Council of Teachers of English, 1973.

Olson, Carol Booth. "Personalizing Research in the I-Search Paper," *Arizona English Bulletin*, Vol. 25, No. 1 (November, 1983), 147–63.

Olson, Carol Booth. "Tapping Multiple Intelligences Through the Literature Book Project," *Think*, Vol. 2, No. 2 (December, 1991).

Parker, Robert P., and Vera Goodkin. *Consequences of Writing: Enhancing Learning in the Disciplines.* Portsmouth, N.H.: Boynton Cook Publishers, Inc., 1987.

Perl, Sondra. "Understanding Composing," *College Composition and Communication*, Vol. 31 (December, 1980), 363–69.

Perl, Sondra, and Nancy Wilson. *Through Teachers' Eyes: Portraits of Writing Teachers at Work.* Portsmouth, N.H.: Heinemann Educational Books, 1986.

Probst, Robert E. "Dialogue with a Text," *English Journal*, Vol. 77, No. 1 (January, 1988), 32–38.

Probst, Robert E. *Response and Analysis: Teaching Literature in Junior and Senior High School.* Portsmouth, N.H.: Boynton Cook Publishers, Inc., 1987.

Reading, Thinking and Writing About Multicultural Literature. Edited by Carol Booth Olson. New York: Scott, Foresman & Co., 1996.

Rico, Gabriele. *Writing the Natural Way: Using Right-Brain Techniques to Release Your Expressive Powers.* Los Angeles: J. P. Tarcher, Inc., 1983.

Rico, Gabriele, and Mary Frances Claggett. *Balancing the Hemispheres: Brain Research and the Teaching of Writing* (Monograph). Berkeley: Bay Area Writing Project, University of California, 1980.

Rosenblatt, Louise M. "Language, Literature, and Values," in *Language, Schooling, and Society.* Edited by Stephen N. Tchudi. Upper Montclair, N.J.: Boynton Cook Publishers, 1985.

Rosenblatt, Louise M. *Literature as Exploration* (Fourth edition). New York: Modern Language Association, 1983.

Scardamalia, Marlene. "How Children Cope with the Cognitive Demands of Writing," in *Writing: Process, Development and Communication.* Vol. 2 of *Writing: The Nature, Development, and Teaching of Written Communication.* Edited by Carl H. Frederiksen and Joseph F. Dominic. Hillsdale, N.J.: Lawrence Erlbaum Associates, Publishers, 1981.

Shaughnessy, Mina P. *Errors and Expectations: A Guide for the Teacher of Basic Writing.* New York: Oxford University Press, Inc., 1977.

Stanford, Gene, and Marie Smith. *A Guidebook for Teaching Creative Writing.* Newton, Mass.: Allyn & Bacon, Inc., 1981.

Stone, Jeanne M. *Cooperative Learning and Language Arts: A Multi-Structural Approach.* San Juan Capistrano, Calif.: Kagan Cooperative Learning, 1992.

Strong, William. *Sentence Combining: A Composing Book.* New York: Random House, Inc., 1983.

Thinking/Writing: Fostering Critical Thinking Through Writing. Edited by Carol Booth Olson. New York: HarperCollins College, 1992.

Thomas, Irene, and Owen Thomas. *Sentence Combining I and II.* St. Louis, Mo.: Milliken Publishing Co., 1984.

Wolfe, Tom, and E. W. Johnson. *The New Journalism.* New York: Harper & Row Pubs., Inc., 1973. (Out of print)

91-71 003-0008-95 300 9-95 10M